American Shortline Railway Guide

5th EDITION

RAILROAD REFERENCE SERIES NO. 17

EDWARD A. LEWIS

Editor: George Drury
Copy Editor: Mary Algozin
Art Director: Kristi Ludwig
Book Designer: Mike Schafer/Andover Junction Publications

Fordyce & Princeton 1805, a GP28, leads a freight train
through North Crossett, Arkansas, on October 9, 1990.
Photo by Louis A. Marre.

Published by Kalmbach Publishing Co., 21027 Crossroads Circle, P. O. Box 1612, Waukesha, WI 53187.

First printing 1996

Printed in the United States of America

Publisher's Cataloging in Publication
(Prepared by Quality Books Inc.)

Lewis, Edward A.
  American shortline railway guide / by Edward A. Lewis. — 5th ed.
  p. cm. — (Railroad reference series ; no. 17)
  Includes index.
  ISBN 0-89024-290-9

  1. Railroads—United States—Directories. I. Title. II. Series.
TF23.L48 1996   385.0973
                       QBI96-20326

INTRODUCTION

In the beginning all railroads were short lines. Most early charters were issued for railroads the magnitude of the 17-mile Mohawk & Hudson and the 26-mile Boston & Lowell. Few companies had the ambition of the Baltimore & Ohio: Baltimore to the Ohio River, which turned out to be nearly 400 miles, once they built it and measured it.

Most of the early railroads soon combined with their neighbors to form longer railroads. Seven railroads formed a route from Albany to Buffalo, with a change of company at each major city. From their inception they cooperated in running through passenger service, and in 1853 they merged to form the New York Central Railroad. Similar consolidations and mergers occurred everywhere.

Some short lines remained in existence for a variety of reasons: the owners were making sufficient return on their investment; shippers and passengers were content with local control; if the short line connected with only one large road, the large road was assured of the short line's business; the short line wasn't sufficiently profitable to attract the notice of a larger road.

The dominant trend, though, was for merger and growth, and that trend continued from the beginning of the railroad era in the United States through the 1960s — sometimes faster, sometimes slower, at first to meet competition from other railroads, later to meet competition from other modes of transportation. In 1970 the situation was altered suddenly and drastically.

On June 21, 1970, the Penn Central bankruptcy completely changed U. S. railroading. It triggered the formation of Conrail in 1976 from seven eastern railroads (Penn Central, Reading, Central of New Jersey, Lehigh Valley, Lehigh & Hudson River, and Erie Lackawanna, all bankrupt, and Pennsylvania-Reading Seashore Lines, which for decades had lost money for its parents).

During the same decade two large Midwestern railroads declared bankruptcy: the Rock Island on March 17, 1975, and the Milwaukee Road on December 18, 1977. The Rock Island struggled on for five years before shutting down completely on March 31, 1980. The Milwaukee Road ceased operation west of Miles City, Montana, on March 1, 1980, and in 1982 amputated everything west of Ortonville, Minnesota, and much of the rest of its system. The Milwaukee Road of 1970 had 10,479 route miles on its map; by the end of 1983 it had shrunk to 3,090, less than one-third its 1970 size.

Conrail's predecessors totaled approximately 25,000 route miles; today Conrail operates half that. Milwaukee Road cast off 7,000 route miles, and Rock Island's mileage was about the same. That's 26,000 miles of railroad disposed of. Where did it go? Class 1 railroads picked up a few routes — the largest chunk was Rock Island's Kansas City-Tucumcari line, which became part of the Southern Pacific system — and nature is reclaiming many of the redundant route miles. The rest became the stuff of this book: short lines.

A proliferation of short lines

The formation of Conrail opened the door to simplified, whole-sale abandonment procedures. Conrail needed to streamline its operations. It had duplicate lines and light-density branches that couldn't generate enough revenue to meet the cost of operating them. Its predecessors had been slow to abandon lines, and government — the Interstate Commerce Commission and state commissions — had been even slower to process abandonment petitions.

Some of the lines rejected by Conrail were needed to keep local industries in operation. Those lines were of greater economic value to communities than they were to the railroad, and public money was used to lease or purchase lines that didn't fit Conrail's plans. The lines required operators. With its standard wages and restrictive work rules, Conrail was the high-cost operator. Conrail didn't want to run the marginal branch lines, and shippers and public agencies often wanted to do something different. Short lines with responsive local management were the the way to provide rail service to towns left off Conrail's map.

The trend that started with Conrail soon spread to former Rock Island and Milwaukee Road lines. Short lines proliferated across the Great Plains.

Regional railroads

In the mid-1980s solvent, prosperous railroads began to examine their maps and eliminate routes that were poor sources of revenue or that didn't fit with the rest of the railroad. The routes were sold to become regional railroads.

The champion creator of regional railroads was Illinois Central Gulf. In 1973 ICG was a 9,634-mile railroad; at the end of 1989 it was down to 2,872 route miles. Between 1985 and 1988 ICG sold its major east-west routes and most of the former Gulf, Mobile & Ohio to create several regional railroads ranging from 300 to 1,150 miles in length. At the same time it was equally active in selling smaller pieces to short lines.

Other major railroads did the same. The Soo Line bought what remained of the Milwaukee Road in 1985, merged it in 1986, moved its Chicago-Minneapolis operations to the former Milwaukee route, and sold its own lines (mostly the old Wisconsin Central) to Wisconsin Central Limited, at 2,050 miles the largest of the new regional railroads. In 1986 CSX spun off part of the former Buffalo, Rochester & Pittsburgh to form the Rochester & Southern Railroad and the rest in 1988 to create the Buffalo & Pittsburgh. Burlington Northern leased and sold part of its ex-Northern Pacific main line to form Montana Rail Link and a cluster of ex-NP branches to form the Red River Valley & Western.

The Santa Fe, Southern Pacific, and Union Pacific were the last of the major railroads in the U. S. to begin spinning off branches and secondary lines, and the process has barely begun in Canada.

Divestiture (or downsizing) in the U. S. was made easier by the Staggers Act of 1980 and by changes in ICC procedures; divestiture is necessary if railroads are to compete with trucks (themselves beneficiaries of deregulation). Most independent truckers are nonunion owner-operators, men with lean and hungry operations willing to operate under cost for maximum equipment utilization. Large railroads often have high terminal costs that preclude competitive pricing, and their unions have generally been unwilling to realign wages and work rules to meet new market conditions. Short lines often have less expensive terminal operations and are free of union agreements.

The one constant in railroading these days is change. In the near term there will likely be more and more regional and feeder railroads serving local communities. The trend may stem the erosion of the railroads' share of the freight transportation market, and the future holds opportunities for those railroads that have a solid base and flexible management.

Classification of railroads

There is no official or legal definition of "short line," but the railroad industry as a whole and the American Short Line Railroad Association apply the term to railroads with less than 100 miles of mainline track.

In the ICC classification, a Class 1 railroad is one with annual operating revenue greater than $255.9 million. A Class 2 railroad has annual operating revenue between $20.5 million and $255.9 million, and a Class 3 railroad is one with annual operating revenue under $20.5 million. (Roman numerals are sometimes used to denote the classes.)

The Association of American Railroads classifies railroads as Class 1, Regional, and Local. The AAR agrees with the ICC on what constitutes a Class 1 railroad. A regional railroad is a line-haul railroad with revenues between $40 million and $255.9 million and with more than 350 miles of track; local railroads include line-haul railroads falling below those criteria and switching and terminal railroads.

What does this book contain?

This guide covers shortline and regional railroads reporting to the Interstate Commerce Commission and similar Canadian railroads. The entry for each railroad includes:

• the mailing address, telephone number, and fax number for the principal operating office

• the alphabetic code assigned by the Association of American Railroads Accounting Division, usually used as the reporting mark for freight cars and labeled as such in the entry

• a brief description of the railroad, including location, mileage, connections with other railroads, rail weight, and load limit, if it is outside the usual 263,000- to 270,000-pound range

• the principal commodities carried and approximate number of cars handled each year

• a brief history of the railroad

• the present ownership or control

• the radio frequency used for train operations

• the location of the enginehouse or the place where engines are generally kept. This item is omitted for switching and terminal roads, since they usually operate in only one city.

• a locomotive roster (omitted from listings for regional railroads for reasons of space)

• the number of interchange freight cars, by type if that information is available. Leasing companies indicated may be the lead company participating in the car accounting and revenue collection, but the railroad may also lease cars from other companies.

The omission of an item can usually be taken to mean "none" or "not applicable." The information is accurate for autumn 1995, and most of it was confirmed by the railroads.

All Class 2 and Class 3 railroads have been listed, except for switching and terminal railroads that do not conduct their own operation with their own equipment.

Information sources

To keep current with shortline developments, I recommend the following enthusiast publications:

The Short Line, published bimonthly by G. M. McDonald, P. O. Box 607, Pleasant Garden, NC 27313, is the best source of news about short lines.

Trains Magazine, published monthly by Kalmbach Publishing Co., P. O. Box 1612, Waukesha, WI 53187, carries photos and news, as well as feature articles covering regional railroads and short lines.

Railfan & Railroad Magazine, published monthly by Carstens Publications, P. O. Box 700, Newton, NJ 07860, is similar to *Trains* in its coverage of shortline and regional railroads.

Canadian Trackside Guide, published annually by the Bytown Railway Society, Inc., P. O. Box 141, Station A, Ottawa, ON K1N 8V1, Canada, is an excellent reference work on all aspects of rail operations in Canada.

Several trade magazines are also good sources of information:

Railway Age, published monthly by Simmons-Boardman Publishing Corp., 345 Hudson Street, New York, NY 10014, often carries articles on shortline and regional railroads.

Traffic World, published weekly by the Journal of Commerce, 741 National Press Building, Washington, DC 20005, covers activities at the ICC and traffic developments nationwide.

For reference, the following may be useful:

Railway Line Clearances, an annual list of weight and clearance limits of participating railroads.

The Official Railway Equipment Register, a quarterly list of all freight cars operating on North American railroads.

The Official Railway Guide — North American Freight Service Edition, a bimonthly list of most railroads.

The Pocket List of Railroad Officials, a quarterly list of railroads and their officials, plus an equipment count.

The preceding four periodicals are published by the National Railway Publication Company, 424 West 33rd Street, New York, NY 10001.

Profiles of U. S. Railroads — a computer program from the Department of Economics & Finance, Association of American Railroads, 50 First St, N.W., Washington, DC 20001. It provides basic data on most U. S. railroads.

State rail plans — many states prepare an annual rail plan detailing railroad operations.

The Official List of Open and Prepay Stations, published annually by Station List Publishing Co., 500 North Skinker Boulevard, St. Louis, MO 63130-4836, is a list of all railroads and their stations and junctions.

Compendium of American Railroad Radio Frequencies, compiled by Gary L. Sturm and Mark J. Landgraf, and published by Kalmbach Publishing Co., P. O. Box 1612, Waukesha, WI 53187.

For historical background there are three sources:

The Historical Guide to North American Railroads, by George H. Drury, published in 1991 (revised edition) by Kalmbach Publishing Co., P. O. Box 1612, Waukesha, WI 53187, a guide to major railroads merged or abandoned since 1930.

Railroad Names, edited and published by William D. Edson, 10820 Gainsborough Road, Potomac, MD 20854, a list of all railroad names from the early days to the present along with their predecessors, successors, and dates.

Moody's Transportation Manual, published annually by Moody's Investors Service, 90 Church Street, New York, NY 10007, and its pre-1932 predecessor, *Poor's Manual of Railroads*.

Many railroads have been the subject of books — check advertisements in magazines such as *Trains* and look in bookstores, hobby shops, and libraries.

Acknowledgments

I gratefully acknowledge the assistance provided by the American Short Line Railroad Association, Railway Association of Canada, and the railroads themselves in reviewing these listings. Without their cooperation, this project could not be successfully undertaken. I also thank Garreth M. McDonald and Warren Calloway for their assistance in researching information contained in the locomotive rosters.

The author would like to know of errors or omissions as well as changes as they occur. Please send documented information to: Edward A. Lewis, Editor, *American Shortline Railway Guide*, P. O. Box 505, Aberdeen, NC 28315.

Selected statistics for 1993

Revenue cars carried (233 railroads):

Regional railroads	1,147,071
Local and line haul	1,837,899
Switching and terminal roads	1,753,672
Total cars	4,738,642

Type of traffic:

	Interline terminated	Interline originated	Interline bridged	Local
Regional railroads	29%	27%	28%	17%
Short lines	28%	27%	15%	30%
Switching and terminal roads	29%	27%	14%	38%

Average revenue per car:

Regional railroads	$576.85
Local and line haul	$221.80
Switching and terminal roads	$100.21

Operating ratio
(operating expenses / revenues from operation):

Class 1 railroads	85.1%
Regional railroads	82%
Local and line haul	78.3%
Switching and terminal roads	87.2%

Class of track on short lines:

Excepted	4%
Class 1 (10 mph freight, 15 mph passenger)	9%
Class 2 (25 mph freight, 30 mph passenger)	66%
Class 3 (40 mph freight, 60 mph passenger)	14%
Class 4 (60 mph freight, 80 mph passenger)	7%

Ties replaced per mile of track:

Class 1 railroads	70
Regional railroads	58
Local and line haul	78
Switching and terminal roads	60

Railroad-highway grade crossings:

Railroad Type	Public	Private	Protected
Regional railroads	8,592	4,309	2,676
Local and line haul	9,661	18,351	2,969
Switching and terminal roads	1,465	608	586

Locomotive power distribution (2,129 units):

Under 1000 hp	10%
1000 to 2500 hp	77%
Over 2500 hp	13%

Locomotive age:

Under 10 years old	2%
10 to 20 years old	13%
Over 20 years old	85%

Freight car distribution
(52,310 cars, two-thirds of them leased):

Boxcars	42%
Covered hoppers	17%
Gondolas	15%
Hopper cars	12%
Flatcars	10%
All others	4%

Projected capital investment for the next 5 years:

Road	$ 90 million
Equipment	$70 million
Other	$30 million

Source: 1993 Annual Data Profile of the American Short Line & Regional Railroad Industry: Upper Great Plains Transportation Institute and American Short Line Railroad Association. The data includes information provided by 233 ASLRA members (less than half the industry).

WHOSE LINE WAS IT?

Throughout this book reference is made to former owners of rail lines. Where possible these references are set back a generation or two — even if Conrail sold the track to the short line, it is described as ex-New York Central, or as a former Atlantic Coast Line branch instead of CSX. This should make matters easier for the historically inclined. Younger readers, who have known only Burlington Northern and Norfolk & Western, not Northern Pacific and Wabash, can make use of the table below to follow in general terms the merger histories of the old companies. The table covers only the major railroads referred to in the body of the book and makes no mention of spinoffs, nor does it make allowance for the continued corporate existence of some of the companies.

Atchison, Topeka & Santa Fe	Burlington Northern, 1995		
Atlantic Coast Line	Seaboard Coast Line, 1967	Seaboard System, 1982	CSX, 1986
Baltimore & Ohio	Chesapeake & Ohio, 1987	CSX, 1987	
Boston & Maine	Guilford Transportation Ind., 1983	ST Rail System	
Central of Georgia	Southern Railway, 1963		
Central Railroad of New Jersey	Conrail, 1976		
Chesapeake & Ohio	CSX, 1987		
Chicago & North Western	Union Pacific, 1995		
Chicago, Burlington & Quincy	Burlington Northern, 1970		
Chicago, Milwaukee, St. Paul & Pacific	Soo Line, 1986	CP Rail System	
Chicago, Rock Island & Pacific	abandoned, 1980; portions sold to several railroads		
Colorado & Southern	Burlington Northern, 1981		
Cotton Belt — *see St. Louis Southwestern*			
Delaware & Hudson	Guilford Transportation Ind., 1984	CP Rail System, 1990	
Delaware, Lackawanna & Western	Erie Lackawanna, 1960	Conrail, 1976	
Denver & Rio Grande Western	Southern Pacific, 1988	Union Pacific (pending)	
Detroit, Toledo & Ironton	Grand Trunk Western, 1983		
Erie	Erie Lackawanna, 1960	Conrail, 1976	
Erie Lackawanna	Conrail, 1976		
Frisco — *see St. Louis-San Francisco*			
Great Northern	Burlington Northern, 1970		
Gulf, Mobile & Ohio	Illinois Central Gulf, 1972	Illinois Central, 1988	
Illinois Central	Illinois Central Gulf, 1972	Illinois Central, 1988	
Illinois Terminal	Norfolk & Western, 1981		

Kansas, Oklahoma & Gulf	Texas & Pacific, 1970	Missouri Pacific, 1976	
Lehigh & Hudson River	Conrail, 1976		
Lehigh Valley	Conrail, 1976		
Louisville & Nashville	Seaboard System, 1982	CSX, 1986	
Maine Central	Guilford Transportation Ind., 1981	ST Rail System	
Milwaukee Road — *see Chicago, Milwaukee, St. Paul & Pacific*			
Missouri Pacific	Union Pacific, 1982		
Missouri-Kansas-Texas	Union Pacific, 1988		
Monon	Louisville & Nashville, 1972	Seaboard System, 1982	CSX, 1986
Nashville, Chattanooga & St. Louis	Louisville & Nashville, 1957	Seaboard System, 1982	CSX, 1986
New York Central	Penn Central, 1967	Conrail, 1976	
New York, Chicago & St. Louis	Norfolk & Western, 1964	Norfolk Southern, 1990	
New York, New Haven & Hartford	Penn Central, 1968	Conrail, 1976	
Nickel Plate — *see New York, Chicago & St. Louis*			
Norfolk & Western	Norfolk Southern, 1990		
Norfolk Southern (1942)	Southern Railway, 1974	Norfolk Southern, 1990	
Northern Pacific	Burlington Northern, 1970		
Pennsylvania	Penn Central, 1967	Conrail, 1976	
Pennsylvania-Reading Seashore Lines	Conrail, 1976		
Pittsburgh & West Virginia	Norfolk & Western, 1964	Norfolk Southern, 1990	
Reading Company	Conrail, 1976		
Rock Island — *see Chicago, Rock Island & Pacific*			
Seaboard Air Line	Seaboard Coast Line, 1967	Seaboard System, 1982	CSX, 1986
Southern Pacific	Union Pacific (pending)		
Southern Railway	Norfolk Southern, 1990		
St. Louis Southwestern	Southern Pacific, 1932 (control)	Union Pacific (pending)	
St. Louis-San Francisco	Burlington Northern, 1980		
Tennessee Central	Abandoned, split among Illinois Central, Louisville & Nashville, and Southern Railway		
Texas & Pacific	Missouri Pacific, 1976	Union Pacific, 1982	
Toledo, Peoria & Western	Atchison, Topeka & Santa Fe, 1983	Toledo, Peoria & Western, 1989	
Wabash	Norfolk & Western, 1964	Norfolk Southern, 1990	
Western Maryland	Baltimore & Ohio, 1983	CSX, 1987	
Western Pacific	Union Pacific, 1982		
Wheeling & Lake Erie	New York, Chicago & St. Louis, 1949	Norfolk & Western, 1964	Wheeling & Lake Erie, 1990

SHORTLINE DIESELS

The diesel locomotives in this book range from GE and Plymouth 4-wheelers to a 6600-h.p. DDA40X. In the list below the term "switcher" means "cab at one end"; "road-switcher" means "cab near one end."

Model	H.P.	Wheel arrgt.	Years built	Configuration and notes
Alco — American Locomotive Company				
C-415	1500	B-B	1966-1968	center-cab
C-420	2000	B-B	1963-1968	road-switcher
C-424	2400	B-B	1963-1967	road-switcher
C-425	2500	B-B	1964-1966	road-switcher
C-430	3000	B-B	1966-1968	road-switcher
C-630	3000	C-C	1965-1969	road-switcher
C-636	3600	C-C	1967-1968	road-switcher
MRS-1	1000	C-C	1953	road-switcher
RS-1	1000	B-B	1941-1960	road-switcher
RS-2	1500	B-B	1946-1950	road-switcher
RS-3	1600	B-B	1950-1956	road-switcher
RS-11	1800	B-B	1956-1961	road-switcher
RS-32	2000	B-B	1961-1962	road-switcher
RS-36	1800	B-B	1962-1963	road-switcher
RSD-1	1000	B-B	1942-1945	road-switcher
RSD-12	1800	C-C	1956-1963	road-switcher
RSD-15	2400	C-C	1956-1960	road-switcher
S-1	660	B-B	1940-1950	switcher
S-2	1000	B-B	1940-1950	switcher
S-3	660	B-B	1950-1953	switcher
S-4	1000	B-B	1950-1961	switcher
S-6	900	B-B	1955-1960	switcher
T-6	1000	B-B	1958-1969	switcher
AT&SF — Atchison, Topeka & Santa Fe Railway Shops				
CF7	1500	B-B	1970-1978	road-switcher converted F7
SSB1200	1200	B-B	1974-1979	switcher rebuilt NW2, SW9

Model	H.P.	Wheel arrgt.	Years built	Configuration and notes
BLW — Baldwin Locomotive Works				
AS-616	1600	C-C	1950-1954	road-switcher
DRS-4-4-10	1000	B-B	1948-1950	road-switcher
DRS-6-4-15	1500	A1A-A1A	1946-1952	road-switcher
DRS-6-6-15	1600	C-C	1948-1950	road-switcher
DS-4-4-6	660	B-B	1946-1949	switcher
DS-4-4-7.5	750	B-B	1949-1951	switcher
RS-12	1200	B-B	1951-1956	switcher
S-8	800	B-B	1950-1954	switcher
S-12	1200	B-B	1951-1956	switcher
VO-660	660	B-B	1939-1946	switcher
VO-1000	1000	B-B	1939-1946	switcher
Davenport Locomotive Works				
35-ton	250			
EMD — Electro-Motive Division, General Motors Corp.				
BL2	1500	B-B	1948-1949	road-switcher
DDA40X	6600	D-D	1969-1971	road-switcher
E8	2250	A1A-A1A	1949-1953	cab unit
F7	1500	B-B	1949-1953	cab unit
FP7	1500	B-B	1949-1953	cab unit
F45	3600	C-C	1968-1971	cowl unit
GP7	1500	B-B	1949-1954	road-switcher
GP9	1750	B-B	1954-1959	road-switcher
GP15T	1500	B-B	1982-1983	road-switcher
GP18	1800	B-B	1959-1963	road-switcher
GP20	2000	B-B	1959-1962	road-switcher
GP28	1800	B-B	1964-1965	road-switcher
GP30	2250	B-B	1961-1963	road-switcher
GP35	2500	B-B	1963-1966	road-switcher
GP38	2000	B-B	1966-1971	road-switcher
GP38-2	2000	B-B	1972-1987	road-switcher
GP39	2300	B-B	1969-1970	road-switcher
GP40	3000	B-B	1965-1971	road-switcher
GP40-2	3000	B-B	1972-1986	road-switcher
GP60	3800	B-B	1985-	road-switcher
MP15	1500	B-B	1974-1975	switcher
MP15AC	1500	B-B	1975-1984	switcher

Model	HP	Wheels	Years	Type
MP15DC	1500	B-B	1975-1980	switcher
NW2	1000	B-B	1939-1949	switcher
NW5	1000	B-B	1946-1947	road-switcher
RS1325	1325	B-B	1960	road-switcher
SD7	1500	C-C	1952-1953	road-switcher
SD9	1750	C-C	1954-1959	road-switcher
SD18	1800	C-C	1960-1963	road-switcher
SD35	2500	C-C	1964-1966	road-switcher
SD38	2000	C-C	1967-1971	road-switcher
SD38-2	2000	C-C	1972-1979	road-switcher
SD39	2300	C-C	1968-1970	road-switcher
SDL39	2300	C-C	1969-1972	road-switcher
SD45	3600	C-C	1965-1971	road-switcher
SW1	600	B-B	1939-1953	switcher
SW7	1200	B-B	1949-1951	switcher
SW8	800	B-B	1950-1954	switcher
SW9	1200	B-B	1951-1953	switcher
SW600	600	B-B	1954-1962	switcher
SW900	900	B-B	1954-1965	switcher
SW1000	1000	B-B	1966-1972	switcher
SW1001	1000	B-B	1968-1986	switcher
SW1200	1200	B-B	1954-1966	switcher
SW1500	1500	B-B	1966-1974	switcher

GE — General Electric Company

Model	HP	Wheels	Years	Type
25-ton	150	B		switcher
44-ton	380	B-B	1940-1956	center-cab
45-ton	300	B-B	1940-1959	center-cab
65-ton	400-550	B-B		center-cab
70-ton	600	B-B	1946-1958	switcher
80-ton	600	B-B	1976-	center-cab
110-ton	600	B-B	1974-	center-cab
125-ton	1200	B-B		center-cab
B23-7	2250	B-B	1977-1984	road-switcher
Dash 8-40B	4000	B-B	1988-	road-switcher
U6B	600	B-B		switcher
U18B	1800	B-B	1973-1976	road-switcher
U23B	2250	B-B	1968-1977	road-switcher
U23C	2250	C-C	1968-1970	road-switcher
U28B	2800	B-B	1966	road-switcher
U30B	3000	B-B	1966-1975	road-switcher
U30C	3000	C-C	1967-1976	road-switcher
U33B	3300	B-B	1967-1970	road-switcher

GMD — General Motors Diesel, Ltd.
Canadian subsidiary of Electro-Motive

Model	HP	Wheels	Years	Type
SW1200RS	1200	B-B	1958-1960	switcher

ICG — Illinois Central Gulf Railroad shops

Model	HP	Wheels	Years	Type
GP8	1600	B-B	1967-1977	road-switcher rebuilt GP7
GP10	1850	B-B	1967-1977	road-switcher rebuilt GP9

MLW — Montreal Locomotive Works

Model	HP	Wheels	Years	Type
FPA-4	1800	B-B	1958-1959	cab unit
M420R	2000	B-B	1974-1975	road-switcher
M636	3600	C-C	1969-1975	road-switcher
RS-18	1800	B-B	1956-1968	road-switcher
RSC-14	1400	A1A-A1A		road-switcher

MK — Morrison-Knudsen Company

Model	HP	Wheels	Years	Type
TE-53-1-4E		B-B	1975-1976	road-switcher rebuilt U25B
TE-56-4A	1800, 2000	B-B	1974-1975	road-switcher rebuilt RS-3
TE-47-4E	1200	B-B	1976	switcher rebuilt S2

Plymouth Locomotive Works

Model	HP	Wheels	Years	Type
25-ton	150-175	B		switcher

H. K. Porter, Inc.

Model	HP	Wheels	Years	Type
65-ton		B-B		center-cab

Republic Locomotive Works

RL1500

Whitcomb Locomotive Works

Model	HP	Wheels	Years	Type
20-ton		B		switcher
44-ton		B-B		center-cab
80-ton	400	B-B		center-cab

SHORT LINES AND REGIONAL RAILROADS

A&G RAILROAD, LLC.

P. O. Box 28300
Panama City Beach, FL 32411

Reporting marks: AGRD
Phone: 904-230-8331

The A&G Railroad operates freight service from Abbeville, Alabama, to a connection with CSX at Grimes, 26.7 miles, and then by trackage rights over CSX to Dothan, 6 miles, where interchange is made with CSX, Norfolk Southern, and The Bay Line. A&G carries about 4,300 carloads of wood chips annually.

The line was built by the Abbeville Southern Railway, which opened on December 1, 1893. It was operated by the Alabama Midland, which became part of the Savannah, Florida & Western, then the Atlantic Coast Line in 1902.

CSX sold the property to the Abbeville Grimes Railway, a subsidiary of Stone Container, on March 1, 1989, following abandonment. The railroad was sold to A&G on January 1, 1994.

A&G is controlled by Rail Management & Consulting Corporation and is operated in conjunction with The Bay Line.
Radio frequency: 160.545
Locomotives: supplied by The Bay Line
Freight cars: 100 boxcars

A&R LINE

123 Depot Street
P. O. Box 40
Wawaka, IN 46794

Reporting marks: ARE
Phone: 219-761-3311

The A&R operates from Winamac, Indiana, to a connection with the Toledo, Peoria & Western at Kenneth, then to Logansport, where it connects with the TP&W again and with Norfolk Southern and Winamac Southern. Rail is predominantly 130 pound. The road expects to move about 1,500 cars of grain annually in unit trains.

The line was part of the Pennsylvania Railroad's line Between Columbus, Ohio, and Chicago. The Winamac Southern Railway acquired it from Conrail in March 1993 and sold it to the A&R line on September 1, 1995. A&R is owned by Daniel Frick, who also owns the Winamac Southern and the JK Line.
Location of enginehouse: Winamac, Ind.
Locomotives: 1

No.	Builder	Model	New	Builder No.
7302	EMD	SD18	1/63	27600

ABERDEEN & ROCKFISH RAILROAD CO.

101 East Main Street
P. O. Box 917
Aberdeen, NC 28315

Reporting marks: AR
Phone: 910-944-2341
Fax: 910-944-9738

The Aberdeen & Rockfish operates from Aberdeen, North Carolina, through Raeford to Fayetteville and River Terminal, 46.9 miles. It connects with CSX at Aberdeen and Fayetteville, Norfolk Southern at Fayetteville, and Laurinburg & Southern at Raeford. Rail is 70 to 100 pound. Traffic is about 4,500 cars a year of chemicals, coal, lumber, scrap, paper, and other general commodities.

The company was incorporated on June 22, 1892, and the railroad was opened from Aberdeen to Raeford in 1898, to Hope Mills in 1903, and to Fayetteville in 1912. A branch from Raeford to Wagram was built before 1909 and sold to the Laurinburg & Southern Railroad in November 1921. Regular passenger service ended in 1951. Aberdeen & Rockfish operates the Pee Dee River Railway and Dunn-Erwin Railway as divisions.

The Blue family interests control the company.

Radio frequencies: 160.530, 161.280
Location of enginehouse: Aberdeen, N. C.
Locomotives: 7

No.	Builder	Model	New	Builder No.	Rebuilt
205	EMD	GP7	10/51	14572	
210	EMD	GP7U	2/53	17758	1989
300	EMD	GP18	8/63	28357	
400	EMD	GP38	6/68	34029	
1797	EMD	GP8	12/51	14979	1981
2486	AT&SF	CF7	1/75		
2594	AT&SF	CF7	11/72		

Freight cars: 27 boxcars, 25 gondolas

Aberdeen & Rockfish GP38 No. 400 pulls the daily Fayetteville freight through Montrose, North Carolina. Photo by Warren Calloway.

ABERDEEN, CAROLINA & WESTERN RAILWAY CO.

115 West Main Street
P. O. Box 398
Aberdeen, NC 28315

Reporting marks: ACWR
Phone: 910-944-3165
Fax: 910-944-3174

The Aberdeen, Carolina & Western operates freight service from a connection with CSX at Aberdeen, North Carolina, to Star, 34.46 miles. Rail is 70 to 85 pound.

The company also leases and operates Norfolk Southern's Charlotte-Star-Gulf line, 104 miles. That line connects at Charlotte and Gulf with Norfolk Southern and at Norwood with Winston-Salem Southbound. Rail is 85 to 110 pound.

Traffic includes grain, wood chips, brick, lumber, pulpwood, latex, limestone, and LP gas — about 11,000 cars a year.

The Aberdeen–Star line was built as a private logging line in the 1880s. It was reorganized in 1893 as the Aberdeen & West End Railroad, then became part of the Aberdeen & Asheboro Railroad in 1897. In 1914 the A&A was acquired by the Raleigh, Charlotte & Southern. That road was in turn merged by the original Norfolk Southern, which was renamed Carolina & Northwestern in 1982. C&NW sold the line to the Aberdeen & Briar Patch Railway on August 1, 1983, following their decision to abandon the line. The Aberdeen, Carolina & Western purchased the assets of the ABP and began operations June 19, 1987. The company leased NS's Charlotte line May 1, 1989. The company is owned by Robert Menzies.

Radio frequencies: 160.680, 461.450, 466.540
Location of enginehouse: Star, N. C.
Locomotives: 20

No.	Builder	Model	New	Builder No.
700	EMD	GP7	11/50	9944
(701) 896	EMD	GP7	5/50	11592
(702) 5820	EMD	GP7	11/52	17041
900	EMD	GP9	11/56	22568
(901) 699	EMD	GP9	4/59	24851
1132	EMD	SW7	1/50	10967
1600	EMD	GP16	9/60	26122
1601	EMD	GP16	9/56	23098
1602	EMD	GP16	2/51	13898
(1603) 1774	EMD	GP16	11/50	12099
(1604) 1783	EMD	GP16	10/50	12898
(1605) 1785	EMD	GP16	12/51	14943
(1606) 1835	EMD	GP16	12/51	14945
1608	EMD	GP18	6/60	25911
(3800) 2010	EMD	GP38	10/67	33328
3801	EMD	GP38	11/67	33708
3802	EMD	GP38	11/67	33364
3803	EMD	GP38	12/67	33728

ACADIANA RAILWAY CO.

597 South Railroad Avenue
P. O. Box 751
Opelousas, LA 70571

Reporting marks: AKDN
Phone: 318-942-4085
Fax: 318-942-4096

The Acadiana operates freight service from a connection with the Southern Pacific at Crowley, Louisiana, to Eunice, 21.6 miles, and then via trackage rights over the Union Pacific to Opelousas, 20.9 miles. The company continues over its own line from Opelousas to Bunkie, 36 miles. It also operates 5 miles of former Southern Pacific switching track at Opelousas. Traffic is agricultural products, edible oil, and general freight — about 6,700 cars a year.

The Eunice line was built by the New Orleans, Texas & Mexico Railway before 1900. The Bunkie line is made up of Texas & Pacific and Southern Pacific lines. Union Pacific sold both branches to the current owner in 1990. Shortline service started on October 15, 1990. The company is controlled by Trac-Work, Inc.

Location of enginehouse: Opelousas, La.
Locomotives: 4

Acadiana Railway GP30 No. 701 pulls a string of tank cars through Savoy, Louisiana, on UP trackage in June, 1994. Photo by Jim Shaw.

No.	Builder	Model	New	Builder No.
101	EMD	NW2	4/48	5512
102	EMD	NW2	12/48	7740
701	EMD	GP30	2/63	28161
1610	EMD	GP9	8/54	19860

ADRIAN & BLISSFIELD RAIL ROAD CO.

708 East Michigan Street
P. O. Box 95
Adrian, MI 49221

Reporting marks: ADBF
Phone: 517-265-6887
Fax: 517-263-6021

The Adrian & Blissfield provides freight and passenger excursion service from a connection with Norfolk Southern at Adrian to a connection with Grand Trunk Western at Riga, Michigan, 15 miles. A 1.7-mile branch runs to Grosvenor. Rail is 90 to 115 pound.

Traffic includes about 700 carloads of grain, fertilizer, and lumber a year. The company started running passenger excursions on April 19, 1991.

This line was built in large part by the Erie & Kalamazoo Railroad, which opened its line from Toledo, Ohio, to Adrian, Mich., in November 1836. The E&K was sold in 1848 to the Michigan Southern, which became the Lake Shore & Michigan Southern, then New York Central. Following the failure of Penn Central, the state of Michigan acquired this line, and it was operated by the Lenawee County Railroad from October 29, 1977, to September 30, 1990. The Adrian & Blissfield leased the line from Michigan

DOT on February 14, 1991. The company is independent.
Radio frequency: 160.650
Location of enginehouse: Adrian, Mich.
Freight cars: 40 flatcars

Locomotives: 2

No.	Builder	Model	New	Builder No.
1751	EMD	GP9	3/57	22853
1752	EMD	GP9	3/57	22843

AKRON BARBERTON CLUSTER RAILWAY CO.

P. O. Box 96
Brewster, OH 44613

Reporting marks: AB
Phone: 216-745-4431
Fax: 216-745-4519

This company is a switching line handling about 4,000 cars annually between Ravenna, Akron, Barberton and Rittman, Ohio, 19.44 route miles (36.83 track miles). Connections are made with Wheeling & Lake Erie at Akron and Kent and with CSX at Barberton. Rail is 100 and 132 pound. Traffic is 2,000 cars a year of scrap, chemicals, and general commodities.

The Akron & Barberton Belt Railroad was incorporated May 6, 1902, as a consolidation of the Barberton, Akron & Eastern Railroad, the Barberton Belt Line Railway, and the Cleveland, Barberton & Western Railroad. On July 21, 1994, the Akron Barberton Cluster Railway took over the assets of the A&BB along with 21 miles of Conrail track from Cuyahoga Falls to Warwick, Ohio, and 11 miles from Kenmore to Wadsworth. The company is owned by the Wheeling Corp., owner of the Wheeling & Lake Erie Railroad.

Radio frequencies: 160.650, 161.550
Locomotives: 3

No.	Builder	Model	New	Builder No.
1203	EMD	SW1200	8/52	17076
1501	EMD	SW1500	6/66	32159
1502	EMD	SW1500	11/67	33541

ALABAMA RAILROAD CO., INC.

1318 South Johanson Road
Peoria, IL 61607

Reporting marks: ALAB
Phone: 309-697-1400

This railroad provides freight service from a connection with CSX at Flomaton, Alabama to Beatrice, 55 miles. Rail ranges from 90 to 130 pound. Traffic is forest products including wood chips, power poles, particleboard, plywood and lumber — about 2,500 cars a year.

The line was built by the Pensacola & Selma Railroad, which was chartered in 1880 to construct a line from Flomaton to Pineapple, Ala. It became part of the Louisville & Nashville that same year and opened as far as Repton in 1881. The line wasn't completed until 1900. L&N became part of the Seaboard System and eventually CSX. On October 28, 1991, CSX sold the line to the Alabama Railroad, which is a subsidiary of Pioneer Railcorp of Peoria, Illinois.

Radio frequencies: 160.500, 160.695
Location of enginehouse: Monroeville, Ala.
Locomotives: 2

No.	Builder	Model	New	Builder No.	Rebuilt
1600	EMD	GP16	12/52	17494	1980
1601	EMD	GP16	12/51	14977	1980

Freight cars: 200 boxcars

ALABAMA & FLORIDA RAILWAY CO.

1318 South Johanson Road
Peoria, IL 61607

Reporting marks: AF
Phone: 309-697-1400

The Alabama & Florida operates freight service from a connection with CSX at Georgiana through Opp to Geneva, Alabama, 78 miles. The company also operates over 2 miles of the Andalusia & Conecuh RR at Andalusia, Ala. Rail is predominantly 90 pound. Traffic includes pulpwood, peanuts, chemicals, plastic, grain and fertilizer — about 2,500 cars a year.

Construction of the Georgiana line was started by the Alabama & Florida Railroad and completed from Georgiana to Graceville, Florida, in March 1901, 2 years after the line had been leased by the Louisville & Nashville. The line was acquired from Seaboard System by Peter Clausen along with a second line running from Crestview, Fla., to Florala, Ala. Independent operation started July 28, 1986. Service on the Crestview line (the Yellow River Railroad) was discontinued in December 1987.

The company was sold to A&F, Inc., of Knoxville, Tennessee, on August 12, 1990; A&F sold the assets to the current owner, Pioneer Railcorp, on November 23, 1992.

Radio frequencies: 160.380, 461.150, 466.150
Location of enginehouse: Opp, Ala.

Locomotives: 4

No.	Builder	Model	New	Builder No.	Rebuilt
902	EMD	GP9	3/56	21489	
1609	EMD	GP16	9/51	14960	1979
1610	EMD	GP16	4/50	11501	
1611	EMD	GP16	6/51	13886	

Freight cars: 29

Alabama & Florida's former CSX GP9s haul a lot of grain and pulpwood, as illustrated by this train shown at Red Level, Alabama. Photo by Jim Shaw.

ALAMEDA BELT LINE

2001 Engineers Road
Oakland, CA 94607

Reporting marks: ABL
Phone: 510-832-8464
Fax: 510-231-2628

Alameda Belt Line operates a switching road at Alameda, California, carrying nearly 1,400 cars of general commodities a year. It has 12.5 miles of track (3.5 route miles) connecting with Santa Fe, Southern Pacific, and Union Pacific. The company has been owned by Santa Fe and Union Pacific (formerly Western Pacific) since it was formed in 1925.

Radio frequency: 160.935

Locomotives: 1

No.	Builder	Model	New	Builder No.	Rebuilt
44	EMD	GP7	11/53	18885	12/78

ALASKA RAILROAD CORP.

P. O. Box 107500
Anchorage, AK 99510-7500

Reporting marks: ARR
Phone: 907-265-2403

The Alaska Railroad provides passenger service from Anchorage north to Fairbanks and south to Seward and Whittier, and freight service from Seward through Anchorage and Fairbanks to Eielson Air Force Base. Three short branch lines extend to Suntran, Palmer and Whittier. A total of 470 miles are operated. All interchange is via car float at Seward or Whittier. Over 76,000 cars a year of coal, chemicals and nonmetallic minerals make up the road's traffic.

The Alaska Railroad was formed in 1916 as a consolidation of the Alaska Northern Railroad (incorporated in 1903 as the Alaska Central and reorganized in 1909) and the Tanana Valley Railroad. The railroad was owned by the United States Government and operated by the Department of Interior for many years. It is now owned by the State of Alaska.
Radio frequencies: 161.355, 161.385, 161.415, 161.445
Employees: 550
Locomotives: 49 (1 F7B, 7 GP7, 51 GP35/38/40/49)
Freight cars: 258
Passenger cars: 30 (plus additional equipment provided by tour operators)
Principal shop: Anchorage, Alaska

ALBANY PORT RAILROAD CORP.

Port of Albany
Albany, NY 12202

Reporting marks: ALBY
Phone: 518-463-8679
Fax: 518-462-2976

The Albany Port Railroad is a switching line operating 18 miles of track at Albany, New York. It connects with Conrail and CP Rail System (Delaware & Hudson). More than 14,000 cars are carried annually. The company began operations in 1932 and is owned jointly by Conrail and Delaware & Hudson.
Radio frequency: 161.355
Locomotives: 2

No.	Builder	Model	New	Builder No.
12	EMD	SW9	3/53	16733
13	EMD	SW9	3/53	16736

ALEXANDER RAILROAD CO.

145 Second Avenue, N.E.
P. O. Box 277
Taylorsville, NC 28681-0277

Reporting marks: ARC
Phone: 704-632-2103
Fax: 704-585-6541

The Alexander Railroad operates freight service from Taylorsville, North Carolina, to a connection with Norfolk Southern at Statesville, N. C., 18.59 miles. Rail is 75 to 100 pound. Traffic includes grain, pulpboard, plastic, fertilizer, sand, cement, LP gas, and lumber — 3,000 cars a year.

The Alexander Railroad was incorporated December 7, 1945, to purchase a Southern branch line that was being abandoned. The line was built as the Statesville & Western Railroad, incorporated

March 3, 1887, and opened in September of that year. The Richmond & Danville Railroad leased the line for 99 years starting October 27, 1888. On September 8, 1894, it was conveyed to Southern. The Alexander Railroad Co. is independent. It has never carried passengers.
Radio frequency: 160.620
Location of enginehouse: Taylorsville, N. C.

Locomotives: 4

No.	Builder	Model	New	Builder No.
3	GE	44-ton	6/51	31111
6	Alco	S-3	9/53	80292
7	Alco	S-3	11/50	78404
8	EMD	SW9	3/52	15968

Alexander Alco S-3 number 6 moves a lone car of freight at Scotts, North Carolina. Most traffic is now handled by EMD SW9 No. 8. Photo by Jim Shaw.

ALGERS, WINSLOW & WESTERN RAILWAY CO.

Highway 64 East
P. O. Box 188
Oakland City, IN 47660

Reporting marks: AWW
Phone: 812-749-4473
Fax: 812-749-6174

AWW operates freight service from a connection with Norfolk Southern and Indiana Southern at Oakland City Junction, Indiana, to Enosville and Algers, 16 miles. Rail is 132 pound. Traffic is outbound coal — 20,000 cars a year.

The present company was incorporated on September 7, 1927, to take over two railroad properties. Common carrier service started in June 1931. The company is jointly owned by Old Ben Coal Co. and Norfolk Southern Corporation.
Radio frequency: 160.575
Location of enginehouse: Oakland City Junction, Ind.
Locomotives: 4

No.	Builder	Model	New	Builder No.
203	EMD	SD9	3/55	20446
204	EMD	SD9	4/55	20447
205	EMD	SD9	6/55	20448
206	EMD	SD9	6/55	20449

ALGOMA CENTRAL RAILWAY, INC.

429 Hudson Street
P. O. Box 9500
Sault Ste. Marie, ON P6A 6Y1
Canada

Reporting marks: AC
Phone: 705-949-2113
Fax: 705-946-7382

Algoma Central operates freight and passenger service from Sault Ste. Marie to Hearst, Ontario, 295.7 miles. A 26-mile branch line extends from Hawk Junction to Michipicoten. Connections are made with Wisconsin Central at Sault Ste. Marie, with CP Rail at Franz and Sault Ste. Marie, and with Canadian National Railways at Oba. Rail is 110 and 115 pound. Traffic is forest products, iron ore, and steel and metal products, about 40,000 cars a year. The company is best known for its scenic passenger excursions.

The Algoma Central Railway was incorporated August 11, 1899. The Ontario government gave the company land grants totaling more than 2 million acres to aid in construction. In addition, the Canadian government provided construction subsidies. The name was changed to Algoma Central & Hudson Bay Railway in May 1901 and back to Algoma Central Railway in May 1965. The railroad was acquired by Wisconsin Central Ltd. on February 1, 1995.
Radio frequencies: 160.530, 160.575, 160.605, 160.995, 161.355
Enginehouse: Sault Ste. Marie, Ont.
Locomotives: pooled with Wisconsin Central
Freight cars: 799

ALIQUIPPA & SOUTHERN RAILROAD

Aliquippa & Southern SW1200 No. 1212 switches a string of hot-metal cars at Aliquippa, Pennsylvania. Photo by Jim Shaw.

200 Woodlawn Drive
P. O. Box 280
Aliquippa, PA 15001

Reporting marks: ALQS
Phone: 412-378-5215
Fax: 412-378-6598

The Aliquippa & Southern is a switching line at Aliquippa, Pennsylvania, operating 27.27 miles of track connecting with the CSX. Rail is 115 pound. It moves more than 7,000 cars a year.

The company was incorporated November 27, 1906, and the railroad was opened in 1910. It is a subsidiary of LTV Steel, Inc.
Radio frequencies: 161.010, 161.100, 161.490
Locomotives: 3

No.	Builder	Model	New	Builder No.
1202	EMD	SW1200	6/54	19532
1204	EMD	SW1200	1955	20636
1205	EMD	SW1200	1955	20637

Freight cars: 25 gondolas

ALLEGHENY & EASTERN RAILROAD CO.

201 North Pine Street
Punxsutawney, PA 15767

Reporting marks: ALY
Phone: 814-938-5500
Fax: 814-938-1537

The Allegheny & Eastern operates freight service from Erie to Emporium, Pennsylvania, 149.2 miles. Connections are made with Conrail at Erie, Corry, and Emporium, with Buffalo & Pittsburgh at Johnsonburg, and with Knox & Kane Railroad at Kane. Rail is 115 to 132 pound. Traffic includes pulpwood, woodpulp, lumber, steel, chemicals, and petroleum products — 5,000 cars a year.

This rail line was built by the Sunbury & Erie Railroad, which was chartered April 3, 1837. Construction started in 1852 and the entire line was opened in 1864 as a reorganization of the Philadelphia & Erie. The property was leased to the Pennsylvania Railroad in 1862 and fully acquired by PRR in 1907.

Although a portion of the line was not included in Conrail in 1976, it was operated by Conrail for a while. Later it was operated by the Johnsonburg, Kane, Warren & Irvine Railroad, and it was acquired by the Allegheny Railroad in May 1985. Operations started September 3, 1985. On November 25, 1992, the property was sold to the current operator. The company is owned by Genesee & Wyoming Industries, Inc.

Radio frequencies: 160.290 (road), 160.425 (yard)
Location of enginehouse: Warren, Pa.
Locomotives: 4

No.	Builder	Model	New	Builder No.
301	EMD	GP40	12/68	34706
302	EMD	GP40	12/68	34715
305	EMD	GP35	5/64	29172
306	EMD	GP35	5/64	29177

ALLEGHENY VALLEY RAILROAD CO.

P. O. Box 28096
Columbus, OH 43228

Reporting marks: AVR
Phone: 614-871-7290
Fax: 614-539-0352

The Allegheny Valley operates from a connection with Conrail at Island Avenue Yard in Pittsburgh to New Kensington, Pennsylvania, 22.65 miles. The rail is predominantly 130 pound. The company expects to move about 2,300 cars a year of scrap and finished paper, food products, and plastic.

The line was built by a previous Allegheny Valley Railroad, which was chartered in 1856 and became part of the Pennsylvania Railroad. Conrail sold the line to the current Allegheny Valley Railroad and operations began on October 28, 1995.

The company is owned by Russell A. Peterson, Philip Larson, and Dennis Larson.

Location of enginehouse: Verona, Pa.
Locomotives: 1

No.	Builder	Model	New	Builder No.
77	EMD	GP10	10/56	21871

ALMANOR RAILROAD CO.

P. O. Box 796
Chester, CA 96020

Reporting marks: AL
Phone: 916-258-2111
Fax: 916-258-4266

The Almanor Railroad operates freight service from Chester, California, to a connection with Union Pacific at Clear Creek Junction, 13 miles. Rail is 60 to 80 pound, and the load limit is 225,000 pounds. Traffic consists of 300 cars a year of outbound lumber and forest products.

The Almanor Railroad was incorporated September 15, 1941, to purchase and operate the private railroad of the Red River Lumber Co. Common carrier service started in May 1942. The company is owned by Collins Pine Co.
Radio frequency: 158.310
Location of enginehouse: Chester, Calif.
Locomotives: 1 (lettered for and owned by Collins Pine Co.)

No.	Builder	Model	New	Builder No.
166	GE	70-ton	6/55	32296

AMADOR CENTRAL RAILROAD CO.

Highway 49
P. O. Box 66
Martell, CA 95654

Reporting marks: AMC
Phone: 209-223-1660
Fax: 209-223-1502

The Amador Central operates freight service from a connection with Southern Pacific at Ione, California, to Martell, 11.79 miles. Rail is 80 to 85 pound and the load limit is 200,000 pounds. Traffic is about 1,000 cars a year of outbound lumber and forest products and inbound wood for fuel.

The railroad was incorporated April 12, 1904 as the Ione & Eastern Railroad. It opened from Ione to Mountain Springs, 6 miles, in 1904 and was extended another 6 miles to Martell the following year. The Amador Central Railroad was incorporated on September 24, 1908, and on January 1, 1909, it took over operation of the Ione & Eastern. Passenger service was discontinued in the 1930s.

The line's track is owned by Georgia Pacific Corporation and leased to the railroad. The company was acquired by Georgia Pacific in June 1988.
Radio frequency: 49.22
Location of enginehouse: Martell, Calif.
Locomotives: 3

No.	Builder	Model	New	Builder No.
9	Baldwin	S12	5/51	75032
10	Baldwin	S12	1/52	75613
1208	EMD	SW1200	6/63	28344

Freight cars: 68 boxcars

Amador Central Baldwin S-12 No. 9 switches cars at Martell, California. Photo by Jim Shaw.

AMERICAN SHORT LINE RAILROAD ASSOCIATION

1120 G Street, N.W., Suite 520
Washington, DC 20005

Phone: 202-628-4500
Fax: 202-628-6430

Starting about 1910, several attempts were made to organize shortline railroads to deal with legislative matters. The most successful of these efforts led to the organization of the Short Line Railroad Association of the Southeast at Atlanta in September 1913. Within a few years, the need for a national organization was apparent, and in March 1917 the American Short Line Railroad Association was organized, with its principal office in Washington, D. C. By 1918, 177 railroads were members. In 1920 the Western Association of Short Line Railroads joined the ASLRA.

The goals of the association are:

• to provide cooperative action in the consideration and solution of problems of management and policy affecting the operation and welfare of shortline and regional railroads
• to promote beneficial federal legislation
• to resist the enactment of laws that would be detrimental to the railroad industry.

Among the services the association provides to its membership are statutory agency information and news; legal, traffic and management assistance; and liaison with congressional and federal agencies.

In addition to its main office in Washington, the American Short Line Railroad Association has a traffic office in Atlanta. Membership is open to U. S. railroads; suppliers may become associate members.

ANGELINA & NECHES RIVER RAILROAD CO.

2225 Spence Street
P. O. Box 1328
Lufkin, TX 75902

Reporting marks: ANR
Phone: 409-634-4403
Fax: 409-639-3879

The Angelina & Neches River operates freight and TOFC service from Lufkin to Keltys and Dunagan, Texas, 15.6 miles. Connections are made with Southern Pacific at Prosser, Dunagan, and Lufkin and with the Texas South-Eastern at Lufkin. Rail is 75 to 113 pound. Traffic is primarily paper and forest products — 5,500 cars a year.

The company was incorporated August 6, 1900, to purchase and operate a private 3-foot gauge logging railroad. A branch line from Dunagan to Chireno, 24 miles, was abandoned in 1963. It was cut back another 2.8 miles from Dunagan to Buck Creek, in October 1994.

Half of the company's stock is held by Champion International and the balance by other parties.

Radio frequency: 161.280
Location of enginehouse: Prosser, Texas
Locomotives: 3

No.	Builder	Model	New	Builder No.
12	Alco	S-4	9/58	82006
1500	EMD	SW1500	11/72	4630-1
2000	EMD	GP38-2	8/80	796383-1

Freight cars: 148 boxcars

The biggest power on the Angelina & Neches River Railroad is well-maintained GP38-2 No. 2000, shown at Lufkin, Texas. Photo by Jim Shaw.

ANN ARBOR RAILROAD

121 South Walnut Street
P. O. Box 380
Howell, MI 48844

Reporting marks: AA
Phone: 517-548-3930
Fax: 517-548-3937

Ann Arbor operates freight service from a connection with Conrail at Ann Arbor, Michigan, to connections with CSX, Conrail, Grand Trunk Western, and Norfolk Southern at Toledo, Ohio, plus a short branch from Pittsfield to Saline, Mich., 53.5 miles in all. Additional connections are made with Norfolk Southern at Milan, Mich., with Grand Trunk Western at Diann, Mich., and with Tuscola & Saginaw Bay at Osmer, Mich. Rail is 115 to 132 pound. Traffic consists of 18,000 cars a year of automobiles, automobile parts, cement, and general commodities.

The State Line Railroad built a line from Toledo to Alexis, Ohio, in 1873. In 1877 the Toledo & Ann Arbor Railroad began construction of a line to run from Alexis to Ann Arbor, Mich. Following its opening the T&AA purchased the State Line Railroad. The company was reorganized in August 1881 as the Toledo, Ann Arbor & Grand Trunk, and 3 years later as the Toledo, Ann Arbor

& Northern Michigan. The Ann Arbor took over in September 1895 and operated the line until April 1976.

Conrail operated the line until Michigan Interstate Railway was designated operator of the 291.8-mile line between Frankfort, Michigan, and Toledo, Ohio, on October 1, 1977. Service was cut back to the current operation in October 1982, and the company was reorganized under bankruptcy between January 1983 and October 1988. Ann Arbor Acquisition Corporation took control on October 7, 1988. The company is controlled by M. J. Barron, P. J. O'Meara and others.

Radio frequencies: 161.490, 161.355
Location of enginehouse: Toledo, Ohio
Locomotives: 3

No.	Builder	Model	New	Builder No.
7771	EMD	GP38	10/69	35400
7791	EMD	GP38	10/69	35420
7802	EMD	GP38	10/69	35431

Freight cars: 2 boxcars, 1 covered hopper

APACHE RAILWAY CO.

P. O. Drawer E
Snowflake, AZ 85937

Reporting marks: APA
Phone: 602-536-4696
Fax: 602-536-4260

The Apache operates freight service from Snowflake, Arizona, to a connection with the Santa Fe at Holbrook, 38 miles. Rail is 110 to 131 pound. It carries nearly 16,000 carloads of recycled fiber, pulpwood, wood chips, coal, paper products, chemicals, and grain annually.

The railroad was incorporated September 6, 1917, and operated in receivership from 1931 to 1936. Passenger service ended during the 1950s. The line was abandoned from Snowflake to McNary in 1984. The company is controlled by Stone Container Corp.

Radio frequencies: 452.900, 457.900, 161.520
Location of enginehouse: west of Snowflake, Ariz.
Locomotives: 6

No.	Builder	Model	New	Builder No.
81	Alco	C-420	6/64	84798
82	Alco	C-420	1/66	3438 1
83	Alco	C-420	8/67	3490-10
84	Alco	C-420	12/64	3397 3
800	Alco	RS-36	9/62	84116
900	Alco	RS-36	9/62	84118

Freight cars: 98 gondolas, 44 flatcars, 65 boxcars

APALACHICOLA NORTHERN RAILROAD CO.

300 First Street
P. O. Box 250
Port St. Joe, FL 32456

Reporting marks: AN
Phone: 904-229-7411
Fax: 904-227-7463

Apalachicola Northern operates freight service from Port St. Joe, Florida, to an interchange with CSX at Chattahoochee, 96.3 miles. Rail is predominantly 115 pound with some 90 and 132 pound. Traffic includes bituminous coal, pulpboard, wood chips, chemicals, and scrap paper — more than 45,000 cars a year.

The AN was incorporated May 9, 1903, and opened from Apalachicola to River Junction (now Chattahoochee) in July 1907. The road operated in receivership from July 1907 until October 1908. An extension from Apalachicola to Port St. Joe was completed on May 10, 1910. The company again operated under bankruptcy protection from May 1914 to February 1916, and from May 1932 until December 1936. The railroad has been owned by St. Joe Paper Co. since September 30, 1940.

Radio frequencies: 160.380 (road), 160.500 (yard)
Location of enginehouse: Port St. Joe, Fla.
Locomotives: 14

No.	Builder	Model	New	Builder No.
709	EMD	SW9	12/52	16952
710, 711	EMD	SW9	11/53	18869-70
712-715	EMD	SW1500	5/69	34972-75
716-719	EMD	SW1500	8/70	36487-90
720-722	EMD	GP15T	4/83	827039-1, -2, -3

Freight cars: 1,102 boxcars, 16 covered hoppers, 55 wood-chip hoppers, 40 pulpwood cars

APPANOOSE COUNTY COMMUNITY RAILROAD, INC.

128 North 12th Street
P. O. Box 321
Centerville, IA 52544

Reporting marks: APNC
Phone: 515-437-7029
Fax: 515-437-0514

The Appanoose County provides freight service from Centerville, Iowa, to connections with Burlington Northern and Norfolk Southern at Albia, 36 miles. Rail ranges from 75 to 130 pound. Traffic is plastic, grain, and scrap metal — 400 cars a year.

The original portion of the line from Centerville to Moulton, 11.8 miles, is made up of former Burlington Northern trackage abandoned in 1982 as well as former Rock Island trackage abandoned in 1980. The Burlington Northern line was built by the Alexandria & Nebraska Railroad and completed to Centerville in 1873. That company was reorganized as the Missouri, Iowa & Nebraska Railroad, then in 1886 as the Keokuk & Western Railroad. Appanoose County operations started on December 19, 1984, following construction of an interchange with the N&W. In April 1993 the railroad acquired 25.9 miles of Norfolk Southern trackage from Moulton to Albia, Appanoose County's only outside connection. The company is controlled by Centerville community interests.

Radio frequency: 161.265
Location of enginehouse: Centerville, Iowa
Locomotives: 2

No.	Builder	Model	New	Builder No.
116	EMD	GP7U	11/51	14993
973	EMD	GP7	11/53	19070

ARCADE & ATTICA RAILROAD CORP.

278 Main Street
P. O. Box 246
Arcade, NY 14009

Reporting marks: ARA
Phone: 716-492-3100

The Arcade & Attica operates freight service from a Conrail connection at Arcade Junction, New York, to North Java, 15 miles. Excursion trains operate between Arcade and Curriers, 7 miles. Rail is 70 pound and the load limit is 200,000 pounds. Freight is primarily grain, fertilizer, and lumber — 300 cars a year. Most of the company's revenue comes from passenger operations.

The Tonawanda Valley Railroad was incorporated on April 5, 1880, and opened a 3-foot gauge line from Attica to Curriers on September 11, 1880. The Tonawanda Valley Extension Railroad extended it to Arcade during 1881. The roads were consolidated to form the Tonawanda Valley & Cuba Railroad, which extended the line to Cuba. In January 1892 operations were cut back from Cuba to Freedom, and the company was reorganized as the Attica & Freedom Railroad. It was again reorganized as the Buffalo, Attica & Arcade Railroad on October 13, 1894. During 1895 the road was relaid to standard gauge. The Arcade & Attica was incorporated May 24, 1917, to purchase and operate the property. Regular passenger service was discontinued in 1951, and the company abandoned 17 miles between Attica and North Java in 1957. Excursion service started in 1962. The company is independent.

Location of enginehouse: Arcade, N. Y.
Locomotives: 5

No.	Builder	Model	New	Builder No.
14	Baldwin	4-6-0	2/17	45083
18	Alco	2-8-0	11/20	62624
110	GE	44-ton	6/41	12947
111	GE	44-ton	4/47	28346
112	GE	65-ton	5/45	27866

Arcade & Attica 44-tonner No. 111 passes through Curriers with a car of grain destined for North Java, New York. Photo by Jim Shaw.

ARIZONA & CALIFORNIA RAILROAD CO., LTD.

1324 California Avenue
P. O. Box AF
Parker, AZ 85344

Reporting marks: ARZC
Phone: 602-669-6662
Fax: 602-669-6666

The Arizona & California provides freight and container service from a connection with the Santa Fe at Cadiz, California, to Matthie, Arizona, 190 miles, and then via trackage rights over the Santa Fe from Matthie to Phoenix, another 57 miles. A branch line runs from Rice through Blythe to Ripley, Calif., 50 miles. Rail runs from 90 to 112 pound.

Traffic is primarily overhead in connection with the Santa Fe,

about 15,000 cars a year. Local traffic includes hay, LP gas, lumber, and solid waste — about 5,000 cars a year.

The line was built by the Arizona & California Railway, chartered September 10, 1903, and opened from Matthie to Parker, in June 1907. The line was completed to Cadiz three years later. It came under control of the Santa Fe, Prescott & Phoenix Railway in November 1905 and was merged into the California, Arizona & Santa Fe Railway, an affiliate of the Santa Fe, in 1911. The Blythe branch was built by the California Southern Railroad. It was completed to Blythe in 1916 and to Ripley in 1921, at which time it was leased by the Santa Fe. The lines were acquired by the

current operator from the Santa Fe on May 9, 1991. The Arizona & California is a limited partnership controlled by David Parkinson and others.

Radio frequency: 160.860

Location of enginehouse: Parker, Ariz.

Locomotives: 13

No.	Builder	Model	New	Builder No.
2001-2005	EMD	GP20	7/60	26045, 26063, 26047, 26046, 26072
3501	EMD	GP35	5/64	29011
3502	EMD	GP35	2/65	30356
3801	EMD	GP38	2/69	34828
3802	EMD	GP38	4/69	34853
3803	EMD	GP38	3/69	34847
3804	EMD	GP38	2/70	35673
9623	EMD	MP15	12/74	75641-3
9628	EMD	MP15	12/74	75641-8

Freight cars: 25 flatcars

Arizona & California's handsome green and tan GP38 No. 3802 heads up a three-unit consist at Big River, California. Most traffic on this desert line is overhead between Santa Fe connections. Photo by Jim Shaw.

ARIZONA CENTRAL RAILROAD, INC.

300 North Broadway
Clarkdale, AZ 86324

Reporting marks: AZCR
Phone: 602-634-4393
Fax: 602-639-1653

The company provides freight service from a connection with the Santa Fe at Drake, Arizona, to Clarkdale, 37.8 miles. Rail is 90 pound. Freight traffic includes about 1,500 cars a year of cement and coal.

Excursion trains through scenic Verde Canyon have run since November 1990. About 60,000 passengers are carried annually.

This line was built by the Verde Valley Railway, which was chartered November 17, 1911. The road was completed in June 1913 and leased to the Santa Fe a short time later. Santa Fe bought the line in 1943 and sold it to the present operator on April 14, 1989. The company is controlled by David L. Durbano (The Western Group).

Radio frequency: 160.560

Location of enginehouse: Clarkdale, Ariz.

Locomotives: 3

No.	Builder	Model	New	Builder No.	Rebuilt
2278	EMD	GP7U	4/57	23140	1980
2279	EMD	GP7U	1/52	15634	1980
3413	EMD	GP9	4/56	21355	1975

ARIZONA EASTERN RAILWAY CO.

P. O. Box Y
Claypool, AZ 85532

Reporting marks: AZER
Phone: 602-473-2447
Fax: 602-473-2449

The Arizona Eastern operates freight service from a connection with Southern Pacific at Bowie to Miami, Arizona, 134 miles. Rail is 75 to 136 pound. Traffic includes copper concentrates, copper rod, and cathode — about 7,000 cars a year.

This line was built by the Gila Valley, Globe & Northern Railway, chartered on January 15, 1895. The line was completed in January 1899. During construction, the company came under control of the Arizona Eastern. Southern Pacific gained control of the AE in 1905 and merged it in 1924. The present operator purchased the property from Southern Pacific and began shortline service on October 11, 1988.

The company is a subsidiary of Kyle Railways Inc.

Radio frequencies: 160.215, 160.245, 161.355, 161.475
Location of enginehouse: Miami, Ariz.
Locomotives: 11

No.	Builder	Model	New	Builder No.	Rebuilt
23	EMD	SW9	12/51	15607	
24	EMD	SW1200	1/64	28747	
25	EMD	SW1200	1/64	28750	
1309	EMD	SW13	12/50	11677	1973
2045	EMD	GP20	1/61	26311	1974
2046	EMD	GP20	12/61	26943	1976
2170	EMD	GP20	5/60	25703	
2171	EMD	GP20	11/60	26291	
2501	EMD	GP35	11/63	28403	1980
2502	EMD	GP35	4/65	30219	1980
2503	EMD	GP35	4/65	30221	1980

Freight cars: 2 flatcars

ARKANSAS & MISSOURI RAILROAD CO.

306 East Emma Street
P. O. Box 303
Springdale, AR 72764

Reporting marks: AM
Phone: 501-751-8600
Fax: 501-751-7603

Arkansas & Missouri operates freight service from connections with Kansas City Southern and Union Pacific at Fort Smith, Arkansas, to a connection with the Burlington Northern at Monett, Missouri, 139.5 miles. An additional Union Pacific connection is made at Van Buren, Ark. Rail is 90 to 132 pound. Seasonal excursion trains operate between Springdale, Van Buren, and Winslow, Ark.

Traffic includes grain and feed supplements, paper products, sand, plastic, food products, scrap steel, lumber, aluminum, and bauxite — about 28,000 cars a year.

This line was part of a route built between 1880 and 1882 by the St. Louis, Arkansas & Texas Railway, an affiliate of the St. Louis-San Francisco. By 1887 the line extended to the coal fields at Paris, Texas. It was SLSF's main route to Texas until 1902 when the Tulsa line was completed. Frisco discontinued passenger service on the line in 1965 and was merged into Burlington Northern in November 1980. The AM was incorporated March 10, 1977, and began operation on September 1, 1986.

The company is owned by J. A. Hannold and others.

Radio frequencies: 160.440, 160.785, 161.475
Location of enginehouse: Springdale and Fort Smith, Ark.
Locomotives: 18

No.	Builder	Model	New	Builder No.
12	Alco	T-6	10/59	83388
14	Alco	T-6	10/59	83385
16	Alco	T-6	1/59	83376
18	Alco	T-6	3/59	82320
20	Alco	RS-1	10/51	79349
22	Alco	RS-1	4/43	70811

No.	Builder	Model	New	Builder No.
42	Alco	RS-32	6/61	83992
44	Alco	C-420	6/65	3418-03
46	Alco	C-420	6/65	3418-04
48	Alco	C-420	6/65	3418-17
50	Alco	C-420	3/63	84721
52	Alco	C-420	12/65	3431-01
54	Alco	C-420	12/65	3431-02
58	Alco	C-420	7/66	3463-03
60	Alco	C-420	10/64	3385-03
62	Alco	C-420	10/64	3385-04
64	Alco	C-420	10/64	3385-09
66	Alco	C-420	10/64	3385-10

Freight cars: 139 hopper cars, 259 gondolas, 70 boxcars

ARKANSAS CENTRAL RAILWAY CO.

600 South Riverside Road
P. O. Box 1089
St. Joseph, MO 64502

Reporting marks: ACRY
Phone: 816-364-6945

The company was formed to provide common carrier switching service over 1.3 miles of track owned by its parent company, Herzog Stone Products, Inc., at Hatton, Arkansas. Rail is 90 pound. Kansas City Southern, which is the sole connection, operates the line under a trackage rights agreement.

Locomotives: 1

No.	Builder	Model	New	Builder No.
5240	GMD	SW9	1/51	A-149

ARKANSAS, LOUISIANA & MISSISSIPPI RAILROAD CO.

P. O. Box 757
Crossett, AR 71635

Reporting marks: ALM
Phone: 501-364-9004
Fax: 501-364-4521

The Arkansas, Louisiana & Mississippi operates freight service from Crossett, Arkansas, to Monroe, Louisiana, a distance of 52.9 miles. Interchange is made with the Union Pacific, Kansas City Southern, Ashley, Drew & Northern, and Fordyce & Princeton railroads. Rail is predominantly 90 pound. About 10,000 cars a year of lumber, paper, forest products, and chemicals make up the road's traffic.

On July 20, 1906, the Arkansas, Louisiana & Gulf Railway

was chartered to build a line from Monroe, La., to Pine Bluff, Ark. The line was opened from Monroe to Hamburg, Ark., 56.2 miles, and from Rolfe Junction to Crossett, Ark., 5.3 miles, on October 1, 1908.

On May 29, 1913, the company was placed in receivership and reorganized in December 1915 as the Arkansas & Louisiana Midland Railroad. The Arkansas & Louisiana Missouri Railway was organized on July 31, 1920, as successor to the A&LM. The present operator bought the assets of the Arkansas & Louisiana Missouri on September 27, 1991. The company is owned by Georgia Pacific Corporation.

Radio frequencies: 160.980 (road), 160.440 (yard)
Locomotives: 3

No.	Builder	Model	New	Builder No.
1001	EMD	NW2	10/49	10598
1815	EMD	GP28	3/74	73662-1
1816	EMD	GP28	9/64	29593

Freight cars: 536 boxcars, 73 flatcars, 21 covered hoppers

ARKANSAS MIDLAND RAILWAY CO., INC.

P. O. Box 696
Malvern, AR 72104

Reporting marks: AKMD
Phone: 501-844-4444
Fax: 501-844-4710

The Arkansas Midland operates four disconnected lines. The two most important run from Mountain Pine, Arkansas, through Hot Springs to a Union Pacific connection at Malvern, 33.3 miles, and from Birds Mill to a UP connection at Gurdon, 52.3 miles. Most of the Birds Mill line is being operated by the Caddo, Antoine & Little Missouri Railroad, which started service April 6, 1994.

The other Arkansas Midland lines run from Galloway to a connection with UP at North Little Rock, 6.6 miles, and from Helena to a connection with UP at Lexa, 12 miles. A total of 104.2 miles is operated. Rail varies from 90 to 112 pound. Traffic is primarily forest and food products, aggregate, building material, chemicals, and soybean and cottonseed oil — about 20,000 cars a year.

The Mountain Pine line was built by the Hot Springs Railroad and opened January 25, 1876, as a 3-foot gauge line. The Choctaw, Oklahoma & Gulf (Rock Island) purchased the Hot Springs Railroad in 1902. The Gurdon line was built by the Gurdon & Fort Smith Railroad, chartered in 1900. In 1909 it

Former ICG GP8 No. 850 switches cars for the Arkansas Midland at West Helena, Arkansas, in October, 1993. Photo by Jim Shaw.

came under control of the St. Louis, Iron Mountain & Southern (Missouri Pacific). The Carlisle line is a former Rock Island branch. The Helena branch was built by the Iron Mountain & Helena Railroad, chartered in 1879, and purchased by the St. Louis & Iron Mountain in 1882.

All four lines were sold to the current operator by Missouri Pacific on February 23, 1992. Arkansas Midland is a subsidiary of Pinsly Railroad Co., Inc.

Radio frequencies: 160.275, 161.460, 160.905 (yard)
Location of enginehouse: Jones Mills, Ark.
Locomotives: 8

No.	Builder	Model	New	Builder No.	Rebuilt
700	EMD	GP8	1/56	20806	5/74
703	EMD	GP8	3/51	12933	2/74
707	EMD	GP8	4/53	17972	8/74
722	EMD	GP8	4/53	17721	1/77
726	EMD	GP8	4/53	17726	2/77
728	EMD	GP8	8/52	16903	2/77
850	EMD	GP8	4/52	16405	6/73
918	EMD	GP8	3/53	17718	5/78

AROOSTOOK VALLEY RAILROAD CO.

32 Parsons Street
P. O. Box 509
Presque Isle, ME 04769

Reporting marks: AVL
Phone: 207-764-3714
Fax: 207-764-5971

Aroostook Valley operates freight and switching service from a connection with Bangor & Aroostook at Skyway Junction to Presque Isle, Maine, 2.8 miles. Rail is 80 pound.

Traffic includes fertilizer, lumber and forest products, chemicals, paper, pulpboard, and potato meal — less than 250 cars a year.

The company was incorporated July 2, 1902. Construction started in 1909 and the road was opened to Washburn in 1910, Sweden in 1911, and Caribou in 1914. The road was operated by electric power until 1946, when it converted to diesel and passenger service was discontinued. The 18.8-mile Caribou-Washburn Junction line was abandoned in February 1982. The company abandoned its CP Rail connection at Washburn Junction and built a new interchange at Skyway Junction in 1993.

The company has been controlled by Arbox Three Corporation since 1980.

Radio frequency: 160.890
Location of enginehouse: Presque Isle, Maine
Locomotives: 2

No.	Builder	Model	New	Builder No.
10	GE	44-ton	6/45	27799
12	GE	44-ton	9/49	30246

ASHLAND RAILWAY, INC.

489 North Main Street
Mansfield, OH 44901

Reporting marks: ASRY
Phone: 419-525-2822
Fax: 419-525-2864

The Ashland Railway operates freight service from connections with Conrail and CSX at Mansfield to Ashland and West Salem, Ohio, 31.5 miles, and from Mansfield to a CSX connection at Willard, Ohio, 25 miles. Rail is predominantly 130 pound.

Traffic is about 7,000 cars a year of linerboard, plastic pellets, castings, toys, grain, and general commodities.

The Ashland line was built as part of the 6-foot gauge Atlantic & Great Western route from Dayton to the Pennsylvania state line opened in 1864. The line later became part of the Erie's Chicago main line. It was operated by Conrail until February 20, 1986, when it was sold to the Ashland Community Improvement Corporation and shortline service started. The Willard line was acquired from CSX on November 15, 1990.

A second division in New Jersey extends from a Conrail interchange at Lakehurst to Woodmansie, 13.3 miles — that line is not in service. It was a former Central of New Jersey branch purchased from Conrail by Clayton Sand Co. in September 1986 and leased to the Pine Belt Railway (now part of Ashland Railway).

The operating company is controlled by David Crane.

Radio frequencies: 160.965, 452.900 (Ohio)
Location of enginehouse: Ashland, Ohio
Locomotives: 6

No.	Builder	Model	New	Builder No.
32	GMD	GP9	11/56	A1077
33	GMD	GP9	11/56	A1078
34	EMD	GP9	11/56	22600
65	EMD	NW2	7/46	3606
66	EMD	NW2	11/49	7178
4561	EMD	GP9	1/58	23570

Freight cars: 100 gondolas, 50 boxcars

ASHTABULA CARSON JEFFERSON RAILROAD CO., INC.

145 East Walnut Street
P. O. Box 222
Jefferson, Ohio 44047-0222

Reporting marks: ACJR
Phone: 216-576-6346
Fax: 216-576-8848

The Ashtabula Carson Jefferson operates freight service from Jefferson, Ohio, to a Conrail connection at Carson Yard, 6.25 miles. Rail is 105 pound. Limited passenger excursion service is also provided.

Traffic consists of 1,000 cars a year of paper products, stone, aluminum, ore, grains and recyclable materials.

This line is part of the Lake Shore & Michigan Southern's Oil City branch, later New York Central. It was abandoned by Conrail in 1984 and acquired by Ohio DOT. The Ashtabula Carson Jefferson began operations June 27, 1984. The operating company is independent.

Location of enginehouse: Jefferson, Ohio
Locomotives: 1

No.	Builder	Model	New	Builder No.
107	Alco	S-2	6/50	78016

Alco S-2 No. 107 pulls a typical freight train on the 6.25-mile-long Ashtabula Carson Jefferson Railroad near Jefferson, Ohio. Photo by Jim Shaw.

AT&L RAILROAD CO., INC.

Second and Clarence Nash Boulevard
P. O. Box 29
Watonga, OK 73772

Reporting marks: ATLT
Phone: 405-623-5477
Fax: 405-623-2686

The AT&L — named for the owner's grandsons, Austin, Todd, and Ladd Lafferty — operates freight service from Watonga to Geary and El Reno, Oklahoma, 39.7 miles. It connects with Union Pacific at El Reno. A 9.6-mile branch runs from Geary to Bridgeport. Rail is 80, 100, and 112 pound.

Traffic is grain, fertilizer, and agricultural commodities — about 3,000 cars a year. The Central Oklahoma Chapter, NRHS, operates the *Watonga Chief* dinner and excursion train on this line.

The east end of this line was built by the Choctaw Coal & Railway Co. in the 1880s. In October 1894 it was leased to the Choctaw, Oklahoma & Gulf Railroad and in 1904 to the Rock Island. Following the abandonment of the Rock Island, the state acquired the portion of the line from El Reno to Geary. It was operated by the North Central Oklahoma Railroad prior to AT&L taking over in May 1985. AT&L owns the line from Geary to Watonga. The Bridgeport branch has been operated since July 1986.

The company is owned by Wheeler Brothers Grain Co., Inc.
Radio frequency: 160.785
Location of enginehouse: Watonga, Okla.
Locomotives: 4

No.	Builder	Model	New	Builder No.
1127	EMD	SW1200	1/64	28748
1948	EMD	GP9	9/58	24059
2165	EMD	GP7	11/53	18894
2491	AT&SF	CF7		

Freight cars: 8 covered hoppers

ATLANTA, STONE MOUNTAIN & LITHONIA RAILWAY CO.

6978 Rogers Lake Road
Lithonia, GA 30058

Reporting marks: ASML
Phone: 404-482-7231

The company is a switching line at Lithonia, Georgia, operating 4.3 miles of track. Traffic is primarily outbound stone ballast, about 3,400 cars a year. The railroad opened in 1909 and was operated by the Pine Mountain Granite Co. from 1924 to 1945. The company is controlled by Davidson Mineral Properties, Inc.
Radio frequency: 161.025
Locomotives: 1

No.	Builder	Model	New	Builder No.
110	Alco	S-2EM	6/42	69972

ATLANTIC & GULF RAILROAD CO., INC.

1019 Coast Line Avenue
Albany, GA 31705

Reporting marks: AGLF
Phone: 912-435-6629
Fax: 912-436-4571

The Atlantic & Gulf operates freight service from a connection with CSX at Thomasville, Georgia, to Albany and Sylvester, 77 miles. It connects at Albany with Norfolk Southern, Georgia &

Florida and Georgia Southwestern. Rail is predominantly 100 pound. Traffic includes coal, paper, grain, peanut oil, rubber and rubber tires, forest products, aggregate, and other manufactured products — about 12,000 cars a year.

The portion of the line from Thomasville to Albany was built by the South Georgia & Florida Railroad and completed into Albany in June 1870. During the mid-1870s the G&F was absorbed by the Atlantic & Gulf, which became the Savannah, Florida & Western Railway in 1879.

The Albany-Sylvester section was built by the Brunswick & Albany Railroad, which completed its line to Albany about 1872. That company was reorganized as the Brunswick & Western in 1882, and in 1901 it became part of the Savannah, Florida & Western.

The Savannah, Florida & Western became part of the Atlantic Coast Line in 1902. CSX Transportation sold the line to the present operator and shortline service began on February 15, 1991. The company is a subsidiary of Gulf & Ohio Railways (Pete Clausen).

Radio frequencies: 160.500, 161.190
Location of enginehouse: Albany, Ga.
Locomotives: 9

No.	Builder	Model	New	Builder No.	Rebuilt
8068	EMD	GP10	1/55	20147	1970
8090	EMD	GP10	12/55	20757	1975
8104	EMD	GP10	3/55	20283	1975
8274	EMD	GP10	11/54	19764	1972
8302	EMD	GP10	2/54	19213	1977
8311	EMD	GP10	2/54	19231	1977
8331	EMD	GP10	1/58	23855	1977
8395	EMD	GP10	12/55	20840	1976
8421	EMD	GP10			

Freight cars: 398

ATLANTIC & WESTERN RAILWAY, LP.

317 Chatham Street
P. O. Box 1208
Sanford, NC 27330

Reporting marks: ATW
Phone: 919-776-7521
Fax: 919-774-4621

The Atlantic & Western operates freight service from connections with CSX and Norfolk Southern at Sanford to Jonesboro, North Carolina, 3.38 miles. Rail is 70 and 85 pound. Traffic includes sand, scrap, cement, lumber, paper products, and food products — about 900 cars a year.

The Atlantic & Western Railroad was incorporated March 7, 1899, to construct a railroad from Sanford to Goldsboro, N. C., 70 miles, and points beyond. It was opened from Sanford to Broadway in 1905 and to Lillington, 25 miles, in April 1913. It was never extended farther. Trackage from Jonesboro to Lillington was abandoned on December 15, 1961.

The company was acquired by K. E. Durden and others in May 1988. It is now a partnership controlled by Rail Management & Consulting Corporation, general partner.

Radio frequency: 160.275
Location of enginehouse: Sanford, N. C.
Locomotives: 2

No.	Builder	Model	New	Builder No.
100	GE	70-ton	9/50	30452
101	GE	70-ton	1/48	29467

Freight cars: 2,181

AUSTIN & NORTHWESTERN RAILROAD

3007 Longhorn Boulevard, Suite 105
Austin, TX 78758-7632

Reporting marks: AUNW
Phone: 512-873-7713

Austin & Northwestern operates freight service from a connection with the Southern Pacific at Giddings, Texas, through Austin to Scobee, 154.8 miles. A branch extends from Fairland to Marble Falls, 6.2 miles. It also connects with Union Pacific at McNeil and Elgin. Rail is 90, 112, and 132 pound. The ICC approved discontinuance of service from Giddings to Smoot, 53.5 miles, in May, 1995. Traffic includes aggregate, crushed limestone, beer, lumber, and paper — about 8,000 cars a year. The Austin & Texas Central tourist railroad runs over part of this line.

The line from Giddings to Austin was built by the Houston & Texas Central and opened in 1871. The Austin-Scobee line was built by the Austin & Northwestern Railroad, which was chartered April 20, 1881, and opened the following January. The Marble

Falls branch was built by the affiliated Granite Mountain & Marble Falls Railroad. It and the A&NW were merged on September 3, 1901, by the H&TC, which was a Southern Pacific subsidiary. The line was acquired from Southern Pacific by Capital Metro – City of Austin. Short line service started August 15, 1986.

Austin & Northwestern is a subsidiary of RailTex, Inc., but in December 1995 the city of Austin was seeking a new operator.

Radio frequencies: 160.305, 161.520
Location of enginehouse: McNeil, Texas
Locomotives: 4

No.	Builder	Model	New	Builder No.
8	EMD	NW2	12/42	2352
172	EMD	GP9	9/55	20864
173	EMD	GP9	3/59	25105
174	EMD	GP9	5/54	19476

Freight cars: 1 hopper car

The Austin & Northwestern runs some long trains like this three unit affair near Burnet, Texas. Photo by Jim Shaw.

36

BAD WATER LINE

642 South Federal Boulevard
Riverton, WY 82501

Reporting marks: BDW
Phone: 307-956-7480

The company operates a 4-mile switching line from Shoshoni to a connection with Burlington Northern at Bonneville, Wyoming. Rail is 100 pound. Traffic includes liquid sulfur, lumber, and agricultural products such as malt barley, alfalfa, and hay.

The line was built by the Wyoming & North Western Railway, chartered November 12, 1904, and opened from Casper to Lander by 1907. Chicago & North Western controlled the company and absorbed it in 1920. The present owner bought the line from Riverton to Bonneville, 25.7 miles, from C&NW on October 1, 1988. During 1991 the company was given ICC approval to abandon 22.5 miles from Shoshoni to Riverton.

The company is controlled by Ron Vosika and Jim King.
Location of enginehouse: Bonneville, Wyo.
Locomotives: 1

No.	Builder	Model	New	Builder No.
1	EMD	SW1	2/52	16446

BANGOR & AROOSTOOK RAILROAD CO.

Northern Maine Junction Park
R.R. 2, Box 45
Bangor, ME 04401-9602

Reporting marks: BAR
Phone: 207-848-4200
Fax: 207-848-4343

The Bangor & Aroostook provides freight service over 419 route miles in eastern and northern Maine. The main line runs from Searsport north through Northern Maine Junction (where it

Bangor & Aroostook GP38 No. 94 heads up the consist near Presque Isle, Maine. BAR used to haul potatoes but now depends on paper and forest products for a living. Photo by Jim Shaw.

connects with ST Rail System's Maine Central) and Brownville Junction (connection with Canadian American) to St. Leonard, New Brunswick (connection with Canadian National). The company operates nearly a dozen branch lines. Traffic is primarily paper, forest products, coal, and oil, about 41,000 cars a year.

The company was chartered on February 13, 1891, to build a railroad from Brownville to Caribou. BAR's earliest component dates from 1836. The railroad completed dieselization by 1952 and ceased operating rail passenger service September 4, 1961.

The company was purchased by Iron Road Railways in March 1995 and is affiliated with the Canadian American Railroad Co. Radio frequencies: 160.440, 160.740, 160.920, 160.685

Employees: 340
Locomotives: 40 (2 BL2, 1 F3A, 37 GP7/9/38)
Freight Cars: 3,306
Principal shop: Northern Maine Junction, Maine

BATTEN KILL RAILROAD CO., INC.

1 Elbow Street
Greenwich, NY 12834

Reporting marks: BKRR
Phone: 518-692-2160
Fax: 518-692-2160

The Batten Kill Railroad operates 32.4 miles extending from a connection with the CP Rail System (Delaware & Hudson) at Eagle Bridge to Thompson, New York. Rail is 80 to 90 pound.

Traffic is under 500 cars annually and consists primarily of feed grain, fertilizer, and wood pulp. Seasonal *Batten Kill Rambler* passenger excursions are also operated.

Rail service on this line was first provided by the Greenwich & Johnsonville Railroad, which was incorporated March 26, 1864, and opened from Greenwich to Johnsonville on August 31, 1870. The company was reorganized as the Greenwich & Johnsonville Railway on September 10, 1879. The company absorbed the Battenkill Railroad in 1903. In 1982, the Delaware & Hudson sold the G&J to the newly formed Batten Kill Railroad, which began operations October 22 of that year.

The D&H line from Eagle Bridge to Salem, N. Y., was acquired by the Eagle Bridge-Thompson Development Corp., and has since been transferred to the Northeast New York Railroad Preservation Group, a non-profit corporation. The property is operated by the Batten Kill Railroad.

The company is controlled by R. E. Crowd and others.

Radio frequency: 160.905
Location of enginehouse: Greenwich, N. Y.
Locomotives: 2

No.	Builder	Model	New	Builder No.
605	Alco	RS-3	11/50	78369
4116	Alco	RS-3	9/52	80316

BAUXITE & NORTHERN RAILWAY CO.

Cyanamid Road
P. O. Box 138
Bauxite, AR 72011

Reporting marks: BXN
Phone: 501-776-4619
Fax: 501-776-4558

The Bauxite & Northern operates freight service between Bauxite, Arkansas, and and a Union Pacific connection at Bauxite Junction, 3 miles. Rail is 115 pound. Traffic is about 3,600 cars a year of bauxite, aluminia, clay, and cement.

The company was incorporated November 13, 1906. Construc-tion started during April 1907 and the road opened shortly afterward. The company has been owned by Aluminum Company of America since it was built.
Radio frequency: 160.500
Location of enginehouse: Bauxite, Ark.
Locomotives: 2

No.	Builder	Model	New	Builder No.
15	EMD	MP15DC	11/74	74621-1
16	EMD	MP15DC	11/74	74621-2

BAY COLONY RAILROAD CORP.

420 Washington Street
Braintree, MA 02184

Reporting marks: BCLR
Phone: 617-380-3556
Fax: 617-380-4820

The Bay Colony railroad provides freight service over six disconnected routes, all of them in southeastern Massachusetts, totaling 122 miles:
• Middleboro to Hyannis and South Dennis, with a branch to Falmouth, 63.4 miles
• Braintree to North Plymouth, with a branch to West Hanover, 35 miles
• Medfield Junction to Newton Highlands and Millis, 12.9 miles
• Weir Junction to Dean Street in Taunton, 1.3 miles
• North Dartmouth to Watuppa, 6.1 miles.
• West Concord to Acton, 4.9 miles.
    Bay Colony connects with Conrail at Middleboro, Braintree,

Bay Colony GP9 No. 1751 sets off three gondolas for fly ash loading at the Canal Electric power plant at Sandwich, Massachusetts. Photo by Jack Armstrong.

Medfield Junction, Weir Junction, and North Dartmouth, and with Boston & Maine (ST Rail System) at West Concord. The affiliated Cape Cod Scenic Railroad and Amtrak operate seasonal passenger service over the Middleboro line. Massachusetts Bay Transportation Authority commuter trains operate over a portion of the Medfield line. Rail is 107 to 115 pound.

Traffic includes municipal solid waste, lumber, cement, LP gas, building materials, salt, plastic, scrap steel, and military hardware — 5,500 cars a year.

These lines opened as early as the 1840s and in time became components of the Old Colony Railroad, which was leased by the New Haven in 1893. The commonwealth of Massachusetts acquired ownership of the lines in the late 1970s and early 1980s, and upgraded BCLR's Middleboro Hyannis line to FRA Class IV after Amtrak began operating New York-Cape Cod passenger service.

In 1981 Conrail planned to abandon freight service over most of the lines. Bay Colony leased its lines on June 12, 1982.

The operating company was created by a special act of the Massachusetts legislature in 1977 and is controlled by Gordon H. Fay and George E. Bartholomew.

Radio frequencies: 160.305, 161.265, 161.355
Location of enginehouse: East Wareham, Mass.
Locomotives: 10

No.	Builder	Model	New	Builder No.
410	GE	44-ton	9/49	30250
411	GE	44-ton	10/56	32664
412	GE	44-ton	1953	
1052	Alco	S-2	8/43	70244
1058	Alco	S-4	10/50	78419
1061	Alco	S-4	9/50	78235
1064	Alco	RS-1	1/52	79580
1501	EMD	GP7	2/53	17843
1751	EMD	GP9	10/55	20897
2443	AT&SF	CF7	1977	

Freight Cars: 9 boxcars, 23 gondolas, 16 municipal waste cars

---

THE BAY LINE RAILROAD, LLC.

2605 Thomas Drive
P. O. Box 28300
Panama City Beach, FL 32411

Reporting marks: BAYL
Phone: 904-230-8331
Fax: 904-230-8848

The Bay Line operates freight and TOFC service from Panama City, Florida, to Dothan, Alabama, a distance of 81 miles. A 7-mile branch runs from Campbellton to Graceville, Fla. Connections are made at Dothan with CSX, Norfolk Southern, A&G Railroad and H&S Railroad and at Cottondale, Fla., with CSX. Rail is 90 to 115 pound. More than 30,000 cars a year of wood chips, paper products, chemicals, petroleum products and agricultural products make up the railroad's traffic.

The Atlanta & St. Andrews Bay Railway was incorporated February 14, 1906, and was completed between Dothan and Panama City on July 15, 1908. Passenger service ended on July 15, 1956. The Graceville branch opened July 14, 1971.

The Bay Line Railroad purchased the assets of the A&StAB from its owner, Stone Container Corp., on January 1, 1994. The company also operates the affiliated A&G Railroad.

The Bay Line is controlled by Rail Management & Consulting Corporation.

Radio frequencies: 160.455, 160.770, 160.815, 161.295
Location of enginehouse: Panama City, Fla.
Locomotives: 12

No.	Builder	Model	New	Builder No.
102	EMD	GP9	6/56	21722
500, 501	EMD	GP38	8/69	35176, 35170
502	EMD	GP38	8/69	35389
503	EMD	GP38	9/69	35410
504-507	EMD	GP38	10/69	35419, 35421, 35440, 35448

No.	Builder	Model	New	Builder No.
508, 509	EMD	GP38-2	5/73	72686-1, 72686-2
510	EMD	GP38-2	6/75	75623-1
511	EMD	GP38	8/69	35378

Freight Cars: 539 boxcars, 175 woodchip gondolas, 46 woodchip hoppers

BC RAIL

221 West Esplanade
P. O. Box 8770
North Vancouver, BC V6B 4X6
Canada

Reporting marks: BCOL
Phone: 604-986-2012
Fax: 604-984-5004

BC Rail is a regional railroad operating from North Vancouver to Chetwynd, British Columbia, 658.5 miles. Principal branch lines run from Odell to Chipmunk, 309.5 miles; Chetwynd to Fort Nelson, 320.9 miles; Chetwynd to Dawson Creek, 61.1 miles; Kennedy to Mackenzie, 25 miles; and Wakely to Quintette, 82.3 miles. It connects with Canadian National, CP Rail, Southern Railway of British Columbia, Burlington Northern, and Union Pacific.

Regular passenger service is provided between North Vancouver, Lillooet, and Prince George. Royal Hudson steam-powered excursions run between North Vancouver and Squamish. Freight traffic is primarily forest products (60 percent) plus coal, minerals, and metal concentrates — more than 200,000 cars a year.

The Pacific Great Eastern Railway was incorporated February 27, 1912, to build a railroad from Vancouver to Prince George. By 1918 the government of British Columbia had acquired the capital stock of the company and it has remained under provincial control ever since. The Fort Nelson line was opened in 1971. The name was changed to British Columbia Railway on April 1, 1972, and the current name was adopted in April 1985.

The company is owned by the Province of British Columbia, which is currently considering privatization of the railroad. BC Rail also operates Vancouver Wharves, Ltd., Westel Telecommunications, Ltd., and trucking lines.

Radio frequencies: 159.570, 161.370, 161.235, 160.695, 161.520
Enginehouse: North Vancouver, B. C.
Locomotives: 116
Freight Cars: 8,943

BEAUFORT & MOREHEAD RAILWAY, INC.

1213 Bridges Street
P. O. Box 3608
Morehead City, NC 28557

Reporting marks: BMH
Phone: 919-726-1777
Fax: 919-726-3759

The Beaufort & Morehead operates freight service from a connection with Norfolk Southern at Morehead City to Beaufort, Marsh Island, and Radial Island, 3.1 miles. Rail is 75 and 100 pound, and the load limit without special arrangements is 200,000 pounds. Traffic includes 6,000 cars a year of aviation fuel, ordnance material, lumber, and miscellaneous commodities.

The Beaufort & Morehead Railroad Co. acquired this line from the Norfolk Southern in 1937. Regular passenger service was discontinued May 2, 1944. The railroad property was sold to the North Carolina Ports Railway Commission in May 1990 and leased to the current operator. The operating company is controlled by A. T. Leary, Jr.

Radio frequency: 160.260
Location of enginehouse: Beaufort, N. C.
Locomotives: 1

No.	Builder	Model	New	Builder No.
1203	EMD	SW1200	11/55	20668

BEE LINE RAILROAD CO., INC.

The company, whose reporting marks are BL, purchased a Conrail line extending from a Norfolk Southern connection at Handy to Stewart, Indiana, 10.6 miles. It was part of a larger segment (from Schneider to Danville) that Conrail was conditionally authorized to abandon on August 26, 1994. The sale was consummated on August 26, 1994. The company is owned by Stewart Grain Co. and the railroad is being operated by the Kankakee, Beaverville & Southern Railroad.

BEECH MOUNTAIN RAILROAD CO.

P. O. Box 2327
Elkins, WV 26241

Reporting marks: BEEM
Phone: 304-636-8320
Fax: 304-636-8271

The Beech Mountain extends from Star Bridge to a CSX connection at Alexander, West Virginia, 8 miles. Rail is 80 to 131 pound. The line carries about 5,600 cars of coal annually. The company was incorporated by the Peerless Coal Co. on December 28, 1953, to purchase and operate a private railroad. It is controlled by Carter-Roag Coal Co., Inc.

Radio frequency: 160.260
Location of enginehouse: Alexander, W. Va.
Locomotives: 1

No.	Builder	Model	New	Builder No.
113	Alco	S-2	9/46	74797

BELFAST & MOOSEHEAD LAKE RAILROAD CO.

One Depot Square
P. O. Box 555
Unity, ME 04988

Reporting marks: BML
Phone: 207-948-5500
Fax: 207-948-5903

BML operates freight service and seasonal passenger excursions between Belfast, Maine, and a connection with ST Rail System (Maine Central) at Burnham Junction, 33.07 miles. Rail ranges from 75 to 90 pound.

Most of the railroad's revenue comes from excursion service. Freight service was suspended in 1992 but resumed in 1995. The line expects to haul about 300 carloads of plastic a year.

The BML was chartered February 28, 1867. Construction started in August 1868 and was completed on December 23, 1870. The line was immediately leased to and operated by the Maine Central until January 2, 1926, when MEC dropped the lease and independent operations started. Regular passenger service ended March 9, 1960. The company started operating passenger excursions in 1987.

Charles Sturtevant and others acquired the city of Belfast's controlling interest in the company on July 3, 1991.

Radio frequencies: 160.710, 160.715, 161.385

Location of enginehouse: Belfast and Thorndike, Maine

Locomotives: 6

No.	Builder	Model	New	Builder No.
50	GE	70-ton	11/46	28567
52	GE	70-ton	4/51	30846
53	GE	70-ton	1/47	28514
54	GE	70-ton	12/48	30032
55	GE	70-ton	12/48	30033
1109	SJ*	4-6-0	1913	

*Swedish State Railways

The Belfast & Moosehead Lake Railroad hauls mostly passengers, but scenes like this one may be repeated as the line finds new freight customers. Photo by James Gunning.

BELVIDERE & DELAWARE RIVER RAILWAY CO., INC.

105 John Ringo Road
P. O. Box 22
Ringoes, NJ 08551

Reporting marks: BDRV
Phone: 908-782-9600

The Belvidere & Delaware River Railway operates freight service from Milford, New Jersey, to a connection with Conrail at Phillipsburg, 16.2 miles. Rail is 130, 131, and 155 pound. Traffic includes lumber, plywood, and forest products amounting to about 1,150 cars a year. The line was built by the Belvidere Delaware Rail Road — chartered in 1836, opened in 1854, and part of the Pennsylvania Railroad by 1872. Conrail sold the line in November 1995. The company is affiliated with the Black River & Western Railroad.
Radio frequency: 161.085
Location of enginehouse: Milford, N. J.
Locomotives: 3

No.	Builder	Model	New	Builder No.
752	EMD	GP9	2/56	21428
782	EMD	GP7	1/50	10546
820	EMD	NW2	11/49	8914

BERLIN MILLS RAILWAY

650 Main Street
Berlin, NH 03570-2489

Reporting marks: BMS
Phone: 603-342-2550
Fax: 603-342-2553

The company operates a terminal line at Berlin, New Hampshire. Its 10.3 miles of track connect with the Atlantic & St. Lawrence and New Hampshire & Vermont railroads. Rail is 80 pound and loadings are restricted over two bridges. About 2,500 cars of paper products and chemicals are switched in and out annually.

This line was formed in 1911 as a department of its paper mill owner. The line is now part of James River Paper Co.
Radio frequency: 160.650
Location of enginehouse: Berlin, N. H.
Locomotives: 3

No.	Builder	Model	New	Builder No.
731	EMD	SW1	5/49	6408
741	EMD	SW1	7/48	5383
745	EMD	SW1	4/49	6759

BESSEMER & LAKE ERIE RAILROAD CO.

General office:
135 Jamison Lane
P. O. Box 68, Monroeville, PA 15146
Operating office:
P. O. Box 471, Greenville, PA 16125

Reporting marks: BLE
Phone: 412-829-6000

The Bessemer & Lake Erie operates freight service from Mifflin Junction, Pennsylvania, north to Erie, Pa., and Conneaut, Ohio. There are branch lines to Annandale and Kaylor as well as additional lines in the Pittsburgh area. A total of 204 miles are operated. B&LE interchanges with Conrail, CSX, Norfolk Southern, Wheeling

& Lake Erie, and several switching and shortline carriers. Traffic is primarily coal, iron ore, and steel — 55,000 cars a year. Passenger service ended on March 5, 1955.

B&LE's history dates from 1865. By 1892 it reached from Butler to Erie and Conneaut. In 1897 it became the Pittsburg, Bessemer & Lake Railroad (incorporated 1897 as successor to the Pittsburgh, Shenango & Lake Erie and the Butler & Pittsburgh railroads). The B&LE was incorporated December 31, 1900, by Carnegie Steel; it leased the Pittsburgh, Butler & Lake Erie in 1902. The company is controlled by Transtar, Inc. (USX Corporation owns 44 percent).

Radio frequency: 160.830 (road), 161.310 (yard)
Employees: 340
Locomotives: 42 (mostly SD units)
Freight Cars: 3,480
Principal shop: Greenville, Pa.

BI-STATE DEVELOPMENT AGENCY RAILROAD CO.

103 North Oak Street
P. O. Box 99
O'Fallon, IL 62269

Reporting marks: BSDA
Phone: 618-632-4400
Fax: 618-632-4562

Bi-State Development Agency provides local switching service over 2 miles of track in St. Louis, Missouri, connecting with Union Pacific. The line is former Southern Railway track acquired from Norfolk Southern. Shortline service started June 17, 1989. Traffic is under 500 cars a year. This line is operated by Railroad Switching Service of Missouri, Inc., an affiliate of Ironhorse Resources, Inc.

Locomotives: 1

No.	Builder	Model	New	Builder No.
1209	EMD	SW1200	12/55	20674

BIRMINGHAM SOUTHERN RAILROAD CO.

6200 E. J. Oliver Blvd.
P. O. Box 579
Fairfield, AL 35064

Reporting marks: BS
Phone: 205-783-2821
Fax: 205-783-4507

Birmingham Southern provides switching service in Birmingham, Alabama, and the surrounding area. It operates 84 miles of track and connects with Burlington Northern, CSX, and Norfolk Southern. Rail is 100 to 115 pound. Over 120,000 carloads of general commodities are handled annually.

The company was incorporated March 3, 1899, and is owned by Transtar, Inc. In 1966 the company acquired the Federal Barge Line Railroad from Port Birmingham to Fairfield, 18 miles.

Radio frequency: 160.290, 160.890
Location of enginehouse: Fairfield, Ala.
Locomotives: 33
1 NW2, 1 SW7, 3 SW9s, 3 SW1000s, 12 SW1001s, 1 SW1200s, 3 MP15s, 5 GP38s, 4 SD9s
Freight Cars: 5 boxcars, 54 gondolas, 198 hopper cars

BLACK RIVER & WESTERN CORP.

Route 579
P. O. Box 200
Ringoes, NJ 08551

Reporting marks: BRW
Phone: 908-782-9600
Fax: 908-782-8251

Black River & Western operates freight service from a connection with Conrail at Three Bridges, New Jersey, to Flemington and Lambertville, 16 miles. Rail is 100 to 130 pound. Freight traffic consists of about 500 cars a year of chemicals, plastic, bulk transfer, and general commodities. Seasonal passenger excursion trains are operated out of Flemington and Ringoes. Much of the company's income comes from excursions.

The company was incorporated January 24, 1961. On May 16, 1965, it leased a portion of the Pennsylvania Railroad's Flemington branch from Flemington to Ringoes and started excursion service. On March 16, 1970, it took over the balance of the branch to Lambertville and started freight operations over the entire line. On April 1, 1976, the company acquired Central of New Jersey's Flemington branch from Three Bridges to Flemington as well as other Penn Central trackage in the Lambertville area. Rail service on the Flemington line dates from 1854 when the Flemington Railroad & Transportation company opened the line into Flemington.

The company is controlled by Nicholas Burenga and others.

Radio frequency: 161.085
Location of enginehouse: Ringoes, N. J.
Locomotives: 3

No.	Builder	Model	New	Builder No.
42	AT&SF	CF7	2/78	
60	Alco	2-8-0	9/37	69021
780	EMD	GP7	4/50	8879

BLOOMER LINE (BLOOMER SHIPPERS CONNECTING RAILROAD CO.)

Route 9 West
P. O. Box 546
Gibson City, IL 60936

Reporting marks: BLOL
Phone: 217-784-4923
Fax: 217-784-5965

The Bloomer Line operates from Colfax to Kempton, Illinois, 36 miles, and from Risk (Strawn) to Gibson City. It connects with the Toledo, Peoria & Western at Chatsworth and Illinois Central and Norfolk Southern at Gibson City. Rail is 75, 85, and 115 pound. Traffic includes grain, fertilizer, plastic, and lumber — about 3,500 cars a year.

The Colfax-Kempton route was built by the Kankakee & Southwestern Railroad in 1878. In time it became Illinois Central's Bloomington District (thus the name "Bloomer Line"). It was operated by ICG until June 1, 1981. Shipper opposition to abandonment led to the formation of the new railroad. The track between Barnes and Herscher was purchased by the Bloomer Shippers Railway Redevelopment League in 1985, and short line service started on June 3 of that year. The Strawn-Gibson City line, once part of Wabash's Chicago-Decatur route, was acquired from Norfolk & Western on May 22, 1990.

The operating company is owned by shippers along the line.

Radio frequency: 161.355
Location of enginehouse: Gibson City, Ill.
Locomotives: 3

No.	Builder	Model	New	Builder No.
55	EMD	SW1200	3/65	29793
91	EMD	GP9	6/58	24060
92	EMD	GP9	2/56	20981

BLUE MOUNTAIN RAILROAD, INC.

709 North Tenth Street
Walla Walla, WA 99362

Reporting marks: BLMR
Phone: 509-522-1464
Fax: 509-522-8213

The Blue Mountain Railroad operates freight service from a connection with Union Pacific at Zanger Junction to Walla Walla, Washington, 30 miles. Branches run from Dayton through Walla Walla to Weston, Oregon, 65 miles, and from Walla Walla to Walair, 4 miles. Traffic is primarily food products — about 2,500 cars a year.

The line was leased from Union Pacific on November 20, 1992. The operating company is controlled by Charles R. and Kaye L. Webb and it is affiliated with the Palouse River Railway.

Radio frequency: 160.785
Location of enginehouse: Walla Walla, Wash.
Locomotives: 2

No.	Builder	Model	New	Builder No.
784	EMD	GP35	11/63	28400
790	EMD	GP35	12/63	28407

Blue Mountain's two GP35s team up to pull a train through the dry country near Valley Grove, Washington, in September 1993. Photo by Jim Shaw.

BLUE RAPIDS RAILWAY CO.

Bestwall, Kansas

Reporting marks: BLUR

The Blue Rapids Railway has acquired a line extending from connections with Union Pacific and Northeast Kansas & Missouri at Marysville, Kansas, to Bestwall, 10.12 miles. Rail is 90 pound. Traffic is gypsum and gypsum products.

This line was built by the Omaha & Republican Valley Railroad, chartered in January 1877. The company was merged into Union Pacific in 1898, and the line was operated by the Union Pacific until the summer of 1993, when portions were washed out and service suspended. Blue Rapids restored the line in 1994, then leased it to the Northeast Kansas & Missouri Railroad Division of MidMichigan Railroad (RailTex). Blue Rapids is owned by Georgia Pacific Corporation.

BLUE ROCK TRANSPORTATION CO.

10815 State Route 41
North Greenfield, OH 45123

Reporting marks: BRT
Phone: 614-335-4332

Blue Rock operates for limited freight service from Blue Rock Limestone Quarry to Thrifton, Ohio, 4.24 miles, connecting with the Indiana & Ohio Central near Thrifton.

The line was built about 1877 by the Springfield, Jackson & Pomeroy Railroad, reorganized in 1879 as the Springfield Southern, in 1881 as the Ohio Southern, in 1901 as the Detroit Southern, and in 1905 as the Detroit, Toledo & Ironton. The line was acquired by Blue Rock following its abandonment by the DT&I. ICC operating authority was granted November 28, 1983. The company is owned by CSR American Aggregates Corp.

Location of enginehouse: Blue Rock Quarry (near Thrifton, Ohio)

Locomotives: 1

No.	Builder	Model	New	Builder No.
12335	Whitcomb	65-Ton	1/44	60363

BORDER PACIFIC RAILROAD CO.

804B West Main Street
P. O. Drawer 156
Rio Grande City, TX 78582-0156

Reporting marks: BOP
Phone: 210-487-5606
Fax: 210-487-4678

Border Pacific Railroad operates freight service from Rio Grande City to Mission, Texas, 31.6 miles, where a connection is made with Union Pacific via the Rio Valley Railroad. Rail is 90 pound.

Traffic includes aggregates, silica sand, ballast, crushed stone, asphalt, scrap paper, and feed grains — 1,000 cars a year.

This line was built by the St. Louis, Brownsville & Mexico Railroad and opened in 1925. The line came under Missouri Pacific Railroad control and was absorbed by that company in 1956. Shortline service started February 2, 1984.

The company is independent.

Location of enginehouse: Rio Grande City, Texas

Locomotives: 1

No.	Builder	Model	New	Builder No.	
96	EMD	GP7	3/50	11123	1973

BRADFORD INDUSTRIAL RAIL, INC.

201 North Penn Street
Punxsutawney, PA 15767

Reporting marks: BR
Phone: 814-938-5500

Bradford Industrial Rail has acquired 3.7 miles of Conrail trackage extending from East Bradford to Bradford, Pennsylvania, along with trackage rights over Conrail from Bradford to Salamanca, New York, 14.3 miles, where connection is made with Conrail and Buffalo & Pittsburgh. Service started in May 1993. Traffic runs about 1,000 cars a year. The company is a subsidiary of Genesee & Wyoming Industries, Inc. Equipment is supplied by the Buffalo & Pittsburgh.

BRANDON CORPORATION

28th and N Streets
Omaha, NE 68107

Reporting marks: BRAN
Phone: 402-734-1490
Fax: 402-731-0990

Brandon Corporation operates a 17.3-mile switching and terminal railroad at South Omaha, Nebraska. It connects with Burlington Northern, Chicago & North Western, and Union Pacific and carries under 500 cars a year.

The line was opened as the Union Stock Yards Co. of Omaha in 1897. It became the South Omaha Terminal Railway in July 1927 and was operated by that company until Brandon took over in 1978, operating at first under an ICC emergency service order issued April 4, 1978. Brandon Corporation is independent.

Locomotives: 4

No.	Builder	Model	New	Builder No.
3	Alco	S-1	6/45	73356
71	Alco	S-3	10/50	78395
423	Alco	C-415	11/66	3451-9
427	EMD	NW2	12/49	9461

BRANDYWINE VALLEY RAILROAD CO.

50 South First Avenue
Coatesville, PA 19320

Reporting marks: BVRY
Phone: 610-383-3202
Fax: 610-383-2734

Brandywine Valley operates 12 miles of track (3.65 route miles) between Coatesville and Valley Township, Pennsylvania, serving Lukens Steel and eight other shippers. It connects with Conrail and Delaware Valley Railroad (CSX connection). Rail is 115 and 130 pound. Nearly 25,800 cars (including 15,500 local cars) are switched yearly.

The line was built in part by the Wilmington & Reading Railroad, which was chartered in 1870. In 1877 that company was

Brandywine Valley NW2 No. 8202, a former Conrail engine, rests near the mill of its owner, Lukens Steel Company, at Coatesville, Pennsylvania. Photo by Jim Shaw.

reorganized as the Wilmington & Northern, and in 1900 it was absorbed by the Philadelphia & Reading system.

Conrail acquired the line from the Reading and sold it in 1982 to the Brandywine Valley, which is owned by Lukens, Inc.

Radio frequencies: 467.7625/462.7625, 469.5625/464.5625

Freight Cars: 260 gondolas, 92 flatcars

Locomotives: 7

No.	Builder	Model	New	Builder No.
8201	EMD	NW2	11/45	3392
8202	EMD	NW2	1949	9230
8203	EMD	SW7	6/50	10434
8204	EMD	SW1200	3/64	28760
8205	EMD	SW1200	3/57	22907
8206	EMD	SW7	3/50	10404
8207	EMD	SW7	11/50	13016

BRISTOL INDUSTRIAL TERMINAL RAILWAY CO.

P. O. Box 1271
Bristol, PA 19007

Reporting marks: BITY
Phone: 908-966-3733
Fax: 908-996-6912

Bristol Industrial Terminal Railway operates 1.7 miles of industrial switching track extending from a connection with Conrail at Bristol to Barre (Bristol Industrial Park), Pennsylvania. Traffic is primarily intermodal transfer and is less than 1,500 cars a year. Service started on August 25, 1992. The company is controlled by John Nolan (Transrail Company).

Locomotives: 2

No.	Builder	Model	New	Builder No.
361	GE	U36B	7/70	37428
1102	Alco	RSC-2	5/49	76815

BROWNSVILLE & RIO GRANDE INTERNATIONAL RAILROAD

Texas Highway 48 and F.M. 511
P. O. Box 3818
Brownsville, TX 78523-3818

Reporting marks: BRG
Phone: 210-831-7731
Fax: 210-831-2142

The company is a terminal switching railroad at the Port of Brownsville, Texas, operating 33 miles of track and connecting with the Union Pacific and via UP with Southern Pacific and National Railways of Mexico. Rail ranges from 80 to 132 pounds. Traffic is 8,000 cars a year of agricultural products, food products, and general commodities.

This line was operated by the Missouri Pacific until 1984, when its owner, the Brownsville Navigation District, took it back and leased it to the Brownsville & Rio Grande International Railroad, which is a political subdivision of the state of Texas. Service started February 26, 1984.

Radio frequency: 161.565

Locomotives: 3

No.	Builder	Model	New	Builder No.
237	EMD	SW1200	10/55	20551
1130	EMD	SW1200	2/64	28751
1145	EMD	SW1200	4/66	31219

Freight Cars: 58 covered hoppers

BSDA RAILROAD CO. — *See Bi-State Development Agency Railroad*

BUCKINGHAM BRANCH RAILROAD CO.

U. S. Route 15
P. O. Box 336
Dillwyn, VA 23936

Reporting marks: BB
Phone: 804-983-3300
Fax: 804-983-3270

Buckingham Branch Railroad provides freight service over 17.3 miles of track extending from Dillwyn to a connection with CSX at Bremo, Virginia (actual interchange takes place at Strathmore). Rail is 100 pound. About 2,000 cars a year of kyanite ore, pulpwood, crossties, and industrial sand and aggregates make up the road's traffic.

This line was built in part by the Buckingham Railroad, which was chartered on March 3, 1879, to run from Bremo to Arvon. Upon opening on May 1, 1885, the property was leased to the Richmond & Allegheny Railroad, which became part of the Chesapeake & Ohio. By the turn of the century the branch was extended to Dillwyn and Rosney, 21 miles.

Following abandonment, CSX sold the property to the present operator on March 3, 1989, and shortline service started 3 days later. The company also operates the nearby Shenandoah Valley Railroad. The railroad is owned by Robert and Annie Bryant.

Radio frequency: 160.470
Location of enginehouse: Dillwyn, Va.
Locomotives: 3

No.	Builder	Model	New	Builder No.	Rebuilt
40	EMD	GP9	8/55	20849	
101	EMD	GP7	6/53	18265	
8851	EMD	GP7U	4/51	12390	

Freight Cars: 31 boxcars, 8 covered hoppers, 1 hopper car

A Buckingham Branch train crosses the high bridge at New Canton, Virginia. The line uses a caboose because of a short run on CSX to make interchange. Photo by Jim Shaw.

BUFFALO & PITTSBURGH RAILROAD INC.

General office: 3 Parkway
P. O. Box 247
Leicester, NY 14481
Operating office: 201 North Penn Street
Punxsutawny, PA 15767

Reporting marks: BPRR
Phone: 716-382-3220
Fax: 716-382-2222
Phone: 814-938-5500
Fax: 814-938-1537

The Buffalo & Pittsburgh operates a line from Buffalo Creek, New York, to Eidenau, Pennsylvania, 255.3 miles, then by trackage rights on CSX 25 miles to New Castle. In addition the company operates several branch lines totaling 55.5 miles including WS Tower to Bruin, Pa., 17.2 miles, and C&M Junction to Clearfield, Pa., 25.7 miles. A total of 400 miles is operated. The company has secured trackage rights over Conrail from Machias Junction to Buffalo in anticipation of abandonment from Ashford to Buffalo. The main line is predominantly 115- to 132-pound welded rail.

The company has 100 customers and handles a diverse selection of commodities including coal, fuel oil, lumber, pulp, paper products, salt, grain, and steel — about 44,000 cars a year.

Buffalo & Pittsburgh connects with Allegheny & Eastern, Bessemer & Lake Erie, Buffalo Southern, Canadian National, CP Rail System, Conrail, CSX, Delaware & Hudson (CP Rail), Knox & Kane, New York & Lake Erie, Norfolk Southern, Pittsburg & Shawmut, Rochester Southern, and South Buffalo.

This former CSX line was partly leased and partly purchased on July 19, 1988. It was part of the old Buffalo, Rochester & Pittsburgh Railroad, was built between Ashford Junction and Buffalo by the Rochester & Pittsburgh Railroad in 1882 and 1883. The line from Ashford Junction through Salamanca was built by the Rochester & State Line Railroad in the late 1870s. The lines south of Salamanca were completed by September 1883.

The Rochester & State Line was reorganized as the Rochester & Pittsburgh in February 1881. In 1883 the R&P became the Buffalo, Rochester & Pittsburgh, which was acquired by the Baltimore & Ohio in 1932. The Buffalo & Pittsburgh is owned by Genesee & Wyoming Industries, Inc.

Radio frequencies: 160.230, 160.320, 160.530, 160.785
Employees: 140
Location of enginehouse: Butler, Pa.
Locomotives: 28 (pooled with other GWI lines)

No.	Builder	Model	New	Builder No.
201	EMD	GP9	8/56	22201
202	EMD	GP9	12/55	21190
203	EMD	GP9	4/56	21533
204	EMD	GP9	8/56	22203
206	EMD	GP9	9/56	22052
207	EMD	GP9	10/56	22036
208	EMD	GP9	12/55	21193
209	EMD	GP9	11/55	21040
626	EMD	GP9	10/58	24778
874	EMD	GP9	7/59	24883
886, 887	EMD	GP9	8/59	24895, 24896
922, 926	EMD	GP18	1/60	24931, 24935
2000	EMD	GP38		
2001, 2002	EMD	GP38	7/70	36322, 36331
2003	EMD	GP38	5/71	36729
3000	EMD	GP40	9/71	38505
3001	EMD	GP40	12/65	30938
3100	EMD	GP40	10/67	33511
3102	EMD	GP40	11/67	33507
3106	EMD	GP40	10/67	33491
3107	EMD	GP40	8/67	33236
3111	EMD	GP40	9/68	34314
3119	EMD	GP40	10/67	33498
7803, 7822	EMD	GP38	10/69	35438, 35457
9621, 9622	EMD	MP15	12/74	74641-1, 74641-2

Freight Cars: 113 boxcars, 24 gondolas

BUFFALO SOUTHERN RAILROAD, INC.

8600 Depot Street
Eden, NY 14057

Reporting marks: BSOR
Phone: 716-992-4979
Fax: 716-992-4979

Buffalo Southern operates freight service from Gowanda, New York, to Buffalo Creek Junction, 31 miles. Interchange is made at the latter point with Buffalo & Pittsburgh, Conrail, CSX, CP Rail System, and Norfolk Southern. Buffalo Southern also connects with the New York & Lake Erie at Gowanda. Rail is 100 pound. Traffic includes grain, lumber, scrap steel, and cement — about 1,500 cars a year. The company also preforms contract switching for ConAgra in Buffalo and Dunlap Tire in Tonawanda.

This is a former Erie branch built by the Buffalo & Southwestern Railroad and operated by Conrail until 1981, when operations were turned over to the New York & Lake Erie Railroad. Erie County Industrial Development Authority acquired the property in 1982 and effective May 1, 1982, designated Buffalo Southern to operate it. The operating company is controlled by E. R. Winter, K. N. O'Gorman and M. Riefler.

Radio frequency: 160.260
Location of enginehouse: Hamburg, N. Y.
Locomotives: 9

No.	Builder	Model	New	Builder No.
28	Alco	RS-3	10/51	80531
29	Whitcomb	35-ton	7/47	60731
30	GE	44-ton	1946	
81	Alco	S-2	8/48	75919
87	GE	50-ton	9/47	29053
107	Alco	S-2	8/42	69953
701	Alco	S-1	1942	
2010	Alco	C-420	12/67	3384-01
5010	Alco	RS-11	5/61	83689

BURLINGTON JUNCTION RAILWAY

1510 Bluff Road
P. O. Box 37
Burlington, IA 52601

Reporting marks: BJRY
Phone: 319-753-6157
Fax: 319-753-9811

BRJY operates 1.5 miles of track in Burlington, Iowa, connecting with Burlington Northern. Rail is 90 pound. Traffic is 2,000 cars a year of machinery, grain, fertilizer, lumber, and wallboard.

The line is former Rock Island track operated by Burlington Northern from October 1978 until Burlington Junction took over operations on March 4, 1985. The company is independent.

Radio frequency: 160.395
Locomotives: 2

No.	Builder	Model	New	Builder No.
44	GE	44-ton	12/41	15041
1007	Alco	S-2	9/50	78031

C&S RAILROAD CORP.

2 Lehigh Avenue
P. O. Box 66
Jim Thorpe, PA 18229

Reporting marks: CSKR
Phone: 717-325-8412
Fax: 717-325-2699

The C&S Railroad provides freight service between Conrail connections at Packerton Junction and Haucks, Pennsylvania, 18 miles. Rail is 100 to 135 pound. Traffic includes coal, plastic, chemicals and floor and building products — about 1,500 cars a year.

This line was built by the Lehigh & Susquehanna and leased to the Central Railroad of Pennsylvania (part of the Central Railroad of New Jersey). When the CNJ ended operations in Pennsylvania in 1972, the property was sold to the Reading and operated by Lehigh Valley. Conrail served as designated operator from 1976 to 1983, when the line was acquired by the Carbon County Railroad Commission and leased to the Panther Valley Railroad. PVAL began operations August 1, 1983, and operated the line until March 10, 1990, when the commission leased it to the current operator.

C&S is controlled by a local management group including Betsy Ahner and James Zurn.

Locomotives: 2

No.	Builder	Model	New	Builder No.
2717	GE	U23B	8/72	38523
5771	GE	U36B	10/71	38043

CADDO, ANTOINE & LITTLE MISSOURI RAILROAD CO.

P. O. Box 150
Dardanelle, AR 78234-0150

Reporting marks: CALM
Phone: 501-968-6455

The Caddo, Antoine & Little Missouri operates freight service from a connection with Union Pacific at Gurdon, Arkansas, to Bird's Mill, 52.9 miles. Rail is 75, 80, and 90 pound. Traffic includes roofing granules and byproducts, lumber, and crushed gravel — about 1,500 cars a year.

The Gurdon line was built by the Gurdon & Fort Smith Railroad, which was chartered in 1900. In 1909 it came under control of the St. Louis, Iron Mountain & Southern (Missouri Pacific).

MP sold this line and several others to the Arkansas Midland on February 23, 1992. AM ran the Gurdon line until flood damage in December 1993 made it inoperable. On April 6, 1994, the Caddo, Antoine & Little Missouri was given an ICC directed service order to operate the line. The company restored the track and began service. In 1995 the ICC awarded operation of the line to the Glenwood & Southern Railroad, but the Caddo, Antoine & Little Missouri has appealed and continues to operate the line.

The company is a subsidiary of Arkansas Short Lines, Inc., and is affiliated with the Dardanelle & Russellville Railroad (William Robbins).

Location of enginehouse: PK Junction (Antoine), Ark.

Locomotives: 4

No.	Builder	Model	New	Builder No.	Rebuilt
306	Alco	RS20M	5/51	78857	1976
319	Alco	C424	1963	84558	
320	Alco	C424	1963	84553	
321	Alco	C424	1963	84557	

CAIRO TERMINAL RAILROAD CO.

38th and Commercial Avenue
P. O. Box 871
Cairo, IL 62914

Reporting marks: CTML
Phone: 618-734-2190
Fax: 618-734-2191

Cairo Terminal operates 3 miles of track connecting with Illinois Central at Cairo, Illinois. Rail is 90 pound. Traffic includes clay, chemicals, and railcar clean-out — under 500 cars a year.

The company began operations on 2.5 miles of former Conrail (New York Central) line at Cairo in April 1982. In mid-1983 the company acquired 17.5 miles of an Illinois Central Gulf branch from Davis to Elco, Ill. but has since discontinued operation on that line. The company is controlled by A. R. Jackson and others.

Radio frequencies: 161.070, 161.190
Location of enginehouse: Cairo, Ill.
Locomotives: 1

No.	Builder	Model	New	Builder No.
102	EMD	SW1	6/50	11783

Freight cars: 48 boxcars

CALDWELL COUNTY RAILROAD CO.

2114 Williams Wood Drive
Morganton, NC 28655

Reporting marks: CWCY
Phone: 704-433-7409

Caldwell County Railroad operates freight service from a connection with Norfolk Southern at Hickory, North Carolina, to Lenoir (Valmead), 22.7 miles. Rail is 85 pound. Traffic consists of about 1,000 cars a year of furniture, plastic, scrap metal, grain, and lumber.

The Chester & Lenoir Railroad, chartered in 1874, opened its 3-foot gauge line between Hickory and Lenoir on June 2, 1884. The company was reorganized as the Carolina & Northwestern Railway in March 1895 and came under Southern Railway control. It was relaid to standard gauge in 1902.

The line was leased to the Carolina & Northwestern Railroad under NS's Thoroughbred Short Line Program on May 29, 1990. The lease was assigned to Caldwell County Railroad on September 26, 1994. Caldwell County Economic Development Commission bought the line from Norfolk Southern on January 26, 1995. The operating company is a subsidiary of Southeast Shortlines, Inc. (Don McGrady).

Location of enginehouse: Lenoir, N. C.
Locomotives: 1

No.	Builder	Model	New	Builder No.	Rebuilt
1747	EMD	GP16	9/52	17376	1979

CALIFORNIA NORTHERN RAILROAD CO., LP.

129 Klamath Court
American Canyon, CA 94589

Reporting marks: CFNR
Phone: 707-557-2868
Fax: 707-557-2941

California Northern operates three separate lines in north central California:

• from a Southern Pacific connection at Suisun-Fairfield to Napa Junction, Schellville, and Willits, 126.9 miles, with a 13-mile branch from Vallejo through Napa Junction to Rocktram. Additional connections are made with the Napa Valley Railroad at Rocktram and with the California Western and North Coast railroads at Willits.

• between Southern Pacific connections at Davis and Tehama, 110.7 miles, with a 19-mile branch from Wyo to Hamilton. Another connection is made with the Yolo Shortline at Woodland.
• from a Southern Pacific connection at Tracy to Los Banos, 58.2 miles.

Total mileage operated by California Northern is 354 miles. Rail ranges from 90 to 132 pound. Traffic includes about 36,000 cars a year of lumber, sugar beets, agricultural products, steel pipe, manufactured goods, and trash.

The Schellville-Willits line was part of the Northwestern Pacific Railroad, which was merged by Southern Pacific in October 1992. The NWP was formed in 1907 by Southern Pacific and Santa Fe as a consolidation of a number of small railroads, the oldest of which was the Petaluma & Haystack Railroad, chartered in 1864. Southern Pacific bought out Santa Fe's interest in the NWP in 1929.

The Los Banos and Davis lines were built by Southern Pacific in the late 1880s. They are leased from Southern Pacific under a long-term agreement. Shortline service started on September 26, 1993.

The railroad is a limited partnership controlled by David Parkinson, William Frederick, and Parksierra Corporation. The line is affiliated with the California & Arizona Railroad.

Radio frequencies: 161.295, 161.385, 160.635

Location of enginehouses: Willits, Petaluma, Napa, Tracy, Woodland, and Corning, Calif.

Locomotives: 18

No.	Builder	Model	New	Builder No.
100-113	EMD	GP15-1	12/55	757142-12–757142-25
200	EMD	SD9	2/58	23918
201	EMD	SD9	4/58	23936
202, 203	EMD	SD9	1/55	20223/8

CALIFORNIA WESTERN RAILROAD

Foot of Laurel Street
P. O. Box 907
Fort Bragg, CA 95437

Reporting marks: CWR
Phone: 707-964-6371

CWR operates freight and passenger excursion service from Fort Bragg to Willits, California, 40 miles. Connections are made with the California Northern and North Coast railroads at Willits. The load limit is 210,000 pounds.

Freight traffic is outbound lumber and forest products totaling under 500 cars a year. The company derives most of its income from its *Skunk* excursion trains.

The Fort Bragg Railroad opened in 1885 and was renamed the California Western Railroad & Navigation Co. on July 1, 1905.

The line was completed December 19, 1911. The present name was adopted December 19, 1947.

The company was purchased from Georgia Pacific by the Mendocino Coast Railway, a subsidiary of Kyle Railways, in June 1987.

Radio frequency: 160.650

Location of enginehouse: Fort Bragg, Calif.

Locomotives: 3

No.	Builder	Model	New	Builder No.
45	Baldwin	2-8-2	10/24	58045
62	Alco	RS-11	4/59	83416
64	EMD	GP9	1/55	20132

CAMAS PRAIRIE RAILROAD CO.

325 Mill Road
P. O. Box 1166
Lewiston, ID 83501

Reporting marks: CSP
Phone: 208-743-2115
Fax: 503-249-2653

The Camas Prairie operates freight service on five routes totaling 244.81 miles:
• Lewiston, Idaho, to Riparia, Washington, 70.02 miles
• Lewiston to Arrow, Idaho, 15.96 miles
• Arrow to Kooskia, Idaho, 61 miles
• Orofino to Revling, Idaho, 31 miles
• Spalding, Idaho, to Grangeville, 66.83 miles

Connections are made with Union Pacific and Burlington Northern at Riparia. Traffic includes grain, lumber, forest products, and chemicals — 19,000 cars a year.

The company was incorporated November 4, 1909, to operate a line of railroad jointly owned by the Northern Pacific (later Burlington Northern) and the Oregon-Washington Railroad & Navigation Co. (a subsidiary of the Union Pacific) and including the line of the Clearwater Short Line Railroad.

Camas Prairie is jointly owned by BN and UP. The owners supply the locomotives and cars.

Radio frequencies: 160.515, 161.100, 161.250

CAMP CHASE INDUSTRIAL RAILROAD CORP.

4200 Sullivant Avenue
P. O. Box 28096
Columbus, OH 43228

Reporting marks: CCRA
Phone: 614-871-7254
Fax: 614-539-0352

This company provides switching service from a connection with Conrail at Columbus (Camp Chase) to Lilly Chapel, Ohio, 14 miles. Rail is 127 pound. Traffic includes newsprint, grain, flour and lumber — 3,000 cars a year.

This former Conrail line was part of the New York Central (Big Four) Cincinnati-Cleveland main line. Camp Chase Industrial Railroad acquired the property from Conrail on October 11, 1994. The company is controlled by Phillip Larson, Russell Peterson, and Dennis Larson.

Radio frequency: 161.040
Location of enginehouse: Columbus, Ohio
Locomotives: 1

No.	Builder	Model	New	Builder No.
1855	EMD	GP16	6/51	13873

CANADA & GULF TERMINAL RAILWAY CO.

206 Rue Hebert, C. P. 578
Mont-Joli, PQ G5H 3L3
Canada

Reporting marks: CGT
Phone: 418-775-4373
Fax: 418-775-8661

The Canada & Gulf Terminal is operated by Canadian National Railways from Mont-Joli to Matane, Quebec, 30 miles. The railroad also provides car ferry service across the St. Lawrence River to Baie-Comeau, Que. Rail is 85, 100, and 115 pound. Traffic includes newsprint, aluminum, and forest products, about 9,000 cars a year.

CGT was chartered March 26, 1902, as the Matane, Gaspe Railway under Quebec laws. The current name was adopted prior

to the start of operations in 1911. The company has been controlled by Canadian National Railways since 1975.
Radio frequencies: 161.415, 160.665, 160.935, 161.205
Location of enginehouse: Mont-Joli, Que.

Locomotives: 1

No.	Builder	Model	New	Builder No.
104	GMD	SW1200RS	7/59	A-1806

CANADIAN AMERICAN RAILROAD CO.

c/o Bangor & Aroostook Railroad Co.
Northern Maine Junction Park
Rural Route 2, Box 45
Bangor, ME 04401-9602

Reporting marks: CDAC
Phone: 207-848-4250

Canadian American operates freight service from a connection with CP Rail System at Sherbrooke, Quebec, through Brownville Junction to a connection with the New Brunswick Southern Railway at McAdam, New Brunswick, 288 miles. Additional connections are made with Bangor & Aroostook at Brownville Junction, Maine, with Canadian National at Lennoxville, Quebec, and (via New Brunswick Southern) at Saint John, N. B., and with ST Rail (Maine Central) at Mattawamkeag, Maine. Rail is predominantly 100 to 115 pound.

Traffic is primarily overhead freight moving between the CP and the BAR and New Brunswick Southern railroads. Local traffic is mostly forest products (pulp). About 21,000 cars a year are expected.

The Atlantic & Northwestern Railroad opened this line between Sherbrooke and Mattawamkeag in January 1889. In June 1890 it was leased to Canadian Pacific for 550 years. In September 1988, CP Rail set up the Canadian Atlantic Railway (CAR) to operate this and other eastern lines in hopes of reducing expenses, improving service, and generating net income from the operation. The effort was not successful and CAR was abandoned on December 31, 1994.

Canadian American restored service on January 6, 1995, following purchase of the property from Brownville Junction west. Another firm, Eastern Maine Railway, purchased the line from Brownville Junction east to the New Brunswick border near McAdam and has leased the property to Canadian American.

Canadian American is controlled by Iron Road Railways (which also controls Bangor & Aroostook).
Radio frequencies: 161.355, 160.875
Location of enginehouses: Brownville Junction and Northern Maine Junction, Maine

CANEY FORK & WESTERN RAILROAD, INC.

401 Bridge Street
P. O. Box 451
McMinnville, TN 37110

Reporting marks: CFWR
Phone: 615-473-4910
Fax: 615-473-4910

No.	Builder	Model	New	Builder No.
531	EMD	GP9	5/54	18725
979	EMD	GP7	9/52	17371
2345	EMD	GP7	2/51	11238

Caney Fork & Western operates freight service from a connection with CSX at Tullahoma, Tennessee, to Sparta, 61 miles. Rail is 80 to 90 pound. The company also switches the Arnold Engineering & Development Center's 15 miles of industrial trackage at Tullahoma. Traffic includes about 1,600 cars a year of grain, fertilizer, wood chips, forest products, plastic, steel, and carbon black.

This line was built by the McMinnville & Manchester Railroad, which was chartered February 4, 1850. Construction started in 1853, and the first 34.5 miles to McMinnville were opened in November 1856. During the Civil War, General Grant had Union soldiers remove 25 miles of rail from the line for use on the Nashville & Chattanooga Railroad. In addition, all stations were burned and a number of bridges destroyed.

After the war, the line was rebuilt and in 1871 it was sold to the Memphis & Charleston Railroad, which sold it to the Nashville, Chattanooga & St. Louis in 1877. The line was extended to Sparta in 1885.

Seaboard System abandoned the line in 1983, and in December 1983 the property was acquired by the Tri-County Railroad Authority and leased to the Caney Fork & Western. Shortline service started December 27, 1983. The operating company is controlled by shippers located along the line.

Radio frequency: 160.545
Location of enginehouse: McMinnville, Tenn.
Freight cars: 1,011 covered hoppers
Locomotives: 3

Caney Fork & Western's GP9 No. 531 heads through the Tennessee countryside near Summitville with a string of gons, woodchip cars, pulpwood cars and a box car. Photo by Jim Shaw.

CANTON RAILROAD CO.

6610 Tributary Street, Suite 204
Baltimore, MD 21224

Reporting marks: CTN
Phone: 410-633-9200
Fax: 410-633-8720

The Canton Railroad is a switching line in the Canton section of Baltimore, Maryland. It operates 4.88 route miles (16.26 track miles) and connects with CSX and Conrail. Rail is 90 and 132 pound. About 5,000 cars are switched annually.

The company was incorporated May 11, 1906, and its stock was acquired by the state of Maryland in April 1987. On April 23, 1993, the company began service over its Southwest Division, 6 miles from Clifford to Glen Burnie — the former Baltimore & Annapolis Railroad line now owned by the Maryland Transit Authority.

Radio frequency: 160.980
Locomotives: 3

No.	Builder	Model	New	Builder No.
1201	EMD	SW1200	11/54	20055
1501	EMD	SW1500	9/67	33147
1751	EMD	GP16	9/52	17393

Canton Railroad 1201 switches cars at its Baltimore terminal in November, 1991. Photo by Jim Shaw.

CAPE BRETON & CENTRAL NOVA SCOTIA RAILWAY

13 Water St.
Bag No. 4444
Port Hawkesbury, Nova Scotia B0E 2V0
Canada

Reporting marks: CBNS
Phone: 902-625-5715
Fax: 902-625-5722

Cape Breton & Central Nova Scotia operates from a connection with Canadian National at Truro to Sydney, Nova Scotia, 245 miles. At Sydney, a connection is made with Devco Railway. Rail is predominantly 110 to 115 pound. Traffic includes coal, woodpulp, chemicals, newsprint, and railway equipment.

The first portion of this line was built by the Halifax & Cape Breton Railway, chartered in 1876 and opened from Mulgrave to New Glasgow in 1879. The company was acquired by the provincial government and later leased to the Eastern Extension Railway, an affiliate of the Intercolonial Railway. The Intercolonial was part of the group of railroads that were consolidated to form Canadian National Railways in 1922.

Canadian National sold the line to the current operator for $20 million. Shortline service started October 1, 1993. The company is a subsidiary of RailTex.

Radio frequencies: 161.310, 160.050
Location of enginehouses: Sydney and Truro, N. S.

Locomotives: 14

No.	Builder	Model	New	Builder No.
1756	MLW	RSC-14	1960	83244
2003	MLW	C630M	1967	M3491-02
2015, 2016	MLW	C630M	1968	M3491-14, M3491-15
2029	MLW	C630M	1968	M3491-28
2032	MLW	C630M	1968	M3491-31
2034, 2035	MLW	C630M	1968	M3491-33, M3491-34
2039	MLW	C630M	1968	M3491-38
3267	MLW	RS-18	1957	82138
3275	MLW	RS-18	1957	82217
3716	MLW	RS-18	1958	82479
3842	MLW	RS-18	1958	82523
3852	MLW	RS-18	1960	83232

CAPE FEAR RAILWAYS, INC.

Knox Street, Building 8-4205
P. O. Box 70090
Fort Bragg, NC 28307

Reporting marks: CF
Phone: 910-497-5008
Fax: 910-497-9124

Cape Fear Railways operates freight and TOFC service from a connection with CSX at Fort Junction to Fort Bragg, North Carolina, 5 miles. Track is in place between Skibo and Fort Bragg, but service between those points has been suspended for several years. Rail is 115 pound. Traffic is jet fuel and military supplies, about 3,000 cars a year.

The railroad was built as a streetcar line from Fayetteville to Fort Bragg. In 1926, it became a common carrier and abandoned its track between Fayetteville and Cains. In March 1930 Cape Fear Railways took over operation of all the track within Fort Bragg. Most of Cape Fear's track is leased from the U. S. Army and CSX. The company is controlled by Seaboard Corporation.

Radio frequency: 160.860
Location of enginehouse: Fort Bragg, N. C.
Locomotives: 2 (leased from U. S. Army)

No.	Builder	Model	New	Builder No.	Rebuilt
4604	EMD	GP10	1/57	22326	1977, 1990
4605	EMD	GP10	12/57	23832	1977, 1990

CAROLINA COASTAL RAILWAY, INC.

1 Park West Circle — Suite 203
Midlothian, VA 23113

Reporting marks: CLNA
Phone: 804-379-4664
Fax: 804-379-4668

Carolina Coastal Railway operates for freight service from a connection with Norfolk Southern at Pinetown, North Carolina, to Belhaven, 17 miles. Traffic includes grain, lime, and agricultural products, about 1500 cars a year.

The line was built by the Norfolk & Southern in 1908 and includes terminal trackage at Belhaven constructed after 1887. The line was leased to the current operator under the Norfolk Southern Thoroughbred ShortLine Program. Shortline service started on February 6, 1989.

The company is a subsidiary of Rail Link, Inc.

Location of enginehouses: Pinetown and Belhaven, N. C.
Locomotives: 1

No.	Builder	Model	New	Builder No.	Rebuilt
127	Baldwin	S-12M	1/47	72800	1959

Carolina Coastal 127, a Baldwin S-12 with an EMD prime mover, pulls a string of coal cars through Belhaven, North Carolina. Photo by Jim Shaw.

CAROLINA PIEDMONT DIVISION, SOUTH CAROLINA CENTRAL RAILROAD

268 East Main Street
Laurens, SC 29360

Reporting marks: CPDR
Phone: 864-984-0040
Fax: 864-984-0043

Carolina Piedmont operates freight service from a connection with CSX at Laurens, South Carolina, to East Greenville, 34 miles. Rail is 80 pound. About 6,000 cars a year of lumber, minerals, plastic, chemicals, paper, scrap, and food products make up the road's traffic.

This line was built by the Charleston & Western Carolina Railroad in the 1890s. C&WC became part of the Atlantic Coast Line System in 1897 and was merged into ACL in 1959. CSX sold the line to the present operator, and service began on November 2, 1990. The company is a subsidiary of RailTex.

Radio frequencies: 160.770, 161.085
Location of enginehouse: Laurens, S. C.
Locomotives: 3

No.	Builder	Model	New	Builder No.	Rebuilt
8379	EMD	GP10	12/58	25031	1974
8383	EMD	GP10	4/53	17974	1974
8387	EMD	GP10	12/58	25039	1974

Carolina Piedmont carries a variety of commodities over a well-maintained branch of the old Charleston & Western Carolina. The train is passing through Fountain Inn, South Carolina, in June, 1994. Photo by Jim Shaw.

CAROLINA RAIL SERVICES, INC.

100 Terminal Road/State Port
Morehead City, NC 28557

Reporting marks: CRIJ
Phone: 919-247-2332
Fax: 919-247-5463

This company provides switching service at Morehead City, North Carolina, connecting with Norfolk Southern. The company operates North Carolina Ports Railway Commission trackage leased in October 1986. Traffic consists of about 6,000 cars a year of wood chips, borate, potash, steel, asphalt, and linerboard. CRIJ is affiliated with Morehead City Terminals, Inc.

Radio frequency: 160.320
Locomotives: 2

No.	Builder	Model	New	Builder No.
1201	EMD	SW1200	3/66	31111
1202	EMD	SW1200	4/66	31218

CAROLINA SOUTHERN RAILROAD CO.

103 South Wilson Street
P. O. 368
Chadbourn, NC 28431

Reporting marks: CALA
Phone: 910-654-4134
Fax: 910-654-3635

Carolina Southern operates freight service from a connection with CSX at Mullins, South Carolina, to Whiteville, North Carolina, 37 miles. A branch runs from Chadbourn, N. C., to Conway, S. C., 38.9 miles, where interchange is made with the Waccamaw CoastLine Railroad. Rail is 90 to 132 pound.

Traffic includes stone, coal, lumber and wood chips, brick, and fertilizer — 13,000 cars a year.

The main line was built by the Wilmington, Columbia & Augusta and Wilmington & Manchester railroads, and the Conway branch was built by the Wilmington, Chadbourn & Conway Railroad. The railroads became part of the Atlantic Coast Line system. CSX sold the line to Duval Transportation, and independent service began March 28, 1987. Duval was renamed Mid-Atlantic on November 4, 1987. Mid-Atlantic was sold to the current operator and renamed Carolina Southern Railroad on February 7, 1995. The company is owned by Ken Pippin.

Radio frequencies: 160.470, 161.505
Location of enginehouse: Chadbourn, N. C.
Locomotives: 4

No.	Builder	Model	New	Builder No.	Notes
950, 951	EMD	GP18	7/61	26791, 26792	
958	EMD	GP18	8/61	26799	
959	EMD	GP18	1/60	25450	ex-No. 100

Freight cars: 70 boxcars

CARTIER RAILWAY CO.

Road 138
Port Cartier, PQ G5B 2H3
Canada

Reporting marks: QCM
Phone: 418-768-2494

The Cartier Railway operates freight service from Fermont (Mont-Wright) and Gagnon to Port Cartier, Quebec, 260 miles total. Rail is 132 to 136 pound. Traffic, primarily iron ore, totals more than 180,000 cars a year. The company was formed and the railroad was built in 1961 by U. S. Steel. It is now a subsidiary of Quebec Cartier Mining Co.

Radio frequencies: 161.130, 160.800
Enginehouse: Port Cartier, Que.
Locomotives: 32

No.	Builder	Model	New	Builder No.
34	Alco	C630	1966	3440-2
41-45	MLW	M636	1970	M6037-01–M6037-05
46, 47	MLW	M636	1970	M6037-12, M6037-13
48, 49	MLW	M636	1970, 1971	M6037-19, M6052-02
62-68	MLW	RS-18	1959-1960	83196-831201, 83229
71, 73	MLW	M636	1972	M6058-01, M6058-03
74-76	MLW	M636	1973	M6072-01–M6072-03
77-79	Alco	C636	3/68	6008-03, 6008-02, 6008-01
81-85	MLW	M636	3/75	M6085-01–M6085-05
86-87	MLW	M636	3/71	M6052-11, M6052-12

Freight cars: 383 (local use only)

CEDAR RAPIDS & IOWA CITY RAILWAY CO.

2330 12th Street, S. W.
P. O. Box 2951
Cedar Rapids, IA 52406

Reporting marks: CIC
Phone: 319-398-4597
Fax: 319-398-4171

The Cedar Rapid & Iowa City operates a 24.71-mile line between Cedar Rapids and Iowa City, Iowa, plus 6.3 miles from Iowa City to Hills and 21 miles from Cedar Rapids to Middle Amana. Direct connections include Chicago & North Western, Chicago Central & Pacific, Iowa Northern, and Iowa Interstate. A haulage agreement with Iowa Interstate gives the company additional connections in Illinois and Iowa. Rail is 90 to 115 pound. Traffic includes coal and general commodities — about 18,000 cars a year.

The road was built and operated as part of the Iowa Railway & Light Co. in 1904. In 1914 a branch was built from Cedar Rapids to Mount Vernon; it was abandoned in 1928. Operation of the railroad was separated from the electric company on January 1, 1950, and the present corporation was formed. On May 30, 1953, passenger service was discontinued and the railroad dieselized.

The Hills branch was added in 1980 and the Amana branch in 1981. The company is owned by IES Transportation Co.
Radio frequencies: 160.500, 161.055
Location of enginehouse: Cedar Rapids, Iowa
Locomotives: 14

No.	Builder	Model	New	Builder No.	Rebuilt
91	EMD	SW8	10/53	18784	1989
94	EMD	SW900	8/59	25443	1977
95	EMD	SW9	3/51	14101	1980
96	EMD	SW8	6/53	18352	1978
97	EMD	SW1200	3/66	31239	
99	EMD	SW1200	4/66	31220	
100, 101	EMD	GP9	3/59	25300, 25303	
102, 104	EMD	GP9	6/59	25299, 25297	
104	EMD	GP9	1/59		
105	EMD	GP9	1/59	25048	
107, 108	EMD	SW14			

Freight cars: 35 boxcars, 41 gondolas, 113 covered hoppers

Four CR&IC switchers pull a string of coal cars near Cou Falls, Iowa. The acquisition of larger power means that scenes like this will become less frequent. Photo by Jim Shaw.

CEDAR RIVER RAILROAD CO.

P. O. Box 657
Waterloo, IA 50704-0657

Reporting marks: CEDR
Phone: 319-236-9200
Fax: 319-236-9259

The Cedar River operates freight service from Albert Lea, Minnesota, 6.79 miles to Glenville by trackage rights, thence 94.32 miles to Mona Junction, then via trackage rights over Chicago Central & Pacific into Waterloo, Iowa. There is also a 7.21-mile branch from Stacyville Junction to Stacyville. Total mileage is 102. Connections include Chicago Central & Pacific at Waterloo; CP Rail System and Charles City Rail Lines at Charles City, Iowa; Chicago & North Western and Dakota, Minnesota & Eastern at Glenville, Minn.; and CP Rail System at Lyle, Minn. The Iowa Star Clipper dinner train operates out of Waverly, Iowa, on Cedar River rails. Traffic includes agricultural products, coal, corn syrup, and scrap metal, about 6,000 cars a year.

The line is a former Illinois Central Gulf branch that traces its history from 1858, when the Cedar Falls & Minnesota Railroad was chartered. In 1866 the property in Iowa was leased by the Dubuque & Sioux City Railroad and the Minnesota portion by the Albert Lea & Southern Railroad. The Stacyville branch was built by the Stacyville Railroad in 1897.

ICG sold the line to Cedar Valley Railroad on September 20, 1984. Cedar Valley filed for bankruptcy protection and suspended operations on May 22, 1991. Chicago, Central & Pacific operated the line under a directed service order until they could organize the Cedar River Railroad, a Chicago, Central & Pacific subsidiary, which acquired the line on December 31, 1991.

Radio frequencies: 160.605, 161.535
Location of enginehouse: Osage, Iowa
Locomotives: supplied by Chicago, Central & Pacific

CEN-TEX RAIL LINK LTD.

3811 Turtle Creek Boulevard, Suite 380
Dallas, TX 75219

Reporting marks: CTE
Phone: 214-528-2888
Fax: 214-528-0770

Cen-Tex operates freight, TOFC, and COFC service between Santa Fe connections at Birds (Fort Worth) and Ricker, Texas, 135 miles. The company has trackage rights over Santa Fe from Ricker to San Angelo Junction, where a connection is made with the affiliated South Orient Railroad. An 18-mile branch extends from Cresson to Cleburne, and a 24-mile branch runs from Gorham to Dublin.

Connections are also made with Burlington Northern, Southern Pacific, Union Pacific and Fort Worth & Western at Fort Worth and with the Santa Fe at Cleburne and Brownwood. Rail is 115 pound.

Traffic includes animal feed, fertilizer, plastics, milk products, steel, cement, and chemicals (including chlorine). In addition, the company expects to handle substantial overhead traffic between Fort Worth and the affiliated South Orient Railroad.

This line was built by the Fort Worth & Rio Grande Railway, chartered in June 1887 and opened from Fort Worth to Brownwood in 1890. The company came under the control of the St. Louis-San Francisco from 1902 until 1937, when it was sold to the Santa Fe. The Cleburne branch was built by the Gulf, Colorado & Santa Fe.

Santa Fe sold the line to Cen-Tex Rural Rail District, and shortline service started on May 20, 1994. This company began operating the Texas Central Railroad by trackage rights effective August 15, 1994.

The company is controlled by Joel Williams III, Roy Coffee, and Rafael Fernandez-MacGregor and is affiliated with the South Orient Railroad.

Radio frequencies: 160.440, 161.490
Location of enginehouses: Cresson and Dublin, Texas
Locomotives: pooled with South Orient Railroad

CENTRAL CALIFORNIA TRACTION CO.

1645 North Cherokee Road
Stockton, CA 95205

Reporting marks: CCT
Phone: 209-466-6927
Fax: 209-466-1204

Central California Traction operates freight service between Stockton and Sacramento, California, 52.1 miles. It connects with the Santa Fe, Union Pacific, Southern Pacific, and Stockton Terminal & Eastern railroads. Traffic is 2,000 cars a year of food, steel, lumber, and general commodities.

The company was incorporated August 7, 1905. The line opened from Stockton to Lodi in September 1907 and to Sacramento in August 1910. Passenger service was discontinued February 5, 1933, and the railroad was dieselized in 1946. The railroad has been owned jointly by Santa Fe, Southern Pacific and Union Pacific (formerly Western Pacific) since 1928.

Radio frequencies: 160.305, 161.415
Location of enginehouse: Stockton, Calif.
Locomotives: 3

No.	Builder	Model	New	Builder No.
60	EMD	GP7	8/52	16906
1790	EMD	GP18	2/60	25683
1795	EMD	GP18	10/61	26938

Freight cars: 2 hopper cars

CENTRAL INDIANA & WESTERN RAILROAD CO.

P. O. Box 456
Lapel, IN 46051

Reporting marks: CEIW
Phone: 317-534-3398
Fax: 317-546-4324

Central Indiana & Western operates freight service from Lapel, Indiana, to a connection with Conrail at South Anderson, 9 miles. Rail is 70 to 105 pound. Traffic includes grain, glass sand, and soda ash — about 2,300 cars a year.

The company began operations November 4, 1986, over track acquired from Conrail. The line was built by the Anderson, Lebanon & St. Louis Railroad, which opened between Anderson and Noblesville in 1876. The company was reorganized as the Cleveland, Indiana & St. Louis Railroad in 1882, and a year later the property was sold to the Midland (Indiana) Railway. That in turn was reorganized in 1892 as the Chicago & Southeastern and in 1903 as the Central Indiana Railroad. It came under control of the Pennsylvania Railroad in 1921. The company is independent.

Radio frequency: 160.335
Location of enginehouse: Lapel, Ind.
Locomotives: 1

No.	Builder	Model	New	Builder No.
88	EMD	SW7	2/50	9453

CENTRAL KANSAS RAILWAY, INC.

1825 West Harry Street
Wichita, KS 67213

Reporting marks: CKRY
Phone: 316-263-3113
Fax: 316-263-8346

The Central Kansas Railway operates 887 miles of former Santa Fe branch lines in south central Kansas:
• Abilene to Salina and Osborne, 104 miles
• McPherson to Great Bend and Scott City, 184 miles
• Great Bend to Jetmore, 83 miles
• Rago and Harper to Belvidere and Englewood, 150 miles
• Wellington to Blackwell, 35 miles
• Lyons to Galatia, 52 miles
• Wichita to Pratt, 80 miles

The railroad connects with Santa Fe, Kansas Southwestern, Southern Pacific, Union Pacific, Kyle Railroad, and Hutchinson & Northern. It hauls about 30,000 cars of grain, fertilizer, aggregate, LP gas, and wood chips a year.

The Central Kansas Railway started service on January 1, 1993. The company is a subsidiary of OmniTRAX, Inc. The railroad is operated in conjunction with the Kansas Southwestern Railway.

Radio frequency: 161.085

Location of enginehouse: Wichita, Kan.
Locomotives: 18

No.	Builder	Model	New	Builder No.	Rebuilt
101	EMD	SW8	11/52	29783	
713	EMD	GP7			
1777	EMD	GP7		21083	
2016	EMD	GP7U	11/53	18887	1981
2083	EMD	GP7U	11/53	18900	1974
2084	EMD	GP7U	9/52	16999	1974
2085	EMD	GP7U	12/52	17647	1974
2087	EMD	GP7U	12/52	17700	1975
2105	EMD	GP7U	12/53	18908	1977
2179	EMD	GP7U	10/50	12198	1979
2199	EMD	GP7U	3/53	17015	1980
2230	EMD	GP7U	10/52	17458	1981
2232	EMD	GP7U	9/52	17307	1981
2233	EMD	GP7U	2/52	15818	1981
2238	EMD	GP7U	2/51	12204	1981
2239	EMD	GP7U	11/52	17625	1981
2242	EMD	GP7U	2/52	15815	1981
2243	EMD	GP7U	10/52	17457	1981

CENTRAL MICHIGAN RAILWAY CO.

1410 South Valley Center Drive
Bay City, MI 48706-9998

Reporting marks: CMGN
Phone: 517-684-5088
Fax: 517-684-5260

Central Michigan Railway provides freight service from Owosso to Durand and Bay City, Michigan, 70 miles, and from Midland through Bay City to Essexville, 21 miles. It connects with CSX at Bay City, Midland, and Saginaw, with Grand Trunk Western at Durand, with Huron & Eastern at Harger, with Lake States at Bay City, and with TSBY at Durand and Owosso. Rail is 100 to 130 pound. Traffic includes auto parts, chemicals, grain, lumber, sugar, beet pulp, coal, and general commodities. About 25,000 cars a year are carried.

The Bay City line was started by the Toledo, Saginaw &

Mackinaw, chartered in 1889 and reorganized the following year as the Cincinnati, Saginaw & Mackinaw Railroad. It became part of Grand Trunk Western in January 1929.

Central Michigan started service on September 4, 1987, following purchase from Grand Trunk Western. The company also purchased a line from Owosso to Muskegon, but it has since been abandoned and portions sold to other operators. The company is controlled by the Straits Corporation.

Radio frequencies: 161.280, 161.310
Location of enginehouse: Bay City, Mich.
Locomotives: 11

No.	Builder	Model	New	Builder No.	Rebuilt
4502	GE	U23B	1/73	38760	
8801	EMD	GP38	2/69	34831	
8802	EMD	GP38	2/69	348341	
8803	EMD	GP38	3/69	34850	
8804	EMD	GP38	3/69	34843	
8902	GE	U23B	1/73	38764	
8903	GE	U23B	1/73	38758	
8904	GE	U23B	1/73	38759	
8905	GE	U23B	1/73	38762	
9209	EMD	GP8	1953	18490	1978
9210	EMD	GP8	10/50	11839	1978

CENTRAL MONTANA RAIL, INC.

1 Railroad Way
P. O. Box 868
Denton, MT 59430

Reporting marks: CM
Phone: 406-567-2223
Fax: 406-567-2223

Central Montana Rail operates freight service from Geraldine, Montana, to a connection with Burlington Northern at Moccasin Junction, a distance of 84.2 miles. Rail is predominantly 75 pound. Traffic is about 1,500 cars a year and includes grain and agricultural commodities.

The line is part of Milwaukee Road's Great Falls-Lewistown route, which was donated to the state of Montana by Burlington Northern in February 1983. It is leased by the state to Central Montana Rail. Short line service began June 5, 1985. The operating company is a non-profit community development corporation.

Radio frequencies: 160.800, 160.860
Location of enginehouse: Denton, Mt.
Locomotives: 6

No.	Builder	Model	New	Builder No.
1809	EMD	GP9	4/54	19365

Central Montana Rail's GP9 No. 1809 pulls a string of covered hoppers past a grain elevator at Danvers, Montana in September, 1991. Photo by Jim Shaw.

No.	Builder	Model	New	Builder No.
1810	EMD	GP9	4/54	19366
1814	EMD	GP9	3/54	19347
1817	EMD	GP9	3/54	19350
1824	EMD	GP9	4/54	19357
1838	EMD	GP9	4/56	21259

CENTRAL NEW ENGLAND RAILROAD CO.

44 Cedar Ridge Road
Newington, CT 06111

Reporting marks: CNZR
Phone: 860-666-1636
Fax: 860-665-1540

The Central New England provides freight service from a connection with Conrail at South Windsor, Connecticut, to East Windsor Hill and Enfield, 13.5 miles. Rail is 74 to 80 pound. Traffic is primarily fertilizer. The road expects to handle 100 cars per year initially. There is potential for other traffic.

The line was built between 1874 and 1876 by the Connecticut Valley Railroad. Ownership passed in succession to Connecticut Central, New York & New England, New Haven, Penn Central, and Conrail. The railroad, which began service on November 15, 1995, is controlled by Amedee Belliveau.

Location of enginehouse: East Windsor, Conn.
Locomotives: 3

No.	Builder	Model	New	Builder No.	Rebuilt
0670	Alco	RS-1	11/48	76212	1964
0825	GE	25-ton	6/44	27611	
1922	EMD	GP9	2/57	22769	

CENTRAL OF TENNESSEE RAILWAY & NAVIGATION CO., INC.

150 Fourth Avenue North, Suite 1210
Nashville, TN 37219-2417

Reporting marks: CTRN
Phone: 615-256-7245
Fax: 615-244-4508

Central of Tennessee operates a line extending northwest from a connection with CSX at Nashville to Chapmansboro, Tennessee, 19 miles. Rail runs from 70 to 112 pound. About 1,000 cars a year of lumber, scrap paper, volcanic ore, plastic, and brick make up the road's traffic.

The line is a part of the former Tennessee Central Railway that opened about 1903. After the abandonment of the TC in May 1968 the line was owned, leased, or operated successively by Illinois Central Gulf, the Nashville & Ashland City Railroad, the Cheatham County Rail Authority, the Walking Horse & Eastern Railroad, and the McCormick, Ashland City & Nashville Railroad. Central of Tennessee, a privately held company, took over operations in 1992.

Radio frequency: 160.635
Location of enginehouse: Nashville, Tenn.
Locomotives: 2

No.	Builder	Model	New	Builder No.
5	EMD	SW900	1/53	16286
4286	EMD	GP7	1/52	16851

Freight cars: 945 hopper cars, 177 coil steel cars

CENTRAL OREGON & PACIFIC RAILROAD, INC.

706 East Sheridan
Roseburg, OR 97470

Reporting marks: CORP
Phone: 503-957-5966
Fax: 503-957-0696

The Central Oregon & Pacific operates freight service on a former Southern Pacific line from Eugene, Oregon, through Roseburg and Grants Pass to Black Butte, California, 303 miles. A branch runs from Eugene to the Oregon coast at Coquille, 138 miles. A total of 439 miles are operated.

It also connects with the Longview, Portland & Northern at Gardiner Junction, Ore., with the WCTU Railway at White City, Ore., with the Willamette & Pacific at Eugene, and with Yreka Western at Montague, Calif. Rail ranges from 90 to 130 pounds. Traffic is primarily forest products and paper plus some chemicals, steel, LP gas, and miscellaneous commodities — about 40,000 cars a year are expected.

The main line from Eugene to Black Butte was built in large part by the Oregon & California Railroad, which started building south from Eugene in the 1870s. The line reached Ashland in 1884. It was leased to Southern Pacific and completed to a connection with the California & Oregon building northward in 1887. The Coos Bay branch was built by a Southern Pacific affiliate, the Willamette Pacific, after 1910. Southern Pacific sold these lines to this RailTex affiliate on December 31, 1994.

Radio frequency: 160.320
Location of enginehouses: Cottage Grove, Roseburg, Medford, Coos Bay, and Grants Pass, Ore.
Locomotives: 29

No.	Builder	Model	New	Builder No.
1335	EMD	GP40	4/66	31875
1338	EMD	GP40	4/66	31878
1342	EMD	GP40	4/66	31882
1345	EMD	GP40	4/66	31885
1348	EMD	GP40	4/66	31888
3075	EMD	GP40	2/69	34823
3076	EMD	GP40	2/69	34827
3077	EMD	GP40	2/69	34836
3079	EMD	GP40	3/69	34839
3081	EMD	GP40	3/69	34846
3082	EMD	GP40	3/69	34848
3083	EMD	GP40	3/69	34851
3084	EMD	GP40	4/69	34862
5039	EMD	GP38	10/67	33357
5041-5043	EMD	GP38	11/67	33359-33361
5047	EMD	GP38	11/67	33365
5054	EMD	GP38	11/67	33685
5057	EMD	GP38	11/67	33688
5183	EMD	GP38	4/67	33065
5528	EMD	GP38	8/69	35388
5529	EMD	GP38	8/69	35398
5532	EMD	GP38	9/69	35412
5533	EMD	GP38	9/69	35414
5534	EMD	GP38	8/69	35377
5535	EMD	GP38	8/69	35382
5536	EMD	GP38	10/69	35422
6440	EMD	GP9	5/55	20444

CENTRAL RAILROAD CO. OF INDIANA

500 North Buckeye Street
P. O. Box 554
Kokomo, IN 46903

Reporting marks: CIND
Phone: 317-459-3196
Fax: 317-457-4107

The Central of Indiana provides freight service from connections with Conrail, CSX, Norfolk Southern, Grand Trunk Western, and the Indiana & Ohio Railroad at (or near) Cincinnati, Ohio, to Shelbyville, Indiana, 81 miles, where a connection is made with Conrail. In addition the company has trackage rights over Conrail from Shelbyville to Indianapolis and Frankfort, Ind., 76.3 miles.

Mainline rail is 127 pound. Traffic is primarily grain, fertilizer and agricultural products, chemicals, plastics, sand, and soda ash, about 10,000 cars a year.

The Cincinnati-Shelbyville line was built by the Indianapolis & Cincinnati Railroad, chartered in 1853. That company was reorganized in 1867 as the Indianapolis, Cincinnati & LaFayette Railway and in 1880 became the Cincinnati, Indianapolis, St. Louis & Chicago. In 1899 it became part of the Cleveland, Cincinnati, Chicago & St. Louis (Big Four) which was leased by New York Central in 1907 and absorbed into NYC in 1930. Conrail sold the line on December 30, 1991.

The company is a subsidiary of Central Properties, Inc., and is affiliated with the Central Railroad Company of Indianapolis.
Radio frequencies: 160.545, 161.415
Locomotives: pooled with Central Railroad of Indianapolis

CENTRAL RAILROAD CO. OF INDIANAPOLIS

500 North Buckeye Street
P. O. Box 554
Kokomo, IN 46903

Reporting marks: CERA
Phone: 317-459-3196
Fax: 317-457-4107

Central Railroad of Indianapolis provides freight service from a Norfolk Southern connection at Frankfort, Indiana, through Kokomo to a Conrail connection at Marion, 53 miles (plus another 14 miles from Marion to Amboy operated on behalf of Kokomo Grain Co.) and from a Norfolk Southern connection at Tipton through Kokomo to Peru, 35 miles. The company connects with Winamac Southern at Kokomo and with Central Railroad of Indiana at Frankfort. In addition the company subleases its line from Peru to Argos, 36 miles, to Indiana-Hi Rail. Rail is 90 to 112 pound. Traffic is 12,000 cars a year of grain, fertilizer, sand, soda ash, lumber, newsprint, clay, and general commodities.

The Frankfort-Marion line was built by the Frankfort & Kokomo Railroad, which was organized in 1870 and consolidated with the Toledo, Delphos & Burlington Railroad in May 1879. The line eventually became part of the Nickel Plate's main line to St. Louis. The Peru line was built by the Peru & Indianapolis Railroad which was completed to Tipton in 1846 and to Peru in 1853. The line north of Peru was built by the Cincinnati, Peru & Chicago Railway; it became part of the Nickel Plate's Lake Erie & Western line. The Kokomo Rail Co. line to Amboy was acquired from CSX in December 1991. The company is owned by Central Properties, Inc. It began operations August 14, 1989, under a lease with NS's Thoroughbred Shortline Program.
Radio frequencies: 160.455, 161.295
Location of enginehouse: Kokomo, Ind.
Locomotives: 14 (power is pooled with affiliated lines)

No.	Builder	Model	New	Builder No.
1201	EMD	SW9	3/53	17581
1202	EMD	SW9	12/52	16744
1750	EMD	GP7U	11/51	14988
1751	EMD	GP7U	12/52	17082
1752	EMD	GP10	10/50	11042
1753	EMD	GP10	6/51	13352
1754	EMD	GP9	6/59	24866
1755	EMD	GP9	4/54	19201
2251	EMD	GP30	8/62	27385
2252	EMD	GP30	10/63	27578
2253	EMD	GP30	10/63	28580
2254	EMD	GP30	10/62	27443
2255	EMD	GP30	10/63	28587
7302	EMD	SD18	1/63	27600

Freight cars: 3

CENTRAL WESTERN RAILWAY CORP.

P. O. Box 1030
Stettler, AB T0C 2L0
Canada

Reporting marks: CWRL
Phone: 403-742-2503
Fax: 403-742-1477

Central Western Railway operates freight service from a Canadian National connection near Morrin, Alberta, 106.5 miles to a second CN connection at Ballast Pit, south of Camrose. A second line runs from a CP Rail connection at West Stettler to Compeer, 176 miles. Rail ranges from 60 to 110 pound.

Traffic is primarily grain — about 3,000 cars a year. In addition, Alberta Prairie Railway Excursions operates out of Stettler to various destinations along Central Western's lines.

The Morrin-Ballast Pit line was built by Canadian Northern between 1909 and 1911, and the Compeer line is a former CP Rail branch built by Canadian Pacific between 1909 and 1915. Central Western acquired the Morrin line from CN on October 11, 1986, and started operations. The CP line was acquired in 1992. The company is independent.

Radio frequencies: 161.445, 160.590
Location of enginehouse: Stettler, Alta.
Locomotives: 4

No.	Builder	Model	New	Builder No.
3708	EMD	GP9	1959	25631
4301	EMD	GP7U	1951	15477
4302	EMD	GP7U	1951	15476
7438	GMD	GP9	1957	A-1083

CHAMPAGNE RAILROAD, INC.

P. O. Box 323
Cohocton, NY 14826

Reporting marks: CGNE
Phone: 716-384-9169

The Champagne Railroad operates freight service from a connection with Conrail at Bath, New York, to Hammondsport, 9.23 miles, and from Bath to Wayland, 22 miles. Rail is 80 to 132 pound. Traffic includes about 340 carloads of wine and related products, fertilizer, and general commodities annually. Seasonal "Champagne Trail" excursions are operated between Bath and Cohocton.

The Bath & Hammondsport Railroad was chartered January 17, 1872, and opened a 3-foot gauge line between Bath and Hammondsport on June 30, 1875. It was relaid to standard gauge about 1889. The Erie Railroad controlled and operated the company from 1903 to May 28, 1936, when it was taken over by local businessmen. Passengers were carried until 1917, when the Keuka Lake steamers ended service.

On April 1, 1976, the state of New York designated the B&H to operate the Wayland branch of the former Erie Lackawanna from Bath to Wayland; it had been acquired by the Steuben County Industrial Development Agency. The agency acquired the assets of the Bath & Hammondsport on February 25, 1993, and leased the entire property to the Champagne Railroad on March 21, 1993.

The railroad is owned by Stanley Clark.

Location of enginehouse: Cohocton, N. Y.
Locomotives: 2

No.	Builder	Model	New	Builder No.
4	Alco	S-1	6/50	78139
5	Alco	S-1	3/50	77077

THE CF7

About 1970 the Santa Fe found itself with several hundred F7 freight diesels that had been bumped from mainline freight duties by high-horsepower hood units. Their carbody configuration made them unsuitable for branchline and local work, where they were needed.

Santa Fe couldn't afford new units for that service, but the mechanical components of the Fs were still good. The road decided to convert the F7s to hood units. Influencing that decision were a desire to keep the Cleburne, Texas, shop busy, and the tax advantages of a capital rebuild program, which lets a railroad depreciate rebuilt locomotives over a period of several years.

The basic difference between a cab unit and a hood unit complicated the rebuilding. A cab unit is designed so that the sides carry part of the load of the machinery. Remove the sides and the frame will sag. Fabricating new frames was a major part of the conversion of the F7s to CF7s.

At first glance, the CF7 looks like a chopnosed GP7, but the short hood is shorter and the cab is longer; also the side members of the frame are quite different. Mechanically, the CF7 is the same as a GP7.

Santa Fe built 233 CF7s between 1970 and 1978. In the early 1980s the road began to phase them out and discovered a ready market for the CF7 in the short lines, where they are proving to be useful locomotives.

Florida Northern No. 50, shown at Ocala, Florida, is a late CF7, with a flat cab roof and an air conditioner atop it. Early CF7s have a curved cab roof. Photo by Jim Shaw.

CHATTAHOOCHEE INDUSTRIAL RAILROAD

Highway 370
P. O. Box 253
Cedar Springs, GA 31732

Reporting marks: CIRR
Phone: 912-372-4531
Fax: 912-372-5811

The Chattahoochee Industrial Railroad operates freight and TOFC service from a connection with Norfolk Southern at Hilton, Georgia, to a connection with CSX at Saffold, 15.4 miles. Rail is 100 to 112 pound. Traffic consists of about 35,000 cars annually of coal, pulpwood, wood chips, plywood, pulpboard, chemicals, fuel oil, steel, and waste paper.

The company, which is owned by Georgia Pacific Corporation, was incorporated in January 1961 to build a new railroad. Operations started July 15, 1963.
Radio frequencies: 160.620, 160.860, 161.235

Location of enginehouse: Cedar Springs, Ga.
Locomotives: 7

No.	Builder	Model	New	Builder No.
1	EMD	GP10	1/59	20147
11	EMD	SW1200	3/50	11232
12	EMD	SW1200	1/52	15636
14	EMD	SW1200	1/53	17365
1500	EMD	SW1500	5/73	72649-1
1505	EMD	SW1500	5/73	72649-9
1830	EMD	GP7	5/51	9662

Freight cars: 902

Chattahoochee Industrial Railroad GP9 1830 switches at Saffold, Georgia, in December, 1992. Photo by Jim Shaw.

CHATTOOGA & CHICKAMAUGA RAILWAY CO.

413 West Villanow Street
Lafayette, GA 30728

Reporting marks: CCKY
Phone: 706-638-9552
Fax: 706-638-9553

Chattooga & Chickamauga operates freight service from Alton Park Junction, Tennessee, to Lyerly, Georgia, 48.9 miles, and to Hedges, Tennessee, 19.3 miles. Connection is made with Norfolk Southern at Shipp yard in Chattanooga. Rail is 90 and 100 pound. Traffic includes plastic, pulpwood, chemicals, grain, and steel — 1,600 cars a year.

The Chattooga & Chickamauga was authorized to begin common-carrier operations over 2 miles of trackage rights on the Columbus & Greenville between Davis and Waters, Mississippi, on June 14, 1989.

The Lyerly line is former Central of Georgia trackage, and the Hedges line was part of Tennessee, Alabama & Georgia Railway. The lines were acquired by the company from Norfolk Southern under their Thoroughbred ShortLine Program. Service started September 11, 1989. The company is a subsidiary of CAGY Industries, owner of the Columbus & Greenville Railway.

Radio frequencies: 160.455, 160.695
Location of enginehouse: Lafayette, Ga.
Locomotives: 2

No.	Builder	Model	New	Builder No.
102	EMD	GP7	9/52	16892
103	AT&SF	CF7	10/73	

CHENEY RAILROAD CO., INC.

1 Graystone Road
P. O. Box 309
Allgood, AL 35013

Reporting marks: CHNY
Phone: 205-625-3031

The Cheney Railroad operates freight traffic from Greens, Alabama, to Carnes (near Ivalee), 54.5 miles. Interchange is made with CSX at Mt. Pinson via trackage rights over the Cheney Railroad. Rail is 115 to 132 pound. Traffic is under 250 cars a year of miscellaneous commodities.

This line was part of the Alabama Mineral Railroad, which was absorbed by the Louisville & Nashville in 1893. The property was acquired from CSX on June 16, 1989. The company is owned by the Cheney family.

Location of enginehouse: Graystone, Ala.
Locomotives: 1

No.	Builder	Model	New	Builder No.
65	GE	65-ton	9/42	7392

CHESAPEAKE RAILROAD CO.

P. O. Box 586
Ridgely, MD 21660

Reporting marks: CHRR
Phone: 410-482-2330
Fax: 410-482-7075

The Chesapeake Railroad operates freight and passenger excursion service from a connection with Conrail at Clayton, Delaware, to Easton, Maryland, 45.3 miles. A branch line extends from Queen Anne to Denton, Md., 8.8 miles. A total of 54.1 miles is operated. Rail runs from 100 to 130 pound.

Passenger excursion service started October 29, 1994, and freight service resumed on January 31, 1995. Freight traffic is expected to include potash, aggregate, grain, fertilizer, and lumber.

This line was built in the 1860s by the Maryland & Delaware Railroad, which was reorganized as the Delaware & Chesapeake Railroad in 1878. By 1882 it was leased to a Pennsylvania Railroad affiliate, the Philadelphia, Wilmington & Baltimore. It was operated successively by the Pennsylvania Railroad, Penn Central, Conrail, and the Maryland & Delaware until February 1983, when service ended. The property was acquired by Maryland Department of Transportation (Mass Transit Administration) after Conrail discontinued service. Chesapeake Railroad leases the property from Maryland DOT. The operating company is controlled by William Bartosh.

Radio frequencies: 160.935, 161.145, 161.175
Location of enginehouse: Greensboro, Md.
Locomotives: 3

No.	Builder	Model	New	Builder No.
85	Whitcomb	80-ton	6/44	60511
95	Whitcomb	80-ton	6/46	60682
4302	Vulcan	8-ton	11/40	4302

CHESAPEAKE & ALBEMARLE RAILROAD CO.

1500 Lexington Drive
P. O. Box 1849
Elizabeth City, NC 27909

Reporting marks: CA
Phone: 919-332-2778

The Chesapeake & Albemarle Railroad operates a line extending from a connection with Norfolk Southern and Norfolk & Portsmouth Belt at Chesapeake (Portlock Yard), Virginia, to Edenton, North Carolina, 73.1 miles. Rail is 105 to 130 pound. Traffic includes aggregate, lumber, scrap, and agricultural products, about 7,000 cars a year.

This line was built by the Elizabeth City & Norfolk Railroad, which opened its line from Norfolk (Berkley) to the Albemarle Sound at Edenton on December 15, 1881. The EC&N was renamed Norfolk Southern Railroad in 1883 and reorganized in 1891 as Norfolk & Southern Railroad. The company eventually became part of Southern Railway. The railroad is leased and operated under NS's Thoroughbred ShortLine Program. Shortline service started April 2, 1990.

The Chesapeake & Albemarle is a subsidiary of RailTex Inc.
Radio frequency: 161.310
Location of enginehouse: Elizabeth City, N. C.
Locomotives: 2

No.	Builder	Model	New	Builder No.	Rebuilt
2158	EMD	GP7	8/52	16978	1979
2190	EMD	GP7	11/52	17628	1980

Chesapeake & Albemarle CF7 No. 2158 heads south out of Moyock, Virginia, with a typical freight train in July 1994. Photo by Jim Shaw.

CHESAPEAKE WESTERN RAILWAY

290A Chesapeake Drive
P. O. Box 231
Harrisonburg, VA 28801

Reporting marks: CHW
Phone: 703-434-7352

The Chesapeake Western operates freight service from a Norfolk Southern connection at Shenandoah, Virginia, via trackage rights on NS south 6 miles to Elkton, then west to a connection with the Shenandoah Valley Railroad at Pleasant Valley, 23.8 miles. Branches extend from Harrisonburg southwest to Dayton, 3 miles, northeast to Mount Jackson, 27.5 miles. Rail is 80 to 115 pound. Traffic is grain and farm related products, paper, and manufactured and miscellaneous commodities.

The company was incorporated January 22, 1892, as the Chesapeake, Shendun & Western Railroad. On May 14, 1895, the name was changed to Chesapeake & Western Railroad. The road opened from Elkton to Bridgewater, 26.67 miles, on April 29, 1896, and was leased to the Chesapeake Western Railway (incorporated March 3, 1900) on May 1, 1902, for 99 years. A branch line was opened from Bridgewater to North River Gap, 13.96 miles, on June 1, 1902.

The Chesapeake & Western and Chesapeake Western merged to become the Chesapeake Western Railway on December 31, 1943. The company purchased Baltimore & Ohio's Harrisonburg-Staunton branch in 1943.

Norfolk & Western purchased the entire capital stock of the Chesapeake Western on November 10, 1954. The company purchased Southern Railway's Harrisonburg-Mount Jackson branch on April 15, 1989. The railroad was abandoned south of Pleasant Valley in 1992, and that track has been acquired by the Shenandoah Valley Railroad.

Radio frequencies: 161.250, 161.490, 161.190
Locomotives: supplied by Norfolk Southern

CHESTNUT RIDGE RAILWAY CO.

401 Delaware Avenue
Palmerton, PA 18071

Reporting marks: CHR
Phone: 610-826-8617
Fax: 610-826-8775

The Chestnut Ridge operates freight service from a connection with Conrail at Palmerton, Pennsylvania, to Little Gap, 7.2 miles. Rail ranges from 80 to 100 pound. Traffic, 1,500 cars a year, includes zinc products, chemicals, and waste. Passenger service ended in 1935. The Chestnut Ridge Railroad Co. of Pennsylvania was incorporated by Jacob Astor, J. Pierpont Morgan, Chauncey

Chestnut Ridge Alco S-2 No. 11 switches around the New Jersey Zinc plant at Palmerton, Pennsylvania. Photo by Jim Shaw.

M. DePew, and others on March 8, 1898, and it opened for service in January 1900. It was known as the "millionaires road" because it had two millionaires on its board of directors for each mile of track. The company was sold under foreclosure on November 30, 1901, to become the Chestnut Ridge Railway. New Jersey Zinc Company has owned the railroad since 1901.

Radio frequency: 154.515
Location of enginehouse: Palmerton, Pa.
Locomotives: 1 (plus leased New Jersey Zinc Co. engines)

No.	Builder	Model	New	Builder No.
11	Alco	S-2	12/46	73901

CHICAGO & ILLINOIS MIDLAND RAILWAY CO.

15th and North Grand Avenue
P. O. Box 139
Springfield, IL 62705-0139

Reporting marks: CIM
Phone: 217-788-8601
Fax: 217-788-8658

Chicago & Illinois Midland operates freight service from East Peoria, Illinois, to Taylorville, 121 miles. Connections are made with Santa Fe, Burlington Northern, Chicago & North Western, Conrail, Gateway Western, Iowa Interstate, Illinois Central, Keokuk Junction, Norfolk Southern, Southern Pacific, St. Louis Southwestern, Toledo, Peoria & Western, and Peoria & Pekin Union. Rail is 115 to 131 pound.

Coal makes up 90 percent of C&IM's traffic; general commodities bring the total to about 48,000 cars a year.

The Central Illinois Railway Company was incorporated on July 17, 1905. Its name was changed to Chicago & Illinois Midland Railway on January 22, 1906, when it absorbed the Pawnee Railroad. In 1926 the company purchased the Springfield-Pekin line of the defunct Chicago, Peoria & St. Louis.

The C&IM was owned by Commonwealth Edison from 1907 until it was sold by Illinois Midland Transportation Co. to QF, Ltd., in December 1989.

Radio frequencies: 160.950 (road), 160.290 (switching)
Location of enginehouse: Springfield, Ill.
Locomotives: 12

No.	Builder	Model	New	Builder No.
18	EMD	SW1200	4/55	20363
20-23	EMD	SW1200	11/55	20678-20681
30, 31	EMD	RS1325	9/60	25773, 25774
50	EMD	SD9	11/55	20691
52	EMD	SD9	11/55	20693
54	EMD	SD9	11/55	20695
60	EMD	SD18	12/61	26668
61	EMD	SD18	6/62	27392

Freight cars: 414 gondolas

Austere-looking SD9 No. 54, shown at Springfield, Illinois, is typical of Chicago & Illinois Midland power. Photo by Jim Shaw.

CHICAGO, CENTRAL & PACIFIC RAILROAD CO.

402 East Fourth Street
P. O. Box 1800
Waterloo, IA 50704

Reporting marks: CC
Phone: 319-236-9200

The Chicago Central provides freight service from the Chicago area across Illinois and Iowa to Omaha, Nebraska, 517 miles. A 129-mile branch runs from Tara, west of Fort Dodge, to Sioux City, Iowa, 135 miles. Several additional short branch lines are located in Iowa and Illinois. A total of 774 miles are operated.

Traffic consists of 120,000 carloads annually of coal, agricul-tural products, lumber, and intermodal shipments.

The company acquired its line (it was former Illinois Central trackage) from Illinois Central Gulf in December 1985 at a cost of $75 million for track and equipment. The transaction was financed by General Electric Credit Corporation. Service started on December 24th. On September 1, 1987, CC filed for Chapter 11 protection. The company was released from protection the following month following a restructuring of its debt obligations.

The company is owned by a management group and Cimmred Corp. (Midwest Energy). As this book went to press, Illinois Central was negotiating to purchase the CC&P.
Radio frequencies: 160.755, 161.190, 160.410, 161.460
Employees: 490
Locomotives: 43
Freight cars: 2,390
Principal shop: Waterloo, Iowa

CHICAGO-CHEMUNG RAILROAD CORP.

P. O. Box 69
Crystal Lake, IL 60039-0069

Reporting marks: CCUO
Phone: 815-459-1600

This company provides switching service over a former Chicago & North Western line from a connection with C&NW at Harvard, Illi-nois, to Chemung, 3.5 miles. Service started in October 1987. The company is independent.
Locomotives: 1

No.	Builder	Model	New	Builder No.
202	EMD	SW7	3/50	10295

CHICAGO RAIL LINK

2778 East 104th Street
Chicago, IL 60617

Reporting marks: CRL
Phone: 312-721-4000
Fax: 312-374-7713

CRL operates a switching line between Chicago, Blue Island, and Kensington, Illinois, 56.9 miles. Over 20,000 cars a year of scrap, steel, grain, and overhead cars make up the road's traffic.

The company was originally the LaSalle & Bureau County Railway, which was organized August 29, 1890. The Chicago area trackage was acquired from the Rock Island around 1980 and the present name was adopted May 1, 1985. The original LS&BC route between LaSalle and Midway, Illinois, has since been abandoned. Chicago Rail Link is a subsidiary of OmniTRAX, Inc.
Radio frequencies: 160.635, 161.610
Location of enginehouse: Chicago, Ill.

Locomotives: 14

No.	Builder	Model	New	Builder No.		No.	Builder	Model	New	Builder No.
14	EMD	GP18	1/60	25456		52	EMD	SW1200	2/65	29783
15	EMD	GP18	1/60	25463		58	EMD	GP7	2/58	24373
18	EMD	SW1500	12/72	7343-1		59	EMD	GP7	2/58	24374
19	EMD	SW1500	12/72	7343-3		613	EMD	GP9	5/53	18444
28	EMD	GP9	1951	16879		614	EMD	GP9	5/53	18452
29	EMD	GP9	1951	14297		617	EMD	GP9	9/51	14229
51	EMD	SW9	10/52	16427		4297	EMD	GP7	1951	14305

Freight cars: 549 gondolas, 115 hopper cars

CHICAGO SHORT LINE RAILWAY CO.

9746 South Avenue N
Chicago, IL 60617

Reporting marks: CSL
Phone: 312-768-6405

Radio frequency: 160.335
Locomotives: 4

No.	Builder	Model	New	Builder No.
28	EMD	SW1001	9/74	74616-1
29	EMD	SW1001	9/74	74616-2
30	EMD	SW1500	9/68	34126
31	EMD	SW1500	7/71	37078

Freight cars: 50 gondolas

The Chicago Short Line is a switching railroad operating 28 miles of track in the Calumet district between South Chicago, Illinois, and Indiana Harbor, Indiana. Rail is 90 and 115 pound.

The company was incorporated December 8, 1900, and operations started in 1903. It is owned by LTV Steel Company, Inc.

CHICAGO SOUTHSHORE & SOUTH BEND RAILROAD

505 North Carroll Avenue
Michigan City, IN 46360-5082

Reporting marks: CSS
Phone: 219-874-9000
Fax: 219-879-3754

The SouthShore provides freight service between Chicago and South Bend, Indiana. A total of 91 miles are operated. Connections are made with Conrail, CSX, Elgin, Joliet & Eastern, Illinois Central, Grand Trunk Western, Norfolk Southern, Union Pacific, and several switching companies including Indiana Harbor Belt, Baltimore & Ohio Chicago Terminal, and Belt Railway of Chicago.

Traffic includes coal, steel, and manufactured products — about 50,000 cars a year. Passenger service is operated over the line by a local transit authority, the Northern Indiana Commuter Transportation District.

The line was built by the Chicago & Indiana Air Line Railway, incorporated in December 1901 and reorganized in 1925 as the Chicago, Lake Shore & South Bend Railway. It was purchased at foreclosure on July 14, 1925, by the Chicago South Shore & South Bend Railroad. SouthShore owns, leases, and operates the Kensington & Eastern Railroad Co., which extends from Kensington,

Ill., east to the state line. Venango River Corp. purchased the Chicago South Shore & South Bend from the Chesapeake & Ohio Railway on September 28, 1984. Venango River went bankrupt in 1990 and sold the physical plant and the passenger operations to Northern Indiana Commuter Transportation District. Freight operations and all track used exclusively for freight service were acquired by Anacostia & Pacific Corporation as the Chicago SouthShore & South Bend.

Radio frequency: 161.355
Locomotives: 11

No.	Builder	Model	New	Builder No.
206	EMD	SW8	12/51	15742
2000-2009	EMD	GP38-2	1/81	796333-1–796333-10

Freight cars: 680

CHICAGO, WEST PULLMAN & SOUTHERN RAILROAD CO.

2728 East 104th Street
Chicago, IL 60617

Reporting marks: CWP
Phone: 312-374-4800
Fax: 312-374-7713

The Chicago, West Pullman & Southern is a switching road operating between West Pullman and Irondale, Illinois, 25 miles. Rail is 90 pound. Traffic runs about 1,500 cars a year.

The company was incorporated October 28, 1909, as a consolidation of the Chicago, West Pullman & Southern Railway (incor-porated in 1901) and the Calumet & South Eastern Railroad (incorporated 1908). The company is a subsidiary of OmniTRAX, Inc. and is operated in conjunction with Chicago Rail Link.

Radio frequency: 160.215
Locomotives: 1

No.	Builder	Model	New	Builder No.
43	EMD	SW8	11/52	16825

Freight cars: 25 boxcars, 123 gondolas

CHILLICOTHE-BRUNSWICK RAIL MAINTENANCE AUTHORITY

909 Main Street
Trenton, MO 64683

Reporting marks: CBRM
Phone: 816-359-5086
Fax: 816-359-3096

Chillicothe-Brunswick operates freight service from a connection with the Norfolk Southern at Brunswick, Missouri, to a connection with CP Rail System (Soo Line) at Chillicothe, 37.6 miles. It also connects with Burlington Northern at Sumner. Traffic is primarily agricultural commodities, about 1,200 cars a year.

The line was built by the Brunswick & Chillicothe Railroad in 1871 and leased to the Wabash Railroad in 1878. It became part of a through route from Brunswick to Council Bluffs, Iowa. It was abandoned by the Norfolk & Western in 1984 and acquired by the Green Hills Rural Development Authority, which leased it to the Northern Missouri Railroad on February 13, 1984.

Floods and washouts cut the Northern Missouri, and the southern portion was reorganized as the Chillicothe Southern Railroad on January 13, 1986. The CS failed and the Chillicothe-Brunswick Authority took over operations on September 20, 1986. It ran the line until April 1, 1990, when it was leased to the

Wabash & Grand River Railroad. W&GR ended service during the summer of 1993 due to flood damage. The authority again took back its railroad and more than $1.1 million was required for repairs before trains resumed service in April 1994.

Location of enginehouse: Trenton, Mo.
Locomotives: 1

No.	Builder	Model	New	Builder No.
4485	EMD	GP7	5/53	18236

CINCINNATI TERMINAL RAILWAY CO.

2856 Cypress Way
P. O. Box 12576
Cincinnati, OH 45212-0576

Reporting marks: CTER
Phone: 513-531-4800

Cincinnati Terminal Railway operates from Cincinnati to Red Bank and Evendale, Ohio, 16.25 miles. Rail is 131 pound and heavier. Norfolk Southern has trackage rights over the line. Traffic includes chemicals, paper products and other commodities, about 2,000 cars a year.

The line was part of the Pennsylvania Railroad and was included in Conrail. Cincinnati Terminal and Southwest Ohio Regional Transportation Authority jointly acquired the line from Conrail for $4 million. Cincinnati Terminal started operations on June 24, 1994. It is a wholly owned subsidiary of the Indiana & Ohio Rail Corp.
Radio frequency: 161.385
Location of enginehouse: Cincinnati, Ohio
Locomotives: supplied by the I&O

CITY OF PRINEVILLE RAILWAY

185 East Tenth Street
Prineville, OR 97754

Reporting marks: COP
Phone: 503-447-6251
Fax: 503-447-1631

The City of Prineville Railway operates freight and TOFC service from a connection with the Union Pacific and Burlington Northern at Prineville Junction to Prineville, Oregon, 18.34 miles. Rail is 112 pound. Traffic consists of about 2,000 carloads annually of lumber, forest products, and general commodities. The Crooked River Railroad Company runs passenger excursions and dinner trains over the line.

The City of Prineville's two diesels team up to move a train to the UP and BN connection at Prineville Junction, Oregon. Photo by Jim Shaw.

The railway was constructed during 1918. It is a department of the city of Prineville and is managed by a commission appointed by the city council. Regular passenger service was discontinued in 1939.
Radio frequency: 161.190
Location of enginehouse: Prineville, Ore.

Locomotives: 3

No.	Builder	Model	New	Builder No.	Rebuilt
1	Lima	3-truck Shay	1923	3233	
985	EMD	GP9U	6/54	19569	1974
989	EMD	GP9U	11/54	20029	1974

Freight cars: 182 boxcars

CLAREMONT CONCORD RAILROAD CORP.

P. O. Box 1598
Claremont, NH 03743

Reporting marks: CCRR
Phone: 603-542-5166
Fax: 603-542-9035

Claremont Concord Railroad operates freight service from a connection with ST Rail (Boston & Maine) and New England Central at Claremont Junction to Claremont, New Hampshire, 2 miles. Rail is 70 to 85 pound. Traffic includes lumber, salt, and scrap metal, about 500 cars a year.

The Claremont & Concord Railway was incorporated July 12, 1954, to purchase the Claremont-Concord branch of the B&M and the Claremont Railway, an electric line operating from Claremont to West Claremont. Passenger service was discontinued soon after it began operation, and the line was abandoned between Newport and East Claremont on September 1, 1977.

The Claremont-Claremont Junction line dates from 1848, when the Concord & Claremont Railroad was chartered. The line was opened in September, 1872.

The Claremont Railway & Lighting Co was chartered in 1901 and opened its line in August 1903. At its height it operated more than 15 miles of track in Claremont.

The present company was formed to acquire the assets of the Claremont & Concord on October 19, 1988. It is independent.
Radio frequency: 160.950
Location of enginehouse: Claremont Junction, N. H.
Locomotives: 2

No.	Builder	Model	New	Builder No.
30	GE	44-ton	12/42	15757
119	GE	44-ton	6/48	29974

CLARENDON & PITTSFORD RAILROAD CO.

53 Park Street
Rutland, VT 05701

Reporting marks: CLP
Phone: 802-775-4356
Fax: 802-658-2553

The Clarendon & Pittsford operates freight and TOFC service in conjunction with the Vermont Railway over a former Delaware & Hudson branch from Whitehall, New York, to Rutland, Vermont, 23.7 miles. It also operates a 1-mile line, part of its original line,

from a connection with the Vermont Railway at Florence Junction to Florence, Vt.

Traffic, about 9,000 cars a year, is overhead moving between the Vermont Railway and the Green Mountain at Rutland and CP Rail System (D&H) at Whitehall, as well as limestone and mineral products.

The Clarendon & Pittsford was incorporated September 10, 1885, and opened between Rutland and West Rutland in July

1886. It purchased the Brandon & West Rutland Railroad on May 13, 1911, and the Pittsford & Rutland on November 13, 1911. Limited passenger service ended in 1925. The company has been run as an affiliate of the Vermont Railway since November 1972. D&H's Rutland & Whitehall branch was acquired in December 1983. The company is controlled by the owners of the Vermont Railway.

Radio frequencies: 160.290, 160.010
Location of enginehouse: Rutland, Vt.

Locomotives: 4

No.	Builder	Model	New	Builder No.
30	GE	44-ton	12/42	15757
119	GE	44-ton	6/48	29974
202	EMD	GP38-2	10/74	75603-1
203	EMD	GP38	11/66	32664
502	EMD	SW1500	2/68	33521
802	EMD	GP16	5/50	10220

Freight cars: 12 boxcars

Clarendon & Pittsford GP9 No. 752 heads up train RW-2 (Rutland to Whitehall) at West Rutland, Vermont. Photo by Jack Armstrong.

CLINTON TERMINAL RAILROAD CO.

P. O. Box 11
Clinton, NC 28328

Reporting marks: CTR
Phone: 910-862-6339

The Clinton Terminal Railroad operates 3.5 miles of switching track at Clinton, North Carolina, connecting with CSX. The railroad began operation in July 1994 as the Clinton Division of the Waccamaw Coast Line, and adopted its present name in September 1995. The operating company is controlled by L. Gray Tuttle.

Radio frequencies: 461.450, 466.450
Location of enginehouse: Clinton, N. C.
Locomotives: 1

No.	Builder	Model	New
2480	AT&SF	CF7	2/76

COE RAIL, INC.

26795 Captains Lane
Franklin, MI 48025

Reporting marks: CRLE
Phone: 810-960-9440
Fax: 810-960-9444

Coe Rail operates excursion trains and limited freight service between Wixom and West Bloomfield, Michigan, 8.1 miles, connecting with CSX at Wixom.

Freight traffic, less than 400 cars a year, includes plastic and lumber. The Michigan Star Clipper Dinner Train operates on Coe Rail's line.

This line was built by the Michigan Air Line Railway and opened about 1883. It became part of the Grand Trunk Western and was acquired by Coe Rail in 1984 when GTW abandoned it. The company is owned by Larry I. Coe.

Radio frequency: 161.025
Location of enginehouse: Walled Lake, Mich.
Locomotives: 4

No.	Builder	Model	New	Builder No.	Rebuilt
70	Alco	S-1	6/45	73354	
105	Whitcomb	20-ton	1/42	13214	
725	EMD	F7A	2/53	17909	
1002	Alco	CS-9	9/55	81405	1981

Freight cars: 2,492 (leased from Greenbrier)

COLONEL'S ISLAND RAILROAD CO.

U. S. Route 17 North
P. O. Box 2406
Savannah, GA 31402

Reporting marks: CISD
Phone: 912-964-3987
Fax: 912-964-3969

The Colonel's Island Railroad operates freight service from a connection with CSX and Norfolk Southern at Anguilla, Georgia, to Mydharris, south of Brunswick, 12 miles. Rail is 100 pound.

Traffic includes minerals and automobiles for transloading to and from ships. About 3,000 cars are carried annually.

This line was built by the state of Georgia in 1969 as part of a port development project. There was little activity on it until August 1980. The track is owned by the Georgia Port Authority.

Radio frequencies: 808.465, 852.4375
Location of enginehouse: Mydharris, Ga.
Locomotives: 2

No.	Builder	Model	New	Builder No.
8235	EMD	GP7	4/51	14570
8239	EMD	GP7	1/53	17676

COLORADO & WYOMING RAILWAY CO.

P. O. Box 316
Pueblo, CO 81002

Reporting marks: CW
Phone: 719-561-6359
Fax: 719-561-6837

The Colorado & Wyoming operates a 4.5-mile switching line at Minnequa, Colorado (near Pueblo), connecting with Santa Fe, Burlington Northern, and Southern Pacific. Rail is 75 and 115 pounds. Traffic consists of coal, ore, and steel products — 15,000 cars a year.

The company was incorporated May 9, 1899, by the Colorado Fuel & Iron Co. It quickly built what came to be its Northern Division to iron mines north of Guernsey, Wyoming, from a connection with the Colorado & Southern. The Northern Division was shut down in 1980.

The Southern Division from Jansen to New Elk Mine, 26.7 miles, opened in 1901. That line was sold to the Trinidad Railway in 1992. The Middle Division was formed in 1902 when C&W took over switching duties at CF&I's Minnequa Works from the railroads. The present operation consists of the former Middle Division. Oregon Steel Corporation owns the railroad.

Radio frequency: 161.250

Location of enginehouse: Minnequa, Colo.
Locomotives: 10

No.	Builder	Model	New	Builder No.	Rebuilt
102	EMD	GP7	3/51	13552	
103	EMD	GP7	12/51	15746	
104	EMD	GP7	12/51	15747	
201	EMD	SW8	12/51	15737	
203	EMD	SW8	12/51	15739	
205	EMD	SW8	12/51	15741	
208	EMD	SW8	12/51	15744	
209	EMD	SW8	12/51	15745	
210	EMD	SW8	3/52	15940	
211	EMD	SW8	3/52	15941	

Freight cars: 89 flatcars, 5 gondolas

COLUMBIA & COWLITZ RAILWAY CO.

P. O. Box 209
Longview, WA 98632

Reporting marks: CLC
Phone: 206-636-6535
Fax: 206-636-6489

The Columbia & Cowlitz operates freight service from Columbia Junction to Ostrander Junction, Washington, 8.49 miles, connecting with the Burlington Northern and Union Pacific at Rocky Point. Rail is 112 pound. Traffic consists of lumber, forest products, paper, and chemicals, about 15,000 cars a year.

The company was incorporated April 9, 1925, and the railroad was built between 1926 and 1928. The owner, Weyerhaeuser Company, also operates a 35-mile logging line in connection with the Columbia & Cowlitz.

Radio frequencies: 161.385, 160.425, 161.115
Location of enginehouse: Longview, Wash.
Locomotives: 2

No.	Builder	Model	New	Builder No.	Rebuilt
700	EMD	GP7U	7/53	18599	1976
701	EMD	GP7U	8/53	18604	1977

Freight cars: 760

COLUMBIA TERMINAL

15 North Seventh Street
P. O. Box N
Columbia, MO 65205

Reporting marks: CT
Phone: 314-874-7325
Fax: 314-443-6875

Columbia Terminal operates freight service from Columbia, Missouri, to a connection with Norfolk Southern at Centralia, 21.4 miles. Rail is 90 to 115 pound. Annual traffic is 1,000 cars a year of coal, grain, plastic resin, lumber, wax, steel, and general commodities.

The line was built by the Boone County & Jefferson City Railroad, which was chartered January 30, 1857. Ground was broken in 1866, and the railroad was completed from Centralia to Columbia on October 29, 1867. The railroad was leased to the North Missouri Railroad until April 23, 1873, when it was reorganized as the Boone County & Booneville Railroad. It was leased to the St. Louis, Kansas City & Northern Railway in May, 1875; that became part of the Wabash system.

Norfolk Southern sold the Columbia-Centralia line to the City of Columbia on October 2, 1987. The operating company is a division of the Water & Light Department of the city of Columbia.
Location of enginehouse: Columbia, Mo.
Locomotives: 1

No.	Builder	Model	New	Builder No.
1	EMD	SW1200	1/65	29871

COLUMBUS & GREENVILLE RAILWAY

201 19th Street, N.
P. O. Box 6000
Columbus, MS 39701

Reporting marks: CAGY
Phone: 601-329-7710
Fax: 601-329-7724

The Columbus & Greenville operates freight service from Columbus, Mississippi, to Greenville, 175 miles. It connects at Columbus with Burlington Northern, Norfolk Southern, Kansas City Southern (and CSX via KCS), and Golden Triangle Railroad. It connects at Greenwood and Winona with Illinois Central, at West Point with KCS, and at Great River Junction with the Great River Railroad.

The company also operates several former Illinois Central Gulf lines acquired in May 1985:
• Greenville to Metcalf, 7.37 miles
• Metcalf to Leland, 7.31 miles
• Cleveland to Hollandale, 49.22 miles.

Total mileage operated is 230. Rail includes 80, 85, 90, and 112 pound. Traffic includes about 11,000 cars a year of lumber, steel, grain, agricultural products, manufactured goods, and general commodities.

The first construction between Columbus and Greenville was undertaken by the Greenville, Columbus & Birmingham Railroad in 1878. The 3-foot gauge line was sold to the Georgia Pacific in 1881. The company then came under control of the Richmond & Danville and was reorganized August 31, 1894, as the Southern Railway in Mississippi. The Southern operated the company until September 12, 1924, when the Columbus & Greenville Railway was formed by local interests to acquire the line. Independent operations continued until September 29, 1972, when the company was purchased by ICG. On August 2, 1974, the ICG entered into an agreement to sell the line to local interests once again. The ICC authorized the resumption of local management effective July 4, 1975, and service started October 30, 1975.

The company is independent, controlled by local interests.

Radio frequencies: 160.245 (road), 160.230 (switching)
Location of enginehouse: Columbus, Miss.
Locomotives: 23

No.	Builder	Model	New	Builder No.
601*	Baldwin	DRS-6-4-1500	9/51	72624
608	EMD	GP7	9/52	17345
614	EMD	GP7	10/52	17351
615	EMD	GP7	10/52	17352
618	EMD	GP7	10/52	17355
621	EMD	GP7	10/52	17358
701	EMD	GP9	7/55	20587

No.	Builder	Model	New	Builder No.
702	EMD	GP9	7/55	20586
704	EMD	GP9	7/55	20590
801-810	AT&SF	CF7	1977	(except 804)
1000	EMD	GP7	9/52	16891
1001	EMD	GP7	4/51	14317
1002	EMD	GP7	5/53	18248
1003	EMD	GP7	9/52	16893

* 601 is on display at Columbus
Freight cars: 1,175

COLUMBUS & OHIO RIVER RAILROAD CO.

136 South Fifth Street
Coshocton, OH 43812

Reporting marks: CUOH
Phone: 614-622-8092
Fax: 614-622-8097

The Columbus & Ohio River operates freight service between Conrail connections at Columbus and Gould Siding, Ohio, 140.9 miles. Branch lines run from Cadiz Junction to Georgetown Mine, 12.8 miles, and from Heath to Hebron, 5.5 miles. It connects with CSX at Newark and Heath, with Ohio Central at Coshocton, with R. J. Corman at Uhrichsville, and with Wheeling & Lake Erie at Jewett. Main line rail is 132 to 155 pound. Traffic includes crude oil, asphalt, and paper, and there is potential for significant coal movements. Traffic presently runs about 11,500 cars a year.

The line was built in two sections. The Steubenville & Indiana built the east end of the line to Newark about 1854, and the Central Ohio opened the line from Newark to Columbus several years earlier. The Pittsburg, Cincinnati & St. Louis (Panhandle Line) took over the route in May 1868. PC&StL was under Pennsylvania Railroad control. The line became part of Pennsy's Pittsburgh-St. Louis main line and was part of the original Conrail system.

Conrail sold the property for $7.45 million to Caprail I, Inc., in April 1992. Caprail leased it to the Ohio Department of Transportation, which subleased it to the Columbus & Ohio River. Shortline service started on April 17, 1992. The Columbus & Ohio River is controlled by Jerry Jacobson and is part of the Ohio Central Railroad System.

Radio frequency: 160.845
Location of enginehouses: Coshocton and Heath, Ohio
Locomotives: 5

No.	Builder	Model	New	Builder No.	Rebuilt
3216	EMD	GP40	11/68	34657	
3217	EMD	GP40	11/68	34658	
5407	EMD	GP8	8/53	18635	1976
5408	EMD	GP8	12/50	12008	1976
6606	EMD	GP35	1/65	29711	

Freight cars: 35 boxcars, 5 gondolas

COMMONWEALTH RAILWAY, INC.

1 Park West Circle — Suite 203
Midlothian, VA 23113

Reporting marks: CWRY
Phone: 804-379-4664

Commonwealth Railway operates freight service from a connection with Norfolk Southern at Suffolk, Virginia, to West Norfolk, 16.5 miles. Rail is 112 pound. Traffic consists of 1,000 cars a year of aggregate, chemicals and plastic.

Shortline service started August 24, 1989, following sale and lease from Norfolk Southern. The company, a subsidiary of Rail Link, Inc., owns the line from West Norfolk to Churchland and leases it between Churchland and Suffolk.

Radio frequency: 469.550
Location of enginehouse: Suffolk, Va.
Locomotives: 1

No.	Builder	Model	New
517	ATSF	CF7	7/74

CONEMAUGH & BLACK LICK RAILROAD CO.

1 Locust Street
Johnstown, PA 15909

Reporting marks: CBL
Phone: 814-533-6424

The Conemaugh & Black Lick provides switching service on 33 miles of track at Johnstown, Pennsylvania. It connects with Conrail and CSX and moves about 2,000 revenue cars a year. The company began operations in 1907 and is owned by Bethlehem Steel Corporation.

Radio frequencies: 161.100, 161.250
Locomotives: 13

No.	Builder	Model	New	Builder No.
100-102	EMD	NW2	7/49	9749-9751
104	EMD	NW2	1/50	10304
110, 111	EMD	SW7	8/49	9755, 9756
112, 114	EMD	SW7	11/49	9915, 9917
116	EMD	SW7	10/50	12917
122	EMD	NW2	12/48	8412
125	EMD	NW2	7/45	2066
127	EMD	SW1200	12/64	29638
128	EMD	SW1200	5/65	30243
129	EMD	SW1200	11/57	24141

CONNECTICUT CENTRAL RAILROAD CO.

Rapallo Avenue
P. O. Box 1022
Middletown, CT 06457

Reporting marks: CCCL
Phone: 203-346-8698
Fax: 203-344-9719

Connecticut Central operates freight service from a connection with Conrail at Cedar Hill (New Haven) to Middletown, Connecticut, 19.4 miles. The company also operates short branch lines from Middletown to Portland, Cromwell, Laurel, and North Middletown. Interchange is also made with Providence & Worcester at Middlefield. Total owned trackage is 17.4 miles. Rail varies from 105 to 115 pound. Traffic is 1,400 cars a year of sludge, steel, paper (pulpboard), brick, fertilizer, and other commodities.

The railroad was built by the New Haven, Middletown & Willimantic Railroad and opened August 13, l873. In 1875 the property was reorganized as the Boston & New York Air Line and later became part of the New Haven, and still later, Penn Central and Conrail. Shortline service started May 26, 1987. The company is privately owned.

Radio frequencies: 160.695 (road), 160.290 (yard and maintenance of way)

Location of enginehouse: Middletown, Conn.

Locomotives: 3

No.	Builder	Model	New	Builder No.	Rebuilt
35	Alco	S-4	1959	82008	
36	Alco	S-4	11/53	80941	
53	EMD	GP9	5/54	19485	1978

COPPER BASIN RAILWAY, INC.

Highway 177
P. O. Drawer I
Hayden, AZ 85235

Reporting marks: CBRY
Phone: 602-355-7730

Copper Basin Railway operates freight service from a connection with the Southern Pacific at Magma, Arizona, to Winkelman, 54 miles. It connects with the San Manuel Arizona Railroad at Hayden. A branch line extends from Ray Junction to Ray, 7 miles. Rail is 112 to 136 pound. Traffic includes copper concentrates, copper ore, and finished copper along with sulfuric acid, lumber, coal, military equipment, and gypsum rock — about 107,000 cars a year.

The Magma-Winkelman line was the east end of the Phoenix & Eastern Railroad, which was chartered October 1, 1901, opened in 1905, and leased to a Southern Pacific subsidiary, the Arizona Eastern Railroad, in March 1910.

The Ray branch was built by the Ray & Gila Valley Railroad, which opened in October 1910. It was a common carrier until December 1943 when it became a private railroad. Copper Basin purchased the branch from Kennecott Copper Co. Copper Basin Railway started service August 15, 1986. It is controlled by Rail Management & Consulting Corporation.

Radio frequencies: 160.545, 161.505
Location of enginehouse: Hayden Junction, Ariz.
Freight cars: 764

Copper Basin GP18 No. 201 and GP39 No. 403 pull a train through the desert near Ray Junction, Arizona. Photo by Jim Shaw.

Locomotives: 13

No.	Builder	Model	New	Builder No.
201, 202	EMD	GP18	10/63	28632, 28631
203	EMD	GP18	2/61	26648
204	EMD	GP9	2/55	20336
205	EMD	GP9	3/54	19355
206	EMD	GP9	2/56	21089
207	EMD	GP9	7/56	21233
208	EMD	GP9	6/54	19613
401, 402	EMD	GP39	6/70	36792, 36793
403	EMD	GP39	12/80	796398-1
501, 502	EMD	GP39	10/78	776116-2, 776116-27

CORMAN, R. J. — *See R. J. Corman*

COUNCIL BLUFFS RAILWAY

200 29th Avenue and High Street
Council Bluffs, IA 51501

Reporting marks: CBGR
Phone: 712-328-3755
Fax: 712-323-2276

In May 1991, Council Bluffs Railway acquired the Iowa Southern Railroad's 30-mile terminal switching operation at Council Bluffs, Iowa. The previous owner was National Railway Systems, which had operated this ex-Norfolk & Western line (formerly Wabash)

as the Council Bluffs & Ottuma Railway from 1989 through 1992.

The Council Bluffs Railway is owned by Great Western Railway Company of Iowa (OmniTRAX).

Radio frequency: 160.845
Locomotives: 2

No.	Builder	Model	New	Builder No.
714	EMD	GP7U	10/50	13162
992	EMD	NW5	12/46	3485

CRAB ORCHARD & EGYPTIAN RAILROAD

514 North Market Street
Marion, IL 62959

Reporting marks: COER
Phone: 618-993-5769
Fax: 618-993-8057

The Crab Orchard & Egyptian operates freight and TOFC service from a connection with Union Pacific and Burlington Northern at Marion, Illinois, to Mande and Ordill, 8.53 miles. A separate 5-mile branch operates from a Burlington Northern connection at Herrin. Rail is 100 pound and heavier.

Traffic includes piggyback, grain, fertilizer, lumber, coal, paper, steel, plastic, oil products, chemicals, scrap iron, beer, clay, and manufactured goods — 1,500 cars a year.

The railroad was incorporated July 2, 1971, and began steam-powered excursion service using trackage rights over an Illinois

Central Gulf branch in 1973. The property was acquired by the Crab Orchard & Egyptian in October 1977, with freight service starting October 18. Excursions ended in 1978. The Herrin line was acquired Sept. 11, 1987.

The company is owned by American Rail Heritage, Ltd.

Radio frequency: 160.350
Location of enginehouses: Marion and Herrin, Ill.
Locomotives: 3

No.	Builder	Model	New	Builder No.
6	EMD	SW1	11/53	53673
1136	EMD	SW1200	3/66	31096
1161	EMD	SW1200	4/65	29799

Freight cars: 68 flatcars

CUYAHOGA VALLEY RAILWAY CO.

3060 Eggers Avenue
P. O. Box 6073
Cleveland, OH 44101

Reporting marks: CUVA
Phone: 216-398-3507
Fax: 216-429-7272

The Cuyahoga Valley provides switching service over 15.9 miles of track in Cleveland, Ohio. It connects with Conrail, CSX, Norfolk Southern, and the Newburgh & South Shore. More than 24,000 cars are handled yearly.

The company was incorporated May 18, 1905, and first reported to the ICC in 1911. It is owned by LTV Steel Corp. In June 1986, the company acquired 2.2 miles of the Newburgh & South Shore Railroad between Cleveland and Newburgh Heights.

Radio frequencies: 160.260, 160.290, 160.380
Locomotives: 25

No.	Builder	Model	New	Builder No.
110	EMD	SW1001	1973	786279-2
421, 422	EMD	SW1001	1974	73688-1, 73688-2
423	EMD	SW1001	1975	74672-1
424, 425	EMD	SW1001	1976	756061-1, 756061-2
800-802	EMD	SW8	12/53	19071-19073
855	EMD	SW8	1/53	17924
960, 961	EMD	SW900	1956	21596, 21597
962	EMD	SW900	1954	19520
1003	EMD	SW1001	1970	36160
1050	EMD	SW1000	11/66	32494
1051	EMD	SW1001	2/73	72679-1
1052	EMD	SW1001	10/79	786279-2
1201	EMD	SW1200	1954	19529
1207	EMD	SW1200	1955	20639
1209	EMD	SW1200	1956	21560
1212	EMD	SW1200	1957	23079
1213	EMD	SW1200	1957	23080
1280, 1281	EMD	SW1200	3/56	21598, 21599
1286	EMD	SW1200	10/62	30490

Freight cars: 45 gondolas

D&I RAILROAD CO.

313 South Philips
P. O. Box 5829
Sioux Falls, SD 57117-5829

Reporting marks: DAIR
Phone: 605-334-5000
Fax: 605-334-3656

D&I operates freight service from Dell Rapids, South Dakota, to Sioux City, Iowa, 138 miles. It connects with Burlington Northern at Sioux Falls, S. D., and with Burlington Northern, Chicago & North Western, and Chicago Central & Pacific at Sioux City. Rail is 90 pound. Annual traffic is 13,000 cars per year of sand, gravel, grain, and fertilizer.

Operations started in April 1982. The line from Dell Rapids to Sioux Falls is a former Milwaukee Road branch line that is owned by L. G. Everist Co., owner of the D&I. The balance of the track is also ex-Milwaukee Road. It is owned by the state of South Dakota and the Sioux Valley Regional Railroad Authority.

Radio frequency: 161.190
Location of enginehouse: Dell Rapids, S. D.
Locomotives: 12

No.	Builder	Model	New	Builder No.
1	EMD	GP9	2/54	19149
2	EMD	GP9	8/54	19787
3	EMD	GP20	11/60	26287
5	EMD	GP9	7/59	25323
7	EMD	GP9	6/59	25318

No.	Builder	Model	New	Builder No.	No.	Builder	Model	New	Builder No.
8	EMD	GP9	5/59	25298	22	EMD	GP9	7/57	21241
19	EMD	GP9	6/54	19617	23	EMD	GP9	2/57	22784
20	EMD	GP20	4/61	26602	24	EMD	GP9	2/56	21431
21	EMD	GP9	8/59	25467					

Six D&I Geeps power an aggregate train through Hawarden, Iowa. Photo by Jim Shaw.

DAKOTA, MINNESOTA & EASTERN RAILROAD CORP.

337 22nd Avenue, S.
P. O. Box 178
Brookings, SD 57006

Reporting marks: DME
Phone: 605-697-2400
Fax: 605-697-2499

The Dakota, Minnesota & Eastern operates freight service from Winona, Minnesota, to Rapid City, South Dakota. Branch lines run to Mason City, Iowa, and Aberdeen and Watertown, S. D. A total of 917 miles are operated. The railroad connects with Burlington Northern, Chicago & North Western, Cedar River Railroad, and Iowa Northern. Traffic consists of 51,000 cars a year of grain, agricultural products, paper, forest products, and cement.

This line was acquired from the Chicago & North Western in September 1986 at a cost of $26 million. Service started on September 25. A $25 million rehabilitation program was completed in 1990. The company was put together by L. B. Foster, Inc., and financing was provided by Westinghouse Credit Corporation. The company is controlled by a management group.
Radio frequencies: 160.395 (road), 160.965 (yard)
Employees: 240
Principal shop: Huron, S. D.
Locomotives: 46
Freight cars: 231 covered hoppers

DAKOTA, MISSOURI VALLEY & WESTERN RAILROAD, INC.

2101 East Broadway
Bismarck, ND 58501

Reporting marks: DMVW
Phone: 701-223-9282

The Dakota, Missouri Valley & Western operates 364 miles of line in North Dakota. One line extends west from Oakes, in the southeast part of the state, to Wishek, then northwest through Bismarck to Washburn, with a branch south from Wishek to Ashley. The other runs west from Flaxton, in the northwest corner of the state, to Whitetail, Montana. The lines, which total 304 miles, are leased from Soo Line under a 20-year agreement. DMV&W operates an additional 60 miles by trackage rights on Burlington Northern.

Principal connections are with CP Rail System (Soo Line) at Flaxton, Washburn, and Oakes and with Burlington Northern at Bismarck. Rail is 60 to 90 pound. Traffic is primarily grain and agriculture related — 10,000 cars a year. The company is controlled by Larry Wood and others.

Employees: 40
Radio frequencies: 160.305, 161.265
Location of enginehouses: Bismarck, Crosby, and Wishek, N. D.
Locomotives: 8

No.	Builder	Model	New	Builder No.
281	EMD	GP9	3/59	25276
316	EMD	GP16	8/61	
318	EMD	GP9	8/59	
321	EMD	GP20	2/61	26573
323	GMD	GP35	8/64	A-2061
324	EMD	GP35R	4/64	28972
856	EMD	GP35	3/65	29772
862	EMD	GP35	3/65	29778

A Dakota, Missouri Valley & Western grain train headed by GP35 No. 323 arrives in Bismarck, North Dakota. Photo by Jim Shaw.

DAKOTA RAIL, INC.

25 Adams Street, North
Hutchinson, MN 55350-2653

Reporting marks: DAKR
Phone: 612-587-4018
Fax: 612-587-0875

Dakota Rail's line extends from a connection with Burlington Northern at Wayzata to Hutchinson, Minnesota, 44 miles. Rail is 56, 60, 72, and 90 pound.

Traffic includes grain, fertilizer, plastic pellets and tanks, lumber, and alcohol, about 1,000 cars a year.

The line was built by the St. Paul, Minnesota & Manitoba Railway in the 1880s and became part of the Great Northern in 1890. The line, known as the Little Crow line, was acquired from Burlington Northern November 14, 1985.

Dakota Rail began operations on a former Milwaukee Road line in South Dakota in June 1982. Operations on that segment were turned over to the Sisseton Southern Railway in July 1987. Dakota Rail filed for Chapter 11 bankruptcy protection in March 1988 and was sold two years later. The company was acquired in September 1995 by RailAmerica.

Radio frequencies: 160.275, 161.055
Location of enginehouses: Hutchinson and Spring Park, Minn.
Locomotives: 4

No.	Builder	Model	New	Builder No.
81A	EMD	F7A	1/49	6309
81C	EMD	F7A	1/49	6308
1206	EMD	SW1200	1954	20044
1208	EMD	SW1200	1954	20048

DAKOTA SOUTHERN RAILWAY CO.

East Prospect Street
P. O. Box 436
Chamberlain, SD 57325

Reporting marks: DSRC
Phone: 605-734-6595
Fax: 605-734-6595

Dakota Southern operates freight service from a connection with Burlington Northern at Mitchell, South Dakota to Kadoka, 187 miles. Rail is mostly 65 pound with some 75, 85, and 90 pound sections. Traffic is about 2,000 cars a year of grain and aggregate.

The line is part of a former Milwaukee Road secondary main line from Marquette, Iowa, to Rapid City, S. D. It was built between 1880 and 1907. The company also operated a line from Napa to Platte, S. D., from November 1985 to January 1989.

The Kadoka line is owned by the state of South Dakota, leased to the MRC Regional Rail Authority, and operated by Dakota Southern under a long-term contract. The operating company is controlled by A. and D. Huff.

Radio frequency: 161.535
Location of enginehouse: Chamberlain, S. D.
Locomotives: 6

No.	Builder	Model	New	Builder No.
75	GE	70-ton	9/47	29090
213	Alco	C-420	4/64	84784
506	EMD	SD9	5/52	15618
512	EMD	SD7	6/52	16491
522	EMD	SD7	10/53	18308
6925*	EMD	DDA40X	6/70	35499

*6925 is on display at Chamberlain
Freight cars: 165 covered hoppers, 33 hopper cars

DALLAS, GARLAND & NORTHEASTERN RAILROAD, INC.

425 North Fifth Street
Garland, TX 75040

Reporting marks: DGNO
Phone: 214-487-8180
Fax: 214-487-7980

The Dallas, Garland & Northeastern operates from Trenton to Garland, Texas, 62 miles (including 4.5 miles of trackage rights over Dallas Area Rapid Transit at Garland). It connects with Texas Northeastern at Trenton, Burlington Northern, Union Pacific, and Southern Pacific at Dallas, and Kansas City Southern at Greenville. Rail is 90 to 112 pound.

Traffic includes aggregate, agricultural products, and food products as well as traffic being bridged from the affiliated Texas Northeastern to Garland (Dallas), about 12,000 cars a year.

The company leases the line the line between Greenville and Garland and has purchased the former Missouri-Kansas-Texas line (abandoned in 1987) from Greenville to Trenton. Shortline service started February 9, 1992. The company is a subsidiary of RailTex.

Radio frequencies: 160.455, 161.085
Location of enginehouse: Garland, Texas
Locomotives: 9

No.	Builder	Model	New	Builder No.	Rebuilt
66	EMD	GP38	12/63	28722	
107	EMD	GP7	2/51	12065	
115	EMD	GP7	11/51	14992	
171	EMD	GP9	4/58	24104	
201	EMD	GP9	4/55	20518	
205	EMD	GP9			
2013	EMD	GP7	3/54	18789	1981
2022	EMD	GP7	10/52	17459	1981
4161	EMD	slug			

Four units headed by GP30 No. 66 head up a Dallas, Garland & Northeastern freight at Dallas, Texas, in June, 1994. Photo by Jim Shaw.

DANBURY TERMINAL RAILROAD CO.

P. O. Box 537
Old Saybrook, CT 06475

Reporting marks: DTRR
Phone: 203-388-4426
Fax: 203-388-6402

Danbury Terminal operates freight service from a connection with Conrail at Beacon, New York, through Hopewell Junction, N. Y., to a second connection with Conrail at Derby, Connecticut, 74.7 miles. Branch lines run from Wassaic, N. Y., to White Plains, 53.6 miles and from Berkshire Junction, Conn., to a connection with the Housatonic Railroad at New Milford, 13.6 miles. 157 miles are operated. Portions of the Beacon and White Plains lines are being abandoned.

Traffic includes wood pulp, lumber, and general commodities totaling about 5,000 cars a year.

The Beacon-Derby line was part of the New Haven; various portions trace their ancestry to the Dutchess & Columbia, New York & New England, and Housatonic railroads. The Hopewell Junction-Derby portion was part of NH's Maybrook line, its principal freight with railroads west of the Hudson River.

The White Plains-Wassaic line was built by the New York & Harlem Railroad in the 1850s and is still owned by that company, though it was operated for most of its existence by the New York Central. Passenger service is operated on that line by Metro-North Railroad.

All the lines were part of Penn Central, and they were acquired by Conrail in 1976. DTRR will lease or purchase most of the lines except for the Beacon-Derby line, which is being acquired by Maybrook Properties.

Danbury Terminal is controlled by Housatonic Transportation Co. and is affiliated with the present-day Housatonic Railroad.
Radio frequencies: 160.395, 161.505
Location of enginehouse: New Milford, Conn.
Locomotives: supplied by Housatonic Railroad

DANSVILLE & MOUNT MORRIS RAILROAD CO.

3 Parkway
P. O. Box 247
Leicester, NY 14481

Reporting marks: DMM
Phone: 716-382-3220

The Dansville & Mount Morris operates freight service from Dansville, New York, to a connection with the Genesee & Wyoming at Groveland, 7.8 miles. Rail is 60 to 90 pound. Traffic includes steel and machinery, less than 100 cars a year.

The Erie & Genesee Valley Railroad was incorporated in January 1868. It was completed in 1872 and leased to the Erie until October 21, 1891, when it was returned to local management as the Dansville & Mount Morris Railroad. The company operated in receivership from 1894 until September 30, 1927. Passenger service ended in 1939.

The company was acquired by the Genesee & Wyoming July 23, 1985, and is operated with Genesee & Wyoming equipment.

DARDANELLE & RUSSELLVILLE RAILROAD CO.

North Dardanelle Loop Road
P. O. Box 150
Dardanelle, AR 72834-0150

Reporting marks: DR
Phone: 501-968-6455
Fax: 501-968-2634

The Dardanelle & Russellville operates freight and excursion service from North Dardanelle, Arkansas, to a connection with the Union Pacific at Russellville, 4.8 miles. Rail is 75 pound.

More than 1,000 cars a year of pulpboard, lumber, plastic, and petroleum products make up the road's traffic.

The Dardanelle & Russellville Railway was chartered in 1883 and opened on August 15 of that year. The company was reorganized under its present name on January 13, 1900. Regular passenger service ended about 1950.

The company is owned by Arkansas Shortline Railroads, Inc. (William K. Robbins, Jr.).
Radio frequencies: 160.365, 161.280
Location of enginehouse: North Dardanelle, Ark.
Locomotives: 6

No.	Builder	Model	New	Builder No.
4	Baldwin	2-6-2	12/13	40958
15	EMD	SW1	4/49	8613
16	EMD	SW1	1/42	1474
17	EMD	SW7	6/50	10526
18	Alco	S-1	11/48	75901
19	Alco	S-3	6/50	78140

Freight cars: 21 boxcars

D&R SW1 No. 16 brings a cut of grain cars into Russellville, Arkansas. Photo by Jim Shaw.

DECATUR JUNCTION RAILWAY CO.

1318 South Johanson Road
Peoria, IL 61607

Reporting marks: DT
Phone: 309-697-1400

Decatur Junction operates lines from Decatur, Illinois, south to Assumption and northeast to Cisco, 42.1 miles in all. Between Elwin and Green's Switch near Decatur the company operates on Illinois Central using trackage rights. Rail is 90 pound. Traffic includes grain, fertilizer, and lumber, about 3,000 cars a year.

The portion of the line from Decatur to Assumption is part of Illinois Central's original route, completed in 1856. It and the line to Cisco were operated by Indiana Hi-Rail from 1986 to December 3, 1993, when they were turned over to Decatur Junction.

The line to Assumption is owned by Central Illinois Shippers, Inc.; the line to Cisco by Cisco Cooperative Grain Co. Decatur Junction is a subsidiary of Pioneer Railcorp.
Radio frequency: 160.380
Location of enginehouse: Assumption, Ill.
Locomotives: 3

No.	Builder	Model	New	Builder No.	Rebuilt
702	EMD	GP7	2/51	11241	
1607	EMD	GP16	11/55	21522	1980
1608	EMD	GP16	11/51	14969	1980

Freight cars: 38 covered hoppers

DELAWARE-LACKAWANNA RAILROAD CO., INC.

701 Wyoming Avenue
Scranton, PA 18509

Reporting marks: DL
Phone: 717-343-4580
Fax: 717-343-4583

Delaware-Lackawanna operates freight service from Scranton, Pennsylvania, to Carbondale, 19.1 miles, and to Mount Pocono, 33 miles. It connects with Conrail at Pittston and Analomink, and with CP Rail System (Delaware & Hudson) at Taylor. Rail is 112 to 115 pound on the Carbondale line and 131 pound on the Mount Pocono line.

Traffic includes about 2,300 cars a year of plastic, perishables, lumber, chemicals, brick, munitions, and other commodities.

The Carbondale line is former Delaware & Hudson trackage built in the 1860s. The line was sold to the Lackawanna County Railroad Authority on April 15, 1985, and was operated for a while by the Lackawanna Valley Railway.

The Mount Pocono line was built as the main line of the Delaware, Lackawanna & Western between 1853 and 1855. Conrail sold the line to the Lackawanna County Rail Authority in September 1991 and it was operated initially by the Lackawanna Railway. On August 27, 1993, the Rail Authority turned both lines over to the current operator.

The company is a subsidiary of Genesee Valley Transportation Co. of Batavia, New York.
Radio frequency: 161.460
Location of enginehouse: Scranton, Pa.
Locomotives: 6

No.	Builder	Model	New	Builder No.
5	Alco	S-1	3/47	75225
426	EMC	SC	3/35	517
802	Alco	C-425	10/64	3392-02
811	Alco	C-425	10/64	3392-11
901	GE	U30B	12/67	36439
5019	Alco	RS-36	1/63	84401

DELAWARE VALLEY RAILWAY CO., INC.

505 South Broad Street
P. O. Box 128
Kennett Square, PA 19348-0146

Reporting marks: DV
Phone: 610-444-1630
Fax: 610-444-1633

Delaware Valley operates freight service from connections with Conrail at Wilmington and with CSX at Elsmere, Delaware, to a connection with the Brandywine Valley Railroad at South Modena, Pennsylvania, 30 miles. A branch line extends from Chadds Ford Junction southwest to Avondale and Nottingham, Pa., 26 miles. Rail is 100 to 130 pound. Traffic includes mushroom composting materials, steel, feed, lumber, food products, and scrap — about 1,500 cars a year.

The Wilmington-South Modena line was opened by the Wilmington & Reading Railroad in 1874. The company was reorganized as the Wilmington & Northern Railroad in 1877 and leased to the Philadelphia & Reading in 1900. It was operated as part of the Reading thereafter. The line was not included in Conrail. On January 20, 1977, the Pennsylvania Department of Transportation designated the Octoraro Railway to operate the line.

The Chadds Ford Junction-Nottingham line was built by the Philadelphia & Baltimore Central Railway in the 1860s. The Pennsylvania Railroad acquired the P&BC. In 1971 a washout isolated the line and service was discontinued. It was acquired by Southeastern Pennsylvania Transportation Authority for future passenger use, and freight service was restored by the Octoraro Railway from Chadds Ford Junction to Kennett Square on July 4, 1977.

The Octoraro Railway ceased operation July 1, 1994, following bankruptcy, and the Delaware Valley Railway took over under a Pennsylvania DOT lease.

Delaware Valley is a subsidiary of RailAmerica.
Radio frequencies: 160.545, 160.605
Location of enginehouse: Kennett Square, Pa.
Locomotives: 4

No.	Builder	Model	New	Builder No.	Rebuilt
211	Alco	RS-32	3/62	84027	
212	Alco	RS-32	6/62	84035	
341	EMD	GP7R	5/51	13203	1980
346	EMD	GP7R	11/53	18904	1979

DELRAY CONNECTING RAILROAD CO.

7819 West Jefferson Avenue
P. O. Box 32538
Detroit, MI 48232

Reporting marks: DC
Phone: 313-841-2851
Fax: 313-841-2420

Delray Connecting is a switching and terminal line operating 15.46 miles of track in the Downriver district of Detroit, Michigan. It switches about 12,000 cars yearly and interchanges with CSX, Conrail, Grand Trunk Western, and Norfolk Southern. Rail is 100 to 115 pound.

The company was incorporated March 25, 1904, and is owned by National Steel Corporation.
Radio frequencies: 153.050, 153.080
Locomotives: 3

No.	Builder	Model	New	Builder No.
1	GMD	SW9	3/52	A-341
2	GMD	SW9	3/52	A-342
3	EMD	SW1	1954	

DELTA SOUTHERN RAILROAD CO.

P. O. Box 1709
Tallulah, LA 71284-1709

Reporting marks: DSRR
Phone: 318-574-5420
Fax: 318-574-4029

Delta Southern operates freight service from a connection with Union Pacific at McGehee, Arkansas, to a Kansas City Southern connection at Tallulah, Louisiana, 103.4 miles. Rail is 85 pound. A second disconnected line runs from a UP connection at Monroe, La., to Sterlington, 15 miles. Rail is 115 pound.

Traffic on the McGehee line includes cotton, grain, agricultural products, coal, and chemicals totaling about 2,500 cars a year. The McGehee line also serves a Mississippi River barge transfer port. Traffic on the Monroe line includes forest products, fertilizer, chemicals, and sand clay.

The McGehee line was built as the Memphis, Helena & Louisiana line of the St. Louis, Iron Mountain & Southern Railroad and opened on December 1, 1903. (The Iron Mountain became part of Missouri Pacific in 1917.) Delta Southern acquired the property from Union Pacific, successor to the Missouri Pacific, and shortline service started January 14, 1989.

The Monroe line was built by the Little Rock & Monroe Railway between 1904 and 1906. That company was acquired by the St. Louis, Iron Mountain & Southern in 1909. Delta Southern bought the line from Huttig, Ark., south to Sterlington from MP on January 7, 1991 and abandoned it in July 1993. It leases the Sterlington-Monroe segment of the line. Delta Southern is affiliated with National Railway Equipment Co.

Radio frequencies: 160.335, 161.220
Location of enginehouse: Tallulah and Sterlington, La.
Locomotives: 7

No.	Builder	Model	New
100, 101, 103-107	AT&SF	CF7	1973

DELTA VALLEY & SOUTHERN RAILWAY CO.

1 Park Street
P. O. Box 308
Wilson, AR 72395

Reporting marks: DVS
Phone: 501-655-8311
Fax: 501-655-8106

Delta Valley Southern operates freight service from a connection with Burlington Northern at Delpro, Arkansas (about 2 miles southwest of Wilson), to Elkins, 2 miles. Rail is 60 to 70 pound and the load limit is 200,000 pounds. Traffic — farm related commodities and manufactured goods — amounts to about 600 cars a year.

The line was built in 1887 to serve the timber industry. It eventually became part of the St. Louis-San Francisco Railway.

The Delta Valley Southern was incorporated June 27, 1934, to purchase the branch extending from Delpro to Tyronza, 18.1 miles. The line was cut back to its present size on March 17, 1947, when the ICC authorized abandonment between Tyronza and Elkins.

The company is owned by the Wilson family.

Radio frequencies: 160.335, 161.220
Location of enginehouse: Evadale, Ark.
Locomotives: 1

No.	Builder	Model	New	Builder No.
50	GE	45-ton	5/54	32129

Freight cars: 223 boxcars

DENVER ROCK ISLAND RAILROAD

3400 East 56th Avenue
Commerce City, CO 80022

Reporting marks: DRIR
Phone: 303-296-0900

Denver Rock Island owns a 4.1-mile switching line at Denver, Colorado, formerly operated by Denver Terminal Railroad, Platte Valley Railway, Denver Terminal Railway, Denver Union Stockyards' Terminal, and the Rock Island. Connections are made with Burlington Northern (Stockyards Division) and Southern Pacific (Air Lawn Division). Traffic is under 500 cars a year. The company is owned by Tom Mars.

Locomotives: 1

No.	Builder	Model	New	Builder No.
996	EMD	NW2	6/58	6252

DEPEW, LANCASTER & WESTERN RAILROAD CO., INC.

8364 Lewiston Road
Batavia, NY 14020-1245

Reporting marks: DLWR
Phone: 716-343-5398
Fax: 716-343-4369

The Depew, Lancaster & Western operates two divisions. The Lancaster Division runs from Lancaster, New York, to a connection with Conrail at Bison Yard (Cheektowaga), 3.1 miles plus 2 miles of interchange access rights over Conrail. Rail is 115 pound.

The Batavia Division covers 5 miles of track in and around Batavia, N. Y., connecting with Conrail. Under 500 cars a year of paper products, recycled materials, lumber, grain, aggregates, and plastic make up the road's traffic.

The Lancaster line is part of the former Delaware, Lackawanna & Western main line, which was not included in Conrail. It was purchased by the Erie County Industrial Development Authority and run by Conrail under contract until April 1988, when service ended. On August 1, 1989, the DL&W was designated to operate the line. The Batavia division is former Lehigh Valley and New York Central trackage purchased from Conrail in August 1983.

The operating company is a subsidiary of GVT Rail (Genesee Valley Transportation Co.).

Radio frequency: 160.920
Location of enginehouses: Batavia and Lancaster, N. Y.
Locomotives: 4

No.	Builder	Model	New	Builder No.	Rebuilt
1801	Alco	RS-18	4/58	82258	1980
3600	Alco	RS-11	8/56	81934	
3603	Alco	RS-11	8/56	81937	
3604	Alco	RS-11	8/56	81939	

DE QUEEN & EASTERN RAILROAD CO.

412 East Lockesburg
De Queen, AR 71832

Reporting marks: DQE
Phone: 501-642-1309
Fax: 501-642-1368

The De Queen & Eastern operates freight service from West Line, Arkansas, through De Queen to Perkins, 45.3 miles. It connects with Texas, Oklahoma & Eastern at West Line, Kansas City Southern at De Queen, and Union Pacific at Perkins. Rail is 90 to

115 pound. Traffic, about 27,000 cars per year, is forest products, gypsum board, grain, and paper.

The De Queen & Eastern was incorporated September 22, 1900. It opened from De Queen to Provo in 1903 and to Dierks in September 1906. The entire line was open by 1921 except for the final 10 miles into Perkins, which opened in 1957. Passenger service was discontinued in 1948.

Weyerhaeuser Company owns the company.

Radio frequencies: 160.230 (road), 160.785, 161.445, 161.505
Location of enginehouses: De Queen and Dierks, Ark.
Locomotives: 4

No.	Builder	Model	New	Builder No.
D-6	EMD	GP35	5/64	29359
D-7	EMD	GP40	8/66	31855
D-27	EMD	GP38	2/81	796388-1
D-28	EMD	GP38	2/81	796388-2

DeQueen & Eastern GP35 No. D-6 pulls a train of forest products through Valliant, Oklahoma. Photo by Jim Shaw.

DEVCO RAILWAY

P. O. Box 2500
Sydney, NS B1P 6K9
Canada

Reporting marks: DVR
Phone: 902-564-7613

Devco Railway operates freight service from a connection with the Cape Breton & Central Nova Scotia at Sydney, Nova Scotia, to Caledonia, 18.8 miles, and from Rail Center to Lingan, 16.2 miles. Rail is 135 pound. Traffic is primarily coal, about 40,000 plus cars a year.

Devco Railway includes lines built by the Sydney & Louisburg Railroad as early as 1895. The S&L went out of business in 1961, and its properties in the Sydney area were acquired by Cumber-land Railway & Coal Co., which was in turn acquired by Devco in 1968. The railroad is a subsidiary of Cape Breton Development Corp. — Transportation Division (a Crown corporation).

Radio frequencies: 160.305
Enginehouse: Sydney, N. S.
Locomotives: 13

No.	Builder	Model	New	Builder No.
216-219	GMD	GP38-2	1979	A-3684–A-3687
220-223	GMD	GP38-2	1981	A-4063–A-4066
224-227	GMD	GP38-2	1982	A-4278–A-4281
228	GMD	GP38-2	1983	A-4347

Freight cars: 560 (local use only)

DODGE CITY, FORD & BUCKLIN RAILROAD CO.

P. O. Box 714
Dodge City, KS 67801

Reporting marks: DCFB
Phone: 316-227-3232
Fax: 316-225-0196

The Dodge City, Ford & Bucklin operates freight and excursion service between Dodge City and Bucklin, Kansas, 26.5 miles. It connects with the Santa Fe and the St. Louis Southwestern (Southern Pacific) at Bucklin. Freight traffic is agricultural, and most revenue comes from the passenger excursions and dinner train service.

The line was built by the Bucklin & Dodge City Railroad in 1880. It became part of the Rock Island and was operated by the St. Louis Southwestern after the demise of the RI until it was acquired by the Ford County Historical Railroad Preservation group. It is currently privately owned.

Location of enginehouse: Dodge City, Kan.
Locomotives: 2

No.	Builder	Model	New	Builder No.
1	GE	45-ton	5/41	13059
6601	Alco	S-1	6/41	69407

DONIPHAN, KENSETT & SEARCY RAILWAY

Reporting marks: DKS

The Doniphan, Kensett & Searcy is operated by the Union Pacific for freight service between Doniphan and Searcy, Arkansas, 5.51 miles. It connects with the Union Pacific at Kensett. Rail is 56 to 90 pound.

The railroad was incorporated March 20, 1906 as the Doniphan, Kensett & Searcy Railroad. It opened between Doniphan and Kensett in January 1907 and was reorganized under its present name on May 22, 1909. It came under Missouri Pacific control in December 1931. Equipment is furnished by UP.

DUBOIS COUNTY RAILROAD CORP.

P. O. Box 150
French Lick, IN 47432

Reporting marks: DCRR
Phone: 812-936-2626
Fax: 812-936-2904

Dubois County Railroad operates freight service from a connection with Norfolk Southern at Huntingburg, Indiana, to Dubois, 16.4 miles. Traffic includes feed, fertilizer, lumber, and furniture. The railroad expects to handle about 500 cars a year.

The line was built in the early 1890s by the Louisville, New Albany & Chicago Railroad, which was reorganized in 1898 as the Louisville, Evansville & St. Louis. By 1901 the line was part of the Southern Railway System.

The line is owned by Norfolk Southern. Dubois County Railroad started service July 14, 1993, under trackage rights granted by Indiana Hi-Rail. The company is part of the Indiana Railway Museum.

Location of enginehouse: Dubois, Ind.
Locomotives: 1

No.	Builder	Model	New	Builder No.
1	Alco	S-4	4/53	79818

DULUTH & NORTHEASTERN RAILROAD CO.

207 Avenue C
P. O. Box 510
Cloquet, MN 55720

Reporting marks: DNE
Phone: 218-879-1029
Fax: 218-879-6558

Duluth & Northeastern operates freight switching service at Cloquet, Minnesota, connecting with Burlington Northern and CP Rail System. Rail is 85 to 100 pound. Annual traffic is 5,000 cars of pulpwood, pulp, paper, and related products plus chemicals.

The company was incorporated on September 30, 1898, and built a line from Cloquet to Hornby, 75 miles including branches. It was cut back to Saginaw, 10 miles from Cloquet, about 1941 and to the present size in May 1991. Potlatch Corporation acquired control of the railroad in May 1964.

Radio frequency: 161.490
Location of enginehouse: Cloquet, Minn.
Locomotives: 4

No.	Builder	Model	New	Builder No.
31	EMD	SW1	11/41	1403
32	EMD	SW1	12/40	1236
33	EMD	SW1	10/41	1399
35	EMD	SW1000	2/67	32399

Duluth & Northeastern SW1 No. 33 switches a car of pulpwood into the Potlatch mill at Cloquet, Minnesota. Photo by Jim Shaw.

DULUTH, MISSABE & IRON RANGE RAILWAY CO.

500 Missabe Building
Duluth, MN 55802

Reporting marks: DMIR
Phone: 218-723-2115

The Duluth, Missabe & Iron Range provides freight service over 293 miles of line extending from Duluth into the Mesabi and Vermilion ranges of northeast Minnesota. It connects with Burlington Northern, Canadian National, CP Rail, Chicago & North Western, and Wisconsin Central.

The company is the largest iron ore carrier in the United States, handling 470,000 revenue carloads annually.

The DM&IR was formed on July 1, 1937, as a consolidation of the Duluth, Missabe & Northern Railway (incorporated May 1891) and the Spirit Lake Transfer Railway (incorporated October 1907 and leased to DM&N from August 1915). On March 22, 1938, DM&IR acquired the assets and property of the Duluth & Iron Range Railroad. The DM&N and D&IR had both been owned by U. S. Steel since 1901. Passenger service ended July 15, 1961.

The company is controlled by Transtar Corp. (USX Corporation owns 44 percent).

Radio frequencies: 160.350, 160.800
Principal shops: Proctor, Minn.
Locomotives: 61
Freight cars: 47

DUNN-ERWIN RAILWAY

101 East Main Street
P. O. Box 917
Aberdeen, NC 28315

Reporting marks: DER
Phone: 910-944-2341

The Dunn-Erwin Railway operates from a connection with CSX at Dunn to Erwin, North Carolina, 5.4 miles. Rail is 70 pound. Traffic is about 600 cars a year of coal, grain, and cement.

This line was built by the Cape Fear & Northern Railroad, which opened between Durham and Dunn on June 30, 1904. The company was reorganized as the Durham & Southern on January 13, 1906, and it operated until November 1981, when it was acquired by Seaboard Coast Line. CSX sold the segment of the line between Dunn and Erwin to the Aberdeen & Rockfish Railroad in December 1987, and A&R organized the Dunn-Erwin Railway, Inc., to provide service starting on December 17 of that year. Dunn-Erwin was merged into the Aberdeen & Rockfish Railroad on January 1, 1990, and is now operated as a division of the A&R.

Radio frequencies: 161.280, 160.530
Location of enginehouse: Dunn, N. C.
Locomotives: 1

No.	Builder	Model	New	Builder No.
5072	EMD	NW2	6/49	10373

DURHAM TRANSPORT, INC.

P. O. Box 479
Stockton, NJ 08559

Phone: 215-862-9267
Fax: 215-862-0225

Durham Transport provides switching service over 11 miles of industrial track at Raritan Center Industrial Park in Edison, New Jersey. Interchange is made with Conrail. Traffic is primarily food products, about 1,500 cars a year. Service started August 2, 1994. The company is controlled by David Crane.

Locomotives: 1

No.	Builder	Model	New	Builder No.
66	EMD	NW2	11/49	7178

EAST CAMDEN & HIGHLAND RAILROAD CO.

P. O. Box 3180
East Camden, AR 71701

Reporting marks: EACH
Phone: 501-574-0770
Fax: 501-574-2838

East Camden & Highland operates freight and TOFC service from a connection with the Cotton Belt (Southern Pacific) at Eagle Mills, Arkansas, to East Camden, 18.43 miles. Rail is 75 to 112 pound. Traffic includes chemicals, synthetic bulk rubber, lumber, paper products, and scrap metal — 1,200 cars a year.

The company was incorporated December 8, 1971, to take over switching operations at the former Shumaker Ordnance Depot at East Camden, which was being converted into the Highland Industrial Park. Operations started August 21, 1972.

The company operated a former Rock Island line from El Dorado, Ark., to Lille, Louisiana, from 1983 to October 1990, when it was sold to the Dardanelle & Russellville Railroad (for operation by the Ouachita Railroad). The East Camden & Highland is owned by Highland Resources, Inc.

Radio frequency: 160.380
Location of enginehouse: East Camden, Ark.
Locomotives: 3

No.	Builder	Model	New	Builder No.	Rebuilt
60	EMD	SW1200M	3/49	7424	1980
61	EMD	SW1200M	6/45	8604	1980
62	EMD	SW1200M	1/41	1313	1980

Freight cars: 24 boxcars

EAST COOPER & BERKELEY RAILROAD CO.

540 East Bay Street
P. O. Box 279
Charleston, SC 29402

Reporting marks: ECBR
Phone: 803-727-2067
Fax: 803-727-2005

The East Cooper & Berkeley operates freight service from a connection with CSX at State Junction (Cordesville) to Charity Church, South Carolina, 15.5 miles. Rail is 132 pound. Traffic is petrochemicals — 4,000 cars annually.

The railroad is a joint undertaking by the South Carolina Public Railway Commission and Amoco. Application to build the line was approved by the ICC on July 15, 1977, and construction was completed the following year. The company is now owned and operated by the South Carolina Public Railways Commission.
Radio frequency: 160.980

Location of enginehouse: Charity Church, S. C.
Locomotives: 2

No.	Builder	Model	New	Builder No.
2001	EMD	SW1001	12/77	776017-1
5105	Alco	S-4	8/53	80629

Freight cars: 1 gondola

EAST ERIE COMMERCIAL RAILROAD CO.

1300 Lawrence Parkway
P. O. Box 7305
Erie, PA 16510

Reporting marks: EEC
Phone: 814-875-6572
Fax: 814-875-5858

East Erie Commercial operates a switching and terminal line at Erie, Pennsylvania. About 1,000 cars and locomotives are carried annually. The Eastern Division has multigauge track for testing locomotives and transit cars built by General Electric.

It connects with Conrail, Norfolk Southern, Allegheny & Eastern (via Conrail), and Bessemer & Lake Erie (via Conrail or Norfolk Southern). Rail is 100 pound. The company, which is owned by General Electric, was incorporated October 17, 1907. The Eastern Division opened in 1915.
Radio frequencies: 160.590, 161.100
Location of enginehouse: Erie, Pa.
Locomotives: 2

No.	Builder	Model	New	Builder No.
21	GE	85-ton	3/80	41152
22	GE	85-ton	3/80	41153

EAST JERSEY RAILROAD & TERMINAL CO.

250 East 22nd Street
Bayonne, NJ 07002

Reporting marks: EJR
Phone: 201-437-2200
Fax: 201-339-4637

East Jersey Railroad & Terminal is a switching and terminal line operating 2.39 miles of track at Bayonne, New Jersey. It connects with Conrail. Traffic is mostly petrochemicals, about 1,500 cars a year. The railroad began operations in 1903 and is privately owned.
Locomotives: 4

No.	Builder	Model	New	Builder No.
18	GE	65-ton	3/50	30497
19	GE	80-ton	8/48	29995
321	EMD	SW8	2/53	16196
8634	EMD	SW900	12/55	20938

EAST MAHANOY & HAZLETON RAILROAD CO.

P. O. Box 237
Clinton, PA 19549

Reporting marks: EMHR
Phone: 215-562-2606

The East Mahanoy & Hazleton operates freight service from a connection with the Reading, Blue Mountain & Northern at York Junction, Pennsylvania, to Ashmore Junction and Jeddo, all in the Hazleton area. A total of 9.6 miles are operated. Traffic is 950 cars a year, primarily anthracite coal. The line is mostly former Lehigh Valley trackage purchased from Conrail. Service started July 24, 1992. The company is owned by Andrew Muller, Jr., and is operated by the affiliated Reading, Blue Mountain & Northern Railroad.
Locomotives: furnished by Reading, Blue Mountain & Northern

EAST PENN RAILWAYS, INC.

P. O. Box 102
Pennsburg, PA 18073

Reporting marks: EPRY
Phone: 215-679-0555

East Penn Railways operates three former Reading Company branches in southeast Pennsylvania: Topton to Kutztown, 4.12 miles; Pottstown to Boyertown, 8.6 miles; and Emmaus to Pennsburg, 15.8 miles. Rail is 90 to 100 pound on the Kutztown and Boyertown lines and 130 pound on the Pennsburg line. East Penn connects with Conrail at Topton, Pottstown, and Emmaus.

Traffic includes foundry material, plastic, grain, paper, lumber, and motor vehicles. The company expects to move 1,400 cars a year.

The commonwealth of Pennsylvania owns the three lines. The Kutztown line was built by the Allentown Railroad, which was chartered April 19, 1853, and opened from Topton to Kutztown in 1870. The Boyertown line was built by the Colebrookdale Railroad, which was chartered March 23, 1865, and completed in 1869. The Pennsburg line was built by the Perkiomen Railroad, which was chartered March 23, 1865, and opened in 1875.

All three lines were leased to the Philadelphia & Reading Railroad and operated by the Reading until 1976 when Conrail became designated operator.

Pennsylvania first leased these lines to the Anthracite Railway on August 1, 1983. The leases were then given to the Blue Mountain & Reading between October 1988 and June 1989. The current operator took over July 1, 1995.

The company is controlled John Nolan (Bristol Industrial Terminal Railway)
Radio frequency: 160.935
Location of enginehouses: Pennsburg, Boyertown, and Topton, Pa.
Locomotives: 5

No.	Builder	Model	New	Builder No.	Rebuilt
52	EMD	SW900	7/37	649	1955
55	GE	50-ton	1951		
92	EMD	SW1200	1965		
182	Alco	RS-18	11/59	83189	
8990	EMD	SW9	2/53	16312	

EAST PORTLAND TRACTION CO.

9001 SE McBrod Avenue
P. O. Box 22548
Portland, OR 97269

Reporting marks: EPTC
Phone: 503-659-5452
Fax: 503-652-9032

East Portland Traction provides switching service over 4.28 miles of track extending from East Portland to Milwaukie, Oregon. It connects with Burlington Northern, Southern Pacific, and Union Pacific. Traffic includes paper, plastic, and food products, about 1,200 cars a year. The company also operates seasonal "Samtrak" excursions.

This road is former Portland Traction Co. trackage acquired April 1, 1991. Rail runs from 70 to 132 pound. The company is affiliated with Samuels Pacific Industries and is owned by Richard Samuels.

Radio frequencies: 160.575, 161.340, 161.550
Location of enginehouse: Milwaukie, Ore.
Locomotives: 6

No.	Builder	Model	New	Builder No.
100	EMD	SW1	2/52	16899
101	GE	80-ton	2/56	32395
102	GE	80-ton	2/56	32413
602	EMD	SW8	7/52	17230
2501	GE	25-ton	6/42	15682
5100	GE	70-ton	3/49	30034

EAST TENNESSEE RAILWAY, LP.

132 Legion Street
P. O. Box 1479
Johnson City, TN 37605

Reporting marks: ETRY
Phone: 615-928-3721
Fax: 615-928-3721

East Tennessee Railway operates freight service from a connection with CSX and Norfolk Southern at Johnson City, Tennessee, to Elizabethtown, 11.2 miles. Rail ranges from 70 to 112 pound. Traffic is about 3,500 cars a year and includes coal, chemicals, and general commodities.

The East Tennessee & Western North Carolina Railroad Co. was incorporated May 24, 1866, to build a 3-foot gauge line from Johnson City to Cranberry, North Carolina. The line opened July 3, 1882. In 1905 and 1906 a portion of the line between Johnson City and Hampton was relaid to standard gauge. In October 1950 service on the narrow gauge to Cranberry was discontinued and the line was later abandoned.

The East Tennessee Railway was formed in 1983 to acquire the rail operations of the ET&WNC. The company has been controlled by K. E. Durden, Green Bay Packaging, and others since June 1983. It is currently a partnership controlled by Rail Management, general partner.

Radio frequency: 160.425
Location of enginehouse: Johnson City, Tenn.
Locomotives: 2

No.	Builder	Model	New	Builder No.	Rebuilt
7735	EMD	GP10	10/51	13318	1975
7736	EMD	GP8	11/50	11992	1975

Freight cars: 20 boxcars, 15 gondolas

EASTERN ALABAMA RAILWAY

2413 Hill Road
P. O. Box 658
Sylacauga, AL 35150

Reporting marks: EARY
Phone: 205-249-1196
Fax: 205-249-1198

Eastern Alabama Railway operates freight service from Gantts Quarry, Alabama, to a connection with Norfolk Southern at Sylacauga and on to a connection with CSX at Talladega, 25.2 miles. Rail is 80, 90, and 100 pound. Traffic consists of about 8,000 cars a year of limestone, urea, paper, and corn syrup.

The Sylacauga-Talladega line was built as a narrow gauge railroad by the Anniston & Atlantic Railroad, which was founded on May 24, 1883. It came under control of Louisville & Nashville's Alabama Mineral Railroad on July 19, 1889.

The line and another running from Wellington to Anniston were sold to the Eastern Alabama Railway on November 26, 1990. The Wellington line was abandoned in November 1992. Eastern Alabama Railway is a subsidiary of Kyle Railways, Inc.

Radio frequency: 161.070
Location of enginehouse: Sylacauga, Ala.
Locomotives: 4

No.	Builder	Model	New	Builder No.
1510	EMD	GP7	9/51	14573
1511	EMD	GP7	4/53	17979
1550	GMD	GP7	8/53	A-417
1551	GMD	GP7	5/53	A-414

EASTERN IDAHO RAILROAD, INC.

618 Shoshone Street W.
Twin Falls, ID 83301

Reporting marks: EIRR
Phone: 208-733-4686
Fax: 208-733-1720

Eastern Idaho Railroad operates two separate clusters of former Union Pacific branch lines in southern Idaho. The lines in the northern cluster are:
• Idaho Falls through St. Anthony to Ashton, 51 miles
• Orvin to Lincoln and Newdale, 39 miles
• Lincoln to Ammon, 4 miles
• Ucon to Menan, 11 miles
• St. Anthony to Edmonds, 12 miles
  Total mileage is 116. The sole connection is with Union Pacific at Idaho Falls.

The southern cluster comprises 154 miles:
• Minidoka through Twin Falls to Buhl, 75 miles
• Rupert to Wendell, 58 miles
• Burley to Martin, 11 miles
• Burley to Declo, 9 miles
  Total mileage in the southern group is 154 miles. It connects with UP at Minidoka.

Rail is predominantly 133 pound. Traffic includes grain and agricultural products, food products, limestone, aggregate and chemicals — about 40,000 cars a year.

The St. Anthony Railroad, incorporated in May, 1889, opened a line from Idaho Falls to St. Anthony in November 1899. It was extended through Ashton to West Yellowstone, Montana, by the Yellowstone Park Railway in 1906. Both companies were acquired in 1910 by the Oregon Short Line Railroad, a subsidiary of the Union Pacific.

The line from Minidoka to Buhl was built by the Minidoka & Southwestern Railroad, incorporated in January 1904, and opened in May 1905. It was acquired by the Oregon Short Line in 1910. OSL built the Rupert-Wendell and Burley-Martin lines about 1912.

Eastern Idaho Railroad, which is controlled by Charles R. Webb of Coffeyville, Kansas, bought the lines from Union Pacific on November 22, 1993.

Radio frequencies: 160.845 (yard), 161.370 (train)
Location of enginehouses: Twin Falls, Rupert, Pocatello, and Idaho Falls, Idaho
Locomotives: 24

No.	Builder	Model	New	Builder No.	Rebuilt
782	EMD	GP35			
785	EMD	GP35	11/63	28398	
786	EMD	GP35	11/63	28399	
788	EMD	GP35	11/63	28401	
791	EMD	GP35	11/64	29031	
793	EMD	GP35	3/65	30218	
798	EMD	GP35	3/65	30223	

No.	Builder	Model	New	Builder No.	Rebuilt
1004	EMD	GP7	8/52	16795	
2174	EMD	GP7	2/52	15820	1979
2178	EMD	GP7	9/52	17006	1979
2186	EMD	GP7	4/53	17018	1980
2191	EMD	GP7	4/53	17017	1980
2204	EMD	GP30	3/63	28112	
2225	EMD	GP30	4/63	28133	
2228	EMD	GP30	4/63	28136	
2242	EMD	GP30	5/63	28150	
2274	EMD	GP30	4/62	27121	
3133	EMD	SD45	11/67	33556	
3167	EMD	SD45	3/70	36116	
3144	EMD	GP40	7/67	33221	
3145	EMD	GP40	7/67	33222	
3669	EMD	GP35	8/65	30595	
6513	EMD	SD45	7/84	827041-8	
6525	EMD	SD45	7/84	837073-5	

EASTERN ILLINOIS RAILROAD CO.

730 Elm Street
P. O. Box 1132
Charleston, IL 61920

Reporting marks: EIRC
Phone: 217-345-4832
Fax: 217-345-4846

Eastern Illinois Railroad provides freight service from a connection with the Illinois Central at Neoga, Illinois, northeast to a connection with CSX at Metcalf, 52.9 miles. Rail is 110, 112, and 115 pound. Traffic includes about 3,000 cars a year of grain, lumber, and plastic.

The line was built in the early 1880s by the narrow gauge Toledo, Delphos & Burlington Railroad. In time it became part of Nickel Plate's line to St. Louis, then Norfolk & Western, then Norfolk Southern. Norfolk Southern sold the Neoga-Metcalf line to

GP9 No. 4541, the only engine owned by the Eastern Illinois Railroad, is shown pulling a grain train near Charleston, Illinois, in July 1994. Photo by Jim Shaw.

NRG, Inc., in 1988. It was leased to and operated by Indiana Hi-Rail from May 1988 until March 31, 1991, when NRG decided to take over operations. Eastern Illinois Railroad, a subsidiary of NRG, Inc., began service on April 1, 1991.
Radio frequency: 160.815

Location of enginehouse: Charleston, Ill.
Locomotives: 1

No.	Builder	Model	New	Builder No.
451	EMD	GP9	1/59	25053

Freight cars: 13 covered hoppers

EASTERN MAINE RAILWAY CO.

11 Gifford Road
P. O. Box 5666
Saint John, NB E2L 5B6
Canada

Reporting marks: EMRY
Phone: 506-632-5813

Eastern Maine Railway provides freight service from a connection with the Canadian American and Bangor & Aroostook railroads at Brownville Junction, Maine, to a connection with the New Brunswick Southern at McAdam, New Brunswick, 99.2 miles. Interchange is also made with ST Rail System (Maine Central) at Mattawamkeag, Maine. Rail is predominantly 100 pound.

Traffic is primarily overhead paper and forest products moving between the New Brunswick Southern and the other connections — up to 15,000 cars a year are expected.

The line east of Mattawamkeag was built by the European & North American Railway and opened in 1871. It became part of the Maine Central and, by trackage rights, part of Canadian Pacific's Montreal-Saint John route. Maine Central sold the line east of Mattawamkeag to CP in 1974. The line from Brownville Junction to Mattawamkeag was built by Canadian Pacific in the late 1880s.

In September 1988 CP Rail turned the Montreal-Saint John line over to a subsidiary, Canadian Atlantic Railway. Canadian Atlantic was unable to operate the line profitably and closed on December 31, 1994. Eastern Maine Railway purchased the line from CP and initially contracted with Canadian American Railroad to run it on their behalf. Eastern Maine then decided to run the line and started service on April 10, 1995.

The company is controlled by J. D. Irving Ltd. and is affiliated with the New Brunswick Southern Railway.
Radio frequencies: 161.355, 160.935, 161.205
Location of enginehouses: Brownville Junction, Maine, and McAdam, N. B.
Locomotives: supplied by New Brunswick Southern and other lessors

EASTERN SHORE RAILROAD, INC.

P. O. Box 312
Cape Charles, VA 23310

Reporting marks: ESHR
Phone: 804-331-1094
Fax: 804-331-2772

Eastern Shore operates freight service from a connection with Conrail at Pocomoke City, Maryland, to Cape Charles, Virginia, 64.1 miles, and from Cape Charles by car float to Little Creek and Norfolk, 26 miles, interchanging there with Norfolk Southern, CSX, and Norfolk & Portsmouth Belt Line. Rail is 130 pound. Traffic includes grain, fertilizer, chemicals, and overhead traffic moving between Conrail on the north and Norfolk Southern, CSX, and N&PBL on the south — 10,000 cars a year.

The line was built by the New York, Philadelphia & Norfolk Railroad, which was chartered September 27, 1881, and opened on November 17, 1884. That company was acquired by the Pennsylvania Railroad. Much later the line became part of Penn Central, but it was not included in Conrail. In 1977 the Virginia & Maryland Railroad was designated to operate the Virginia portion of the line.

The Eastern Shore Railroad was incorporated October 1, 1981, to take over from the Virginia & Maryland. It is owned by Canonie Atlantic Company, which in turn is owned by Accomack Northampton District Transportation Authority.

Radio frequencies: 160.695, 160.980, 161.445

Location of enginehouses: Little Creek and Cape Charles, Va.
Locomotives: 8

No.	Builder	Model	New	Builder No.	Rebuilt
1600	EMD	GP8	8/50	11993	
1603	EMD	GP8	2/52	15052	
2000	EMD	GP10	1/57	22315	
2001	EMD	GP10	1/58	23862	
2085	Alco	MRS-1	10/53	80401	
2090	Alco	MRS-1	10/53	80406	
8066	EMD	GP10	12/54	19908	8/69
8096	EMD	GP10	3/55	20175	6/69

Freight cars: 20 covered hoppers

EASX RAILROAD CORP.

40 Furnace Street
New Castle, PA 16101

Reporting marks: EASO
Phone: 412-654-9900

EASX owns two former Pittsburgh & Lake Erie branch lines at New Castle, Pennsylvania. The New Castle and Big Run branches total 3.24 miles and connect with CSX at New Castle. EASX acquired them from Three Rivers Railway Co. (CSX) on September 10, 1993. They are being operated under contract by ISS Rail, Inc.

EL DORADO & WESSON RAILWAY CO.

900 S. West Avenue
P. O. Box 46
El Dorado, AR 71731

Reporting marks: EDW
Phone: 501-863-7100

El Dorado & Wesson operates freight service from a connection with the Union Pacific at El Dorado, Arkansas, to Newell, 5.5 miles. Rail ranges from 70 to 90 pound. Traffic consists of petroleum products, chemicals, and grain — 6,000 cars a year.

The company was incorporated September 17, 1905, and opened a 10-mile line to Wesson in October 1907. Passenger service ended about 1953. The line was abandoned between Wesson and Oil Hill, 7 miles, in January 1959, only to be reopened from Oil Hill to Newell, 2 miles, in 1961. The company is independent.

Enginehouse: El Dorado, Ark.
Locomotives: 2

No.	Builder	Model	New	Builder No.
25	EMD	SW7	11/50	13426
26	EMD	SW7	11/51	9796

ELGIN, JOLIET & EASTERN RAILWAY CO.

1141 Maple Road
Joliet, IL 60432

Reporting marks: EJE
Phone: 815-740-6900

The "J" runs from Waukegan, Illinois, through Joliet to Gary, Indiana, 120 miles. A branch runs from Walker to Goose Lake, Ill., 19.5 miles. A total of 169 miles are operated. Traffic includes 260,000 cars a year of coal, steel, petroleum products, and general commodities.

The railroad was incorporated in 1887 to expand the Joliet, Aurora & Northern Railway into a belt line around Chicago. The EJ&E bought the JA&N the following year; other components of the J were the Chicago, Lake Shore & Eastern, Gardner, Coal City & Northern, and the Waukegan & Southwestern railroads.

Until 1988 the EJ&E was owned by U. S. Steel, which had a huge steel mill at Gary. In 1988, the road was acquired (along with U. S. Steel's other railroads) by Transtar Corporation. USX, successor to U. S. Steel, holds a 44 percent interest in Transtar.
Radio frequencies: 160.350, 160.260
Principal shops: Joliet, Ill.
Locomotives: 58
Freight cars: 4,217 cars

ELLIS & EASTERN CO.

1201 West Russell
P. O. Box 84140
Sioux Falls, SD 57118

Reporting marks: ELE
Phone: 605-336-8464

The Ellis & Eastern operates a former Chicago & North Western branch extending from Ellis to Brandon, South Dakota, 16.5 miles, a portion of the line between Sioux Falls and Mitchell. It connects with Burlington Northern and D&I Railroad at Sioux Falls, 8 miles east of Ellis. Private contract service started in May 1989. Traffic includes aggregate and cement, 3,500 cars a year. The Ellis & Eastern is owned by Sweetman Construction Co.
Radio frequency: 161.385
Location of enginehouse: Sioux Falls, S. D.
Locomotives: 2

No.	Builder	Model	New	Builder No.
7	EMD	SW1200	4/57	22827
17	GMD	SW900	4/55	A-678

ESCANABA & LAKE SUPERIOR RAILROAD CO.

One Larkin Plaza
Wells, MI 49894

Reporting marks: ELS
Phone: 906-786-0693
Fax: 906-786-8012

The Escanaba & Lake Superior operates 342 miles of track in upper Michigan and Wisconsin:

- Wells to Escanaba, Mich., 4 miles
- Green Bay, Wis., to Ontonagon, Mich., 210.5 miles
- Crivitz, Wis., to Menominee, Mich., 22.3 miles
- Channing to Republic, Mich., 21.8 miles
- Stiles Junction to Oconto Falls, Wis., 4.7 miles

It connects with Chicago & North Western and Wisconsin

Central. Rail is 90 to 100 pound. Traffic is lumber, paper, ore, and general commodities and runs about 12,000 cars a year.

The company was incorporated as the Escanaba & Lake Superior Railway on November 17, 1898, and reorganized under the present name February 12, 1900. It opened from Escanaba to Watson in January 1900 and to Channing in November 1900. Passenger service was discontinued December 12, 1956.

E&LS leased the lines from Channing to Green Bay, Ontonagon, and Republic in March 1980 and purchased them from the Milwaukee Road in 1984. E&LS abandoned its original Wells-Channing line in May 1994.

The railroad has been controlled by W. W. Larkin, J. Larkin, and others since 1978.

Radio frequency: 160.320
Location of enginehouse: Wells, Mich.
Locomotives: 15

No.	Builder	Model	New	Builder No.
101	Baldwin	DS-4-4-660	11/47	73367
201	Baldwin	DRS-4-4-1000	7/48	73956
202	Baldwin	DRS-4-4-1000	7/48	73957
210	Baldwin	RS-12	1/53	75766
212	Baldwin	RS-12	5/52	75480
213	Baldwin	RS-12	1/53	75765
300	Baldwin	RS-12	1/53	75767
400	EMD	GP38	10/69	75430
401	EMD	GP38	10/69	75438
402	EMD	GP38	10/69	75440
1200	EMD	SW8	6/52	16925
1201	EMD	SW8	6/52	16971
1220	EMD	SD9	6/55	19989
1223	EMD	SD9	5/56	21066
1224	EMD	SD9	12/56	22417

Freight cars: 492 boxcars, 46 flatcars, 4 gondolas

Few Baldwin diesels remain active, but one such unit is Escanaba & Lake Superior RS-12 No. 300, shown at Lambert, Michigan. Photo by Jim Shaw.

117

ESQUIMALT & NANAIMO RAILWAY (CP RAIL)

Reporting marks: EN

The E&N was incorporated September 27, 1883, and leased to the Canadian Pacific Railway on July 1, 1912, for 99 years. It retains its name but is operated by CP Rail as part of the CP system. It owns all the track on Vancouver Island. VIA Rail Canada operates passenger service on the line between Victoria and Courtenay.

ESSEX TERMINAL RAILWAY CO.

1601 Lincoln Road
P. O. Box 24025
Windsor, ON N8Y 4Y9
Canada

Reporting marks: ETL
Phone: 519-973-8222
Fax: 519-973-7234

Essex Terminal provides switching service between Windsor and Amherstburg, Ontario, 21 miles. Rail is predominantly 115 pound. Connections are made with Canadian National, CP Rail, CSX, and Norfolk Southern. Traffic consists of agricultural products, grain, chemicals, salt, machinery, automotive parts, and lumber — between 25,000 and 30,000 cars a year.

Essex Terminal Railway was incorporated on May 15, 1902.

The first section of the line was opened in 1902, and it reached its current configuration by 1918. The company is controlled by a local group, Essex Morterm Holdings Ltd.

Radio frequencies: 160.605, 160.905
Enginehouse: Essex, Ont.
Locomotives: 4

No.	Builder	Model	New	Builder No.
102	GMD	GP9	1963	A-2019
105	GMD	SW1200	1956	A-949
107	EMD	SW1500	1971	7436
108	GMD	GP9	1960	A-1822

EVERETT RAILROAD CO.

P. O. Box 361
Claysburg, PA 16625

Reporting marks: EV
Phone: 814-239-5757

The Everett Railroad operates freight service over two disconnected lines in south-central Pennsylvania:
- From a connection with the Hollidaysburg & Roaring Spring Railroad at Brookes Mills to Sproul, 7.9 miles. Rail is 100 pound.
- The Morrison's Cove Railroad from a connection with the H&RS at Roaring Spring to Martinsburg and Curryville, 6.8 miles. Rail is 85 to 100 pound.

Everett has trackage rights over the H&RS from Brookes Mills and Roaring Spring, 10 miles, to a connection with Conrail at Hollidaysburg. Traffic consists of about 1,500 cars a year of feed, ore, woodpulp, and paper.

The Everett Railroad was incorporated April 1, 1954, to acquire and operate several miles of the abandoned Huntingdon

& Broad Top Mountain Railroad near Everett. The company operated that line until October 1982, when Conrail discontinued connecting service.

The company was dormant until the Sproul line was acquired from Conrail in May 1984. The Martinsburg line (ex-PRR) was operated by the Allegheny Southern Railroad from September 3, 1982, until January 1, 1985, when the Everett Railroad leased the line from its owner, Morrison's Cove Railroad, Inc.

Alan Maples controls the company, which is affiliated with the Hollidaysburg & Roaring Spring Railroad.

Radio frequency: 160.365
Location of enginehouse: Claysburg, Pa.
Locomotives: 4

No.	Builder	Model	New	Builder No.
4	GE	80-ton	11/43	18065
1927	GE	U18B	11/73	39392
6051	EMD	GP9	6/56	21688
8933	EMD	SW9	5/51	14045

Everett's former CR SW9 No. 8990 brings the daily freight into Roaring Springs, Pennsylvania, in August, 1993. Photo by Jim Shaw.

FARMRAIL CORP.

1601 West Gary Boulevard
P. O. Box 1750
Clinton, OK 73601

Reporting marks: FMRC
Phone: 405-323-1234
Fax: 405-323-4568

Farmrail operates freight service from Elk City to Clinton and Weatherford, Oklahoma, 47 miles, connecting with Grainbelt Corporation at Clinton. In addition the company provides contract haulage west of Elk City to Sayre and Erick. Farmrail also operates a line from Westhom through Clinton and Altus to Elmer, 102 miles. Connections at Altus include Burlington Northern, Hollis & Eastern, and Wichita, Tillman & Jackson. A total of 187 miles are operated. Rail ranges from 70 to 110 pound. Traffic includes wheat, oil field materials, fertilizer, and sulfur — about 2,500 cars a year. Farmrail also operates freight car storage facilities on its lines.

The company started operations November 19, 1981, over a former Rock Island line between Clinton and Elk City (part of RI's Memphis-Tucumcari route). The Westhom-Elmer line (ex-Santa Fe; long ago, Kansas City, Mexico & Orient) was run by the Texas & Oklahoma Railroad until January 1993, when it was purchased by the state of Oklahoma and leased to Farmrail.

All of Farmrail's lines are owned by the Oklahoma Department

Two attractive brown-and-cream Farmrail GP9s Nos. 286 and 280 head up a grain train at Foss, Oklahoma. Photo by Jim Shaw.

of Transportation and are operated under a long-term contract by Farmrail.

Farmrail Corporation is owned by Farmrail System, Inc., which is employee-owned, and is operated in connection with the affiliated Grainbelt Corporation.

Radio frequency: 161.100
Location of enginehouse: Clinton, Okla.
Locomotives: 7

No.	Builder	Model	New	Builder No.	Rebuilt
280	EMD	GP9	3/59	25275	
286	EMD	GP9	3/59	25281	
297	EMD	GP9	5/59	25292	
316	EMD	GP9	1959	25311	
317	EMD	GP9	1959	25312	
331	EMD	GP9	1959	36116	
8251	EMD	GP10	12/54	19769	1973

FINGER LAKES RAILWAY CORP.

North Street
P. O. Box 1099
Geneva, NY 14436

Reporting marks: FGLK
Phone: 315-781-1234
Fax: 315-781-1234

Finger Lakes Railway operates several lines located in the Finger Lakes region of New York. The main line extends from Solvay to Canandaigua, 76 miles. A branch runs from Geneva to Kendaia, 12 miles, and a disconnected line runs from Bellona through Seneca Lake to Watkins Glen, 30 miles. Finger Lakes connects with Conrail at Solvay, Geneva, and Seneca Lake and with the Ontario Central at Manchester. Total mileage is 118 miles. Rail runs from 85 to 152 pound.

Traffic will include salt, paper, plastic, scrap and steel products, aggregate, grain, fertilizer, lumber, and food products — about 6,000 cars a year.

The Solvay-Canandaigua line is part of the former Auburn Road of the New York Central. The Kendaia branch is a short segment of the former Lehigh Valley main line to Buffalo. The Watkins Glen line is former Northern Central/Pennsylvania Railroad trackage.

Service started July 23, 1995. The company is controlled jointly by Rail Systems, Inc., Farmrail Systems, Inc., and G&W Industries, Inc.

Radio frequency: 161.100
Location of enginehouses: Geneva, Solvay, and Auburn, N. Y.
Locomotives: 3

No.	Builder	Model	New	Builder No.
1701	EMD	GP9U	2/59	25018
1702	EMD	GP9U	3/59	25281
1703	EMD	GP9U	1/59	25326

FLORIDA CENTRAL RAILROAD CO.

P. O. Box 967
Plymouth, FL 32768

Reporting marks: FCEN
Phone: 407-880-8500
Fax: 407-880-7748

Florida Central operates freight service from a connection with CSX at Orlando to Umatilla, Florida. Branch lines run from Tavares to Sorrento and from Winter Garden to Forest City. A total of 68.4 miles are operated. Rail is 85 and 100 pound. About 8,900 cars a year of food products, fertilizer, limestone, chemicals, citrus products, and other commodities make up the road's traffic.

The portion of the main line from Orlando to Tavares was built by the Tavares, Orlando & Atlantic Railroad about 1884. That line was acquired by the Florida Central & Peninsular, which became part of the Seaboard Air Line in 1900. The portion from Tavares to Umatilla was built by the St. John & Lake Eustis Rail-way about 1879 and was acquired by Atlantic Coast Line in 1902.

Florida Central began operations November 22, 1986, after acquiring the track from CSX. The main line from Toronto to Orlando, not included in the original transfer, was leased from CSX on September 13, 1990. Florida Central is a subsidiary of Pinsly Railroad Co.

Radio frequencies: 160.545, 161.475
Location of enginehouse: Plymouth, Fla.
Locomotives: 5

No.	Builder	Model	New	Builder No.	Rebuilt
47	AT&SF	CF7	1974		
49	AT&SF	CF7	1974		
55	EMD	GP7	2/51	12208	4/79
57	EMD	GP7	6/53	18557	5/79
207	EMD	GP35	11/63	28622	

FLORIDA EAST COAST RAILWAY CO.

1 Malaga Street
P. O. Drawer 1048
St. Augustine, FL 32085

Reporting marks: FEC
Phone: 904-829-3421

Florida East Coast provides freight, TOFC, and COFC service between Miami and Jacksonville, Florida. The company also operates several short branch lines. A total of 442 miles are operated. About 400,000 carloads of food products and general commodities are carried annually.

In 1885 Henry M. Flagler acquired the narrow gauge Jacksonville, St. Augustine & Halifax River Railway. In 1893 he consolidated it and several other railroads to form the Jacksonville, St. Augustine & Indian River Railway, which in September 1895 was renamed the Florida East Coast Railway. Its rails reached Miami in 1896 and Key West in 1912. During the 1920s the FEC underwent a major upgrading and re-equipping just before the Florida land boom collapsed. The Great Depression sent the company into receivership in 1931, and a hurricane in 1935 destroyed the Key West extension. The company emerged from bankruptcy in 1961 under the control of the St. Joe Paper Co. (Alfred I. duPont estate).

Radio frequencies: 160.530, 160.770, 161.190
Locomotives: 73
Freight cars: 2,629
Principal Shop: St. Augustine, Fla

FLORIDA MIDLAND RAILROAD CO., INC.

P. O. Box 967
Plymouth, FL 32768

Reporting marks: FMID
Phone: 407-880-3200
Fax: 407-880-7748

Florida Midland operates three disconnected lines in central Florida. One runs from a CSX connection at Wildwood to Leesburg, 12.1 miles. The longest runs from a CSX connection at West Lake Wales to Frostproof, 14.8 miles. The shortest is from a CSX connection at Winter Haven to Gordonville, 7.2 miles. Rail is 85 and 100 pound. Traffic includes limestone, gravel, forest products, citrus products, and chemicals — about 4,500 cars a year.

The Leesburg line is a former Seaboard Air Line branch. The Gordonville line was built by Atlantic Coast Line. The Frostproof branch includes both ACL and SAL trackage. CSX sold these lines to Florida Midland in November 1987.

The company is a subsidiary of Pinsly Railroad Co.

Radio frequencies: 160.545, 161.175
Location of enginehouses: Wildwood, West Lake Wales, and Winter Haven, Fla.
Locomotives: 3

No.	Builder	Model	New
53	AT&SF	CF7	9/74
63	AT&SF	CF7	4/71
64	AT&SF	CF7	1/71

FLORIDA NORTHERN RAILROAD CO., INC.

P. O. Box 967
Plymouth, FL 32768

Reporting marks: FNOR
Phone: 407-880-3200
Fax: 407-880-7748

Florida Northern operates freight service from Candler, Florida, through Ocala to Lowell, 24.3 miles, plus 2.68 miles of switching track at Ocala. It connects with CSX at Ocala. Rail is 85 pound. Traffic includes limestone products, fertilizer, and coal totaling about 2,000 cars a year.

The line was built by the Florida Southern Railroad and opened in the 1880s as part of a route from Leesburg to Gainesville. In 1903 the company was leased to Atlantic Coast Line. CSX sold the line to the present operator and shortline service started November 29, 1988.

The company is a subsidiary of Pinsly Railroad Co.

Radio frequencies: 160.545, 161.475
Location of enginehouse: Ocala, Fla.
Locomotives: 1

No.	Builder	Model	New
50	AT&SF	CF7	8/74

FLORIDA WEST COAST RAILROAD CO.

104 N.W. Lancaster Street
P. O. Box 1267
Trenton, FL 32693

Reporting marks: FWCR
Phone: 904-463-1103
Fax: 904-463-1104

Florida West Coast provides freight service from a connection with CSX at Newberry to Cross City, Florida, 33 miles. Rail is 80 to 100 pound. Traffic is primarily grain, about 1,500 cars a year.

The line was built by the Atlantic Coast Line and opened to Wilcox in 1906. The line from Wilcox northwest to Cross City was part of ACL's Perry Cutoff, opened in 1914. CSX sold the lines to Florida West Coast in December 1987, and shortline service started December 13, 1987. A branch from Wilcox southeast to Chiefland, also part of the former Perry Cutoff, was abandoned in 1992. The company is controlled by CSF Acquisitions Co. (Clyde S. Forbes, Jr., and others).
Radio frequencies: 160.980, 161.190
Location of enginehouse: Trenton, Fla.
Locomotives: 2

Until recently, one of the principal commodities hauled by the Florida West Coast was wood chips for Georgia-Pacific, as indicated in this photo of a train at Eugene, Florida. GP18 No. 1337 now pulls more grain than anything else. Photo by Jim Shaw.

No.	Builder	Model	New	Builder No.
1337	EMD	GP18	1/60	25454
1353	EMD	GP18	10/61	26942

Freight cars: 2 insulated boxcars

FORDYCE & PRINCETON RAILROAD CO.

P. O. Box 757
Crossett, AR 71635

Reporting marks: FP
Phone: 501-364-9004
Fax: 501-364-4521

Fordyce & Princeton operates freight service from a connection with the Cotton Belt at Fordyce, Arkansas, to Whitlow Junction, 52 miles, then by trackage rights 5 miles over the Ashley, Drew & Northern to Crossett. Fordyce & Princeton also connects with the Arkansas, Louisiana & Mississippi. Rail ranges from 85 to 112 pound. Annual traffic is about 10,000 cars of lumber and paper products.

The Fordyce & Princeton was incorporated February 25, 1890, and built a narrow gauge line from Fordyce to Toan, 9.4 miles. The line was converted to standard gauge in October 1907. Additional spurs added another 17 miles to the railroad, but by 1962 the F&P had been reduced to a 1.14-mile switching line at Fordyce. When the Rock Island was abandoned, the company acquired the Rock's line to Crossett and started service on it in

January 1981. The company has applied to purchase the Ashley, Drew & Northern line between Whitlow Junction and Crossett upon which it operates now by trackage rights. The company has been owned by the Georgia Pacific Corporation since 1963.

Radio frequencies: 160.770, 161.535

Location of enginehouse: Fordyce, Ark.

Locomotives: 3

No.	Builder	Model	New	Builder No.
1503	EMD	SW1500	5/70	36656
1504	EMD	SW1500	7/66	31746
1805	EMD	GP28	8/64	28944

Freight cars: 93 pulpwood cars, 1 boxcar, 32 gondolas

FORT SMITH RAILROAD CO.

1318 South Johanson Road
Peoria, IL 61607

Reporting marks: FSR
Phone: 309-697-1400

The Fort Smith Railroad provides freight service from connections with Union Pacific, Kansas City Southern, and Arkansas & Missouri at Fort Smith, Arkansas, to Fort Chaffee, 17 miles. Rail is 85 to 112 pound. Traffic includes grain, food products, paper products, scrap and finished steel, lumber, peanuts, alcohol, military materials, and charcoal — about 10,000 cars a year.

The line was built by the Arkansas Central Railroad, which was incorporated on April 29, 1897. Within two years the company came under control of the St. Louis, Iron Mountain & Southern (Missouri Pacific) and was completed east to Paris, Ark., in May 1900. Union Pacific leased the line to Fort Smith Railroad on July 7, 1991. The line from Fort Chaffee to Paris, 31 miles, is now inactive. The Fort Smith Railroad is a subsidiary of Pioneer Railcorp.

Radio frequency: 160.380

Location of enginehouse: Fort Smith, Ark.

Locomotives: 3

No.	Builder	Model	New	Builder No.	Rebuilt
102	Alco	RS-3M	4/53	80243	1979
900	EMD	GP9	7/56	21241	
901	EMD	GP9	8/57	22720	

Freight cars: 115 boxcars, 60 gondolas

FORT WORTH & DALLAS RAILROAD CO.
FORT WORTH & DALLAS BELT RAILROAD
FORT WORTH & WESTERN RAILROAD CO.

6300 Ridglea Place
Suite 1200
Fort Worth, TX 76116

Reporting Marks: FWDR, FWDB, FWWR
Phone: 817-763-8297
Fax: 817-738-9657

The Fort Worth & Western acquired 8.25 miles of Burlington Northern switching trackage in Fort Worth, Texas, and started service in October 1988. The Fort Worth & Dallas acquired an additional 1.5 miles from Union Pacific in November 1988, and the Fort Worth & Dallas Belt purchased 1.5 miles in June 1994. A total of 11.25 miles is operated. Rail is predominantly 112 pound. The companies interchange with Santa Fe, Burlington Northern, Cotton Belt, and Union Pacific. About 4,000 cars a year are handled. The railroad also began operating regular passenger excursion service in January 1992.

These companies are controlled by Tarantula Corporation.

Radio frequencies: 160.215, 160.650, 160.935, 161.100
Locomotives: 4

No.	Builder	Model	New	Builder No.
938	Alco	4-6-2	11/10	48510
1744	Baldwin	2-6-0	11/01	19671
2248	Cooke	4-6-0	1896	
4299	EMD	GP7	9/52	16872

FOX VALLEY & WESTERN LTD.

200 Dousman Street
P. O. Box 2527
Green Bay, WI 54306

Reporting marks: FVW
Phone: 414-436-7200

On August 27, 1993, Fox Valley & Western acquired the property (507 miles) of the Green Bay & Western Railroad, the Fox River Valley Railroad, and the Ahnapee & Western Railroad, 507 miles in all, for $62.2 million from Itel Rail Corporation. The company is controlled by and operated in conjunction with the Wisconsin Central Ltd. Traffic is about 30,000 cars a year.
Locomotives: pooled with Wisconsin Central

FREMONT & ELKHORN VALLEY RAILROAD

1835 North Somers Street
Fremont, NE 68025

Reporting marks: FEV
Phone: 402-727-0615

The Fremont & Elkhorn Valley owns a 16.5-mile route from Hooper, Nebraska, to a connection with the Chicago & North Western at Fremont. Rail is 100 to 115 pound. Passenger excursions and a dinner train are operated.

The line was built by the Fremont, Elkhorn & Missouri Valley Railroad, which was chartered in 1880 and absorbed by the Chicago North Western system in 1903. Chicago & North Western sold the line to the Fremont, West Point & Pacific Railway in November 1987; that company became the Fremont & Elkhorn Valley in 1989. It is controlled by the Eastern Nebraska Chapter, National Railway Historical Society.
Radio frequencies: 160.245, 161.265
Location of enginehouse: Hooper, Neb.
Locomotives: 1

No.	Builder	Model	New	Builder No.
1219	EMD	SW1200	3/62	27148

GALVESTON RAILROAD, LP.

37th and Old Industrial Boulevard
P. O. Box 1108
Galveston, TX 77553

Reporting marks: GVSR
Phone: 409-762-8861
Fax: 409-762-6605

EMD SW1001 No. 304 switches a cut of covered hoppers at the Port of Galveston, Texas, on the Galveston Railway. Photo by Jim Shaw.

Galveston Railroad operates 43.3 miles of track at Galveston, Texas. It connects with Santa Fe, Burlington Northern, Southern Pacific, and Union Pacific. About 50,000 cars are carried annually.

The line began operations in 1900 as the Galveston Wharves Railway and is owned by the city of Galveston. The city leased the line to the present operator in November 1987.

The company is affiliated with Rail Switching Services (Earl Durden) and is a partnership controlled by Rail Management, general partner.

Radio frequencies: 160.830, 161.355
Locomotives: 5

No.	Builder	Model	New	Builder No.
301, 302	EMD	SW1001	10/75	756080-1, 756080-2
303	EMD	SW1001	12/77	776052-1
304, 305	EMD	SW1001	7/80	796304-1, 7996304-2

Freight cars: 3,176

GARDEN CITY WESTERN RAILWAY

106 North Sixth Street
P. O. Box 838
Garden City, KS 67846

Reporting marks: GCW
Phone: 316-275-6161
Fax: 316-275-8433

Garden City Western operates freight service from a connection with the Santa Fe at Garden City, Kansas, to Wolf, 13.87 miles, and to Shallow Water, 30.59 miles. Rail is 70 to 85 pound on the Wolf line and 70 to 90 pound on the Shallow Water line. About 3,000 cars a year of farm and agriculture related products make up the road's traffic.

The company was incorporated as a freight railroad on May 29, 1915. It opened for business from Garden City to Wolf on January 12, 1916.

A second affiliated company, the Garden City Northern Railway, took over the Shallow Water line of the Santa Fe (which was built in 1907 by the Garden City, Gulf & Northern Railway) on September 7, 1989. Garden City Northern was merged into Garden City Western on September 1, 1991.

The Garden City Western has been owned by the Garden City Co-op since 1982.

Radio frequency: 152.990
Location of enginehouse: Garden City, Kan.
Locomotives: 2

No.	Builder	Model	New	Builder No.	Rebuilt
200	EMD	GP9	2/57	22783	1990
201	EMD	GP9	6/52	16349	1974

Garden City Western SW1 No. 202 has been replaced by GP9s. Photo by Jim Shaw.

GATEWAY EASTERN RAILWAY CO.

15 Executive Drive
Fairview Heights, IL 62208

Reporting marks: GWWE
Phone: 618-624-4700
Fax: 618-624-4731

Gateway Eastern operates freight service between East St. Louis and East Alton, Illinois, 16.7 miles, plus industrial tracks at Alton and East St. Louis. Main line rail is 115 pound. Traffic includes petroleum products, lumber, grain, and scrap metal — about 2,000 cars a year.

This line was built by the Terre Haute, Alton & St. Louis Railroad in the 1850s. Following a number of reorganizations, the line became part of the New York Central System. The line was included in Penn Central and was sold by Conrail to Gateway Eastern on January 28, 1994.

Gateway Eastern is a wholly owned subsidiary of Gateway Western Railroad.

Location of enginehouse: Willows, Ill.
Locomotives: 1

No.	Builder	Model	New	Builder No.
2000	EMD	GP38	9/69	35406

GATEWAY WESTERN RAILWAY

15 Executive Drive
Fairview Heights, IL 62208

Reporting marks: GWWR
Phone: 618-624-4700
Fax: 618-624-4731

Gateway Western provides freight service on its main line from Kansas City, Missouri, to Springfield, Illinois; a branch from Roodhouse, Ill., to East St. Louis; and two branch lines to Jacksonville, Ill. and Fulton, Mo. A total of 600 miles are operated. Traffic includes farm products, lumber, food products, and general commodities as well as haulage for the Santa Fe — about 18,000 cars a year.

During the 20th century the line was an east-west line of several north-south railroads in succession: Chicago & Alton; Alton; Gulf, Mobile & Ohio; and Illinois Central. The Chicago, Missouri & Western purchased the line from Illinois Central Gulf in April 1987 and filed for bankruptcy protection the following year. Gateway Western began operations on January 9, 1990. The company is controlled by Wertheim Schroeder & Co., which purchased the assets for $24 million.

Radio frequencies: 161.280, 161.460, 160.725, 161.295
Employees: 220
Locomotives: 37 (6 SW1500, 31 GP38/40)
Freight cars: 74 covered hoppers

GENESEE & WYOMING RAILROAD CO.

3546 Retsof Road
P. O. Box 101
Retsof, NY 14539

Reporting marks: GNWR
Phone: 716-243-3770
Fax: 716-243-3607

Genesee & Wyoming operates freight service from Groveland to Rochester, New York, 47.1 miles, and from G&W Junction to Silver Springs, 44 miles, by trackage rights. It connects with Conrail at Maplewood and Rochester, with Rochester & Southern at P&L Junction, with CP Rail System (Delaware & Hudson) at Silver Springs, and Dansville & Mount Morris at Groveland. Rail is 80 to 115 pound. Traffic includes about 25,000 cars a year of salt and chemicals.

The Genesee & Wyoming Valley Railway was incorporated in 1891 and opened from Retsof to P&L Junction in 1894. The

Near the Retsof, New York, salt mines, Genesee & Wyoming MP15DC No. 46 switches carloads of salt. Photo by Jim Shaw.

company was placed in receivership in November 1898 and sold to the Genesee & Wyoming Railroad, which was incorporated March 24, 1899. On July 30, 1912, Genesee & Wyoming leased the Halite & Northern Railroad (it was abandoned in 1934). The railroad did not come under ICC control until 1921. Passenger service was discontinued in December 1929.

Genesee & Wyoming acquired Conrail's ex-Lackawanna line from Groveland to Greigsville in June 1982. The company extended its operations from P&L Junction to Rochester and Silver Springs in 1985. The company is controlled by the Fuller family and others.

Radio frequencies: 160.770, 160.500 (road), 161.100 (yard)
Location of enginehouse: Retsof, N. Y.
Locomotives: 4 (pooled with other roads in the Genesee & Wyoming family)

No.	Builder	Model	New	Builder No.
45	EMD	MP15 DC	10/80	796350-1
46	EMD	MP15 DC	10/80	796350-2
50	EMD	GP38	5/70	7625
51	EMD	GP38	5/70	7636

Freight cars: 178 boxcars, 294 covered hoppers

GEORGETOWN RAILROAD CO.

5300 H-35 South
P. O. Box 529
Georgetown, TX 78627-0529

Reporting marks: GRR
Phone: 512-863-2538
Fax: 512-869-2649

The Georgetown Railroad operates freight service from a connection with the Union Pacific at Kerr, Texas, to another connection with the UP at Granger, 24.3 miles. A second line runs from a UP connection at Smith to Belton, 5.9 miles. Rail is 90 to 136 pound. Traffic is primarily crushed stone plus cement and lumber — about 41,000 cars a year.

The railroad was incorporated July 25, 1958, to acquire Missouri Pacific's Georgetown branch, which was being abandoned. The company won ICC approval and began operations on January 14, 1959. The Belton line was acquired from the Belton Railroad March 28, 1991. It was a former Missouri-Kansas-Texas branch line sold to the Belton Railroad in 1961.

The Georgetown Railroad is controlled by Bill Snead.

Radio frequency: 160.995
Location of enginehouse: Feld, Texas
Locomotives: 20 plus 1 slug

No.	Builder	Model	New	Builder No.
504	EMD	SW1	6/40	1079
1006	Baldwin	S-12	12/51	75512
1007	Baldwin	S-12	6/52	75193
1009	Baldwin	V-1000	8/46	72798
1010	EMD	SW1500	12/71	7384-1
1012	EMD	MP15AC	11/80	806028
1014	EMD	GP9	6/54	19622
1015	EMD	GP9	6/54	19627
4161	EMD	GP38-2	5/77	766065-2
4162	EMD	GP38-2	5/77	766065-3
4163	EMD	GP38-2	5/77	766065-4
9010-9012	EMD	GP15		
9050	EMD	GP9/20	1/58	23528
9051	EMD	GP9/20	1/58	23531
9052	EMD	GP9/20	1/58	23532
9053	EMD	GP9/20	1/58	23533
9054	EMD	GP9/20	1/58	23535
9055	EMD	GP9/20	1/58	23536
S-1	CRI&P	Slug	5/80	

Freight cars: 765 hopper cars, 384 gondolas

GEORGIA & ALABAMA DIVISION, SOUTH CAROLINA CENTRAL RAILROAD

908 Elm Avenue
Americus, GA 31709

Reporting marks: GAAB
Phone: 912-924-1463
Fax: 912-995-3767

Georgia & Alabama operates freight service from a Norfolk Southern connection at Smithville, Georgia, to White Oak, 73.4 miles. Rail is predominantly 115 pound. Traffic includes peanuts, pulpwood, aggregate, and cement totaling nearly 3,300 cars a year.

This line was part of the South-Western Railroad built in the 1870s and leased to the Central of Georgia. Norfolk Southern leased the line to the current operator under its Thoroughbred Short Line Program effective June 1, 1989.

This company is a subsidiary of RailTex, Inc.
Radio frequencies: 161.085, 160.335, 161.325
Location of enginehouse: Dawson, Ga.
Locomotives: 3

No.	Builder	Model	New	Builder No.	Rebuilt
2077	EMD	GP7U	9/52	16988	1975
2078	EMD	GP7U	9/52	16982	1975
2130	EMD	GP7U	12/52	17636	1978

Georgia & Alabama GP7 No. 2078 pulls a train through Bronwood, Georgia, in December, 1992. Photo by Jim Shaw.

GEORGIA & FLORIDA RAILROAD CO., INC.

1019 Coast Line Avenue
Albany, GA 31705

Reporting marks: GFRR
Phone: 912-435-6629
Fax: 912-436-4571

The Georgia & Florida operates freight service from a connection with the Atlantic & Gulf at Albany, Georgia, to a connection with Norfolk Southern at Adel, 61 miles. The company has trackage rights over Norfolk Southern from Adel to Valdosta and operates the branch from Valdosta to Nashville, Ga., 28 miles. A total of 127 miles are operated including 26 miles of Norfolk Southern trackage rights. Traffic includes grain, peanuts, fertilizer, woodchips, and beer — 10,000 cars a year are expected.

The line from Albany to Moultrie was completed by the Georgia Northern Railroad and 1905. That company was acquired by Southern Railway in 1966 and merged into Southern in 1972.

The Valdosta-Nashville line was built by the Douglas, Augusta

& Gulf, which was consolidated with three other lines in 1906 to form the Georgia & Florida Railway. In 1911 the Georgia & Florida opened a branch from Nashville through Adel to Moultrie (the Nashville-Adel segment was abandoned in the 1960s).

In 1962, the Southern Railway formed the Georgia & Florida Railway (the second company of that name) to acquire the G&F assets. In 1971 the second G&F was merged into Southern Railway. Norfolk Southern sold the line to the Georgia & Florida Railroad and shortline service began April 14, 1995. The company is controlled by Gulf & Ohio Railways (Pete Clausen) and is affiliated with the Atlantic & Gulf Railroad.

Radio frequencies: 160.500, 161.190
Location of enginehouse: Albany, Ga.

Locomotives: 10

No.	Builder	Model	New	Builder No.	Rebuilt
2881	EMD	GP38	6/66	31783	
2882	EMD	GP38	10/66	32308	
2283	EMD	GP38	10/66	32309	
2886	EMD	GP38	7/67	32493	
8006	EMD	GP10	1/56	20794	1977
8050	EMD	GP10	12/58	25026	1977
8067	EMD	GP10	1/57	22328	1973
8136	EMD	GP10	1/58	23858	1977
8265	EMD	GP10	1/57	22326	1973
8330	EMD	GP10	4/54	19259	1977

GEORGIA CENTRAL RAILWAY, LP

200 Main Street, S.E.
P. O. Box 466
Vidalia, GA 30474

Reporting marks: GC
Phone: 912-537-0588
Fax: 912-537-0594

Georgia Central Railway provides freight service from a CSX connection at Savannah, Georgia, to Helena, 121 miles. A branch runs from Vidalia to Macon, 92 miles. Georgia Central also interchanges with Norfolk Southern at Macon, Dublin, and Helena. Rail ranges from 90 to 133 pound. Traffic includes newsprint, clay, chemicals, pulpwood, and forest and agricultural products — as much as 35,000 cars a year.

The main line from Savannah to Helena was built by the Savannah, Americus & Montgomery Railway and opened in 1891. That company was sold under foreclosure to the Georgia & Alabama Railroad in 1895. By 1900 the G&A was part of the Seaboard Air Line System. The Dublin branch was built by the Macon, Dublin & Savannah Railroad, which was chartered in 1885 and completed to Vidalia in the early 1890s. That line came under

No. 1008 and three other GE U-30Bs power a Georgia Central train at Claxton, Georgia, in December, 1992. Photo by Jim Shaw.

control of the Atlantic Coast Line in 1904 but was sold to the SAL in 1906 and merged into SAL in May 1958.

Georgia Central Railway purchased the lines from CSX on

November 21, 1990. The company is a partnership controlled by Rail Management, the general partner.
Radio frequencies: 160.680, 160.800
Location of enginehouse: Lyons, Ga.
Locomotives: 22

No.	Builder	Model	New	Builder No.
1001	GE	U30B	12/66	36122
1002	GE	U30B	10/66	36080
1003	GE	U30B	11/67	36444
1004	GE	U30B	12/71	38222
1005	GE	U30B	10/72	38478
1006	GE	U30B	12/72	38484
1007	GE	U30B	11/72	38486
1008	GE	U30B	11/72	38487
1009	GE	U30B	5/66	35881
1010	GE	U30B	12/74	40073
1011	GE	U30B	11/72	38484
1012	GE	U33B	1/68	36477
1013	GE	U33B	1/68	36481
1014	GE	U33B	1/69	36843
1015	GE	U33B	1/69	36847
1016	GE	U33B	1/69	36848
3602	EMD	GP18	2/60	26934
3614	EMD	GP18	1/60	25451
4929	EMD	GP9	6/55	20316
6049	EMD	GP7	4/52	16207
6052	EMD	GP9	6/56	21689
7011	EMD	SW9	6/52	11166

Freight cars: 16 hopper cars, 2 pulpwood cars

GEORGIA NORTHEASTERN RAILROAD CO., INC.

109 Marr Avenue
Marietta, GA 30060

Reporting marks: GNRR
Phone: 404-428-4784
Fax: 404-428-0592

Georgia Northeastern operates freight service from a connection with CSX at Elizabeth, Georgia, north through Canton to Ellijay, 65.8 miles. Rail is 100 pound. Traffic consists of about 8,500 cars a year of forest products, agricultural products (grain and soy), and minerals.

The first operation on this line was undertaken by the Ellijay Railroad, which opened in 1854. In May 1879 the company was reorganized as the Marietta & North Georgia. The line converted to standard gauge in 1886 and reached the North Carolina state line the following year. In June 1896 the company was reorganized as the Atlanta, Knoxville & Northern Railway; it was acquired by the Louisville & Nashville in 1902 and absorbed in 1905.

CSX sold the line to Georgia Northeastern and shortline service started on December 15, 1988. The Georgia Department of Transportation is buying the CSX line from Ellijay to Blue Ridge, and Georgia Northeastern expects to operate it.

The company was sold to Wilds Pierce in August 1990.
Radio frequencies: 461.250, 466.250
Location of enginehouse: Tate, Ga.
Locomotives: 8

No.	Builder	Model	New	Builder No.
316	EMD	GP20	4/60	25704
372	EMD	GP35	4/65	30117
2097	EMD	GP7	12/52	17703
6516	EMD	GP9	5/57	22990
6576	EMD	GP9	1/58	24360
6585	EMD	GP9	2/58	24369
8704	EMD	GP18	6/60	26024
8705	EMD	GP18	6/60	26031

Freight cars: 931

GEORGIA SOUTHWESTERN DIVISION, SOUTH CAROLINA CENTRAL RAILROAD

908 Elm Avenue
Americus, GA 31709

Reporting marks: GSWR
Phone: 912-924-0812
Fax: 912-928-2619

Georgia Southwestern operates two separate lines, one from Rochelle, Georgia, west through Cordele and Americus to Mahrt, Alabama, 79 miles, and the other from Columbus south to Bainbridge, 127.9 miles. It connects with CSX at Bainbridge and East Cordele, and with Norfolk Southern at Americus, Arlington, and Columbus. Rail is predominantly 100 pound. Traffic includes aggregate, forest products, chemicals, fertilizer, peanuts, and paper — about 9,000 cars a year.

The Rochelle-Americus line was built by the Savannah, Americus & Montgomery Railroad in the 1880s and was absorbed by the Georgia & Alabama Railroad in 1895. In 1901 the line came under control of the Seaboard Air Line Railway. The Columbus-Bainbridge line was part of the main line of the Georgia, Florida & Alabama Railway, built in the 1880s. It came under control of SAL in 1928.

CSX sold the lines to the current operator on June 5, 1989. Included was an 18-mile segment from Rochelle east to Rhine, abandoned in November 1994.

This company is a subsidiary of RailTex, Inc.
Radio frequencies: 161.085, 160.335, 161.325
Location of enginehouses: Americus, Lynn, and Richland, Ga.
Locomotives: 9

No.	Builder	Model	New	Builder No.	Rebuilt
2027	EMD	GP7	5/52	16372	1981
2127	EMD	GP7	5/52	16377	1978
2160	EMD	GP7	5/52	16373	1979
2176	EMD	GP7	5/52	16374	1979
2185	EMD	GP7	8/52	16383	1980
5078	EMD	GP38	11/67	33709	
5124	EMD	GP38	7/70	36670	
8375	EMD	GP10	12/58	25027	1974
8377	EMD	GP10	12/58	25029	1975

Freight cars: 75 wood racks, 47 covered hoppers

GEORGIA WOODLANDS RAILROAD, LLC.

210 Depot Street
P. O. Box 549
Washington, GA 30673-0549

Reporting marks: GWRC
Phone: 706-678-3000
Fax: 706-678-2341

Georgia Woodlands Railroad operates freight service from Washington, Georgia, to a CSX connection at Barnett, 17.33 miles. Rail is 100 pound. Traffic includes about 2,500 cars a year of pulpwood, wood chips, plastic, lumber, fertilizer, and other commodities.

The line is the former Washington branch of the Georgia Railroad, built in 1851 and 1852. Georgia Railroad became part of CSX, which sold the line in February 1987 to the Georgia Eastern

Railroad. Georgia Eastern sold the line to the present operator on June 7, 1988.

Georgia Woodlands Railroad is a subsidiary of OmniTRAX.
Radio frequencies: 160.815, 160.965
Location of enginehouse: Washington, Ga.
Locomotives: 3

No.	Builder	Model	New	Builder No.
45	EMD	SW8	11/52	16827
615	EMD	GP7	9/51	14229
6584	EMD	GP9	2/58	24368

GETTYSBURG RAILROAD CO.

750 Mummasburg Road
Gettysburg, PA 17325

Reporting marks: GETY
Phone: 717-334-2411

Gettysburg Railroad operates freight and excursion service from a connection with CSX at Gettysburg, Pennsylvania, to a connection with Conrail at Mount Holly Springs, 23.4 miles. Rail is 130 pound. Traffic includes agricultural products, containers, and other manufactured goods — 1,600 cars a year.

The company was incorporated as the Blairsville & Indiana Railroad in March 1974. The present name was adopted when the company was designated to operate the former Reading Company's Gettysburg branch.

The line was built by the South Mountain Iron Railroad, which opened in 1873 from Mount Holly Springs, and the Gettysburg & Harrisburg Railroad, which opened from Gettysburg in 1884. The two roads merged to form the Gettysburg & Harrisburg Railway in 1891. They were then leased to the Philadelphia & Reading (later the Reading Company).

The line was not included in Conrail and the property was acquired by Pennsylvania Department of Transportation. The Blairsville & Indiana Railroad, incorporated in 1974, was designated to operate the line starting October 17, 1976. The company changed its name to Gettysburg Railroad. It began operation excursion trains in June 1978.

The company is owned by Sloan Cornell and others.

Radio frequencies: 160.800, 161.235
Location of enginehouse: Gettysburg, Pa.
Locomotives: 5

No.	Builder	Model	New	Builder No.
39	EMD	GP9	4/57	23270
70	Alco	RS-36	4/62	84101
76	Baldwin	2-8-0	12/20	54265
105	EMD	GP9	3/57	22837
1278	CLC	4-6-2	1948	2435

Gettysburg's Alco RS-36 No. 70 heads up a train of food products at Biglerville, Pennsylvania. Photo by Jim Shaw.

GLOSTER SOUTHERN RAILROAD CO.

P. O. Drawer C
Gloster, MS 39638

Reporting marks: GLSR
Phone: 601-225-4889
Fax: 601-225-7276

Gloster Southern operates freight service from a connection with Illinois Central at Slaughter, Louisiana, to Gloster, Mississippi, 34.8 miles. Rail is 90 to 112 pounds. About 3,000 cars a year of lumber, plywood, and aggregates make up the road's traffic.

The Mississippi part of the Gloster line was built by the New Orleans, Baton Rouge, Vicksburg & Memphis Railroad between 1882 and 1884. The Louisiana portion was built by the New Orleans & Mississippi Valley Railroad at the same time. These railroads merged to form the Louisville, New Orleans & Texas Railroad on August 8, 1884. The railroad was acquired by the Yazoo & Mississippi Valley in October 1892, and Y&MV was absorbed by the Illinois Central in July 1946. Gloster Southern, which is owned by Georgia Pacific Corporation, started service on August 5, 1986.

From November 1988 to December 1995 Gloster Southern operated a 28.7-mile line from Silver Creek to Columbia, Miss. It was built by the Gulf & Ship Island Railroad about 1905. Illinois Central Gulf sold the line to the Marion County Railroad Authority in March 1982. It was operated by the Columbia & Silver Creek Railroad from then until November 1, 1988, when operations were transferred to the Gloster Southern. Gloster Southern discontinued service on the Silver Creek line in December 1995.

Radio frequencies: 160.575, 160.770
Location of enginehouse: Gloster and Coss, Miss.
Locomotives: 2

No.	Builder	Model	New
501	AT&SF	CF7	12/74
1502	AT&SF	CF7	7/72

Freight cars: 99 boxcars

GODERICH-EXETER RAILWAY CO. LTD.

1 Maitland Road
P. O. Box 214
Goderich, ON N7A 3Z2
Canada

Reporting marks: GEXR
Phone: 519-524-4024
Fax: 519-524-4026

The Goderich-Exeter Railway operates from a connection with Canadian National Railways at Stratford, Ontario, to Goderich, 45.9 miles, and from Clinton Junction to Centralia, 24.1 miles. Traffic is salt, grain, and heavy machinery, about 7,500 cars a year.

Parts of the line were built in 1856 by the Buffalo & Lake Huron Railway. It eventually became part of Canadian National.

CN sold the line to RailTex (it was RailTex's first Canadian operation) and service started April 6, 1992.

Radio frequency: 161.310
Enginehouse: Goderich, Ont.
Locomotives: 4 engines

No.	Builder	Model	New	Builder No.
177	GMD	GP9	1960	A-1814
178	GMD	GP9	1960	A-1416
179	GMD	GP9	1960	A-1818
180	GMD	GP9	1960	A-1819

GOLDEN TRIANGLE RAILROAD

P. O. Box 2210
Columbus, MS 39703-2210

Reporting marks: GTRA
Phone: 601-243-4804
Fax: 601-243-4802

Golden Triangle operates freight service from Triangle Junction, Mississippi, through Columbus to Trinity, 16.3 miles. At Triangle Junction it connects with Norfolk Southern, and at Columbus with Burlington Northern, Kansas City Southern, and Columbus & Greenville. Rail is 90 pound. Traffic is paper, pulp, chemicals, and paper-mill-related products — about 9,000 cars a year.

The line was built between 1981 and 1982. It is owned by the Weyerhaeuser Company.
Radio frequencies: 160.455, 160.680
Location of enginehouse: Trinity, Miss.
Locomotives: 3

No.	Builder	Model	New	Builder No.
G-1	EMD	MP15AC	10/80	796389-1
810	EMD	GP38-2	1/81	796388-3
819	EMD	GP38-2	1/81	796388-4

Freight cars: 535 boxcars

THE GP16

Between May 1979 and November 1982 the Seaboard Coast Line overhauled 161 GP7s and GP9s. The visible aspects of the overhaul were a four-stack exhaust manifold (the units were built with two stacks) and a cut-down short hood. The new exhaust system allowed a modest horsepower increase to 1600 for the GP7s, but rebuilt GP9s were also rated at 1600 horsepower — thus the GP16 designation.

Although the major portion of the work was done at SCL's Uceta shop in Tampa, Florida — a former Atlantic Coast Line line facility — remanufactured engine components were shipped in from SCL's shop in Waycross, Georgia, and electrical equipment came from General Electric at Chamblee, Georgia. The units were painted at Waycross. SCL numbered the GP16s 4600-4645, 4700-4809, and 4975-4979; CSX numbers were 1706-1860. Many have been sold to short lines.

Four exhaust stacks, barely visible in this view, and chopped short hood are the earmarks of the Seaboard Coast Line's GP16. Photo by Louis A. Marre.

THE GP8 AND GP10

The Illinois Central dieselized its freight trains relatively late with Electro-Motive hood units — 48 GP7s and 348 GP9s. By the mid-1960s the oldest of those units were approaching the time for a major overhaul, so in 1968 IC initiated the country's first major diesel rebuilding program at its Paducah, Kentucky, shops. The rebuilding was extensive, including an increase in power output, low nose (after the first five units), four exhaust stacks, and, again after the first few units, paper air filters, which are housed in a boxy structure atop the hood or on each side of it. The identity of a given locomotive is difficult to trace through the rebuilding program, because the components became fairly well scrambled. The official identity of the predecessor of a given rebuilt locomotive is a matter of accounting rather than of what parts came from which.

The rebuilt GP7s were designated GP8s, and the rebuilt GP9s (and a few GP18s) became GP10s. IC was pleased with the results of the program and eventually bought GP7s and GP9s from other roads to rebuild (and eliminate the Alco diesels acquired when IC merged the Gulf, Mobile & Ohio) and undertook rebuilding for other railroads. Paducah shops turned out a total of 109 GP8s and 327 GP10s for Illinois Central and its successor Illinois Central Gulf between 1967 and 1977, plus many such units for other railroads.

When ICG began spinning off shortline and regional railroads in the mid-1980s, it often offered GP8s and GP10s along with the sales, accounting for their presence on the rosters of such roads as Chicago, Central & Pacific and MidSouth. With a number of units rendered surplus by the line sales, other roads, including Iowa Interstate, also bought them.

Illinois Central Gulf 7901 is a GP8, rated at 1600 horsepower. ICG 8109 is a GP10, rated at 1850 horsepower. It was the first GP10 produced and received its low nose in a subsequent rebuilding. Photos by Charles W. McDonald.

GRAFTON & UPTON RAILROAD CO.

Depot Street
P. O. Box 5
Hopedale, MA 01747

Reporting marks: GU
Phone: 617-853-2849
Fax: 617-853-5977

The Grafton & Upton owns a 15-mile line extending between Conrail connections at Milford and North Grafton, Massachusetts. Currently only 8 miles of track from North Grafton to West Upton is in service. Rail is 85 pound. Traffic consists of grain and rock salt, about 350 cars a year.

The Grafton Center Railroad was chartered October 22, 1873, and opened as a 3-foot gauge line from Grafton Center to Grafton, 3 miles, on August 20, 1874. It was converted to standard gauge in September 1887 and reorganized as the Grafton & Upton

Railroad the following year. It was then extended to West Upton in May 1899 and to Milford in March 1890. It was electrified in 1902, and from then until June 1923 the Milford & Uxbridge Street Railway operated passenger service over the road. G&U operated its own passenger service from 1923 to August 1928. The company is controlled by M. N. Lucey and others.

Radio frequency: 160.245
Location of enginehouses: North Grafton and Hopedale, Mass.
Locomotives: 2

No.	Builder	Model	New	Builder No.
9	GE	44-ton	7/46	28497
1001	Alco	S-4	6/52	77805

GRAINBELT CORP.

1601 West Gary Boulevard
P. O. Box 1750
Clinton, OK 73601

Reporting marks: GNBC
Phone: 405-323-1234
Fax: 405-323-4568

Grainbelt operates 178 miles from Enid, Oklahoma, southwest to Frederick. It connects with the Santa Fe, Burlington Northern, and Union Pacific at Enid, with Farmrail at Clinton, and with Burlington Northern at Snyder. Rail is 90 to 115 pound. In addition, the company has trackage rights over Burlington Northern from Snyder to Quanah, Texas, 59 miles. Traffic includes wheat, gypsum rock and products, oil field materials, petroleum, cotton, fertilizer, vegetable oils, and chemicals — about 6,000 cars a year.

This line is a former Burlington Northern branch (formerly St. Louis-San Francisco). Shortline service started August 31, 1987. The company is owned by Farmrail System, Inc., and is operated in connection with the affiliated Farmrail Corp.

Radio frequencies: 161.100, 161.520
Location of enginehouse: Clinton, Okla.
Locomotives: 12

No.	Builder	Model	New	Builder No.	Rebuilt
3648	EMD	GP9	2/59	25017	
3871	EMD	GP9	2/59	25018	
6083	EMD	GP9	6/56	21720	
8052	EMD	GP10	12/54	19722	1967
8053	EMD	GP10	2/54	19773	1972
8054	EMD	GP10	4/54	19278	1977
8055	EMD	GP10	12/54	19897	1971
8180	EMD	GP10	1/56	20818	
8250	EMD	GP10	1/57	22315	
8267	EMD	GP10	4/56	21393	
8272	EMD	GP10	3/57	22700	1972

Freight cars: 15 hopper cars

GRAND FORKS RAILWAY CO.

Industrial Boulevard
P. O. Box 2676
Grand Forks, BC V0H 1H0
Canada

Reporting marks: GFR
Phone: 604-442-5521
Fax: 604-442-2577

Grand Forks provides switching service over a former Canadian Pacific line extending 3.5 miles from a connection with Burlington Northern at Carson Spur to Grand Forks, British Columbia. The company is owned jointly by its principal shippers, Pope & Talbot Canada and Canpar, Inc. Service started April 12, 1993.

Locomotives: 1

No.	Builder	Model	New	Builder No.
6703	GMD	SW8	12/50	A-113

GRAND RAPIDS & EASTERN RAILROAD, INC.

430 East Grove Street
Greenville, MI 48838

Reporting marks: GR
Phone: 616-754-0990

Grand Rapids & Eastern operates freight service from a connection with Conrail and CSX at Grand Rapids (Penn Junction), Michigan, to Ionia, 43.5 miles. It also connects with the affiliated Mid-Michigan Railroad at Lowell. Rail is 100 pound. Traffic consists of about 3,500 cars a year of chemicals, appliances, cement, plastics, auto parts, and newsprint.

The line was built in part by the Detroit & Pontiac Railroad, chartered in 1838. The company was reorganized as the Detroit & Milwaukee Railroad in 1855 and as the Detroit, Grand Haven & Milwaukee in 1878. It joined the Grand Trunk Western system in 1928.

GTW sold the line to Central Michigan Railway in September 1987. Central Michigan sold the line to the current operator on July 10, 1993. Grand Rapids & Eastern is a subsidiary of RailTex and is operated in conjunction with Mid-Michigan Railroad.

Radio frequency: 161.235
Location of enginehouse: Grand Rapids, Mich
Locomotives: 1 (locomotives are pooled with Mid-Michigan Railroad)

No.	Builder	Model	New	Builder No.
5106	EMD	GP38	8/70	36683

GRAND RIVER RAILWAY CO. (CP RAIL)

Reporting marks: LEN

The Grand River Railway is a former electric line extending north from Galt, Ontario. It is part of the CP Rail system.

GREATER WINNIPEG WATER DISTRICT RAILWAY

598 Plinguet Street
Winnipeg, MB R2J 2W7
Canada

Reporting marks: GWR
Phone: 204-986-4118

The Greater Winnipeg Water District Railway operates freight service from connections with the CP Rail and Canadian National at St. Boniface, Manitoba, to Indian Bay, 97.7 miles. Rail is 60 and 85 pound. Traffic is limited to chemicals and company material carried in one or two trains a week.

This line was built in 1914 to facilitate construction of an aqueduct to the city of Winnipeg. At times it has hauled considerable freight, and passengers were carried until 1983. The railroad is owned by the City of Winnipeg Water & Waste Disposal Department.

Radio frequencies: 169.590/167.670, 169.620/167.700
Location of enginehouse: St. Boniface, Man.
Locomotives: 3

No.	Builder	Model	New	Builder No.
200	MLW	RS-23	5-1960	83289
201	MLW	RS-23	1-1959	82550
202	MLW	RS-23	5-1960	83291

Freight cars: 144 (local service only)

GREAT MIAMI & SCIOTO RAILWAY CO.

7142 Sprucewood Court
Cincinnati, OH 45241

Reporting marks: GMRY
Phone: 513-868-5219
Fax: 513-844-6971

Great Miami GP30 No. 30 and leased Indiana & Ohio GP9 No. 61 pull a train into Hamden, Ohio, on the Great Miami & Scioto Railway. Photo by Jim Shaw.

Great Miami provides freight service from RA Junction (where it connects with CSX) to Red Diamond, Ohio, 44.4 miles. There is also a branch from Hamden to Fire Brick, 32.8 miles. Rail ranges from 90 to 122 pound.

Traffic includes chemicals, logs, auto parts, sand, flour, and tomato paste — about 1,500 cars a year.

The line was part of the Portsmouth Division of the Baltimore & Ohio Southwestern Railroad, later B&O, then CSX. It was purchased by the city of Jackson, Ohio, on April 1, 1987, and was operated by the Indiana & Ohio Eastern Railway from then until January 1, 1994, when the current operator leased the line. Great Miami is controlled by Fred Stout.

Radio frequency: 160.905
Location of enginehouse: Hamden, Ohio
Locomotives: 2

No.	Builder	Model	New	Builder No.
30	EMD	GP30	11/62	27896
35	EMD	GP35	11/64	29660

GREAT RIVER RAILROAD

North Main Street
P. O. Box 460
Rosedale, MS 38769

Reporting marks: GTR
Phone: 601-759-6212

Great River operates freight service from Rosedale, Mississippi, south to a connection with the Columbus & Greenville at Great River Junction, 32.4 miles. Rail is 70 and 90 pound. Traffic amounts to about 200 cars a year of agricultural products, manufactured steel items, and lubricants.

The line was part of the Riverside Division of the Yazoo &

Mississippi Valley Railroad. It became part of the Illinois Central (later Illinois Central Gulf) and was acquired by the Rosedale-Bolivar County Port Commission in December 1979. The Commission operates the railroad.
Radio frequency: 160.680
Location of enginehouse: Rosedale, Miss.
Locomotives: 2

No.	Builder	Model	New	Builder No.
2	Alco	S-2	7/43	70080
8341	Alco	S-1	1941	

Led by an ex-Army Alco, a Great River Railroad work train pauses in a cotton field near Rosedale, Mississippi, to spread ballast. Photo by Louis Saillard.

GREAT SMOKY MOUNTAINS RAILWAY, INC.

1 Front Street
P. O. Box 397
Dillsboro, NC 28725

Reporting marks: GSMR
Phone: 704-586-8811
Fax: 704-586-8806

Great Smoky Mountains Railway provides freight and excursion service over a 66.7-mile line from a connection with Norfolk Southern at Dillsboro, North Carolina, to Murphy. The line is best

known for its scenic route through the Nantahala Gorge and the 4 miles of 4 percent grade to Topton. Rail is 85 to 100 pound. Freight traffic includes lumber, forest products, pallets, aggregate, and grain — under 500 cars a year. Excursions provide most of the revenue — the trains carried 177,000 passengers in 1994.

The line was completed in 1891 by the Western North Carolina Railroad, which was acquired by Southern Railway in 1905.

Heavy grades on the Great Smoky Mountains Railroad require the railroad to doublehead even short freight trains. Two Geeps pull a half dozen loads through Nantahala, North Carolina. Photo by Tom Sink.

Norfolk Southern sold the line to the state of North Carolina on July 19, 1988, following abandonment approval. The property is leased to Great Smoky Mountains Railway, which is independent.

Radio frequencies: 461.575, 463.250
Location of enginehouse: Dillsboro, N. C.
Locomotives: 5

No.	Builder	Model	New	Builder No.
210	EMD	GP35	11/63	28625
223	EMD	GP35	3/64	29223
711	EMD	GP7	1/54	19104
777	EMD	GP7	8/54	19874
1702	Baldwin	2-8-0	9/42	64641

GREAT WALTON RAIL CO., INC.

315 East Lumpkin Street
P. O. Box 711
Monroe, GA 30655

Reporting marks: GRWR
Phone: 770-464-0761
Fax: 770-464-0146

Great Walton provides freight service on three disconnected lines in Georgia. The first runs from a connection with CSX at Social Circle to Monroe, 10 miles. Rail is 75 to 90 pound. The second is a line leased from Norfolk Southern and extending from a connection with NS at Machen to a connection with CSX at Covington, 25 miles. Rail is 80 pound. The newest line runs from a CSX connection at Elberton to a connection with NS at Toccoa, 49 miles. It also connects with the Hartwell Railroad at Bowersville.

Traffic includes about 6,000 cars a year of pulpwood, clay slurry, rosin, plastic, paper products, talc, and feldspar.

The Monroe line was built by the Walton Railroad, chartered in September 1880. The company was consolidated with the Gainesville, Jefferson & Southern Railroad on March 8, 1884, and leased to the Georgia Railroad three days later. It was one of two lines

sold by CSX as a package to the Georgia Eastern Railroad in February 1987; however, the Georgia Eastern sold the line to Great Walton, which began service on March 30, 1987.

The Machen-Covington line is a former Central of Georgia branch line leased under NS's Thoroughbred Short Line Program. Service on that road started April 10, 1989.

The Elberton-Toccoa line was built by the Elberton Air Line, a 3-foot gauge railroad chartered in December 1871 and opened in 1878. The line was leased to the Richmond & Danville in 1894 and became part of the Southern Railway. Norfolk Southern sold the line to the Hartwell Railroad in April 1995 and Hartwell designated Great Walton to operate it. Service started on April 10, 1995.

The company is controlled by Benny Ray Anderson, who also owns the Hartwell Railroad.

Radio frequencies: 160.815, 160.995
Location of enginehouse: Social Circle, Covington, and Bowersville, Ga.
Locomotives: 8

No.	Builder	Model	New	Builder No.
136	EMD	GP35	8/65	30508
2594	EMD	GP30	10/63	27564
4537	EMD	GP9	3/59	25164
5093	EMD	SW9	1/53	19299

No.	Builder	Model	New	Builder No.
6243	EMD	GP9	8/57	23505
6400	EMD	GP9	5/54	19548
6525	EMD	GP9	5/57	22999
6580	EMD	GP9	1/58	24364

GREAT WESTERN RAILWAY CO. (COLORADO)

Taylor Avenue
P. O. Box 537
Loveland, CO 80539

Reporting marks: GWR
Phone: 303-667-6883
Fax: 303-667-1444

Great Western operates freight service from Loveland, Colorado, to Longmont, 29 miles, with branch lines from Officer Junction to Windsor, 6 miles, and from Welty through Johnstown to Milliken, 8.8 miles. The railroad has trackage rights over Union Pacific from Kelim to LaSalle. It connects with Union Pacific at Kelim and with Burlington Northern at Longmont, Loveland, and Windsor. Rail runs from 60 to 115 pound. Traffic is 4,200 cars a year of agricultural, manufactured, and forest products.

The company was incorporated October 16, 1901, by the Great Western Sugar Company and started operations a short time later. Passenger service ended about 1927. The company was acquired from Great Western Sugar by the Castile Corporation (BROE Corporation) in June 1986. It is now owned by OmniTRAX of Denver.

Radio frequencies: 160.260, 160.875
Location of enginehouse: Loveland, Colo.
Locomotives: 5

No.	Builder	Model	New	Builder No.	Rebuilt
211	EMD	GP9	1/54	19097	
296	EMD	GP9	9/54	19893	
705	EMD	GP7	10/52	17028	
711*	EMD	GP7	9/52	16983	1973
1845*	Alco	S-4	4/55	81319	

* Out of service

GREAT WESTERN RAILWAY (OREGON)

1410 South Third Street
Lakeview, OR 97630

Reporting marks: GWR
Phone: 503-947-2444

Great Western's Oregon line provides freight service from Lakeview, Oregon, to a connection with the Southern Pacific at Alturas, California, 54.4 miles. Rail is 90 pound. Traffic is primarily lumber and forest products — about 1,000 cars a year.

The line was part of the narrow gauge Nevada-California-Oregon Railway, which was absorbed by Southern Pacific. SP operated the Lakeview-Alturas line until January 18, 1986, when Great Western purchased it.

The company is a subsidiary of OmniTRAX.

Radio frequency: 160.875
Location of enginehouse: Lakeview, Ore.
Locomotives: 2

No.	Builder	Model	New	Builder No.
1621	EMD	GP7	6/54	19604
3416	EMD	GP9	5/54	19477

GREEN MOUNTAIN RAILROAD CORP.

8 Depot Street
P. O. Box 498
Bellows Falls, VT 05101-0498

Reporting marks: GMRC
Phone: 802-463-9531
Fax: 802-463-4084

Green Mountain Railroad operates freight service from Rutland to Bellows Falls, Vermont, and across the Connecticut River to North Walpole, New Hampshire, 52.2 miles. It connects at Rutland with the Vermont Railway and the Clarendon & Pittsford and at Bellows Falls with the New England Central and ST Rail (Boston & Maine). It also operates seasonal excursion trains. Rail is 90 to 105 pound. Annual freight traffic is about 4,500 cars of talc and related mineral products, roofing granules, forest products, limestone, fly ash, paper, beer, oil, and salt.

The line was built by the Rutland & Burlington Railroad in the late 1840s. It became part of the Rutland Railroad, and when the Rutland abandoned operations following a long strike, its assets were sold to the state of Vermont. Green Mountain Railroad was incorporated April 3, 1964, to lease and operate the line. The ICC approved operations effective April 2, 1965.

The company has been employee owned since 1967.

Radio frequencies: 160.605, 161.355, 161.445
Location of enginehouse: North Walpole, N. H.
Locomotives: 7

Green Mountain GP9 No. 1848 with westbound XR-1 passes over the high bridge at East Wallingford, Vermont, on its way to Rutland. Photo by Jack Armstrong.

No.	Builder	Model	New	Builder No.	Rebuilt
400	Alco	RS-1	5/48	75839	
405	Alco	RS-1	11/51	79575	
1848	EMD	GP9	6/54	19553	
1849	EMD	GP9	6/55	20310	
1850	EMD	GP9	11/56	22564	
1851	EMD	GP9	10/55	21015	
4265	EMD	F7A	3/49	8478	

Freight cars: 43 boxcars, 92 covered hoppers

GREENVILLE & NORTHERN RAILWAY CO.

222 Cox Street
P. O. Box 2165
Greenville, SC 29602

Reporting marks: GRN
Phone: 864-232-6441
Fax: 864-232-9027

Greenville & Northern operates freight service from a connection with CSX and Norfolk Southern at Greenville, South Carolina, to Travelers Rest, 11.3 miles. Rail ranges from 60 to 80 pounds. Traffic includes scrap iron, cotton waste, vermiculite, peat moss, paper, lumber, and chemicals — about 2,000 cars a year.

The Carolina, Knoxville & Western Railway was chartered in 1887 to build a line from Augusta, Georgia, to Knoxville, Tennessee. By November 1888, it had been completed from Greenville to Marietta, 15 miles. The line was extended another 8 miles to River Falls, then abandoned in March 1899. In 1907 the Greenville & Knoxville Railroad was formed to revive the railroad. It operated until 1914 when it was reorganized as the Greenville & Western, which was renamed Greenville & Northern in 1920. The line was cut back to Travelers Rest in the mid 1950s.

The company was acquired by Pinsly Railroad Company in July 1957.
Radio frequency: 160.425
Location of enginehouse: Greenville, S. C.
Locomotives: 2

No.	Builder	Model	New	Builder No.	Rebuilt
1	EMC	SW1	8/39	905	
704	EMD	GP8	1/57	22302	1974

Freight cars: 25 boxcars, 102 gondolas

GULF, COLORADO & SAN SABA RAILWAY

207 South Cook Street, Suite 200
Barrington, IL 60010

Reporting marks: GCSR
Phone: 708-382-0500
Fax: 708-382-0540

The Gulf, Colorado & San Saba operates freight service from a connection with Santa Fe at Lometa, Texas, to Brady, 67.5 miles. Rail is 90 to 112 pound. Traffic includes frac sand (used for making glass), grain, fertilizer, and feed products. About 2,500 cars a year are expected.

The line was built by the Gulf, Colorado & Santa Fe in 1911. Santa Fe sold the property to the current operator on May 10, 1993. The company is a subsidiary of American Railroads Corporation.
Location of enginehouse: Brady, Texas
Locomotives: 2

No.	Builder	Model	New	Builder No.
4303	EMD	GP7	11/56	22822
4308	EMD	GP7	4/57	22982

GWI SWITCHING SERVICES

P. O. Box 340
Dayton, TX 77535

Reporting marks: GWSW
Phone: 409-258-4030
Fax: 409-258-4031

This company operates the Sjolander Car Storage Yard at Dayton, Texas, including 10 miles of incidental trackage rights over Southern Pacific in the Dayton area. Service began on April 6,

1994. About 4,000 cars of chemical traffic a year are handled. GWI Switching Services is affiliated with Genesee & Wyoming Industries, Inc.
Locomotives: 5

No.	Builder	Model
1510-1514	AT&SF	CF7

145

H&S RAILROAD CO., INC.

401 Henley St., Suite 5
Knoxville, TN 37902

Reporting marks: HS
Phone: 615-525-9400

H&S operates limited freight service from a connection with CSX, Norfolk Southern, and The Bay Line at Dothan, Alabama, to Taylor, 8 miles. Rail is 100 pound. Traffic consists primarily of railroad cars moving from and to a car repair shop.

The Chattahoochee & Gulf Railroad was chartered on July 7, 1899. That company opened a line from Dothan to Sellersville, 47 miles, on November 1, 1900. Eventually the railroad was extended and operated from Columbia to Lockhart, 91 miles. It was leased by the Central of Georgia in 1900. About 1940 the line was abandoned west of Hartford, and in the early 1950s the Central of Georgia decided to abandon the line from Hartford to Dothan.

The Hartford & Slocomb Railroad was incorporated on August 1, 1953, to purchase and operate the line, and it started service February 16, 1954.

The line was abandoned from Taylor to Hartford in April 1992, and Pete Claussen (Gulf & Ohio Railways) purchased the remaining property from the Rail Division of Itel Corporation on July 1, 1992, to become the H&S Railroad.

Radio frequencies: 161.250, 161.490
Location of enginehouse: Malvern, Ala.
Locomotives: 2

No.	Builder	Model	New	Builder No.
110	EMD	GP7	11/51	14987
119	EMD	SW1	8/49	7511

Freight cars: 5,881 (additional reporting marks: FRDN and LNAC)

HAMPTON & BRANCHVILLE RAILROAD CO.

11 Lightsey Street
P. O. Box 56
Hampton, SC 29924

Reporting marks: HB
Phone: 803-943-3334
Fax: 803-943-5779

The Hampton & Branchville operates freight service from a connection with CSX at Hampton, South Carolina, to Canadys, 40 miles. A short branch runs from Stokes to Walterboro. Rail is 85, 100, and 132 pound.

Traffic includes unit coal trains and forest and agricultural products — 7,000 cars a year.

The company was chartered on December 16, 1891, as the successor to a short 3-foot gauge logging road opened in the late 1880s. In October 1925, the road was authorized to extend its line to Cottageville, 48 miles from Hampton. Passenger service ended in 1957.

Most of the Cottageville line was built to serve the timber industry, and the line has been cut back as lumbering in the area has turned to trucks. The portion of the line from H&B Junction through Stokes to Walterboro and the Stokes-Canadys branch were former Atlantic Coast Line branches purchased by the Colleton County Railroad from CSX on November 1, 1986. Colleton County was merged into Hampton & Branchville on January 1, 1988.

The railroad is owned by the Lightsey family.
Radio frequencies: 49.26, 48.80
Location of enginehouse: Miley, S. C.
Locomotives: 8

No.	Builder	Model	New	Builder No.
120	EMD	SW1000	8/67	33184
667	EMD	GP9	2/59	24819
686	EMD	GP9	3/59	24838
859	EMD	GP9	6/59	24868
906	EMD	GP9	8/59	24915
5943	EMD	GP9	8/55	20852
6025	EMD	GP9	3/56	21503
6249	EMD	GP9	8/57	23511

Hampton & Branchville's SW1000 No. 120 pulls a short train of pulpwood and tank cars into Hampton, South Carolina, in December 1992. Photo by Jim Shaw.

HAMPTON RAILWAY, INC.

9400 S.W. Barnes Road, Suite 400
Portland, OR 97225-6698

Reporting marks: HLSC
Phone: 503-297-7691
Fax: 503-297-6690

The Hampton Railway operates a switching line running from a connection with the Willamette & Pacific at Willamina, Oregon, to Fort Hill — 5.2 miles. Rail is 90 to 112 pound. Traffic is forest products — less than 500 cars a year.

The line was built in 1922 and operated by the Willamina & Grand Ronde Railway until 1955, when the Longview, Portland & Northern Railroad acquired it. In March 1980 when it was sold to the Willamina & Grand Ronde Railroad, which was merged into the Willamette Valley Railroad on March 10, 1986, and sold again on March 1, 1988. The Hampton Railway purchased the Willamina-Fort Hill line in 1995, but the Willamina & Grand Ronde remains in business at Willamina.

The Hampton Railway has contracted with the Willamette & Pacific to operate the line.

HARBOR BELT LINE RAILROAD

340 Water Street
Wilmington, CA 90744

Reporting marks: HBL
Phone: 213-834-8511

The Harbor Belt Line is a switching road operating 69 miles of track in the harbor area of Los Angeles, connecting with Santa Fe, Southern Pacific, and Union Pacific. About 22,000 cars a year are handled.

The line was formed in June 1929 and is owned jointly by the City of Los Angeles and Santa Fe, SP, and UP.
Radio frequency: 160.980
Locomotives: 2

No.	Builder	Model	New	Builder No.
101	EMD	GP7	1952	16858
102	EMD	GP7	5/53	18228

HARDIN SOUTHERN RAILROAD, INC.

Railroad & Second Street
P. O. Box 20
Hardin, KY 42048

Reporting marks: HSRR
Phone: 502-437-4555
Fax: 502-437-4200

Hardin Southern operates seasonal excursion and irregular freight service from Hardin to a connection with the KWT Railroad at Murray, Kentucky, 8.34 miles. Rail is 90 to 110 pound. Freight traffic is outbound grain, agricultural products, and lumber — under 400 cars a year.

The line was built by the Paducah, Tennessee & Alabama Railroad, opened through Hardin in 1890 and completed between Paducah and Lexington on October 23, 1892. In 1895 the line was acquired by the Louisville & Nashville. J&J Railroad, Inc., was incorporated June 24, 1983, and purchased the property from Seaboard System in July 1983 following abandonment. Shortline service started October 11, 1983. Hardin Southern, which is controlled by Karl Koenig, acquired the assets of J&J on October 1, 1993.

Radio frequency: 161.055
Location of enginehouse: Hardin, Ky.
Locomotives: 1

No.	Builder	Model	New	Builder No.
863	EMD	SW1	4/40	1048

HARTWELL RAILROAD

Depot and Jackson Streets
P. O. Box 429
Hartwell, GA 30643

Reporting marks: HRT
Phone: 706-376-2627
Fax: 706-376-1121

The Hartwell Railroad operates freight service from Hartwell, Georgia, to a connection with Great Walton Railroad at Bowersville, 9.6 miles. Rail is 90 pound. Traffic includes lumber, fertilizer, grain, scrap, oil, sand, and stone — under 500 cars a year.

The railroad was chartered in 1878 as the Hartwell Railroad. The company opened its 3-foot gauge line in October 1879 and was bankrupt within 7 years. The company was reorganized as the Hartwell Railway in February 1898 and came under Southern Railway control in 1902. It was relaid to standard gauge in 1905. Southern operated the railroad until 1924 when it was sold to

The Hartwell Railroad operates this former Amtrak SW1, now numbered 7, into Bowersville, Georgia. Photo by Edward A. Lewis.

local interests, which in turn sold the assets of the company to Benny Ray Anderson in May 1990.

Hartwell Railroad purchased the Norfolk Southern's Elberton-Toccoa line (formerly Southern Railway) on April 10, 1994, and designated the Great Walton Railroad, also owned by Anderson, to operate it.

Radio frequency: 158.240
Location of enginehouse: Hartwell, Ga.
Locomotives: 1

No.	Builder	Model	New	Builder No.
7	EMD	SW1	6/49	6405

HIGH POINT, THOMASVILLE & DENTON RAILROAD CO.

206 North Spruce Street
P. O. Box 20204
Winston-Salem, NC 27120-0204

Reporting marks: HPTD
Phone: 910-723-3671
Fax: 910-882-5924

The High Point, Thomasville & Denton is operated for freight service by the Winston-Salem Southbound Railway. It extends from High Point, North Carolina, to High Rock, 34 miles. It connects with Norfolk Southern at High Point and Thomasville and with Winston-Salem Southbound at High Rock. Rail is 80 to 100 pound. About 3,900 cars a year of forest products, paper products, pulpboard, chemicals, and general commodities make up the railroad's traffic.

The Carolina & Yadkin River Railway was chartered February 19, 1903. The company changed its name to Carolina, Glen Anna & Pee Dee Railway & Development Co. in 1905 and to Carolina Valley Railway in 1907. It was reorganized as the Piedmont Railway in 1909, and the name was again changed in 1912 to the Carolina & Yadkin River Railway. The C&YR failed and entered receivership April 18, 1922. It was sold under foreclosure in May 1923 and emerged as the High Point, Thomasville & Denton Railroad. It was not until July 1, 1924, that the line began common carrier operation.

The Winston-Salem Southbound Railway acquired all the stock of the company in June 1960. Locomotives are supplied by Norfolk Southern and CSX, joint owners of WSSB.

Radio frequencies: 161.250, 160.590

HOLLIDAYSBURG & ROARING SPRING RAILROAD CO.

P. O. Box 361
Claysburg, PA 16625

Reporting marks: HRS
Phone: 814-239-5757

The Hollidaysburg & Roaring Spring operates freight service from a connection with Conrail at Hollidaysburg, Pennsylvania, to Roaring Spring, 10.2 miles. Rail is 100 pound. Traffic includes woodpulp and chemicals.

The line was part of Conrail's Cove secondary track and was sold to the Hollidaysburg & Roaring Spring on March 31, 1995. Conrail retained trackage rights from Hollidaysburg to a ballast quarry near Roaring Spring. The line is run in conjunction with the affiliated Everett Railroad. Alan W. Maples controls the company.

Locomotives: provided by Everett Railroad

HOLLIS & EASTERN RAILROAD CO.

P. O. Drawer C
Duke, OK 73532

Reporting marks: HE
Phone: 405-679-3971
Fax: 405-679-3921

The Hollis & Eastern operates freight service on an irregular schedule from Duke, Oklahoma, to a connection with Burlington

Former Santa Fe CF7 No. 2520 now serves the Hollis & Eastern and is shown at Victory, Oklahoma. Photo by Jim Shaw.

Northern, Farmrail, and the Wichita, Tillman & Jackson at Altus, 13 miles. Rail is 90 pound. Traffic is 1,500 cars a year of wallboard, building products, grain, and agricultural products.

The railroad is part of a line opened about 1912 by the Wichita Falls & Northwestern Railway (Oklahoma) and the Wichita Falls & Southern Railway (Texas). The two roads were acquired by the Missouri-Kansas-Texas in 1912.

The Hollis & Eastern was incorporated by local interests on October 15, 1958, to purchase and operate the Katy's Wellington branch. Operations started May 15, 1959, between Altus and Hollis, 34 miles. The line was abandoned between Hollis and Duke, 21 miles, in June 1975. Republic Gypsum Co. has controlled the railroad since 1971.

Location of enginehouse: Duke, Okla.
Locomotives: 2

No.	Builder	Model	New	Builder No.
39	EMD	SW1	5/53	18105
2520	AT&SF	CF7	5/74	

Freight cars: 75 flatcars

HONEY CREEK RAILROAD, INC.

P. O. Box 646
Morristown, IN 46461

Reporting marks: HCRR
Phone: 317-763-1215

The Honey Creek Railroad owns a 5.95-mile line from a connection with Norfolk Southern at New Castle, Indiana, to Honey Creek. Rail is 110 pound. Traffic includes grain and fertilizer — under 500 cars a year.

The line was part of the Columbus-Chicago main line of the Columbus, Chicago & Indiana Central Railroad, built in 1867 and 1868. It eventually became part of the Pennsylvania Railroad,

then Conrail. Honey Creek Railroad purchased the line from Conrail on October 1, 1993. It also operates the former Indiana Hi-Rail line from Rushville to Smith, 5.5 miles, as a contract carrier. It is owned by Morristown Grain Co.

Location of enginehouses: Sulfur Springs and Rushville, Ind.
Locomotives: 2

No.	Builder	Model	New	Builder No.
8693	EMD	SW7	8/51	14066
8898	EMD	SW8	6/50	11774

HOOSIER SOUTHERN RAILROAD

847 Sixth Street
P. O. Box 423
Tell City, IN 47586

Reporting marks: HOS
Phone: 812-547-3586
Fax: 812-547-8378

The Hoosier Southern provides freight service from Cannelton, Indiana, to Santa Claus, 19.8 miles, and then by trackage rights, 1.9 miles to Lincoln City, where interchange is made with Norfolk Southern. Rail is 75 pound. Traffic includes chemicals, lumber, and other forest products amounting to about 300 cars a year.

The line was built by the Huntingburg, Tell City & Cannelton Railroad in the late 1880s. It was acquired by the Louisville, Evansville & St. Louis Consolidated Railroad and later became part of the Southern Railway. Norfolk Southern leased the line to Indiana Hi-Rail in 1989 under its Thoroughbred Short Line Program. Service ended in 1991. The line was then acquired by the Perry County Port Authority, which resumed operations on December 15, 1994, under the Hoosier Southern name.
Radio frequency: 160.245
Location of enginehouse: Tell City, Ind.
Locomotives: 1

No.	Builder	Model	New	Builder No.	Rebuilt
464	EMD	GP10	3/53	17747	1968

HOUSATONIC RAILROAD CO., INC.

Route 7
P. O. Box 1146
Canaan, CT 06018

Reporting marks: HRRC
Phone: 203-824-0850
Fax: 203-824-7936

The Housatonic Railroad operates freight service from a connection with Danbury Terminal at New Milford, Connecticut, to a connection with Conrail at Pittsfield, Massachusetts, 72.4 miles Rail is 107 pound. Annual traffic is about 5,000 cars of paper products, plastic, limestone, chemicals, and lumber.

The line was built by the Housatonic Railroad, which was chartered in 1836. That company became part of the New Haven

Housatonic Railroad's southbound freight NX-12 with GP35s 3603 and 3600 passes the former Stockbridge, Massachusetts, station in January 1993. Photo by Jack Armstrong.

system in July 1892. The state of Connecticut purchased the New Milford-Canaan portion of the line from Penn Central in 1980. The Housatonic Railroad was chartered in 1983 to operate it. Housatonic purchased the Canaan-Pittsfield part of the line from Guilford Transportation Industries in January 1991.

The operating company is controlled by Housatonic Transportation Co. (John Hanlon and others). It is affiliated with Danbury Terminal.

Radio frequencies: 160.395, 161.505
Location of enginehouse: Canaan, Conn.

Locomotives: 8

No.	Builder	Model	New	Builder No.
2	GE	45-ton	2/42	15157
3600	EMD	GP35	11/64	29617
3601	EMD	GP35	1/65	30329
3602	EMD	GP35	5/64	29003
3603	EMD	GP35	2/65	30353
3604	EMD	GP35	1/65	30331
7324	EMD	GP9	11/55	20913
9935	Alco	RS-3M	4/51	78578

HUNTSVILLE & MADISON COUNTY RAILROAD AUTHORITY

119 Woodson Street
P. O. Box 308
Huntsville, AL 35804

Reporting marks: HMCR
Phone: 205-535-6516

The Authority owns and operates a line from a connection with Norfolk Southern at Huntsville, Alabama, to Norton, 13.25 miles. Rail is 90 pound. About 400 cars are carried yearly.

This is a former Louisville & Nashville branch line acquired by the Authority following its abandonment by the L&N in 1984. The Alabama Industrial Railroad operated the line until February 1985, when the Authority began operation on its own.

Location of enginehouse: Huntsville, Ala.
Locomotives: 2

No.	Builder	Model	New	Builder No.
527	EMD	NW2	8/46	3626
8923	EMD	SW9	2/51	9962

HURON & EASTERN RAILWAY CO.

3720 East Washington Road
Saginaw, MI 48601

Reporting marks: HESR
Phone: 517-754-2500
Fax: 517-754-8966

Huron & Eastern operates freight service from a connection with CSX at Saginaw, Michigan, to Croswell, with branch lines from Bad Axe to Kinde and from Palms to Harbor Beach, a total of 137 miles. The company also leases and operates 45 miles of state-owned lines from Reese to Vassar, Millington, Colling, and Denmark Junction. Huron & Eastern also connects with the Central Michigan at Harger. Rail is 90 to 131 pound. Traffic includes sugar beet pulp, grain, fertilizer, auto parts, chemicals, plastic, lumber, rubber, and coal — about 10,000 cars a year.

The major portion of the Croswell line was built by the 3-foot gauge Port Huron & Northwestern Railroad in 1882. The Flint & Pere Marquette acquired control in April 1889 and relaid the line to standard gauge. Pere Marquette acquired control in 1900.

CSX sold the line east of Bad Axe to the current operator and shortline service started March 31, 1986. The rest of the line from Saginaw to Bad Axe was purchased from CSX on December 22, 1988. The Vassar cluster consists of former New York Central lines purchased by the state and operated by the Tuscola & Saginaw Bay from 1977 until January 22, 1991, when they were leased to the Huron & Eastern.

The Huron & Eastern is controlled by RailAmerica and is affiliated with the Saginaw Valley Railway.
Radio frequencies: 160.440, 161.355
Location of enginehouses: Bad Axe and Vassar, Mich.
Locomotives: 4

No.	Builder	Model	New	Builder No.
201	EMD	GP38-2	1976	757136-38
202	EMD	GP38-2	1976	757136-39
203	EMD	GP38-2	1976	757136-40
204	EMD	GP38-2	1976	757139-41

HUTCHINSON & NORTHERN RAILWAY CO.

1800 Carey Boulevard
Hutchinson, KS 67501

Reporting marks: HN
Phone: 316-662-0901
Fax: 316-662-0453

The Hutchinson & Northern operates a switching and terminal line from connections with the Santa Fe, Cotton Belt, and Union Pacific at Hutchinson, Kansas, to the Hutchinson Salt Company's mine at Salt Mine, 5.14 miles. About 2,300 cars a year are carried. The railroad was built in 1923 as an electric line. It is owned by North American Salt Company.
Radio frequency: 160.380
Location of enginehouse: Hutchinson, Kan.
Locomotives: 2

No.	Builder	Model	New	Builder No.
6	EMD	SW900	4/57	23298
7	EMD	SW900	7/55	20406

Hutchinson & Northern SW900 No. 6 is ready to switch the salt mine at Hutchinson, Kansas. Photo by Jim Shaw.

IDAHO NORTHERN & PACIFIC RAILROAD CO.

119 North Commercial Street
Emmett, ID 83617

Reporting marks: INPR
Phone: 208-365-6353
Fax: 208-365-6689

Idaho Northern & Pacific provides freight service on three former Union Pacific branches. The Idaho Division consists of two lines. The first runs from the UP at Nampa, Idaho, to Cascade, 94.7 miles, with a 28.7-mile branch from Emmett to a second UP connection at Payette. A separate line runs from a UP connection at Weiser to Rubicon, 84.5 miles. The Oregon Division runs from a UP connection at La Grande, Oregon, to Joseph, 83.6 miles; it is not operated beyond Elgin, 23 miles. Rail is mostly 131 to 133 pound.

Traffic is primarily forest products — rough lumber, logs, finished lumber, woodchips, and plywood — 20,000 cars a year.

The Nampa-Emmett line was completed by the Idaho Northern Railway on March 29, 1902. It came under control of the Union Pacific in 1910 and was merged into the Oregon Short Line Railroad in 1913. In 1914 the line was extended from Emmett to Cascade and beyond. The line from Payette to Emmett was built between 1906 and 1910 by the Payette Valley Railroad (Payette to New Plymouth) and the Payette Valley Extension Railroad (New Plymouth to Emmett). Those lines were acquired by Oregon Short Line Railroad in August 1914. The Weiser-Rubicon line was built by the Pacific & Idaho Northern Railway between 1907 and 1911. It was sold to Oregon Short Line Railroad in 1936.

The Oregon Division was built by the Oregon Railway and Navigation Co. in stages through the 1890s. Union Pacific sold these lines to the Idaho Northern & Pacific on November 15, 1993. The company is a subsidiary of Rio Grande Pacific Corp.
Radio frequencies: 161.190 (yard), 161.265 (road)
Location of enginehouses: Emmett, Idaho; La Grande and Island City, Ore.
Locomotives: 12

No.	Builder	Model	New	Builder No.
1707	EMD	GP16	4/50	11498
4500	EMD	GP40	12/66	32357
4501	EMD	GP40	12/66	32361
4502	EMD	GP40	1/67	32609
4503	EMD	GP40	12/69	35085
4504	EMD	GP40	12/69	35093
4505	EMD	GP40	5/70	35910
4506	EMD	GP40	9/67	33451
4507	EMD	GP40	2/65	29911
4508	EMD	GP40	2/65	29912
4509	EMD	GP40	2/65	29927
4510	EMD	GP40	2/65	29930

INDIAN CREEK RAILROAD CO.

7878 West 600 North
Frankton, IN 46044

Reporting marks: ICRK
Phone: 317-552-7771

Indian Creek operates freight service on a former Conrail line (ex-Pennsylvania Railroad) from a connection with Conrail near Anderson, Indiana, to Frankton, 4.55 miles. Traffic is grain, about 2,000 cars a year.

Operations started July 20, 1980. The company is controlled by Rydman & Fox, a shipper located on the line.
Radio frequency: 151.625
Location of enginehouse: Frankton, Ind.
Locomotives: 1

No.	Builder	Model	New	Builder No.
6002	Alco	RS-11	5/59	83433

INDIANA RAIL ROAD CO.

Senate Avenue Terminal
P. O. Box 2464
Indianapolis, IN 46206

Reporting marks: INRD
Phone: 317-262-5140
Fax: 317-262-3347

Indiana Rail Road operates freight service from a connection with Illinois Central and Indiana Hi-Rail at Newton, Illinois, to Indianapolis, Indiana, 155 miles. The railroad has trackage rights over a branch from Newton to Browns (Grayville), Ill., 57 miles. It connects with Norfolk Southern at Browns, with CP Rail System at Linton, Ind., with Conrail and CSX at Indianapolis, with CSX at Bloomington and Sullivan, Ind., and with Indiana Southern at Switz City, Ind. Rail is 90 to 127 pound.

Traffic includes coal in unit trains for the Indianapolis Power & Light Co., Central Illinois Public Service, and Hoosier Energy as well as lumber, petroleum and petroleum products, grain, and manufactured products — about 65,000 cars a year.

The west end of the line from Sullivan, Ind., to Switz City was built to 3-foot gauge by the Springfield, Effingham & Southeastern between 1880 and 1883. In April 1883, the line was reorganized as the Indiana & Illinois Southern and in 1893 as the St. Louis, Indianapolis & Eastern. That line became the Illinois & Indiana in 1899 and came under control of the Illinois Central.

The central portion of the line was built in 1905 and 1906 by a Illinois Central subsidiary, the Indianapolis Southern Railroad.

Illinois Central Gulf sold the line to the Indiana Rail Road in 1986. Operations started March 18, 1986. Indiana Rail Road operated Norfolk Southern's Tipton branch under its Thoroughbred Short Line Program from 1989 to November 1991. Indiana Rail Road now moves unit coal trains over that line to Noblesville, Ind., for Public Service of Indiana as a contract carrier.

The company was independent until July 1995, when CSX acquired a 40 percent interest.

Radio frequencies: 161.100, 160.260
Location of enginehouse: Indianapolis, Ind.
Locomotives: 16

No.	Builder	Model	New	Builder No.	Rebuilt
600	EMD	SD35	9/65	30524	
1701	EMD	GP16	12/50	13535	1979
1704	EMD	GP16	12/50	12299	1979
1718	EMD	GP16	12/50	12297	1979
1728	EMD	GP16	10/56	22648	1981
1753	EMD	GP16	9/50	11915	1980
1757	EMD	GP16	5/50	11141	1980
1791	EMD	GP16	6/51	13881	1981
2528	AT&SF	CF7	1974		
2543	AT&SF	CF7	1973		
7305	EMD	SD18	1/63	27601	
7308	EMD	SD18	1/63	27603	
7309	EMD	SD18	1/63	27605	
7310	EMD	SD18	1/63	27608	
7314	EMD	SD18	3/63	27612	
7317	EMD	SD18	3/63	27615	

Freight cars: 29 gondolas, 6 boxcars

INDIANA & OHIO RAILROAD, INC.

2856 Cypress Way
P. O. Box 12576
Cincinnati, OH 45212-0576

Reporting marks: INOH
Phone: 513-531-4800
Fax: 513-531-4803

The Indiana & Ohio Railroad operates freight service from a connection with the Central Railroad of Indiana at Valley Junction, Ohio, to Brookville, Indiana, 26.2 miles. Rail is 80 to 90 pound. Traffic is about 1,000 cars a year of roofing material and lumber.

The line was acquired from Penn Central and operations started on June 21, 1979. The line was previously part of New York Central's Whitewater District.

The company is part of the Indiana & Ohio Rail Corporation system.

Radio frequencies: 160.575, 161.385
Location of enginehouse: Brookville, Ind.
Locomotives: 17 (all I&O system engines)

No.	Builder	Model	New	Builder No.
52, 53	EMD	GP7	9/53	18690, 18697
54	EMD	GP7	9/53	18700
55	EMD	GP7	6/50	10133
61	EMD	GP9	6/56	21704
62	EMD	GP9	3/56	21496
63	EMD	GP9	11/56	22561
64	EMD	GP9	12/56	22580
65	EMD	GP9	5/57	23760
71	EMD	GP18	9/60	26118
81, 82	EMD	GP30	8/62	27366, 27370
83	EMD	GP30	5/62	27794
84	EMD	GP30	7/63	28391
85	EMD	GP30	11/62	27895
251	EMD	GP35	12/63	28625
252	EMD	GP35	4/64	29232

Freight cars: 11 covered hoppers

INDIANA & OHIO RAILWAY CO.

2856 Cypress Way
P. O. Box 12576
Cincinnati, OH 45212-0576

Reporting marks: IORY
Phone: 513-531-4800
Fax: 513-531-4803

The Indiana & Ohio Railway operates freight and excursion service from Monroe (Middletown), Ohio, to South Mason, 10.5 miles, plus a 4.4-mile branch from Hageman Junction to Lebanon. The company also operates a separate line running from Blue Ash to McCullough (Norwood), 10.1 miles. It connects with Conrail at Monroe and McCullough and with CSX at Monroe and East Norwood. Rail is 85 and 100 pound. Traffic includes paper, tires, plastic, fertilizer, lumber, talc, chemicals, and foodstuffs — about 3,800 cars a year.

Both lines were acquired from Conrail. Operation on the Mason segment started March 1, 1985, and on the Blue Ash segment on December 19, 1986.

The company is part of the Indiana & Ohio Rail Corporation system.

Radio frequency: 161.385, 160.575
Location of enginehouse: Blue Ash and Mason, Ohio
Locomotives: see the listing for Indiana & Ohio Railroad
Freight cars: 9 boxcars

INDIANA & OHIO CENTRAL RAILROAD, INC.

665 East Front Street
Logan, OH 45040

Reporting marks: IOCR
Phone: 614-385-7551

Indiana & Ohio Central operates three lines in Ohio for freight service:
• from Logan to Valley Crossing, 43.5 miles, then via CSX trackage rights to Columbus where interchange is made with CSX, Conrail, and Norfolk Southern. Rail is 100 pound.
• from the CSX at Midland City to Greenfield and Thrifton, 29.8 miles. Rail is 122 pound.
• from a connection with CSX at Fayne to connections with Grand Trunk Western and Conrail at Springfield, 28.8 miles, and from Springfield to Bellefontaine and Mechanicsburg, 49 miles. Rail ranges from 90 to 115 pound.

Traffic includes more than 8,000 cars a year of chemicals, paper products, auto parts, railway wheels, and agricultural products.

The Logan line was built between 1869 and 1871 by the Columbus & Hocking Valley Railroad, which was reorganized in 1881 as the Columbus, Hocking Valley & Toledo and again in 1899 as the Hocking Valley Railway. In 1911 the company came under control of the Chesapeake & Ohio, which merged it in 1930. The line was acquired from CSX and short line service started July 1, 1987.

The Greenfield line is a former CSX branch that was once part of Baltimore & Ohio's Cumberland-Cincinnati main line. Indiana & Ohio Central took it over in October 1988.

The Springfield-Fayne line is former Grand Trunk Western trackage (previously Detroit, Toledo & Ironton). Service started in October 1990 on that line. The Springfield-Bellefontaine and Mechanicsburg lines are former Conrail property (ex-New York Central) purchased by the West Central Ohio Port Authority on January 14, 1994, and leased to the Indiana & Ohio Central.

The company is part of the Indiana & Ohio Rail Corporation system.
Radio frequencies: 160.695, 161.295
Location of enginehouse: Logan, Ohio
Locomotives: see the listing for Indiana & Ohio Railroad
Freight cars: 75 covered hoppers

INDIANA HI-RAIL CORP.

4301 North State Road 1
Connersville, IN 47331

Reporting marks: IHRC
Phone: 317-825-0349
Fax: 317-825-0453

Indiana Hi-Rail, which was incorporated in 1980, provides switching service on eight unconnected lines in Illinois, Indiana, and Ohio totaling 365 miles.
• Maumee District: Woodburn to Liberty Center, Ohio, 50.4 miles, connecting with Norfolk Southern at Woodburn and CSX at Defiance. Rail is 80 pound.
• St. Marys District: Van Buren, Ind., to Fort Jennings, Ohio, 77.8 miles, connecting with Conrail at Delphos, Ohio, Norfolk Southern at Bluffton, Ind., and the former Spencerville & Elgin at Ohio City, Ohio. Rail is 90 and 100 pound.
• Rochester District: Argos to Rochester, Ind., 15 miles, connecting with Norfolk Southern at Argos. Rail is 90 pound.

• New Castle/Connersville District: From a connection with Norfolk Southern and Conrail at New Castle, Ind., to a connection with CSX at Connersville, 25.4 miles. Rail is 90 to 110 pound. Operations started in December 10, 1981. The Connersville line was the first "Feeder Line" developed under the provisions of the Staggers Act.

• Huntingburg District: From a connection with Norfolk Southern at Lincoln City, Ind., to Santa Claus and Rockport, 21 miles. Rail is 80 pound. The Huntingburg district was leased from Norfolk Southern under its Thoroughbred Short Line Program effective June 30, 1989. A portion of the Huntingburg district from Jasper to DuBois was turned over to the DuBois County Railroad on July 15, 1993.

• Evansville District: From a connection with the Illinois Central at Browns, Ill., to Henderson, Kentucky, 56 miles, plus a 5.7-mile branch from Henderson to Riverport, 5.7 miles. Rail is 90 to 112 pound. The Evansville line was acquired from Illinois Central Gulf in May 1986.

• Olney District: Browns, Ill., to Newton, connecting with Norfolk Southern at Browns and with Illinois Central and Indiana Rail Road at Newton. Rail is 85, 90, and 112 pound.

• Poseyville & Owensville Railroad: Poseyville to Owensville, Ind., 11 miles.

Nearly 15,000 cars a year of a wide variety of commodities make up Indiana Hi-Rail's traffic.

Indiana Hi-Rail's brief history includes several lines it no longer operates:

• Sangamon District: Assumption, Ill., to Decatur (service began on November 11, 1986) and to Cisco (service began in October 1987). The line is now the Decatur Terminal.

• Tiffin District: Woodville to Tiffin, Ohio, on former Pennsylvania Railroad track. Service on the Tiffin line (owned by a port authority) started in 1990.

• Rushville District: Rushville to Smith, Ind., a former Nickel Plate branch, acquired in February 1983. It was turned over to the Honey Creek Railroad on October 1, 1993.

Indiana Hi-Rail is currently operating under bankruptcy reorganization after the ICC rejected its attempt to reorganize as the Wabash & Ohio Railroad and Wabash & Erie Railroad in late 1994.

Employees: 50
Radio frequencies: 160.590, 160.695, 160.845, 161.505
Location of enginehouses: Evansville and Connersville, Ind.
Locomotives: 23

No.	Builder	Model	New	Builder No.	Rebuilt
119	Alco	S-4	7/51	78814	
167	Alco	RS-1	4/50	77476	
203	EMD	GP20	4/59	25564	
216	EMD	SW1200	5/57	23362	
2121	EMD	SW1200	5/57	23367	
223	EMD	SW1200	9/55	20660	
310	Alco	C-420	12/64	3385-07	
311	Alco	C-420	12/64	3385-08	
315	Alco	C-420	9/66	3467-10	
325	Alco	C-425	5/66	3461-03	
327	Alco	C-425	5/66	3461-05	
332	Alco	C-430	8/67	3490-9	
334	Alco	C-430	8/67	3490-11	
342	AT&SF	GP7U	9/52	17005	1980
343	AT&SF	GP7U	6/52	16382	1981
344	AT&SF	GP7U	5/51	13202	1981
345	AT&SF	GP7U	9/52	16986	1981
352	Alco	RS-11	6/60	83590	
365	Alco	C-420	6/65	3418-15	
371	EMD	GP35	1/64	28793	
373	EMD	GP35	8/64	29283	
442	Alco	RSD15	6/60	83578	
443	Alco	RSD15	6/60	83579	

Freight cars: 279 (additional reporting mark GSOR)

INDIANA NORTHEASTERN RAILROAD CO., INC.

50 Monroe Street
P. O. Box 262
Hillsdale, MI 49242

Reporting marks: IN
Phone: 517-439-4677
Fax: 517-439-0222

The Indiana Northeastern operates freight service from Quincy, Michigan, to Montpelier, Ohio, via Jonesville, Hillsdale, and Reading, Mich., and Angola, Pleasant Lake, and Steubenville, Indiana. At Montpelier it connects with Norfolk Southern. A 7-mile branch extends from Jonesville, Mich., northwest to Litchfield, and a 3.6-mile branch runs from Steubenville, Ind., west to Ashley-Hudson. Total mileage is 95.

Traffic consists of 3,400 cars a year of grain, flour, sugar, food products, fertilizer, plastic, and other commodities.

The ancestry of the route goes back to the 1830s and incorporates properties of five distinct railroads. The state of Michigan was an early builder and operator of railroads and a state-owned line entered Hillsdale in 1843. In 1846 it was sold to the Lake Shore & Michigan Southern, and by 1852 was part of a line extending through Coldwater to Chicago. The Fort Wayne, Jackson & Saginaw Railroad opened a line from Jackson, Mich., through Angola to Fort Wayne, Ind., in 1870. In time these Michigan lines became part of the New York Central. They were not included in Conrail in 1976.

The Hillsdale County Railroad was formed in January 1976 and began operations on April 1 that year with 52 miles of line. The company purchased a stretch of former Wabash main line from Montpelier through Steubenville to Ashley-Hudson from the Norfolk & Western in April 1986.

The Coldwater-Quincy line is owned by the Branch & St. Joseph County Rail Users Association, and was leased to the Hillsdale County Railroad in the spring of 1990.

The Indiana Northeastern Railroad purchased Hillsdale County Railroad's rail lines on December 22, 1992, and also acquired the line of the Pigeon River Railroad from Ashley-Hudson west to South Milford, Ind.

The Indiana Northeastern is privately held.

Radio frequency: 161.100
Location of enginehouse: Hillsdale, Mich.
Locomotives: 6

No.	Builder	Model	New	Builder No.
47	EMD	GP7	4/52	16205
1601	EMD	GP7	5/53	18414
1602	EMD	GP7	8/52	16905
1603	EMD	GP9	4/54	19524
1766	EMD	GP9	4/57	22473
1770	EMD	GP9	4/57	22477

INDIANA SOUTHERN RAILROAD, INC.

Illinois Street
P. O. Box 158
Petersburg, IN 47567

Reporting marks: ISRR
Phone: 812-354-8080
Fax: 812-354-8085

Indiana Southern operates freight service from Indianapolis to Evansville, Indiana, 161.9 miles. A 7.3-mile branch line runs from Buckskin to Lynnville. Indiana Southern connects with Conrail at Indianapolis, Norfolk Southern and Algers, Winslow & Western at Oakland City, Indiana Rail Road at Switz City, CP Rail System (Soo Line) at Beehunter, and CSX at Evansville.

Traffic is primarily coal; grain, steel, and plastic help make up the 45,000 cars a year that the railroad hauls.

The north end of the line from Indianapolis to Worthington and Sandborn was built by the Indianapolis & Vincennes Railway after 1869. It was taken over by the Pennsylvania Company in 1879 and became part of the Pennsylvania Railroad system. The line from Worthington to Evansville was built by the Evansville & Indianapolis Railroad, which was chartered in 1886. That company was reorganized several times and in 1930 became part of the New York Central. Conrail sold the route to this RailTex subsidiary on April 11, 1992. The Worthington-Elnora line, 18.2 miles, was abandoned in May 1994. Indiana Southern uses trackage rights on Soo Line between Beehunter and Elnora.

Radio frequency: 160.995
Location of enginehouse: Petersburg, Ind.
Locomotives: 8

No.	Builder	Model	New	Builder No.	Rebuilt
6554	EMD	GP40	2/71	37203	
6556	EMD	GP40	12/71	39246	
6560	EMD	GP40	12/71	39250	
6563	EMD	GP40	12/71	39253	
6573	EMD	GP40	8/71	37889	
6599	EMD	GP40	9/71	38504	
6835	EMD	GP40	7/71	38560	
6853	EMD	GP40	12/71	39244	

RailTex's Indiana Southern GP40 is followed by a slug and a second GP40 on this unit coal train seen passing through Petersburg, Indiana, in May 1994. Photo by Jim Shaw.

IOWA INTERSTATE RAILROAD, LTD.

800 Webster Street
Iowa City, IA 52240

Reporting marks: IAIS
Phone: 319-339-9500
Fax: 319-339-9531

Iowa Interstate operates freight service from Blue Island, Illinois, via Rock Island and Des Moines to Council Bluffs, Iowa, 489 miles — the main line of the former Rock Island. In addition there are several branches:
• Bureau Junction to Peoria, Ill. (the Lincoln & Southern Railroad), 42.66 miles
• Rock Island to Milan, Ill., 10.5 miles
• Altoona to Pella, Iowa, 35.9 miles
• Hancock Junction to Hancock, Iowa, 0.4 mile
• Hancock Junction to Oakland, Iowa, 5.5 miles

Rail ranges from 112 to 136 pound. Total mileage operated is 567. Traffic includes grain, food products, lumber, coal, chemicals, intermodal, and haulage for the Cedar Rapids & Iowa City — 45,000 cars annually. The company operates a major reload center at Blue Island.

The company was formed in 1984 to operate the Blue Island-Council Bluffs line, which had been acquired by the Heartland Rail Corporation (which is owned by the Cedar Rapids & Iowa City Railway and various shippers located along the line). Purchase price of the line was $31 million. In June 1987 Iowa Interstate began leased operation over the Lincoln & Southern Railroad (owned by B. F. Goodrich Company). Heartland Rail Corporation owns 80 percent of the operating company, which has been managed by Rail Development Corporation since February 1, 1991.

Employees: 180
Radio frequencies: 160.305, 161.220
Location of enginehouses: Iowa City and Council Bluffs, Iowa
Locomotives: 30

Three Iowa Interstate GP8s pull a freight into Colfax, Iowa. Photo by Jim Shaw.

No.	Builder	Model	New
250	EMD	SW1200	3/66
303	EMD	GP9	6/56
325	EMD	GP7	10/53
400	EMD	GP7M	1976
401-404	EMD	GP10	1972
405, 407, 408	EMD	GP8	1975
413, 431	EMD	GP10	1969
466, 468, 481	EMD	GP8	1968
483, 4844	EMD	GP10	1969
495	EMD	GP16	1982
600-602	EMD	GP38	10/67
625-628	EMD	GP38AC	3/71
800-802	MLW	M-420R	1974-1975
850	Alco	C-420	1979
900	Alco	RS-36	1/63

Freight cars: 439 covered hoppers, 27 gondolas, 14 hopper cars, 457 flatcars, 1 articulated 10-Pack container car

IOWA NORTHERN RAILWAY

113 North Second Street
P. O. Box 640
Greene, IA 50636

Reporting marks: IANR
Phone: 515-823-5870
Fax: 515-823-4816

Iowa Northern operates freight service from Cedar Rapids, Iowa, to Waterloo and Manly, 126.7 miles. It connects with Chicago & North Western, Chicago Central & Pacific, Cedar Rapids & Iowa City, and CP Rail System (Soo Line). Rail is 110 and 112 pound. Traffic is agriculture related — grain and fertilizer — and totals about 14,000 cars a year.

The major portion of the line was built in the 1870s by the Burlington, Cedar Rapids & Northern Railroad, which became part of the Rock Island. Shortline service from Cedar Rapids to Vinton and from Shell Rock to Nora Springs started August 7, 1981. By mid-1982, the operations had been connected and expanded to the present size. In July 1984 Iowa Northern purchased its line from the Rock Island estate for $5.4 million. In July 1994 the company abandoned a 14-mile branch from Vinton Junction to Dysart.

The company is controlled by Iron Road Railways, Inc.
Radio frequency: 161.385
Location of enginehouse: Waterloo, Iowa
Locomotives: 9

No.	Builder	Model	New	Builder No.
932	EMD	SW1200	10/65	30746
1500	EMD	GP9	3/65	20437
1842	EMD	GP9	3/65	20438
1856	EMD	GP9	6/65	20317
1886	EMD	GP9	7/56	21220
2492	GMD	GP7	6/51	A-167
2493	AT&SF	CF7	11/74	
9016	EMD	GP9	5/54	18813
9239	EMD	GP9	1/57	22304

IOWA TRACTION RAILROAD CO.

Old Highway 106 West
P. O. Box 309
Mason City, IA 50402-0309

Reporting marks: IATR
Phone: 515-424-4600

Iowa Traction extends from connections with CP Rail System (Soo Line) at Mason City, Iowa, and Chicago & North Western at Clear Lake Junction west to Clear Lake, 10.4 miles. Rail is 60, 70, 90, and 112 pound. Traffic includes scrap, potash, food products, chemicals, and lumber — under 500 cars a year.

The Iowa Traction Railroad Co. purchased the Mason City division of the Iowa Terminal railroad in 1987. Iowa Terminal had been formed in 1961 to purchase the property of the Mason City & Clear Lake Railroad, an electric line that had opened in 1897 and provided passenger service until 1936. The company is independent.

Radio frequency: 161.475
Location of enginehouse: Emery, Iowa
Locomotives: 5

No.	Builder	Model	New	Builder No.
50	BLW	50-ton electric	10/20	53784
51	BLW	50-ton electric	5/21	54748
52	BLW	50-ton electric	6/28	56538
53	Texas Electric Railroad	50-ton electric	1928	none
60	BLW	60-ton electric	5/17	45659

Freight cars: 776

ISS RAIL, INC.

200 Industrial Street
New Castle, PA 16102

Reporting marks: ISSR
Phone: 412-652-0822
Fax: 412-652-0554

ISS Rail provides switching service on 11.9 miles of track at New Castle, Pennsylvania, connecting with Buffalo & Pittsburgh, Conrail, and CSX. Rail is predominantly 131 and 132 pound. Traffic runs about 1,200 cars a year.

The company began common carrier service over 7.5 miles of former Conrail trackage on December 21, 1993. The company also operates 4.4 miles of former Pittsburgh & Lake Erie trackage under contract from EASX Corporation of New Castle.

ISS Rail is independent.

Locomotives: 2

No.	Builder	Model	New	Builder No.
1	Alco	S-1	2/43	69860
3003	Alco	S-2	5/45	73359

Freight cars: 23

JK LINES

P. O. Box 68
Monterey, IN 46960

Reporting marks: JKL
Phone: 219-542-2031
Fax: 219-542-4077

JK Lines operates freight service from a connection with CSX at North Judson, Indiana, to Monterey, 16 miles. Rail is 112 to 132 pound. Traffic is grain and fertilizer, about 1,400 cars a year. Unit grain trains are delivered to CSX.

The line was built by the Chicago & Erie Railroad in 1880. The line became the Erie Chicago main line. The Erie Western oper-ated the route from September 1977 to June 1979. It was followed by the Chicago & Indiana Railroad from June through December 1979. The Tippecanoe Railroad took over January 1, 1980, and continued until April 24, 1990, when it was sold to Daniel R. Frick and renamed.

Radio frequency: 153.245
Location of enginehouse: Monterey, Ind.
Locomotives: 1

No.	Builder	Model	New	Builder No.
7311	EMD	SD18	2/63	27609

JAXPORT TERMINAL RAILWAY CO.

2701 Talleyrand Avenue, Building 1
P. O. Box 2217
Jacksonville, FL 32203-2217

Reporting marks: JXPT
Phone: 904-355-8817
Fax: 904-356-9016

Jaxport Terminal Railway provides switching service at Talleyrand Dock in Jacksonville, Florida. It connects with Norfolk Southern and CSX. Traffic includes intermodal, autos, forest products, and chemicals totaling about 17,000 cars a year. Operations started July 24, 1989. The company is controlled by K. R. Nichols (Texas Transportation Consultants) of Victoria, Texas.

Radio frequency: 160.815, 160.545
Locomotives: 2

No.	Builder	Model	New	Builder No.
2054	EMD	GP7	7/53	18560
2057	EMD	GP7	10/52	17461

JEFFERSON WARRIOR RAILROAD CO.

4200 Huntsville Road
P. O. Box 5346
Birmingham, AL 35207

Reporting marks: JEFW
Phone: 205-808-7942
Fax: 205-808-7885

The Jefferson Warrior Railroad provides switching service on 55 miles of track (25 route miles) in North Birmingham, Alabama. It connects with Burlington Northern, CSX, and Norfolk Southern. Rail is 100 pound. Traffic includes about 12,000 cars a year of coal, coke, chemicals, and mineral fiber.

This company operates the former Mary Lee Railroad, a private carrier that was built about 1890. Jefferson Warrior began com-mon carrier service on January 1, 1985. The company is owned by KKR Associates, a New York limited partnership.
Radio frequency: 153.260
Location of enginehouse: Birmingham, Ala.
Locomotives: 6

No.	Builder	Model	New	Builder No.
51-54	EMD	SW1500	8-9/72	72603-1–72603-4
55	EMD	SW9M	2/41	1247
56	EMD	SW9M	5/47	4714

Freight cars: 104 boxcars, 233 hopper cars

JOPPA & EASTERN RAILROAD CO.

P. O. Box 3
Joppa, IL 62953

Reporting marks: JE
Phone: 618-549-7278
Fax: 618-529-3008

Between November 1990 and June 1991 the Joppa & Eastern built a 2.9-mile line from a connection with Burlington Northern near Kelley, Illinois, to the Joppa Steam Electric Station at Powers. Rail is 115 pound. Burlington Northern, Illinois Central, Union Pacific, and Paducah & Louisville can all run trains over the line. Traffic is coal bound for the electric plant. The company is owned by Electric Energy, Inc.

JUNIATA TERMINAL CO.

General office: P. O. Box 412
Narberth, PA 19072
Operating headquarters: 3601 B Street
Philadelphia, PA 19134

Reporting marks: JTFS
Phone: 215-634-7911

Juniata Terminal operates a 1-mile switching line serving a passenger car repair shop and coil steel and bulk paper intermodal transfer facilities in Philadelphia, Pennsylvania. It connects with Conrail and Amtrak at Milepost 83 on Amtrak's Northeast Corridor line. Rail is 130 pound. Service started in 1987.

The company is controlled by Bennett Levin and others.
Locomotives: 1

No.	Builder	Model	New	Builder No.	Rebuilt
9251	EMD	NW2	8/47	5039	2/81

164

KANKAKEE, BEAVERVILLE & SOUTHERN RAILROAD CO.

P. O. Box 136
Beaverville, IL 60912

Reporting marks: KBSR
Phone: 815-486-7260
Fax: 815-486-7264

The Kankakee, Beaverville & Southern operates freight service from Kankakee to Danville, Illinois, and from Iroquois Junction to Hooper, Ill., and to Sheldon, Ill., and Swanington and Lafayette, Indiana. Total trackage is 155 miles. It connects with CSX, Illinois Central, Norfolk Southern, Toledo, Peoria & Western, and Union Pacific. Traffic includes about 6,000 cars a year of grain and agricultural products.

The company was formed in October 1977 to operate the former New York Central line from Kankakee to Sheldon. Service started December 1, 1977. The Hooper-Danville line was acquired from the Milwaukee Road in August 1981 for $2.1 million by the Hooper-Myron Corporation, an affiliated company.

Illiana Railroad Service owns the former NYC line from Sheldon to Lafayette and the former Nickel Plate line from Cheneyville, Ill., to Tempelton, Ind. The Kankakee, Beaverville & Southern leased those lines in 1990 and has since purchased them. The company is owned by Beaverville Grain & Lumber Co.

Radio frequencies: 160.215, 160.800
Location of enginehouse: Iroquois Junction, Ill. (between Donovan and Iroquois)
Locomotives: 7

No.	Builder	Model	New	Builder No.
301	Alco	RS-11	3/58	82864
308	Alco	RS-11	8/56	81931
309	Alco	RS-20	6/55	81287
312	Alco	RS-11	3/56	81469
315	Alco	C-420	8/66	3467-5
318	Alco	RS-11	6/60	83583
321	Alco	RS-11	3/56	81777

Freight cars: 301 covered hoppers

KANSAS SOUTHWESTERN RAILWAY

1825 West Harry
Wichita, KS 67213

Reporting marks: KSW
Phone: 316-263-3240
Fax: 316-263-3254

Kansas Southwestern operates 278 miles of leased line in Kansas including:
- Wichita to Hutchinson and Geneseo, 87 miles
- Wichita to Anthony, Kiowa, and Hardtner, 95 miles
- Conway Springs to Kingman and Radium, 96 miles
- Olcott to Iuka, 20 miles (currently embargoed)

Principal interchange is with the Union Pacific at Wichita and Geneseo. Additional interchange is made with Santa Fe at Wichita and Hutchinson, with Cotton Belt at Hutchinson, and with Hutchinson & Northern at Hutchinson. Traffic includes grain, fertilizer, agricultural products, chemicals, and merchandise — more than 35,000 cars a year.

The Geneseo line was built by the Wichita & Colorado Railroad, which was chartered July 23, 1885. The Hardtner line was opened by the St. Louis, Fort Scott & Wichita Railroad in 1885. The railroad was reorganized in May 1887 as the Fort Scott, Wichita & Western Railway. Both railroads came under the control of the Missouri Pacific by 1888.

The Radium line and the Iuka branch were built by the Denver, Memphis & Atlantic Railroad, which was chartered in October 1883 and became part of the Missouri Pacific system in 1890.

On April 14, 1991, Union Pacific leased these lines to the Kansas Southwestern, which is part of the OmniTRAX group.
Radio frequency: 160.995
Location of enginehouse: Wichita, Kan.
Locomotives: 11

No.	Builder	Model	New	Builder No.
3332	EMD	GP9	3/56	21343
3801	EMD	GP9	4/56	25416

No.	Builder	Model	New	Builder No.
4285	EMD	GP7	6/52	16885
4294	EMD	GP7	6/52	16844
4298	EMD	GP7	1951	14312
4436	EMD	GP9	8/54	19674
4542	EMD	GP9	3/57	22850
4544	EMD	GP9	3/57	22852
4557	EMD	GP9	3/57	22846
4912	EMD	GP9	1/57	22860
4916	EMD	GP9	1/57	22864

Freight cars: 29 covered hoppers

KENTUCKY & TENNESSEE RAILWAY

P. O. Box 368
Stearns, KY 42647

Reporting marks: KT
Phone: 606-376-5367

The Kentucky & Tennessee operates irregular freight service from a connection with Norfolk Southern at Stearns to Oz, Kentucky, 10.49 miles. Rail is 80 to 90 pound. Freight traffic includes coal, lumber, and heavy equipment, about 1,000 cars a year. Seasonal excursions are operated over the line by the Big South Fork Scenic Railway. The company was incorporated as the Kentucky & Tennessee Railroad in May 1902. It opened from Stearns to Rock Creek, 8 miles, in 1903. It was reorganized under its present name January 30, 1904. Regular passenger service was discontinued January 1, 1952. The company is owned by Railum, Inc. (D. King and W. Singleton).
Radio frequency: 160.800
Location of enginehouse: Hemlock, Ky.
Locomotives: 2

No.	Builder	Model	New	Builder No.
102	Alco	S-2	5/44	72051
105	Alco	S-2	1/49	76588

KEOKUK JUNCTION RAILWAY

117 South Water Street
Keokuk, IA 52632

Reporting marks: KJRY
Phone: 319-524-7313
Fax: 319-524-2410

Keokuk Junction operates 38 miles of track extending from Keokuk, Iowa, to a connection with the Santa Fe and Toledo, Peoria & Western at La Harpe, Illinois. A branch runs from Hamilton to Warsaw, Ill. Burlington Northern connects with the line at Keokuk, and connections are made with all roads entering Peoria via a car haulage agreement. Rail is 90 to 100 pound.

Annual traffic is about 4,000 cars a year of fertilizer, grain, corn products, railway car wheels, scrap iron, and coal.

The company started service as a terminal railroad operating over trackage built in 1857 as part of the Keokuk & Des Moines

Valley, the earliest railroad in Iowa. The K&DMV was leased and later purchased by the Rock Island.

In August 1981 Keokuk Junction Railway purchased 4.5 miles of line at Keokuk and started service on September 1, 1981. On December 24, 1986 the company purchased 33.5 miles of Santa Fe (ex-Toledo, Peoria & Western) trackage from Keokuk and Warsaw to La Harpe.

The company is controlled by KNRECO, Inc.

Radio frequencies: 160.395, 160.845

Locomotives: 5

No.	Builder	Model	New	Builder No.	Rebuilt
252	C&NW	HE-15	1979		
405	EMD	NW2	6/49	6651	
469	EMD	GP10	3/53	17728	1969
471	EMD	GP10	3/53	17730	1969
488	AT&SF	CF7	1974		

Freight cars: 68 covered hoppers, 10 insulated boxcars, 6 boxcars

KIAMICHI RAILROAD CO.

800 West Main Street
P. O. Box 786
Hugo, OK 74743

Reporting marks: KRR
Phone: 405-326-8306
Fax: 405-326-6606

The Kiamichi Railroad operates freight service from a connection with Union Pacific and Kansas City Southern at Hope, Arkansas, to Lakeside, Oklahoma, 186 miles, then by trackage rights 20 miles to a connection with Burlington Northern at Madill, Okla. A branch runs from Antlers, Okla., through Hugo to Paris, Texas, 45 miles, connecting there with the Texas Northeastern Division of the Mid-Michigan Railroad. Interchange is also made with Kansas City Southern at Ashdown, Ark., with Texas, Oklahoma & Eastern at Valliant, Okla., and with Santa Fe and Southern Pacific at Fort Worth (via Burlington Northern). Rail ranges from 90 to 132 pound. About 45,000 cars a year of coal, lumber, paper, chemicals, cement, pulpwood, feed, and food products make up Kiamichi's freight traffic. The Hugo Heritage Railroad runs seasonal excursions out of Hugo.

The lines are former Burlington Northern (ex-Frisco) routes. The Paris branch opened about 1887. Short line service started July 22, 1987. The company was controlled by Jack L. Hadley until October 1995 when he sold his interest to States Rail (Peter Kleifgen and others).

Radio frequencies: 160.920, 161.160, 160.425

Two Kiamichi GP9s bring a through freight into Hugo, Oklahoma. Photo by Jim Shaw.

Location of enginehouse: Hugo, Okla.
Locomotives: 20

No.	Builder	Model	New	Builder No.
702	EMD	GP7	10/52	17357
703	EMD	GP7	10/52	17354
704	EMD	GP7	9/52	17347
706	EMD	GP7	10/51	7897
901	EMD	GP9	6/57	23369
902	EMD	GP9	7/58	24052
903	EMD	GP9	8/55	20650
904	EMD	GP9	2/54	19870

No.	Builder	Model	New	Builder No.
905	EMD	GP9	2/51	12066
906, 907	EMD	GP9	5/59	25438, 25439
3801	EMD	GP35	2/65	29810
3802, 3803	EMD	GP35	1/64	28778, 28786
3805	EMD	GP35	9/64	29649
3806, 3807	EMD	GP38	8/69	35384, 35385
3808, 3809	EMD	GP38	9/69	35404, 35407
3810	EMD	GP38	9/69	35405

Freight cars: 120 covered hoppers, 70 boxcars, 40 wood racks, 98 pole cars

KISKI JUNCTION RAILROAD

700 Morovia Street, Room 30
New Castle, PA 16102

Reporting marks: KJR
Phone: 412-657-1268

Kiski Junction Railroad provides switching service on 5.5 miles of track from a connection with Conrail at Kiski Junction, Pennsylvania, to Schenley, near Pittsburgh. Traffic consists of steel products.

The company is owned by Berkman Rail Services, which acquired the former Pennsylvania Railroad track from Conrail and began service about July 1, 1995.

Locomotives: 1

No.	Builder	Model	New	Builder No.
7135	Alco	S-1	2/43	69860

KNOX & KANE RAILROAD CO.

P. O. Box 422
Marienville, PA 16239

Reporting marks: KKRR
Phone: 814-927-6621

The Knox & Kane provides freight service over 65 miles of line between Knox and Kane, Pennsylvania. It connects with the Allegheny & Eastern Railroad at Kane and with the Buffalo & Pittsburgh at Mount Jewett. Rail is 90 pound. Traffic is primarily forest products. Seasonal excursions are operated by the affiliated Knox, Kane & Kinzua Railroad, which operates beyond Kane to the Kinzua trestle.

The line was built as a narrow gauge railroad by the Pittsburgh,

Alco S-6 No. 44 heads up a work train on the Knox & Kane Railroad at Kane, Pennsylvania, in September 1993. Photo by Jim Shaw.

Bradford & Buffalo Railroad in the 1880s. It opened from Knox to Marienville in 1881 and was completed to Mount Jewett 2 years later. At that time it was taken over by the Pittsburg & Western Railroad, which was in turn acquired by the Baltimore & Ohio in 1902. It was relaid to standard gauge by 1911. Passenger service (in mixed trains) ended in 1932. B&O sold the line to the Knox & Kane in January 1982.

The company is controlled by Sloan Cornell and others.

Radio frequencies: 160.800, 161.235
Location of enginehouse: Marienville and Kane, Pa.
Locomotives: 4

No.	Builder	Model	New	Builder No.
1	Porter	50-ton	5/46	7798
38	Baldwin	2-8-0	4/27	59946
44	Alco	S-6	1/57	82295
58	Tang-Shan	2-8-2	1989	

KWT RAILWAY, INC.

908 Depot Street
Paris, TN 38242

Reporting marks: KWT
Phone: 901-642-7942
Fax: 901-642-8767

The KWT operates freight service from a connection with CSX at Bruceton, Tennessee, to a connection with Hardin Southern at Murray, Kentucky, 50 miles. A branch line runs from Paris to Henry, Tenn., 15 miles. Rail is 90, 100, 112, 115, and 132 pound. Traffic includes clay, grain, manufactured products, railway cars, and other commodities — 3,000 cars a year.

The Bruceton-Murray line was built by the Paducah, Tennessee & Alabama Railroad and opened in late 1892. Louisville & Nashville acquired it in 1895 and leased it to the Nashville, Chattanooga & St. Louis. The Paris-Henry branch is a short segment of L&N's Bowling Green-Memphis line.

KWT stands for "Kentucky West Tennessee." It acquired the lines from CSX and began service on February 28, 1987. KWT is affiliated with Rail Management & Consulting Corporation of Panama City, Florida.

Radio frequency: 161.145
Location of enginehouse: Paris, Tenn.
Locomotives: 4

KWT (Kentucky West Tennessee) Railway GP9 No. 302 passes the grain elevator at Puryear, Kentucky, with a short train. Photo by Jim Shaw.

No.	Builder	Model	New	Builder No.
300	EMD	GP7	8/50	11960
301	EMD	GP9	6/59	25313
302	EMD	GP9	7/57	22746
303	EMD	GP18	8/60	26012

Freight cars: 430

KYLE RAILROAD CO.

3rd and Railroad Avenue
P. O. Box 566
Phillipsburg, KS 67661

Reporting marks: KYLE
Phone: 913-543-6527
Fax: 913-543-6530

Kyle Railroad operates 777 miles of track in Colorado and Kansas. The company was set up by L. B. Foster and the track acquired by a local rail authority at a cost of $13 million. The company is controlled by Kyle Railways.

Kyle Railroad started operations in February 1982 over a former Rock Island line from Phillipsburg, Kansas, to Colby, 213 miles. The company currently operates 407 miles extending from Phillipsburg west to Limon, Colorado, and east to Clay Center and Mahaska, Kan. On June 2, 1991, Kyle leased 358 miles of Union Pacific trackage in northwestern Kansas.

Kyle connects with Santa Fe, Burlington Northern, and Union Pacific. Traffic is grain and agriculture-related — about 23,000 cars a year.

The ex-Rock Island lines are owned by a local port authority, and the operating company is a subsidiary of Kyle Railways, Inc.

Employees: 110
Radio frequencies: 160.275, 160.440, 161.325
Location of enginehouse: Phillipsburg, Kan.
Locomotives: 30

No.	Builder	Model	New	Builder No.
1101	EMD	SW8	3/53	18356
1102	EMD	SW8	7/53	18355
1103	EMD	SW8	7/53	18351
1757	EMD	GP9	5/54	19467

No.	Builder	Model	New	Builder No.
1827	EMD	GP28	3/64	28940
1828	EMD	GP28	3/64	28945
1829	EMD	GP28	11/64	29634
2036	EMD	GP20	4/62	27351
2040	EMD	GP20	4/62	26310
2200	EMD	GP30	2/63	28108
2202	EMD	GP30	2/63	28110
2210	EMD	GP30	3/63	28118
2238	EMD	GP30	5/63	28146
2500	EMD	GP35	11/63	28399
5321	GE	U30C	3/72	38351
5322	GE	U30C	3/72	38352
5331	GE	U30C	3/72	38361
5332	GE	U30C	3/72	38362
5794	GE	U30B	3/75	39904
5795	GE	U30B	3/75	40257
5796	GE	U30B	3/75	40258
5799	GE	U30B	3/75	40261
5808	GE	U30C	1973	39291
5810	GE	U30C	1973	39293
5819	GE	U30C	1973	39424
5820	GE	U30C	1973	39425
5821	GE	U30C	1973	39426
5918	GE	U30C	1973	39288
5925	GE	U30C	1973	39435
5928	GE	U30C	1973	39438

Freight cars: 439 covered hoppers

LAKE ERIE & NORTHERN RAILWAY CO.

Reporting marks: LEN

The Lake Erie & Northern was incorporated on May 19, 1911, and leased to the Canadian Pacific for 999 years on December 1, 1914. It is operated as part of the CP Rail.

LAKE STATES RAILWAY CO.

211 Newman Street
P. O. Box 232
Tawas City, MI 48763

Reporting marks: LSRC
Phone: 517-362-3465
Fax: 517-362-4677

Lake States operates freight service from Bay City, Michigan, to La Rocque, 153 miles, and from Pinconning to Gaylord, 103 miles, plus three branch lines:
• Alabaster Junction to Alabaster, 4 miles
• Alpena Junction to Paxton, 10 miles
• Posen to Rogers City, 15 miles
    Total mileage is 275 miles. Lake States connects with CSX and Central Michigan at Bay City. Traffic includes pulp, paper, and related products, lumber, and quarry products — 20,000 cars a year.
    The first rail service in the area was provided by the Tawas & Bay County Railroad, a lumber line incorporated during the late 1870s. The line was absorbed by the Detroit, Bay City & Alpena Railroad, which was chartered February 13, 1880, and had 67 miles of 38-inch gauge track in operation by 1885. On December 29, 1894, the Detroit & Mackinac Railway was incorporated to take over the property of the DBC&A. In 1893 D&M purchased the 29-mile Alpena & Northern Railroad, and in June 1912 it leased the AuSable & Northwestern Railway (and purchased it 2 years later). By 1915 the company was operating 404 miles of line, much of it logging track that has long since been abandoned.

In April 1976, the D&M purchased 72 miles of former Penn Central (New York Central) track extending from Mackinaw City to Sallings. In addition the Michigan Department of Transportation designated the company operator for the southern portion of Penn Central branch from Linwood to Sallings.
    Service to Mackinaw City ended in 1990. The Detroit & Mackinac Railroad was sold to Lake States Railway on February 17, 1992. The company is controlled by management.
Radio frequencies: 161.310, 163.310
Location of enginehouses: Tawas City, Alpena, Bay City, and Cheboygan, Mich.
Locomotives: 12

No.	Builder	Model	New	Builder No.	Rebuilt
468	Alco	RS-2	11/46	74986	
469	Alco	RS-2	11/46	74987	
646	Alco	S-1	6/46	74437	
974	Alco-MK	TE-56-4A	1974	80751	
975	Alco-MK	TE-56-4A	1975	80756	
976	Alco	C-420	2/64	84779	
977	Alco	RS-2	11/49	77571	
1280	Alco	C425M		3433-03	1980
181	Alco	C425M		3433-07	1981
281	Alco	C425M		3433-06	1981
381	Alco	C425M		3433-08	1981

Freight cars: 539 (reporting marks DM)

LAKE SUPERIOR & ISHPEMING RAILROAD CO.

105 East Washington Street
Marquette, MI 49855

Reporting marks: LSI
Phone: 906-228-7979
Fax: 906-228-7983

The Lake Superior & Ishpeming operates freight service from Marquette, Michigan, to Republic Mine, 44.4 miles, and from Eagle Mills to Tilden Mine, 9.2 miles. It connects with Chicago & North Western and Wisconsin Central at Eagle Mills. The predominant rail weight is 132 pounds. Nearly 138,000 cars a year of iron ore, lumber products, propane, and related commodities make up the road's traffic.

The Lake Superior & Ishpeming Railway was formed in 1892, and in 1895 and 1896 it built a line from Presque Isle to Ishpeming. The Munising Railway was organized in 1895 and by 1897 it was open from Little Lake to Munising. In 1900 the Marquette &

Southeastern built a line from Marquette to a connection with the Munising Railway near Lawson. Those two roads, the Munising Railway and the Marquette & Southeastern, merged in 1911 to form the Munising, Marquette & Southern Railway. That company merged with the Lake Superior & Ishpeming Railway in 1923 to form the Lake Superior & Ishpeming Railroad, the present company.

In 1952 the branch to Republic Mine was completed. The Big Bay branch was sold to Marquette & Huron Mountain Railroad in 1963, and most of the line east of Marquette was abandoned. The 5.5-mile Munising branch was sold to Wisconsin Central in 1990.

The company is 99 percent owned by Cleveland Cliffs Iron Co.

Radio frequencies: 160.230, 160.950, 161.490
Location of enginehouse: Eagle Mills, Mich.
Locomotives: 16

No.	Builder	Model	New	Builder No.
3000-11	GE	U30C	12/74	39718
3001	GE	U30C	12/74	39721
3002	GE	U30C	12/74	39725
3003	GE	U30C	12/74	39730
3004	GE	U30C	12/74	39715
3005	GE	U30C	12/74	39714
3006	GE	U30C	12/74	39720
3007	GE	U30C	12/74	39724
3008	GE	U30C	12/74	39729
3009	GE	U30C	12/74	39731
3010	GE	U30C	12/74	39733
3011	GE	U30C	12/74	39735
3050	GE	U30C	4/74	39719
3051	GE	U30C	4/74	39716
3052	GE	U30C	4/74	39728
3053	GE	U30C	4/74	39732

Freight cars: 1,495

A Lake Superior & Ishpeming ore train rumbles through Negaunee, Michigan, with GE U30C No. 3003 on the point. Photo by Jim Shaw.

LAKE TERMINAL RAILROAD CO.

1841 East 28th Street
Lorain, OH 44055

Reporting marks: LT
Phone: 216-277-7222
Fax: 216-277-2788

Lake Terminal provides switching service on 22.31 miles of track at Lorain and South Lorain, Ohio, connecting with CSX, Conrail, and Norfolk Southern. 25,000 cars are switched annually. The company was incorporated September 14, 1895, and is owned by Transtar Corporation.
Radio frequencies: 160.590, 161.040, 160.365, 160.755
Freight cars: 429 gondolas
Locomotives: 16 (plus 3 slugs)

No.	Builder	Model	New	Builder No.
821	EMD	SW8	2/51	13856
825	EMD	SW8	3/51	12996
1011	EMD	NW2	2/48	5265
1015	EMD	NW2	3/48	5269
1016, 1017	EMD	NW2	6/49	7397, 7398
1019, 1020	EMD	NW2	8/49	7400, 7401
1021	EMD	SW1001	9/68	34097
1022	EMD	SW1001	12/69	36161
1023	EMD	SW1001	3/75	74669-2
1201, 1202	EMD	SW9	5/51	14501, 14502
1203	EMD	SW9	4/52	11719
1204, 1205	EMD	SW1200	12/54	20089, 20094

LAMOILLE VALLEY RAILROAD CO.
TWIN STATE RAILROAD CO.

P. O. Box 1267
Trenton FL 32693

Reporting marks: LVRC, TSRD
Phone: 904-463-1103
Fax: 904-463-1104

The Lamoille Valley leases a line from a connection with the New England Central at Fonda Junction, Vermont, to a connection with CP Rail at St. Johnsbury, 96.1 miles. It also operates 27 miles of the former Maine Central Mountain Division from St. Johnsbury to a connection with the New Hampshire & Vermont at Whitefield, New Hampshire, as the Twin State Railroad. Rail is

A Lamoille Valley (Twin State Railroad) train arrives in Whitefield, New Hampshire, with four cars of paper loaded at the paper mill in Gilman, Vermont. Alco RS-3 No. 7803 has been retired, but two sister Alcos continue to operate on the line. Photo by Jim Shaw.

80 to 112 pound. Freight traffic (mostly on the Twin State Railroad) includes chemicals, woodpulp, and paper — about 600 cars a year.

The LVRC traces its history to the Portland & Ogdensburg Line — Vermont Division, formed in 1867 as a consolidation of the Essex County Railroad (incorporated 1864), the Montpelier & St. Johnsbury Railroad (incorporated 1866), and the Lamoille Valley Railroad (incorporated in 1867). The railroad opened from St. Johnsbury to Swanton on July 17, 1877, and failed three months later. The company was reorganized January 1, 1880, as the St. Johnsbury & Lake Champlain Railroad. The line was taken over in time by the Boston & Maine and continued under B&M control until January 24, 1949, when it was sold to the St. Johnsbury & Lamoille County Railroad.

The state of Vermont purchased the property of the company in 1973 following abandonment and leased it to several operators: in succession: Lamoille County Railroad (October 1973-April 1974), St. Johnsbury & Lamoille County Railroad (April 1974-October 1976) and Vermont Northern Railroad (October 1976-December 1977).

The Lamoille Valley took over operation January 1, 1978. The Twin State Railroad started operation in June 1984 and was the result of a settlement agreement between Guilford Transportation Industries and Lamoille Valley following the Maine Central and Boston & Maine control case. The Lamoille Valley took over operation of Central Vermont's Richford branch on March 7, 1988, and discontinued service on that line 14 months later.

The track and fixed assets of the Lamoille Valley are owned by the state of Vermont. The Twin State line is owned by the Maine Central Railroad and leased to the Twin State Railroad.

These companies came under control of CSF Acquisition Corporation (Clyde S. Forbes) on September 1, 1989.

Radio frequencies: 160.230, 161.340
Location of enginehouses: Morrisville and St. Johnsbury, Vt.; Whitefield, N. H.
Locomotives: 2

No.	Builder	Model	New	Builder No.
7801	Alco	RS-3	3/52	79665
7805	Alco	RS-3	8/55	81350

Freight cars: 995 boxcars (LVRC), 1,013 boxcars (TSRD)

LANCASTER & CHESTER RAILWAY CO.

512 South Main Street
P. O. Box 1450
Lancaster, SC 29720

Reporting marks: LC
Phone: 803-286-2100
Fax: 803-286-4158

The Lancaster & Chester operates freight service from Chester to Lancaster, South Carolina, 28.99 miles. It connects with CSX at East Chester and with Norfolk Southern at both ends of the line. Rail is 85 to 131 pound. Traffic consists of more than 7,000 cars

Lancaster & Chester SW900s No. 90 and 92 arrive in Fort Lawn, South Carolina, with the daily freight from Chester. Photo by Jim Shaw.

a year of textile products, coal, chemicals, fertilizer, aggregates, wood products, and fiberglass.

The Cheraw & Chester Railway was chartered February 27, 1873. The 3-foot gauge line was opened from Chester to Fishing Creek in 1877, to Catawba River in 1879, and to Lancaster in December 1894. The Lancaster & Chester Railway was incorporated June 20, 1896, to purchase the property.

The railroad is controlled by the Springs family interests.

Radio frequency: 161.130
Location of enginehouse: Lancaster, S. C.
Locomotives: 3

No.	Builder	Model	New	Builder No.
90	EMD	SW900	10/65	30759
91	EMD	SW900	10/65	30760
92	EMD	SW900	6/59	23454

Freight cars: 37 boxcars, 4 gondolas

LANCASTER NORTHERN RAILWAY CO.

P. O. Box 1271
Bristol, PA 19007

Reporting marks: LANO
Phone: 215-785-6193

The Lancaster Northern operates freight service from a connection with Conrail at Sinking Spring, Pennsylvania, to Ephrata, 12 miles. Rail is 100 and 130 pound. Traffic includes lumber, feed, frozen food, and propane. The company expects to handles about 700 cars a year.

The line was built by the Reading & Columbia Railroad, which was chartered in 1863. The Reading & Columbia was taken over by the Philadelphia & Reading and merged by the Reading Company in 1929. The line was included in Conrail when it was formed in 1976.

The Lancaster Northern acquired the property from Conrail on December 1, 1995. The company is controlled by John Nolan and is affiliated with the Bristol Industrial Terminal Railroad

Location of enginehouse: Denver, Pa.
Locomotives: 1

No.	Builder	Model	New	Builder No.
75	EMD	GP16	9/52	17393

LANDISVILLE RAILROAD, INC.

3900 Nolt Road
P. O. Box 338
Landisville, PA 17538

Reporting marks: AMHR
Phone: 717-898-2271

Landisville Railroad operates freight service on 3 miles of track between a Conrail connection at Landisville and Silver Springs, Pennsylvania. Rail is 80 pound. Traffic includes lumber and railroad cars coming in for repairs.

The line was built as part of the Reading & Columbia Railroad in 1864. It became part of the Reading, then Conrail, and was acquired in 1982 by Amherst Industries prior to its abandonment by Conrail. On January 1, 1985, the company was reorganized as the common-carrier Landisville Railroad. It is owned by Port Amherst Ltd. of Charleston, West Virginia.

Radio frequency: 160.485
Location of enginehouse: Amherst, Pa.
Locomotives: 2

No.	Builder	Model	New	Builder No.	Rebuilt
92	Plymouth	GM-25T	4/28	2861	
8651	EMD	SW900M	5/38	783	1955

LAURINBURG & SOUTHERN RAILROAD CO.

204 Railroad Street
P. O. Box 1929
Laurinburg, NC 28353

Reporting marks: LRS
Phone: 919-276-0786
Fax: 919-276-2853

The Laurinburg & Southern operates freight service from Johns, North Carolina, to Raeford, 27.93 miles, connecting with CSX at Dixie and the Aberdeen & Rockfish at Raeford. Rail is 85 to 90 pound. Traffic includes feed grain, fertilizer, soda ash, building materials, lime, coal, glass, and other commodities — more than 4,000 cars a year. The company is also in the industrial locomotive leasing business and it operates the Red Springs & Northern Railroad.

The Laurinburg & Southern was incorporated March 4, 1909, and opened July 2 of that year. It purchased the Wagram-Raeford branch of the Aberdeen & Rockfish Railroad in November 1921. Passenger service ended in 1946.

The company is controlled by the Evans family.

Radio frequencies: 160.605, 160.980
Location of enginehouse: Laurinburg, N. C
Locomotives: 42

No.	Builder	Model	New	Builder No.
101	GE	70-ton	9/47	29089
103	GE	70-ton	1/51	30837
104	GE	70-ton	9/50	30458
105	GE	70-ton	1/48	29466
107	GE	70-ton	3/49	30038
108	Plymouth	35-ton	12/52	5608
109	GE	70-ton	3/48	29298
110	GE	70-ton	6/48	30013
111	Alco	S-2	6/50	78014
112	Alco	S-4	8/52	80063

No.	Builder	Model	New	Builder No.
113	Alco	S-4	1/52	79518
114, 115	EMD	SW1	6/49	7503, 7505
116, 117	EMD	SW1	8/49	7510, 7512
118, 119	EMD	SW1	8/49	7515, 7511
121	EMD	SW1	3/40	1041
123, 124	EMD	NW2	4/49	7521, 7522
125, 126	EMD	NW2	4/49	7525, 7526
127	EMD	NW2	11/49	8539
128	EMD	NW2	2/49	6691
129	EMD	NW2	11/48	6272
130	EMD	NW2	9/49	10266
131	Alco	S-2	9/48	76169
132	Alco	S-2	7/46	74493
133	EMD	SW1	4/47	4804
134	EMD	SW1	8/46	3617
135	EMD	SW1	6/51	14561
136	EMD	SW1	1/42	1770
137	Alco	S-2	3/48	75662
138	EMD	SW9	11/51	14927
139	EMD	NW2	9/48	5762
140	EMD	SW1	2/52	16116
141	EMD	SW1	10/45	3225
142	EMD	SW1	3/51	14098
143	EMD	SW1	8/51	14559
144	Alco	(Cummins-powered)		
145	Alco	S-4	4/54	81094
146	Alco	S-2	8/43	70273
150	GE	25-ton	1943	17916
151	GE	25-ton	1943	18141

Freight cars: 204 boxcars, 42 covered hoppers, 24 gondolas

LEADVILLE-CLIMAX SHORTLINE RAILWAY CO.

326 East Seventh Street
P. O. Box 916
Leadville, CO 80461

Reporting marks: LCSR
Phone: 719-486-3936

This company owns a 13.74-mile line from a connection with the Denver & Rio Grande Western (Southern Pacific) at Leadville, Colorado, to Climax, at the top of the continental divide. Passenger excursions are operated by an affiliate, the Leadville, Colorado & Southern Railroad. Rail is 90 pound.

Traffic is primarily tourist excursions; however, the molybdenum mine at Climax was scheduled to reopen in 1995, meaning renewed freight traffic.

This line was built by the 3-foot gauge Denver, South Park & Pacific in 1884. It became part of the Colorado & Southern in 1908. In 1937 most of the line from Climax to Denver was abandoned. The orphaned segment between Climax and Leadville was relaid to standard gauge and operated by C&S, then Burlington Northern until 1988, when it was sold to the present operator. Excursions started May 28, 1988.

The company is controlled by Kenneth and Stephanie Olsen.
Enginehouse: Leadville, Colo.
Locomotives: 2

No.	Builder	Model	New	Builder No.
1714	EMD	GP9	8/55	20644
1918	EMD	GP9	8/57	22736

LEWIS & CLARK RAILWAY CO.

1000 East Main Street
P. O. Box 604
Battle Ground, WA 98604

Reporting marks: LINC
Phone: 360-687-2007
Fax: 360-687-4485

Lewis & Clark Railway operates freight and excursion service from a connection with Burlington Northern at Rye, Washington, to Chelatchie, 29.48 miles. About 350 cars are carried annually.

Most of this line was built by the Vancouver, Klickitat & Yakima Railroad starting in 1888. It became the Portland, Vancouver & Yakima Railroad in 1898 and was taken over by the Northern Pacific in 1903. NP sold the branch in 1960 to the Longview, Portland & Northern, which in turn sold the property to the

Lewis & Clark SW8 No. 82 is painted in a scheme reminiscent of the old Northern Pacific. Their train is shown near Brush Prairie, Washington, in June 1990. Photo by Jim Shaw.

Chelatchie Prairie Railroad in 1981. The ICC authorized the Chelatchie Prairie to abandon the line in January 1986; however, Clark County purchased the line in November and leased it to Lewis & Clark Railway on May 1, 1987.

The operating company is independent.

Location of enginehouse: Battle Ground, Wash.

Locomotives: 4

No.	Builder	Model	New	Builder No.
80	EMD	SW8	4/53	17160
81	EMD	SW8	1/54	19495
82	EMD	SW8	7/53	18350
83	EMD	SW8	7/53	18353

LITTLE KANAWHA RIVER RAILROAD

Route 4, Box 179-1A
Marietta, OH 45750

Reporting marks: LKRR
Phone: 614-373-2252
Fax: 614-373-6359

The Little Kanawha River Railroad provides switching service from a connection with CSX at Ohio River Junction, West Virginia, to an Ohio River port at South Parkersburg, 3.2 miles. Rail is 90 pound. About 2,000 cars of petroleum, coal products, coal, and aggregate are handled yearly. The former Baltimore & Ohio line was acquired from CSX and shortline service started September 12, 1989. The company is affiliated with Marietta Industrial Enterprises, Inc.

Equipment: 2

No.	Builder	Model	New	Builder No.
1205	EMD	SW1200	11/55	20670
2646	EMD	GP35	1/65	29901

LITTLE ROCK & WESTERN RAILWAY, LP.

Highway 10
P. O. Box 146
Perry, AR 72125

Reporting marks: LRWN
Phone: 501-662-4878
Fax: 501-662-4783

Little Rock & Western operates freight service from Danville, Arkansas, through Perry to Pulaski, 79 miles, thence over Union Pacific on trackage rights 3 miles to North Little Rock. Connections are with Union Pacific and St. Louis Southwestern at North Little Rock. Rail is 100 to 112 pound. Traffic includes wood and paper products, grain, salt, LP gas, and chemicals — about 6,500 cars a year.

This line was built by the Choctaw & Memphis Railroad, which was purchased by the Choctaw, Oklahoma & Gulf Railroad in June 1900. The Rock Island leased the line in March 1904 and it became part of the Memphis-Tucumcari main line. When Rock Island abandoned operations the line was acquired by the present owners.

Shortline service between Perry and Pulaski started in June 1980. In June 1986 Little Rock & Western was authorized to operate over 35 miles of track from Perry to Danville owned by Continental Grain Company. This railroad is run as a partnership controlled by Rail Management, the general partner.

Radio frequency: 160.965
Location of enginehouse: Perry, Ark.
Locomotives: 3

No.	Builder	Model	New	Builder No.
101	Alco	C-420	2/64	84729
102	Alco	C-420	8/66	3467-1
103	EMD	GP9	4/57	22788

Freight cars: 400 boxcars

LITTLE ROCK PORT RAILROAD

7500 Lindsey Road
Little Rock, AR 72206

Reporting marks: LRP
Phone: 501-490-1523
Fax: 501-490-1800

Little Rock Port Railroad operates 9.77 miles of track at Little Rock, Arkansas, connecting with St. Louis Southwestern and Union Pacific. Construction of the line started in 1967 and it was completed and opened on June 25, 1972. About 5,000 cars a year are handled. The company is owned by the Little Rock Port Authority.

Radio frequency: 453.750
Locomotives: 1 (leased from: Relco)

No.	Builder	Model	New	Builder No.
1017	Alco	S-2	12/47	75550

LIVE OAK, PERRY & GEORGIA RAILROAD CO.

The Live Oak, Perry & Georgia owns a line extending from connection with Norfolk Southern and Georgia & Florida at Adel, Georgia, to Foley, Florida, 80 miles. It also connects with CSX at Quitman and Perry, Ga., and CSX has trackage rights over LOP&G between those points.

Traffic includes wood chips, wood pulp, plywood, lumber, and aggregate. The railroad expects to handle about 6,000 cars a year.

The South Georgia Railroad built from Adel to Perry in the late 1890s. The Live Oak & Perry built from Perry to Foley in 1905 and 1906, and was reorganized as the Live Oak, Perry & Gulf. The two railroads came under the control of the Southern Railway in 1954 and were consolidated in 1972 as the Live Oak, Perry & South Georgia Railroad. Norfolk Southern sold the line on December 15, 1995.

The Live Oak, Perry & Georgia is a subsidiary of Gulf & Ohio Railways and is operated by the affiliated Georgia & Florida Railroad, which provides the locomotives.

Location of enginehouse: Perry, Ga.

LIVONIA, AVON & LAKEVILLE RAILROAD CORP.

3637 Rochester Road
P. O. Box 190-B
Lakeville, NY 14480

Reporting marks: LAL
Phone: 716-346-2090
Fax: 716-346-6454

The Livonia, Avon & Lakeville operates freight service from a connection with Conrail at Avon, New York, to Lakeville, 8.5 miles. Rail is 90 to 110 pound.

Traffic includes 2,000 cars a year of liquid and dry sweeteners, grain, fertilizer, and agricultural products.

The line was built about 1853 by the Buffalo, Corning & New York Railroad, which eventually became part of the Erie. The Livonia, Avon & Lakeville was incorporated May 7, 1964, to purchase an Erie Lackawanna branch slated for abandonment. It began operations in December 1964 and operated excursions from 1965

The Livonia, Avon & Lakeville's biggest engine is Alco C-425 No. 425, shown leaving the Conrail interchange in Avon, New York, with a trainload of sugar and sweeteners bound for Lakeville. Photo by Jim Shaw.

to 1977. A portion of the line from Conesus Lake Junction to Livonia was abandoned in 1981. The company is independent.
Radio frequency: 160.830
Location of enginehouse: Lakeville, N. Y.
Locomotives: 4

No.	Builder	Model	New	Builder No.
20	Alco	RS-1	7/49	76797
72	Alco	S-2	7/41	69535
420	Alco	C-420	6/64	3363-3
425	Alco	C-425	12/64	3398-8

LOGANSPORT & EEL RIVER SHORT LINE CO., INC.

P. O. Box 1005
Logansport, IN 46947

Reporting marks: LER
Phone: 219-753-2644

The Logansport & Eel River provides switching service over 2.2 miles of track connecting with Winamac Southern at Logansport, Indiana. Freight includes lumber, fertilizer, and coal — under 25 cars a year. Service started January 1990. Rail is 100 and 130 pound. The company is independent.
Locomotives: 1

No.	Builder	Model	New	Builder No.
101	GE	80-ton	11/45	28325

LONGVIEW, PORTLAND & NORTHERN RAILWAY CO.

77620 U. S. Highway 101
P. O. Box 22
Gardiner, OR 97441

Reporting marks: LPN
Phone: 503-271-3691
Fax: 503-271-3692

Longview, Portland & Northern Railroad operates freight service from a connection with the Southern Pacific at Gardiner Junction (Tideways), Oregon, to Gardiner, 3.6 miles. Rail is 90 to 133 pound. Traffic is paper, lumber, and forest products — about 3,000 cars a year.

The company was incorporated September 29, 1922, and at one time operated four disconnected lines. The Gardiner line, built in 1952, is the only line remaining under LP&N control. The company is owned by International Paper Company.
Radio frequency: 160.500

Location of enginehouse: Gardiner, Ore.
Locomotives: 2

No.	Builder	Model	New	Builder No.
111	Alco	S-2	8/49	76933
130	EMD	SW1500	12/69	35582

Freight cars: 164 60-foot boxcars, 98 bulkhead flatcars

LP&N Alco S-2 No. 111 pulls a train load of paper and lumber through Gardiner, Oregon. Photo by Jim Shaw.

LOS ANGELES JUNCTION RAILWAY CO.

433 Exchange Avenue
Los Angeles, CA 90058

Reporting marks: LAJ
Phone: 213-587-7961
Fax: 213-587-7923

This company is a terminal and switching line operating 64 miles of track in Los Angeles, connecting with Santa Fe, Southern Pacific, and Union Pacific. It switches about 16,000 cars annually.

The Los Angeles Junction Railway Co. was incorporated May 26, 1923, to lease and operate a private line built by the Central Manufacturing District, Inc. It is controlled by the Santa Fe.

Radio frequency: 161.130
Locomotives: 4

No.	Builder	Model	New
2563	AT&SF	CF7	7/73
2568	AT&SF	CF7	6/73
2571	AT&SF	CF7	5/73
2619	AT&SF	CF7	5/72

LOUISIANA & DELTA RAILROAD, INC.

402 West Washington Street
New Iberia, LA 70560

Reporting marks: LDRR
Phone: 318-364-9625
Fax: 318-364-1486

The Louisiana & Delta Railroad operates four disconnected lines in southern Louisiana, all former Southern Pacific branches:
• New Iberia to Kaplan and Salt Mine, 34.9 miles
• Baldwin to Weeks, 18.8 miles
• Schriever to Houma, 17 miles
• Bayou Sale to Cabot, 4.4 miles

Total mileage operated is 77. Louisiana & Delta connects with SP at New Iberia, Baldwin, Thibodaux Junction, and Bayou Sale. Traffic, which amounts to about 9,000 cars a year, includes carbon black, rice, sugar, salt, wholesale groceries, pipe, and offshore oil well drilling equipment.

The lines out of New Iberia were built by the Louisiana Western starting in 1880. The Houma line was built in part by Morgan's Louisiana & Texas Railroad. These companies all came under the wing of the Southern Pacific. SP sold the lines in March

1987, and the Louisana & Delta Railroad started service on March 16, 1987. The company is a subsidiary of Genesee & Wyoming Industries.
Radio frequency: 161.445
Location of enginehouse: New Iberia, La.

Locomotives: 8

No.	Builder	Model	New	Builder No.
1200	EMD	SW1200	2/64	28895
1500-1506	AT&SF	CF7		

Freight cars: 1 hopper car

LOUISIANA & NORTH WEST RAILROAD CO.

210 West Main Street
P. O. Box 89
Homer, LA 71040

Reporting marks: LNW
Phone: 318-927-2031
Fax: 318-927-2549

Louisiana & North West operates freight service from McNeil, Arkansas, to Gibsland, Louisiana, 61.5 miles. The track from McNeil to Magnolia, 6.5 miles, is leased from the St. Louis Southwestern. It connects with the St. Louis Southwestern at McNeil and the Kansas City Southern at Gibsland. Rail is 75 to 90 pound. Traffic includes lumber, pulp, paper, chemicals, and general commodities — about 5,000 cars a year.

The company was incorporated December 3, 1889, as successor to the Louisiana North & South Railroad. The line opened between Homer and Magnolia, Ark., in November 1898. The St. Louis Southwestern branch from McNeil to Magnolia had been leased several months earlier. By 1904 the line was open from Magnolia south to Natchitoches, La., 117 miles, and was projected to run to Fort Smith, Ark., 225 miles. The company failed in 1913 and operated in receivership until 1922 and again from 1935 to 1939, when the present corporation was formed. Passenger service was ended in 1948.

The company is controlled by Gerald Hausman.
Radio frequencies: 160.530 Road, 160.650 Yard
Location of enginehouse: Gibsland and Homer, La.; McNeil, Ark.
Locomotives: 7

No.	Builder	Model	New	Builder No.	Rebuilt
45	EMD	F7A	7/52	16561	
46	EMD	F7A	7/52	16559	
50	EMD	GP7	6/53	18570	
51	EMD	GP9	1/54	19116	
52	EMD	GP7	6/50	10140	
53	EMD	GP7	1/51	13187	1979
54	EMD	GP35	3/65	29741	

Freight cars: 47 plain and insulated boxcars

LOUISVILLE & INDIANA RAILROAD CO.

2500 Old Highway 31
East Jeffersonville, IN 47130

Reporting marks: LIRC
Phone: 812-288-0940
Fax: 812-288-4977

Louisville & Indiana provides freight service from Louisville, Kentucky, to Avon Yard in Indianapolis, Ind., 111.2 miles. In addition, the railroad operates a line from Jeffersonville, Ind., to the Clark Maritime Centre, 5 miles. It connects with Conrail, CSX,

Indiana Railroad, and Indiana Southern at Indianapolis and with CSX, Norfolk Southern, Paducah & Louisville, and CP Rail System (Soo Line) at Louisville. Additional connections are made with CSX at Jeffersonville and Seymour and with MG Rail at Watson. Rail is predominantly 130 pound.

Annual traffic is about 27,000 cars of grain, agricultural products, fertilizer, and general commodities.

This line was built in two segments. As early as 1835 the Madison & Lafayette Railroad proposed to build a line from from Columbus, Ind., to Indianapolis. In 1843 the project was reorganized as the Madison & Indianapolis Railroad and the road was completed into Indianapolis in 1847. The south end of the line, from Columbus to Louisville, was built by the Jeffersonville Railroad, which opened from Jeffersonville (across the Ohio River from Louisville) in 1852. The two railroads merged to form the Jeffersonville, Madison & Indianapolis Railroad on June 1, 1866. It came under the control of the Pennsylvania Railroad system in 1871 and the bridge into Louisville was completed the following year.

The line was included in Conrail, which sold it to the current owner. Shortline service started on March 12, 1994. The company is controlled by Anacostia & Pacific Co.

Radio frequencies: 161.070 (Louisville area), 160.860
Location of enginehouse: Jeffersonville, Ind.
Locomotives: 10

No.	Builder	Model	New	Builder No.	Rebuilt
1717	EMD	GP16	11/55	21519	1979
1722	EMD	GP16	11/55	21071	
1741	EMD	GP16	10/56	22641	1982
1743	EMD	GP16	11/55	21072	1982
1764	EMD	GP16	9/52	17381	1980
1780	EMD	GP16	12/51	14978	1980
1800	EMD	GP16	6/51	13895	
1840	EMD	GP16	2/51	13917	
1843	EMD	GP16	2/52	15539	
1843	EMD	GP16	6/51	13894	

LOUISVILLE, NEW ALBANY & CORYDON RAILROAD

Walnut and Water Streets
P. O. Box 10
Corydon, IN 47112

Reporting marks: LNAL
Phone: 812-738-3171
Fax: 812-738-3101

The Louisville, New Albany & Corydon operates freight service from a connection with Norfolk Southern at Corydon Junction to Corydon, Indiana, 7.7 miles. Rail is 70, 85, and 100 pound. The company also operates a common carrier truck line between Corydon and Louisville, Kentucky. Traffic is plastic, chemicals, and auto parts, about 4,000 cars a year. The affiliated Corydon Scenic Railroad operates seasonal excursions.

The company was incorporated April 28, 1888, as a reorganization of the Louisville, New Albany & Corydon Railway, which was chartered April 20, 1881, and opened December 1, 1883. Regular passenger service ended in 1948. The company is controlled by Richard Pearson and Charles Owen.

Radio frequency: 160.350
Location of enginehouse: Corydon, Ind.
Locomotives: 4

No.	Builder	Model	New	Builder No.	Rebuilt
1 (*Betty Sue*)	GE	45-ton	8/51	31008	
101	GE	45-ton	2/53	31715	
1000	Alco	S-4/CS9	9/55	81402	1981
1001	Alco	S-4/CS9	9/55	81404	1981

LOWVILLE & BEAVER RIVER RAILROAD CO.

5515 Shadyside Avenue
P. O. Box 261
Lowville, NY 13367

Reporting marks: LBR
Phone: 315-376-2021
Fax: 315-376-7796

The Lowville & Beaver River provides freight service from a connection with the Mohawk, Adirondack & Northern at Lowville to Croghan, New York, 10.44 miles. Rail is 60 to 80 pound. Under 500 cars a year of alum, latex, pulp, and grain make up the railroad's traffic.

The company was incorporated September 17, 1903, and the line opened January 15, 1906. Regular passenger service ended in January 1947. The railroad began operating excursion trains in 1992.

Genesee Valley Transportation Co., Inc., acquired the company in January 1991. It is operated in connection with the Mohawk, Adirondack & Northern.
Radio frequency: 161.460
Location of enginehouse: Lowville, N. Y.
Locomotives: 4

No.	Builder	Model	New	Builder No.
8*	Lima	2-truck Shay	5/18	2977
1947	GE	44-ton	4/47	28345
1950	GE	44-ton	6/50	30461
1951	GE	44-ton	12/50	30847

* Owned by the Railway Historical Society of Northern New York

Because of light rail and light traffic, GE 44-tonner No. 1950 continues to serve shippers on the Lowville & Beaver River. Photo by Jim Shaw.

LUZERNE & SUSQUEHANNA RAILWAY CO.

475 Slocum Road
Exeter, PA 18643

Reporting marks: LS
Phone: 717-693-7565
Fax: 717-693-7571

The Luzerne & Susquehanna Railroad operates 93 miles of main and switching track in and around Wilkes-Barre, Scranton, Avoca, Pittston, and Luzerne, Pennsylvania. It connects with Conrail at Pittston Junction and with CP Rail System (Delaware & Hudson) at Taylor. Traffic includes paper, coal, lumber, plastic, manufactured goods, and other commodities — about 1,500 cars a year.

The lines are former Lackawanna, Central of New Jersey, and Delaware & Hudson trackage. The Pocono Northeast Railway started service on them September 23, 1982, and abandoned operations in November 1983. The property was then operated by the Delaware-Lackawanna Railroad under an ICC emergency service order through August 26, 1994, when the current operator took over. The commonwealth of Pennsylvania plans to spend a substantial sum to upgrade and rehabilitate the line.

The operating company is controlled by Steven May.
Radio frequencies: 160.800, 160.965
Location of enginehouse: Exeter, Pa.
Locomotives: 1

No.	Builder	Model	New	Builder No.
1216	GMD	SW1200	1956	A-757

MADISON RAILROAD

511 State Street
P. O. Box 1102
Madison, IN 47250

Reporting marks: CMPA
Phone: 812-273-4248
Fax: 812-273-5750

The Madison Railroad operates freight service from a connection with CSX at North Vernon, Indiana, to Madison, 25.8 miles. Rail is 70 to 100 pound and the load limit is 230,000 pounds. Traffic consists of about 500 cars a year of coal, lumber, manufactured products, plastic, and general commodities.

This line was built in 1840. Its 6 percent grade from the Ohio River is the steepest on any main line (that is, not an industrial spur) in the United States. The Madison Railway Co., Inc., took over operation of this former Conrail (Pennsylvania Railroad) line as designated operator for the Indiana Department of Transportation on June 13, 1977. It discontinued service on September 15, 1978, and City of Madison Port Authority assumed operations.

The railroad is a division of the city of Madison Port Authority.
Radio frequency: 160.605
Location of enginehouse: North Vernon, Ind.
Locomotives: 2

No.	Builder	Model	New	Builder No.	Rebuilt
2013	EMD	SW8	5/51	15508	1955
3634	EMD	GP10	4/57	22975	1971

MAGMA ARIZONA RAILROAD CO.

P. O. Box M
San Manuel, AZ 85631

Reporting marks: MAA
Phone: 602-385-3456

Magma Arizona operates freight service from a connection with the Southern Pacific at Magma to Superior, Arizona, 28.11 miles. Rail is 70 pound. Traffic is perlite and ore concentrates — about 1,000 cars a year.

The company was incorporated October 13, 1914, and opened a narrow gauge line in 1915. It was converted to standard gauge in April 1923. Passenger service lasted until July 9, 1940. Magma Copper Company owns the company.
Radio frequencies: 452.900, 457.900
Location of enginehouse: Superior, Ariz.
Locomotives: 2

No.	Builder	Model	New	Builder No.
8	Alco	RS-3	8/51	78933
9	Alco	RS-3	8/51	78567

MAHONING VALLEY RAILWAY CO.

P. O. Box 589
Campbell, OH 44405

Reporting marks: MVRY
Phone: 216-742-5658
Fax: 216-742-5865

The Mahoning Valley is a switching line with 21.5 miles of track at Youngstown, Struthers, and Campbell, Ohio. It connects with Conrail and CSX and moves about 2,000 cars a year.

The company started operation over former industrial track in 1981. It is a subsidiary of LTV Steel Co., Inc.
Radio frequencies: 160.245, 160.965, 161.475
Locomotives: 2

No.	Builder	Model	New	Builder No.
466	EMD	SW1	8/49	7513
467	EMD	SW1	8/49	7514

MAINE COAST RAILROAD CORP.

P. O. Box 614
Wiscasset, ME 04578

Reporting marks: MC
Phone: 207-882-7499
Fax: 207-882-7699

Maine Coast Railroad provides freight service from a connection with ST Rail System (Maine Central) at Brunswick, Maine, to Rockland, 55 miles, and to Augusta, 38 miles. Rail runs from 90 to 110 pound. Traffic includes cement, coal, plastic, and perlite — under 500 cars a year. The company also operates excursion service between Wiscasset and Newcastle.

The Rockland line was built by the Knox & Lincoln Railroad in the late 1860s and early 1870s. It was leased by the Maine Central in 1891 and the company was absorbed into MEC ten years later. Maine Central quit operating the branch around 1985. It was acquired by the Maine Department of Transportation in 1990 and was leased to the Maine Coast Railroad, which began service

on October 26, 1990. MEC's Augusta line came under control of Maine Coast Railroad on December 30, 1992. Service on that line started in September 1995. The company is independent.
Location of enginehouse: Rockland, Maine
Locomotives: 4

No.	Builder	Model	New	Builder No.
367	Alco	RS-11	11/58	82958
958	Alco	S-1	10/49	77108
2002	MLW	M420R	2/74	M6075-2
2004	MLW	M420R	5/75	M6086-2

MANUFACTURERS' JUNCTION RAILWAY CO.

2335 South Cicero Avenue
Cicero, IL 60650

Reporting marks: MJ
Phone: 708-863-1717
Fax: 708-863-1719

The Manufacturers' Junction is a 1.78 route-mile (5.5 track miles) switching line at Cicero, Illinois. It connects with Burlington Northern, Belt Railway of Chicago, Baltimore & Ohio Chicago Terminal, Chicago Central & Pacific, Illinois Central, and Wisconsin Central. Rail is 90 pound. 2,000 cars a year are carried.

This company was incorporated January 28, 1903, and the railroad opened in 1906. It is controlled by OmniTRAX.
Radio frequency: 161.475
Locomotives: 2

No.	Builder	Model	New	Builder No.
6	EMD	SW1	1/47	4498
7	EMD	SW1	10/46	3896

Freight cars: 72 boxcars

MANUFACTURERS RAILWAY CO.

2850 South Broadway
St. Louis, MO 63118

Reporting marks: MRS
Phone: 314-577-1700
Fax: 314-577-1814

Manufacturers Railway operates a switching and terminal line with 42.2 miles of track, between St. Louis, Missouri, and East St. Louis, Illinois. It connects with Alton & Southern, Santa Fe, Burlington Northern, Chicago & North Western, Conrail, CSX, Gateway Eastern, Gateway Western, Illinois Central, Norfolk Southern, St. Louis Southwestern, Southern Pacific, Terminal Railroad Association of St. Louis, and Union Pacific. About 17,000 cars a year are carried. The railroad was incorporated in 1887 as

the Manufacturers Railroad. It is owned by Anheuser-Busch, Inc.
Radio frequencies: 160.365, 160.515, 160.740
Locomotives: 7

No.	Builder	Model	New	Builder No.
251	EMD	MP15	8/75	75611-1
252	EMD	MP15	8/75	75611-2
253	MK	TE-47-4E	1977	
254	EMD	MP15	1/83	826025-1
255	EMD	SW1500	11/67	33542
256	EMD	SW1500	10/68	34348
257	EMD	SW1500	1/70	35828

Freight cars: 25 covered hoppers, 168 refrigerator cars

MARYLAND & DELAWARE RAILROAD

106 Railroad Avenue
Federalsburg, MD 21632-1499

Reporting marks: MDDE
Phone: 410-754-5735
Fax: 410-754-9528

The Maryland & Delaware provides freight service over five separate routes:
• from Chestertown and Centreville, Maryland, to a connection with Conrail at Townsend, Delaware, 55 miles
• from Snow Hill, Md., to a Conrail connection at Frankford, Del., 26.5 miles
• from Cambridge and Preston, Md., to a Conrail connection at Seaford, Del., 33 miles
• from Lewes, Del., to a Conrail connection at Georgetown, 16 miles
• from Milton, Del., to a Conrail connection at Ellendale, 7 miles
  Rail ranges from 80 to 115 pound.
  Traffic includes fertilizer, feed and grain, food products, paper, paper products, lumber, chemicals, and plastic totalling about 4,500 cars a year.
  The company was incorporated August 1, 1977, and designated by Maryland and Delaware authorities to operate various former Penn Central branch lines (ex-Pennsylvania Railroad) not included in Conrail. Service started on August 11, 1977, on the Cambridge line, October 1, 1977, on the Centreville segment, and in May 1982 to Snow Hill.
  The Lewes and Milton lines were operated by the Delaware Coast Line until October 1, 1994, when Maryland & Delaware assumed the lease.
  The Snow Hill line is owned by on-line shippers, and the remainder of Maryland and Delaware's trackage is owned by the states. The operating company is controlled by Edward Banks, John Paredes, and Eric Callaway.
Radio frequency: 160.695
Location of enginehouse: Federalsburg, Md.
Locomotives: 5

No.	Builder	Model	New	Builder No.	Rebuilt
1201	Alco	RS-3M	3/52	79667	79
1202	Alco	RS-3M	8/50	78077	79
1203	Alco	RS-3M	3/52	79670	79
2628	AT&SF	CF7	1972		
2630	AT&SF	CF7	1972		

MARYLAND & PENNSYLVANIA RAILROAD CO.

96 South George Street, Suite 400
York, PA 17401

Reporting marks: MPA
Phone: 717-771-1700
Fax: 717-854-6275

The Ma & Pa operates freight service from a connection with Conrail and YorkRail at York, Pennsylvania, to East York (on Ma & Pa's original line) and from York to Hanover on a former Pennsylvania Railroad line, connecting with CSX at Hanover. A total of 26 miles is operated. Rail runs from 80 to 130 pound. Traffic includes about 6,000 cars a year of coal, woodpulp, steel, lumber, food products, and general commodities.
  The Peach Bottom Railway opened a 3-foot gauge line from York to Peach Bottom, 40 miles, in June 1874. It fell on hard times and a receiver was appointed in May 1881, and the company was sold to the York & Peach Bottom Railway. It was then reorganized again as the York Southern Railway and consolidated

with the Baltimore & Lehigh Railway on February 14, 1901, to form the Maryland & Pennsylvania Railroad, running from York to Baltimore, Maryland.

Passenger service was discontinued August 31, 1954, and the line was abandoned between Baltimore and Whiteford, Md., on June 11, 1958. The Whiteford-East York line was abandoned on July 10, 1985. On April 1, 1976, the company purchased a portion of Penn Central's Frederick branch from York to Hanover.

The company is owned by Emons Transportation Group, Inc.

Radio frequencies: 160.695 (yard), 160.335 (road)

Location of enginehouse: York, Pa.
Locomotives: 6 (pooled with Yorkrail)

No.	Builder	Model	New	Builder No.
82	EMD	SW9	11/51	15558
84	EMD	SW9	9/52	16330
1500	AT&SF	CF7	1984	
1502	AT&SF	CF7	1984	
1504	AT&SF	CF7	1984	
1506	EMD	GP7	5/53	18421

Freight cars: 1,480

MARYLAND MIDLAND RAILWAY

40 North Main Street
P. O. Box 1000
Union Bridge, MD 21791

Reporting marks: MMID
Phone: 410-775-7718
Fax: 410-775-2520

Maryland Midland operates freight service from a connection with CSX at Highfield, Maryland, to a second CSX connection at Emory Grove, 50 miles, and from Taneytown to Walkersville, 17 miles — 67 miles in all. Rail on the Highfield line is 115 pound and on Taneytown line it ranges from 85 to 130 pound. Traffic includes cement, coal, lumber, fertilizer, paper, grain, and aggregate — more than 6,000 cars a year.

The Highfield-Emory Grove line is the former main line of the Western Maryland Railway and was acquired in sections from Chessie System starting in October 1983.

The Taneytown line was built in 1872 by the Frederick &

Maryland Midland GP9 No. 200 rounds the bend at Thurmont, Maryland, with a string of cement cars. Photo by Jim Shaw.

Pennsylvania Railroad. In 1875 the company merged with the Hanover & York Railroad to form the York, Hanover & Frederick Railroad, a subsidiary of the Pennsylvania Railroad. This line was not included in Conrail but was operated by the Maryland & Pennsylvania from 1978 to 1980. On May 1, 1980, it was taken over by Maryland Midland.

The Maryland Midland is independent.

Radio frequencies: 160.545, 160.965

Location of enginehouse: Union Bridge, Md.

Locomotives: 6

No.	Builder	Model	New	Builder No.
200	EMD	GP9	5/57	23070
201	EMD	GP9	5/57	23071
202	EMD	GP9	5/57	23265
300	EMD	GP38	10/67	33349
301	EMD	GP38	12/67	33723
302	EMD	GP38	10/67	33314

Freight cars: 139 covered hoppers, 33 hopper cars, 3 gondolas

---

MASSACHUSETTS CENTRAL RAILROAD CORP.

1 Wilbraham Street
P. O. Box 958
Palmer, MA 01069-0958

Reporting marks: MCER
Phone: 413-283-2911
Fax: 413-283-2910

Massachusetts Central operates freight service from a connection with Conrail and the New England Central at Palmer, Massachusetts, to South Barre, 26 miles. A 3-mile branch runs from Forest Lake Junction to Bondsville. Rail is 105 pound. The railroad also operates excursion trains that run between Ware and Barre Plains.

Traffic includes coal, plastic, lumber, paper, and general commodities. MCER operates a United States Customs bonded container handling facility at Palmer and Ware, and container traffic represents the company's principal activity. About 6,000 cars a year are carried.

The Massachusetts Central started operations December 11, 1979, over a former Penn Central (New York Central) branch from Palmer to South Barre. This line was built by the Ware River Railroad in the early 1870s and opened in 1873 from Palmer to Winchendon, 49 miles. Regular passenger service ended in 1948. The rail line is owned by the commonwealth of Massachusetts and leased to Massachusetts Central.

The company is independent.

Radio frequency: 160.470

Location of enginehouse: Palmer, Mass.

Locomotives: 7

No.	Builder	Model	New	Builder No.
21	Alco	RS-1	12/54	80853
201	EMD	GP20M	1/54	18766
202	EMD	GP20M	11/54	20030
401	Whitcomb	44-ton	10/40	60034
1508	EMD	F9A	12/53	19046
2100	EMD	NW5	1/47	3615
2443	AT&SF	CF7	8/77	

MASSENA TERMINAL RAILROAD CO.

Depot Street
P. O. Box 347
Massena, NY 13662

Reporting marks: MSTR
Phone: 315-769-8608
Fax: 315-769-9697

Massena Terminal is a switching road operating 9 miles of track at Massena, New York, connecting with Conrail and Canadian National. Rail is 100 pound. About 3,000 cars of ore and metal products are carried annually.

The company was incorporated April 20, 1900, and has always been owned by the Aluminum Company of America.
Radio frequency: 160.500
Locomotives: 2

No.	Builder	Model	New	Builder No.
14, 15	EMD	MP15	11/74	74622-1, 74622-2

MP15 No. 14 pulls a cut of covered hoppers out of Massena, New York, in August 1993. Photo by Jim Shaw.

MCCLOUD RAILWAY CO.

801 Industrial Way
P. O. Box 1500
McCloud, CA 96057

Reporting marks: MCR
Phone: 916-964-2141
Fax: 916-964-2250

McCloud Railway operates freight service from Mount Shasta, California, to Burney, 77.7 miles. A branch extends from Bartle to Hambone, 19 miles. McCloud Railway connects with Southern Pacific at Mount Shasta and with Burlington Northern at Hambone. Rail is 75 to 90 pound. Traffic is outbound lumber, forest products, and diatomaceous earth (used in filtering) — about 3,000 cars a year.

The McCloud River Railroad was incorporated January 22, 1897, and opened from Mount Shasta to McCloud, 17.8 miles, in 1901. Regular passenger service ended in 1952. It was acquired

by Itel Corporation in 1977 and sold to 4-Rails, Inc. (Jeff and Verline Forbis) on July 1, 1992.
Radio frequencies: 160.025 (train), 160.680 (yard)
Location of enginehouse: McCloud, Calif.
Locomotives: 4

No.	Builder	Model	New	Builder No.
36-38	EMD	SD38	4/69	34880-34882
39	EMD	SD38-2	8/74	74623-1

Freight cars: 1,182

McCloud Railway inherited its SD38s from the McCloud River Railroad. No. 38 passes through Pondosa Junction in October 1993. Photo by Jim Shaw.

MCKEESPORT CONNECTING RAILROAD CO.

135 Jamison Lane
P. O. Box 68
Monroeville, PA 15146

Reporting marks: MKC
Phone: 412-829-3465

McKeesport Connecting is a switching line with 4.82 route miles (16.13 track miles) at McKeesport and Riverton, Pennsylvania. The company connects with Conrail, CSX, and the Union Railroad. Rail is 115 pound. About 4,000 cars a year are carried. The company was incorporated March 20, 1889, and is owned by Transtar, Inc.
Radio frequencies: 160.440, 160.605
Locomotives: leased from Union Railroad
Freight cars: 182 gondolas

MCLAUGHLIN LINE RAILROAD

c/o Metal Service Co., 210 First Street
Vandergrift, PA 15690-1100

Reporting marks: MCLR
Phone: 412-478-3777

McLaughlin Line Railroad provides switching service over 1.86 miles of former Conrail track at Apollo, Pennsylvania, connecting with Conrail. About 900 cars a year are carried. Metal Service Co. owns the company. Rail is 130 pound. Service started in 1985.
Locomotives: 3

No.	Builder	Model	New	Builder No.
4	GE	80-ton	2/58	33342
7	Porter	65-ton	3/44	7570
12	GE	80-ton	3/58	33344

MERIDIAN & BIGBEE RAILROAD CO.

119 22nd Avenue South
P. O. Box 551
Meridian, MS 39301

Reporting marks: MB
Phone: 601-693-4351
Fax: 601-693-6055

The Meridian & Bigbee Railroad operates freight service from Meridian, Mississippi, to Myrtlewood, Alabama, 51 miles. It connects with Kansas City Southern and Norfolk Southern at Meridian, and with Burlington Northern and CSX at Myrtlewood. Rail is 110 to 115 pound.

Annual traffic includes about 25,000 cars a year of pulp, chemicals, paper products, and general commodities.

The Meridian & Bigbee River Railway was incorporated January 24, 1917. Operations started between Meridian and Cromwell on April 16, 1928, and the road was completed on October 15, 1935. In the meantime, a trustee had been appointed in July 1933, and it was not until 1942 that the company was reorganized under its current name.

The company is owned by James River Corporation.

Radio frequency: 160.350
Location of enginehouse: Meridian, Miss.
Locomotives: 5

No.	Builder	Model	New	Builder No.
101	EMD	GP7	8/52	17428
103	EMD	GP7	3/51	14009
104	EMD	GP9	9/57	23600
105	EMD	GP7	8/51	14740
106	AT&SF	CF7	8/77	

Freight cars: 621 boxcars, 95 hopper cars

GP7 No. 103 heads up the daily freight on the Meridian & Bigbee at Pennington, Alabama. Photo by Jim Shaw.

193

MG RAIL, INC.

5130 Port Road
Jeffersonville, IN 47130-8402

Reporting marks: MGRI
Phone: 812-283-9500
Fax: 812-282-5685

MG Rail is a terminal railroad from a connection with CSX and the Louisville & Indiana Railroad at Watson, Indiana, to Jeffersonville (Clark Maritime Center), 7.74 miles.

Traffic includes agricultural products and steel, about 4,000 cars a year.

This is a relatively new line. The track is owned by the Indiana Port Commission, and the operating company by Consolidated Grain & Barge Company.

Locomotives: 2

No.	Builder	Model	New	Builder No.
1221	EMD	SW9	7/55	20658
6140	EMD	GP9	12/56	22049

MICHIGAN SHORE RAILROAD

434 East Grove Street
Greenville, MI 48838

Reporting marks: MS
Phone: 616-754-0434
Fax: 616-754-4444

Michigan Shore Railroad operates a 6-mile switching line at Muskegon, Michigan, connecting with CSX. Rail is 100 pound.

Traffic, 3,000 cars a year, is primarily sand and chemicals.

The line was acquired from the Central Michigan, and includes segments of former Pennsylvania Railroad and Grand Trunk

Western trackage acquired by CM in 1987. Michigan Shore Railroad service started December 14, 1990. Two miles of line were abandoned in April 1992. The company is managed by Mid-Michigan Railroad and is controlled by RailTex, Inc.

Radio frequency: 161.235

Locomotives: 2

No.	Builder	Model	New	Builder No.
73	EMD	SW1200	6/64	29242
1077	Alco	RS-3	9/55	81353

MICHIGAN SOUTHERN RAILROAD CO., INC.

69239 South Kalamazoo Street
P. O. Box 239
White Pigeon, MI 49099

Reporting marks: MSO
Phone: 616-483-9968
Fax: 616-483-9611

Michigan Southern operates freight service from a connection with Conrail at White Pigeon, Michigan, to Coldwater, 42.9 miles.

A track connection with Indiana Northeastern at Coldwater is not currently being used. Rail is 105 pound. Traffic includes fertilizer, plastic, wood, aggregate, and tallow — under 1,000 cars a year. The Little River Railroad runs tourist trains over this line.

The railroad is owned by the Branch & St. Joseph County Rail Users Association, Inc., and was formerly operated by the

Kalamazoo, Lake Shore & Chicago Railway. Michigan Southern started operations on April 9, 1991. The company is controlled by Gordon Morris.

Radio frequency: 160.755
Location of enginehouse: Sturgis, Mich.
Locomotives: 2

No.	Builder	Model	New	Builder No.
66	Alco	S-2	5/54	78725
78	Alco	S-2	6/45	73375

Michigan Southern Alco S-2 No. 66 sits in front of the old depot at Sturgis, Michigan. Photo by Douglas N. Leffler.

MID-MICHIGAN RAILROAD CO.

432 East Grove Street
Greenville, MI 48838

Reporting marks: MMRR
Phone: 616-754-0001
Fax: 616-754-4444

Mid-Michigan operates two separate lines in Michigan. One runs from a CSX connection at Elmdale to Greenville, 32 miles. It connects with Grand Rapids Eastern at Lowell.

The other line extends from a CSX connection at Saginaw (Paines) to a Tuscola & Saginaw Bay connection at Alma and on to Elwell, 35 miles. Rail ranges from 90 to 132 pound. Traffic includes about 8,000 cars a year of grain, fertilizer, appliances, auto parts, and food products.

The Greenville line was built by the Lowell & Hastings Railroad between 1889 and 1893. In 1893 the company became the Central Michigan, and in 1899 it became part of the Pere Marquette.

The Alma line was part of the Saginaw Valley & St. Louis Railroad, which was chartered in 1872. That line was acquired by the Detroit, Lansing & Northern in 1896; it in turn became part of the Detroit, Grand Rapids & Western in 1897. By 1900 the Pere Marquette had gained control of it.

CSX sold the two lines to Mid-Michigan in December 1987, and shortline service started on December 19, 1987.

The company is a subsidiary of RailTex.

Radio frequencies: 161.235, 161.145
Location of enginehouse: Greenville and Alma, Mich.
Locomotives: 2

No.	Builder	Model	New	Builder No.	Rebuilt
24	EMD	GP9	6/58	24508	
5967	EMD	GP9	9/55	20876	

Freight cars: 318 covered hoppers, 65 boxcars

MIDDLETOWN & HUMMELSTOWN RAILROAD CO.

136 Brown Street
Middletown, PA 17057

Reporting marks: MIDH
Phone: 717-944-4435
Fax: 717-944-7758

The Middletown & Hummelstown couples onto its Conrail interchange alongside the former Pennsylvania Railroad main line at Middletown, Pennsylvania. Photo by Edward Lewis.

The Middletown & Hummelstown operates from Middletown to Hummelstown, Pennsylvania, 7 miles, and connects with Conrail at both ends. Rail is 80 to 90 pound. Freight traffic includes about 350 cars a year of chemicals, food products, and scrap. Most of the road's revenue comes from seasonal excursions.

The line was built by the Middletown & Hummelstown Railroad in 1890. That company was absorbed by the Philadelphia & Reading. Reading suspended service in June 1972 because of flood damage. Pennsylvania Department of Transportation owns 4.5 miles of the line.

The company is a reorganization of the Mason City & Clear Lake Railroad, an Iowa interurban line that sold its assets to the Iowa Terminal Co. in 1961. The present name was adopted in 1975 when application was made to the ICC to purchase and run Reading's Middletown branch. The Middletown & Hummelstown began some service on May 3, 1976. It also operated an ex-Conrail (Reading) line at Columbia from 1982 until 1991 when service was discontinued.

The company is controlled by Wendell Dillinger.

Radio frequency: 161.505
Location of enginehouse: Middletown, Pa.
Locomotives: 4

No.	Builder	Model	New	Builder No.
1	GE	65-ton	8/41	13154
2	GE	65-ton	4/55	32228
3	GE	65-ton electric	8/48	29312
91	CLC	2-6-0	4/10	926

MIDDLETOWN & NEW JERSEY RAILWAY CO., INC.

140 East Main Street
Middletown, NY 10940

Reporting marks: MNJ
Phone: 914-343-3435

The Middletown & New Jersey operates limited freight service from a connection with Conrail north of Middletown, New York, to Agway Station. The railroad continues to Slate Hill, with irregular operation, and owns a rail line on to Unionville and M&U Railroad Junction, 14.1 miles. This latter section of track has not been operated since December 1968. Rail is 70 to 80 pound.

Traffic is under 500 cars a year of fertilizer, plastic products, and chemicals.

The Middletown, Unionville & Water Gap Railroad was incorporated May 25, 1866, and opened as a 6-foot gauge line from Middletown to Unionville on May 4, 1868. The line was leased, and operated by the Erie until 1872, when it was leased by the New York & Oswego Midland and relaid to standard gauge. Following reorganization of the Oswego Midland as the New York, Ontario & Western in 1880, the lease was turned over to the New Jersey Midland, which later became the New York, Susquehanna & Western. Susquehanna operated the line until 1913, when it was turned back to its owners.

The company was reorganized as the Middletown & Unionville Railroad on November 14, 1913, and operated independently for the first time. Passenger service was discontinued in 1944. The railroad was sold at foreclosure in 1947 to the Middletown & New Jersey Railway, which was incorporated June 27, 1947. The company is controlled by P. T. Rasmussen.

Enginehouse: Middletown, N. Y.
Locomotives: 3

No.	Builder	Model	New	Builder No.
1	GE	44-ton	4/46	28487
2	GE	44-ton	2/47	28342
11	Alco-Cooke	2-6-0	12/20	62635

MIDLAND TERMINAL CO.

1200 Midland Avenue
Midland, PA 15059

Reporting marks: MDLR
Phone: 412-773-2786
Fax: 412-773-2792

Midland Terminal is a switching line with 11.8 miles of track at Midland, Pennsylvania, connecting with Conrail. Rail is 115 pound. The company handles about 9,000 cars a year.

Midland Terminal started common carrier operations in July 1983 over former LTV Steel Co. industrial trackage. The company is owned by LTV Steel Co.

Radio frequencies: 160.245, 161.220, 161.475
Locomotives: 4

No.	Builder	Model	New	Builder No.
431	EMD	NW2	6/41	1357
432	EMD	NW2	7/46	3431
1200	EMD	SW9	12/53	19074
1215	EMD	SW9	12/53	19089

Freight cars: 18 flatcars

MIDWEST COAL HANDLING CO., INC.

1320 Island Ford Road
Madisonville, KY 42431

Reporting marks: MWCL
Phone: 502-825-0621
Fax: 502-825-0672

Midwest Coal Handling Company provides freight service to the Tennessee Valley Authority from Drakesboro, Kentucky, and via CSX trackage rights to Central City, connecting with CSX at Paradise Junction and with Paducah & Louisville at Central City. Rail is 112 pound. Annual traffic is 34,000 cars a year of coal and limestone rock. Service started in December 1985 for coal, and in mid-May 1989 for limestone. The company is independent.

Radio frequency: 161.295
Location of enginehouse: Drakesboro, Ky.
Locomotives: 5

No.	Builder	Model	New	Builder No.	Rebuilt
2005	EMD	GP7U	5/51	13198	1974
2495	AT&SF	CF7	10/74		
2508	AT&SF	CF7	8/74		
2525	AT&SF	CF7	4/74		
2627	AT&SF	CF7	3/72		

MILFORD-BENNINGTON RAILROAD CO.

62 Elm Street
Milford, NH 03055

Reporting marks: MBRX
Phone: 603-673-7181

The Milford-Bennington Railroad provides freight service over a line from Bennington, New Hampshire, to Wilton, 18.6 miles, and thence by trackage rights over the ST Rail System (Boston & Maine) another 5.4 miles to Milford. Rail is 85 pound. Traffic is primarily aggregate — about 3,200 cars a year.

The line is a Boston & Maine branch that was acquired by the state of New Hampshire following its abandonment in March 1989. The company was formed in 1987 to lease the line from the state; however, protracted negotiations with Guilford Transportation over the trackage rights delayed the opening of the railroad until July 16, 1992. The company is owned by Peter Leishman.

Enginehouse: Wilton, N. H.
Locomotives: 2

No.	Builder	Model	New	Builder No.
901	GMD	SW900	3/58	A-1381
1423	EMD	SW9	5/53	18182

MINNESOTA CENTRAL RAILROAD CO.

1318 South Johanson Road
Peoria, IL 61607

Reporting marks: MCTA
Phone: 309-697-1400

Minnesota Central Railroad extends from a Burlington Northern connection at Hanley Falls, Minnesota, to Norwood, 94.3 miles, thence by trackage rights 42 miles over Chicago & North Western to Bass Lake Yard in Minneapolis, where it connects with Chicago & North Western and CP Rail System (Soo Line). Total mileage is 136.5. Rail is 80 to 100 pound. About 5,000 cars a year of grain, lumber, canned goods, foodstuffs, minerals, fertilizer, and ethanol make up the railroad's traffic. This line was part of the Pacific Division of the Minneapolis & St. Louis Railroad, opened in November 1882. Passenger service ended in 1960, the same year Chicago & North Western purchased the railroad assets of the M&StL. C&NW operated the branch until December 1983.

The Minnesota Valley Regional Rail Authority purchased the property in 1984, and the MNVA Railroad started service in March 1984. MNVA ceased operations on December 13, 1994, and sold its assets to MCTA.

The Minnesota Central is a subsidiary of Pioneer RailCorp.

Radio frequencies: 160.305, 161.265

Location of enginehouse: Morton, Minn.

Locomotives: 7

No.	Builder	Model	New	Builder No.	Rebuilt
291	EMD	GP9	4/59	25286	
298	EMD	GP9	5/59	25293	
315	EMD	GP9	6/59	25310	
322	EMD	SD35	7/65	30448	
426	EMD	NW2	6/49	6876	
904	EMD	SD24	3/63	28170	
1850	EMD	GP16	8/52	17242	1980

Freight cars: 200 covered hoppers, 35 insulated boxcars

MINNESOTA COMMERCIAL RAILWAY CO.

508 Cleveland Avenue, North
St. Paul, MN 55114

Reporting marks: MNNR
Phone: 612-646-2010
Fax: 612-646-8549

The Minnesota Commercial Railway is a switching road in Minneapolis and St. Paul, Minnesota, operating 130 miles of track. The company connects with Burlington Northern, Chicago & North Western, CP Rail System (Soo Line), Twin Cities & Western, and Wisconsin Central. Rail is 90 to 115 pound. The line handles about 40,000 cars a year.

The Minnesota Transfer Railway was incorporated March 10, 1883, under the ownership of the railroads serving the Twin Cities to transfer freight between those railroads. Ownership by the mainline roads continued until February 1, 1987, when it was acquired by the Minnesota Commercial Railway, which is controlled by John Gohmann, and others.

Radio frequencies: 160.560, 160.740

Locomotives: 17

No.	Builder	Model	New	Builder No.	Rebuilt
62	Alco	C424M	5/63	84548	1980
63	Alco	C424M	5/63	84551	1980
66	EMD	GP7	11/50	9939	
100	EMD	NW2	8/52	9947	
110	EMD	SW1200	3/56	21059	
200	EMD	SW1200	11/54	20068	
302	EMD	SW1500	3/68	33898	
306	EMD	SW1500	5/70	36486	
307	Alco	RS-20	6/55	81286	
311	Alco	C424M	9/63	84559	
313	Alco	C424M	1/65	3382-04	
314	Alco	C424M	1/65	3382-08	
316	Alco	RS-27	11/60	83604	
318	Alco	RS-27	11/60	83602	
400	EMD	GP7	8/52	9947	
401	EMD	GP7	8/52	9945	
484	AT&SF	CF7	1/75		

Freight cars: 15 boxcars

MINNESOTA, DAKOTA & WESTERN RAILWAY CO.

101 Second Street
P. O. Box 19
International Falls, MN 56649

Reporting marks: MDW
Phone: 218-285-5290
Fax: 218-283-3000

Minnesota, Dakota & Western operates a 4-mile freight line from International Falls, Minnesota, where it connects with Burlington Northern, to Rainer. Rail is 100 pound. Traffic includes paper products, woodpulp, pulpwood, and chemicals — 7,000 cars a year. The company also operates an intermodal facility.

The International Bridge & Terminal Co. was incorporated October 31, 1902. On January 12, 1912, the company acquired a rail line already under construction, and adopted the present name. At that time, the company intended to build a line from International Falls to Montana. The only extension opened was a 14-mile line from Nakoda Junction to Loman, which has since been abandoned. The company was acquired by Boise Cascade Corporation in 1965.

Radio frequencies: 160.410, 160.530, 160.680
Location of enginehouse: International Falls, Minn.
Locomotives: 5

No.	Builder	Model	New	Builder No.
16	Alco	S-2	9/48	76176
17	Alco	S-2	11/49	77822
18	Alco	S-2	7/47	75360
19	Alco	S-2	3/45	72906
20	Alco	S-2	11/51	79333

Freight cars: 1,312 boxcars, 99 flatcars

Minnesota, Dakota & Western S-2 No. 17 warms up in front of the road's enginehouse at International Falls, Minnesota. The line's ownership is evident. Photo by Roger W. Bee.

MISSISSIPPI & SKUNA VALLEY RAILROAD CO.

Railroad Avenue
P. O. Box 265
Bruce, MS 38915

Reporting marks: MSV
Phone: 601-983-3310
Fax: 601-983-3318

The Mississippi & Skuna Valley operates freight service from a connection with Waterloo Railroad (Illinois Central) at Bruce Junction to Bruce, Mississippi, 21 miles. Rail is 85 to 90 pound. Traffic is primarily lumber, under 500 cars a year.

The railroad was incorporated June 1, 1925, and opened in September 1926. The Weyerhaeuser Company acquired full ownership in March 1973.
Radio frequency: 160.845
Location of enginehouse: Bruce, Miss.

Locomotives: 2

No.	Builder	Model	New	Builder No.
D-4	EMD	SW9	9/52	16331
D-5	AT&SF	CF7	9/71	

Freight cars: 33 flatcars, 40 wood-chip hopper cars

MISSISSIPPI CENTRAL RAILROAD CO.

1318 South Johanson Road
Peoria, IL 61607

Reporting marks: MSCI
Phone: 309-697-1400

Mississippi Central operates freight service from a connection with Norfolk Southern at Grand Junction, Tennessee, through Holly Springs, where it interchanges with Burlington Northern, to Oxford, Mississippi, 56.5 miles. Rail is 85 to 90 pound. Traffic includes about 2,000 cars a year of pulpwood, particleboard, resin, fertilizer, steel, cotton, and cotton seed.

The line was built by the old Mississippi Central Railway, which was chartered in 1852 and eventually became part of Illinois Central's Chicago-New Orleans main line.

The line was sold to a local rail authority as part of ICG divestiture program, and on March 1, 1982, it was sold to a Kyle Railways subsidiary, the Natchez Trace Railroad, under a 20 year lease-purchase agreement. Kyle sold its interest in Natchez Trace early in 1992 to Pioneer Railcorp., which changed the name of the railroad to Mississippi Central on January 12, 1993. Mississippi Central has since acquired full ownership of the line.
Radio frequencies: 160.635, 161.220
Location of enginehouse: Holly Springs, Miss.
Locomotives: 4

No.	Builder	Model	New	Builder No.
700, 701	EMD	GP7	4/53	17976, 17978
909, 910	EMD	GP9	10/57	24080, 24079

Freight cars: 90 boxcars, 20 pulpwood cars, 6 gondolas

MISSISSIPPI DELTA RAILROAD

421 Fourth Street
P. O. Box 1446
Clarksdale, MS 38614

Reporting marks: MSDR
Phone: 601-624-4051
Fax: 601-624-8913

Mississippi Delta interchanges with the Illinois Central at Swan Lake, Mississippi, providing service for the Illinois Central to Lyon (north of Clarksdale), and for its own account to Lula, 18 miles, and from there to Jonestown, 10 miles. Rail is 90 pound on the Swan Lake end, and 110 to 115 pound beyond Clarksdale.

Traffic includes soybeans, soy meal, and soy oil, and cottonseed meal, oil, and hulls, as well as lint, carbon black, and rubber. Traffic amounts to 4,000 cars a year.

The main part of Mississippi Delta's line from Clarksdale to Lula was built as part of the Louisville, New Orleans & Texas

Railroad main line, opened from Memphis to New Orleans in August 1884. The line was under the control of the Yazoo & Mississippi Valley by the end of 1885. Illinois Central acquired control of the Y&MV in 1892. The present operator started service December 31, 1985, and operates the Delta Oil Mills private railroad from Lula to Jonestown. This company is controlled by Gulf & Ohio Railways (Pete Claussen).

Radio frequency: 160.500
Location of enginehouse: Clarksdale, Miss.
Locomotives: 2

No.	Builder	Model	New	Builder No.
7738	EMD	GP8	10/51	13318
8047	EMD	GP10	5/54	19382

Freight cars: 3,124

MISSISSIPPI EXPORT RAILROAD CO.

4519 McInnis Avenue
P. O. Box 8743
Moss Point, MS 39563

Reporting marks: MSE
Phone: 601-475-3322
Fax: 601-475-3337

Mississippi Export operates freight service from a connection with Illinois Central at Evanston, Mississippi, to a connection with CSX at Pascagoula, 41.94 miles. Rail is 90 to 115 pound. Traffic includes coal, chemicals, lumber, paper products, and grain for export — about 18,000 cars a year.

This company was incorporated November 8, 1922, to acquire and operate a portion of the Alabama & Mississippi Railroad. The company is controlled by International Paper Co.

Radio frequencies: 160.500, 161.220, 161.400
Location of enginehouse: Moss Point, Miss.
Locomotives: 5

No.	Builder	Model	New	Builder No.	Rebuilt
60	EMD	GP9	10/57	23985	
64	EMD	SW1500	8/73	73604	
65	EMD	GP38-2	9/75	75645-1	
66	EMD	GP38-2	4/79	786213	
95	EMD	GP40	12/66	32364	1995

Freight cars: 526 boxcars

Mississippi Export GP38-2 No. 65 hauls the daily freight through the delta country near Hurley, Mississippi. Photo by Jim Shaw.

MISSISSIPPIAN RAILWAY CO-OPERATIVE, INC.

Highway 35 South
P. O. Box 476
Fulton, MS 38843

Reporting marks: MSRW
Phone: 601-862-2171
Fax: 601-862-4188

The Mississippian Railway operates freight service from a connection with the Burlington Northern at Amory, Mississippi, to Fulton, 24 miles. Rail is 60 to 90 pound. About 800 cars a year of lumber, wood chips, copper cathodes, and general commodities make up the railroad's traffic.

The Mississippian Railway was incorporated July 30, 1923, and the line was built during 1924. The present operator was formed by the Itawamba County Development Council in October 1986. Regular passenger service was never operated.

Radio frequency: 160.770
Location of enginehouse: Amory, Miss.
Locomotives: 1

No.	Builder	Model	New	Builder No.
261	EMD	SW9	1/52	15595

Freight cars: 480 boxcars, 218 gondolas

MISSOURI & NORTHERN ARKANSAS RAILROAD CO, INC.

514 North Orner Street
P. O. Box 776
Carthage, MO 64836

Reporting marks: MNA
Phone: 417-358-8800
Fax: 417-358-6005

Missouri & Northern Arkansas operates a former Missouri Pacific line from Pleasant Hill, Missouri, to Diaz Junction, Arkansas, plus branch lines:
• Fort Scott, Kansas, through Nevada, Mo., to Clinton, 78.3 miles
• Aurora, Mo., via Burlington Northern to Springfield, 31 miles
• Joplin, Mo., to Carthage, 16.7 miles

In addition the M&NA has trackage rights over Union Pacific from Pleasant Hill to Kansas City, 32 miles. The company operates a total of 560 miles. Most of the main line is 112 to 115 pound welded rail.

M&NA connects with Union Pacific at Pleasant Hill and Diaz Junction, with Kansas City Southern at Joplin, Mo., and with Burlington Northern at Springfield, Lamar, Carthage, Joplin, and Aurora, Mo.

Traffic includes coal, grain, frozen foods, minerals, steel, chemicals, and forest products — about 43,000 cars a year. An intermodal terminal is under construction in Carthage, Mo. It will be able to handle 25,000 trailers and containers a year when fully operational.

Since 1993, the Branson Scenic Railway has run *Ozark Zephyr* excursions out of Branson, Mo. The White River Railway plans to begin excursion service between Flippin and Calico Rock, Ark., in 1995.

The St. Louis, Iron Mountain & Southern opened a branch from Diaz Junction to Batesville, Ark., in 1883. The White River Railway began construction from Batesville to Carthage in 1902. It was not until 1905 that the line was completed. It was then combined with the MP's Lexington & Southern branch to reach Kansas City. Passenger service ended in 1960.

M&NA purchased the line between Bergman, and Guion, Ark., 102 miles, from Union Pacific, and the balance has been leased. MNA started service on December 13, 1992.

The Missouri & Northern Arkansas is a subsidiary of RailTex.
Radio frequencies: 160.635, 160.985
Location of enginehouse: Carthage, Mo.
Locomotives: 20

No.	Builder	Model	New	Builder No.
501-505	EMD	GP40	8/68	34078-34082
507-509	EMD	GP40	8/69	34084-34086
511, 515	EMD	GP40	8/69	34088, 34092
632, 636	EMD	GP40	3/70	36387, 36391
640	EMD	GP40	3/70	36395

No.	Builder	Model	New	Builder No.	Rebuilt
642	EMD	GP40	3/70	36397	
645	EMD	GP40	3/70	36400	
1229	EMD	SW1200	5/53	18195	1979
4202	EMD	GP35M	1/64	28892	
4211	EMD	GP40M	1/67	32620	
4217	EMD	GP40M	2/67	32960	
6527	EMD	GP35	12/63	28469	
4163, 4164		slugs			

Freight cars: 104 covered hoppers, 10 mechanical refrigerator cars

MODESTO & EMPIRE TRACTION CO.

530 11th Street
P. O. Box 3106
Modesto, CA 95353

Reporting marks: MET
Phone: 209-524-4631
Fax: 209-529-0336

M&ET operates freight and switching service from connections with Southern Pacific and Union Pacific at Modesto, California, to Modesto-Empire Junction, 5 miles, where a connection is made with the Santa Fe.

TOFC and COFC service is provided in connection with the Santa Fe. Rail is 90 and 110 pound. Annual traffic consists of about 24,000 cars of food products, wine, syrup, plastic, paper products, and manufactured commodities.

The company was incorporated October 7, 1911. It also owned the Modesto Interurban Railway, which was merged into M&ET in 1993. Passenger service ended in 1918, and the railroad converted from steam to diesel operation in 1953.

The Beard Land & Investment Company has always owned the M&ET.
Radio frequencies: 160.965, 161.175, 161.325, 161.785
Location of enginehouse: Modesto, Calif.
Locomotives: 10

No.	Builder	Model	New	Builder No.
600	GE	70-ton	10/47	29093
601	GE	70-ton	2/49	30031
602	GE	70-ton	2/52	31278
603	GE	70-ton	1/55	32279
604	GE	70-ton	1/50	30390
605	GE	70-ton	2/47	28511
606	GE	70-ton	7/50	30448
607	GE	70-ton	3/52	31284
608	GE	70-ton	8/55	32302
609	GE	70-ton	8/55	32304

Modesto & Empire Traction Company operates a fleet of well-maintained GE 70-ton switchers in and around Modesto, California. Photo by Jim Shaw.

MOHAWK, ADIRONDACK & NORTHERN RAILROAD CORP.

P. O. Box 261
Lowville, NY 13367

Reporting marks: MHWA
Phone: 315-376-2021
Fax: 315-376-7796

Radio frequencies: 160.470, 161.460
Location of enginehouse: Carthage, and Utica, N. Y.
Locomotives: 5

No.	Builder	Model	New	Builder No.
803-806	Alco	C-425	10/64	3392-03–3392-06
408	Alco	C-420	10/64	3385-5

The Mohawk, Adirondack & Northern provides freight service from a connection with Conrail at Carthage, New York, to Lowville, 17.2 miles, and to Newton Falls, 45.7 miles. In addition, the company operates a separate line from a connection with Conrail at Utica to Lyons Falls, 45 miles. The company performs switching service for Conrail at Utica, and Rome. Traffic includes paper, and paper products, grain, chemicals, propane, coal, and food products — about 5,000 cars a year.

The lines from Utica to Lyons Falls and from Lowville to Carthage were built by the Black River & Utica Railroad. It was chartered in 1853, and the line reached Lyons Falls in December 1855. It was extended on to Lowville and Carthage in 1871. The company was leased to the Rome, Watertown & Ogdensburg the following year, and in 1891 the RW&O was leased to the New York Central.

The Carthage-Newton Falls line was built by the Carthage & Adirondack Railway, which was chartered on March 28, 1883, and opened to Benson Mines (near Newton Falls) in August 1889. The line was purchased by the New York Central in 1893.

Conrail sold these lines to the Mohawk, Adirondack & Northern, a subsidiary of Genesee Valley Transportation Corporation, and service started on the Carthage lines June 13, 1991. The Utica and Rome switching operations are owned by the Genesee & Mohawk Valley Railroad, an affiliate, and operated by the Mohawk, Adirondack & Northern under contract.

MA&N Alco C-425 No. 805 still wears colors of former owner, BC Rail, in this view at Aldrich, New York, taken in August 1995. Photo by Jim Shaw.

MOLALLA WESTERN RAILWAY

P. O. Box 22548
Portland, OR 97269

Reporting marks: MWRL
Phone: 503-659-5452

Molalla Western Railway provides freight service over a 10.5-mile line from a Southern Pacific connection at Canby, Oregon, to Molalla. Rail ranges from 75 to 132 pound. Traffic is finished lumber and inbound poultry feed, about 900 cars a year.

The line is a former Southern Pacific branch built about 1912 as part of an electric interurban line. It is owned by Hillvista Investment Company and is affiliated with Samuels Pacific Industries, owned by Richard Samuels. Shortline service, provided under contract by East Portland Traction Co., started February 22, 1993.
Radio frequencies: 160.575, 161.340
Location of enginehouse: Liberal, Ore.
Locomotives: 3

No.	Builder	Model	New	Builder No.
187	EMD	NW5	12/46	3480
801	EMD	SW8	8/51	13305
4501	GE	45-ton	1943	

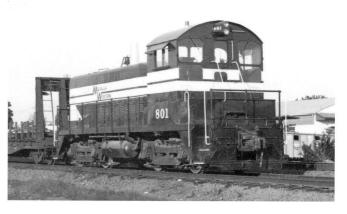

Molalla Western SW7 No. 801 switches pulp flats at Camby, Oregon, in October 1993. Photo by Jim Shaw.

MONONGAHELA CONNECTING RAILROAD CO.

4166 Second Avenue
Pittsburgh, PA 15207

Reporting marks: MCRR
Phone: 412-227-4903
Fax: 412-227-4975

The Monongahela Connecting provides switching service on 20 miles of track at Pittsburgh, Pennsylvania. It connects with CSX. Rail is 115 pound. Traffic is primarily coke, and about 22,000 cars a year are handled.

This line was incorporated April 1, 1885, and opened June 1, 1887. It is now owned by LTV Steel Co.
Radio frequencies: 161.220, 161.400
Locomotives: 3

No.	Builder	Model	New
1000	EMD	SW1001	1973
1001	EMD	SW1001	
1050	EMD	SW1000	1966

MONTANA RAIL LINK, INC.

201 International Way
P. O. Box 8779
Missoula, MT 59807

Reporting marks: MRL
Phone: 406-523-1500

Montana Rail Link operates 542 miles of main line from Huntley, Montana, to Sand Point, Idaho, then 65 miles by trackage rights over Burlington Northern to Spokane, Washington. Including six branch lines, MRL operates 942 miles. It connects with Burlington Northern, Union Pacific, and Montana Western.

Traffic is agricultural and forest products as well as overhead traffic moving from and to Burlington Northern — about 300,000 cars a year.

The line was acquired from Burlington Northern under a reported $150 million lease-sale agreement financed by Bank of America. Service started November 1, 1987. The company is independent.

Radio frequencies: 160.355, 160.950, 160.395
Locomotives: 91
Freight cars: 1,752
Principal shops: Missoula and Laurel, Mont.

Montana Rail Link GP9 heads up a short grain train at Belgrade, Montana, in June 1988. Photo by Jim Shaw.

MONTANA WESTERN RAILWAY CO., INC.

700½ Railroad Street
Butte, MT 59701

Reporting marks: MWRR
Phone: 406-782-1240

Montana Western operates freight service from a connection with Montana Rail Link at Garrison, Montana, to a connection with Rarus Railroad at Butte, 52 miles. It also connects with Union Pacific at Silver Bow. Rail is 115 to 132 pound.

Traffic includes about 11,000 cars a year of lumber, mineral products, and grain.

The line includes some former Oregon Short Line track and the former Northern Pacific passenger main line acquired from Burlington Northern in September 1986. Service started on September 15, 1986. The company is controlled by John W. Greene and William T. McCarthy.

Radio frequencies: 161.430, 161.190
Location of enginehouse: Butte, Mont.
Locomotives: 5 (pooled with Rarus Railway)

No.	Builder	Model	New	Builder No.
201	EMD	GP9	6/57	23909
202	EMD	GP9	12/56	22056
203	GMD	GP9	4/57	A-1082
2010	EMD	GP38-2	4/73	71702-22
2011	EMD	GP38-2	4/73	71702-25

MORRISTOWN & ERIE RAILWAY, INC.

49 Abbett Avenue
P. O. Box 2206
Morristown, NJ 07962

Reporting marks: ME
Phone: 201-267-4300
Fax: 201-267-3138

The Morristown & Erie operates freight service from Morristown, New Jersey, to Roseland, 10 miles. It also operates from Lake Junction to Randolph, 4 miles; Wharton to Rockaway, 6 miles; and Kenvil to Bartley, 7 miles. It has trackage rights on NJ Transit between Morristown and Lake Junction, 14 miles — 29 miles in all. It connects with Conrail at Morristown and Lake Junction. Rail is 80 to 130 pound. Traffic is lumber, food products, paper, corn syrup, starch, plastic, lube oil, and chemicals — about 2,000 cars a year. Whippany Railway Museum operates occasional excursions over parts of this line.

The current corporation is the result of the 1978 reorganization of the Morristown & Erie Railroad, which was formed on August 28, 1903, as a consolidation of the Whippany River Railroad (an operating company), and the Whippany & Passaic River Railroad (a construction company). Although regular passenger service ended in 1928, the company ran excursions from 1965 to 1977.

The Randolph line is former Lackawanna trackage, and the Rockaway and Bartley lines are former Central of New Jersey branches. The Dover & Rockaway and Highbridge lines are owned by Morris County and leased to the Morristown & Erie.

The company is owned by B. J. Friedland and others.
Radio frequencies: 160.230 (road), 161.100 (yard)
Location of enginehouse: Morristown, N. J.
Locomotives: 4

No.	Builder	Model	New	Builder No.
16	Alco	C-430	12/67	3494-05
17	Alco	C-430	12/67	3494-04
18	Alco	C-424	9/64	338201
19	Alco	C-424	9/64	338202

Freight cars: 2 hopper cars

MOSCOW, CAMDEN & SAN AUGUSTINE RAILROAD

P. O. Box 128
Camden, TX 75934

Reporting marks: MCSA
Phone: 409-398-4640
Fax: 409-398-5430

The Moscow, Camden & San Augustine operates freight service from a connection with the Southern Pacific at Moscow, Texas, to Camden, 6.87 miles. Rail is 75 pound. Traffic is outbound lumber — about 1,500 cars a year.

Moscow, Camden & San Augustine SW900 No. 3 pulls a trainload of wood chips into Moscow, Texas. Photo by Jim Shaw.

The railroad was chartered May 28, 1898, to build a line from Moscow to San Augustine, 65 miles. It was completed from Camden to Moscow in 1898 and was never extended. Passenger service was discontinued in 1973.

Champion International acquired the company in 1969.

Radio frequency: 161.205

Location of enginehouse: Camden, Texas
Locomotives: 2

No.	Builder	Model	New	Builder No.
1	EMD	SW1200	2/54	19491
3	EMD	SW900	4/57	23304

Freight cars: 147 boxcars

MOUNT HOOD RAILROAD CO.

110 Railroad Avenue
Hood River, OR 97031

Reporting marks: MH
Phone: 503-386-3556
Fax: 503-386-2140

The Mount Hood Railroad operates freight and seasonal excursion service from a connection with the Union Pacific at Hood River, Oregon, to Parkdale, 21.1 miles. Rail is 75 and 100 pound. Freight traffic includes fruit, lumber, hardboard, and general commodities — about 200 cars a year. Most revenue comes from the excursion trains.

The Mount Hood Railroad was incorporated October 23, 1905, and opened in May 1906. The Mount Hood Railway was chartered by Union Pacific on April 30, 1968, to acquire the assets of the Mount Hood Railroad. The UP company began operations October 16, 1968, and continued until November 2, 1987, when it was sold by Union Pacific to local interests and reorganized under the original name.

Radio frequencies: 160.365, 161.190
Location of enginehouse: Hood River, Ore.
Locomotives: 2

No.	Builder	Model	New	Builder No.
88	EMD	GP9	2/55	19948
89	EMD	GP9	5/59	25301

Mount Hood makes more from passenger service than from freight — but No. 88 does move lumber and produce when traffic warrants. Photo by Jim Shaw.

209

MOUNT VERNON TERMINAL RAILWAY., INC.

P. O. Box 216
Clear Lake, WA 98235

Reporting marks: MVT
Phone: 206-424-8040

Mount Vernon Terminal provides switching service on 2.5 miles of track at Mount Vernon, Washington. It connects with Burlington Northern at North Mount Vernon. Rail is 70 to 100 pound. The road's traffic is under 500 cars a year of fertilizer and frozen fish.

The line was built by the Puget Sound & Cascade Railway in 1916. In 1933 it acquired track in downtown Mount Vernon from the Pacific Northwest Traction Company. In 1939 the PS&C was abandoned, and its track in the Mount Vernon area was turned over to several former railroad workers who started the present company.

The railroad is owned by George and S. Stephenson.
Radio frequency: 160.875
Locomotives: 1

No.	Builder	Model	New	Builder No.
1200	EMD	SW9	4/53	17822

MOUNTAIN LAUREL RAILROAD CO.

One Glade Park East
R. D. 8, Box 45
Kittanning, PA 16201

Reporting marks: MNL
Phone: 412-543-0201
Fax: 412-543-2042

Mountain Laurel Railroad provides freight service from a connection with Conrail at Driftwood, Pennsylvania, to Lawsonham, 104 miles, where it connects with Conrail and the affiliated Red Bank

Five Mountain Laurel GP10s cross the Welch Run trestle at Kingsville, Pennsylvania, in September 1993. Photo by Jim Shaw.

Railroad. A 24-mile branch runs from Rose to Gretchen. Additional connections are made with the Buffalo & Pittsburgh at Falls Creek and with the Pittsburg & Shawmut at Brookville.

Traffic is primarily coal. More than 20,000 local and overhead cars are expected yearly from the Pittsburg & Shawmut and the Buffalo & Pittsburgh.

The main line was the main route of the Allegheny Valley Railroad, surveyed in 1868 and opened for business on May 1, 1874. It was one of three low-grade routes through the Allegheny Mountains. By the time the line was finished the Allegheny Valley had come under control of the Philadelphia & Erie, part of the Pennsylvania Railroad system.

The Gretchen branch was part of a line built by the Franklin & Clearfield Railroad in 1909. It became part of the New York Central system in 1915. Conrail sold the line on December 30, 1991.

This company is owned by the Arthur T. Walker Estate Corporation and Dumaines, a New Hampshire trust, and is affiliated with the Pittsburg & Shawmut Railroad.

Radio frequencies: 160.740, 161.160
Location of enginehouse: Brookville, Pa. (Pittsburg & Shawmut)
Locomotives: 6

No.	Builder	Model	New	Builder No.	Rebuilt
12	EMD	GP10	3/55	20289	1974
13	EMD	GP10	12/55	20757	1975
14	EMD	GP10	12/54	19903	1975
15	EMD	GP10	12/57	23832	1974
16	EMD	GP10	10/56	22249	1974
17	EMD	GP10	12/54	20192	1974

MUNICIPALITY OF EAST TROY, WISCONSIN

222 North Charles Street
Waukesha, WI 53186

Reporting marks: METW
Phone: 414-542-5573

The line is operated for freight service on an irregular basis from East Troy, Wisconsin, to a connection with the Wisconsin Central at Mukwonago, 7.2 miles. Rail is 75 to 80 pound. Traffic consists of under 100 cars a year of feed, fertilizer, lumber, and pipe. The Wisconsin Trolley Museum operates excursion trains on the line.

The line was part of a railroad built by the Milwaukee & Muskego Lake Traction Company, incorporated November 4, 1899. The company was reorganized in 1905 as The Milwaukee Electric Railway & Light Co. When Milwaukee Electric abandoned the line in 1939, the village of East Troy purchased the portion of the line between East Troy and the Soo Line at Mukwonago, and leased it back to Milwaukee Electric for freight operation for 10 years. From 1949 to 1985 the municipality operated the line; in 1985 it leased it to the Wisconsin Trolley Museum, Inc. The Friends of East Troy Railroad Museum purchased the line in January 1995.

Enginehouse: East Troy, Wis.
Locomotives: 2

No.	Builder	Model	New	Builder No.
R4	GE	80-ton diesel	8/48	30004
L9	GE	50-ton electric	1944	

NAPA VALLEY RAILROAD CO.

1275 McKinstry Street
Napa, CA 94559

Reporting marks: NVRR
Phone: 707-258-0504
Fax: 707-253-1546

Napa Valley Railroad provides freight and passenger service from a connection with California Northern at Rocktram, California, to Krug, 21.25 miles. Rail is 90 pound. Freight traffic is under 100 cars a year of agricultural products. The primary business is excursions and dinner trains through the Napa Valley wine country.

The line was opened in 1868 by the Napa Valley Railroad. It quickly became part of the California Pacific Railroad and was soon folded into the Central Pacific, then Southern Pacific. Regular passenger service ended in 1929.

The present owners acquired the line from Southern Pacific in 1987. Excursion service started on September 16, 1989.

The company is owned by Vincent DeDomenico.

Radio frequencies: 160.575, 161.475
Location of enginehouse: Napa, Calif.
Locomotives: 5

No.	Builder	Model	New	Builder No.
52	GE	65-ton	7/43	17871
70	MLW	FPA-4	10/58	82269
71	MLW	FPA-4	2/59	83153
72	MLW	FPA-4	4/59	83165
73	MLW	FPA-4	4/59	83168

NASH COUNTY RAILROAD CORP.

Railroad Street
P. O. Box 487
Spring Hope, NC 27882

Reporting marks: NCYR
Phone: 919-478-3939
Fax: 919-478-7079

Nash County Railroad operates freight service from a CSX connection at Rocky Mount, North Carolina, to Spring Hope, 20 miles. Rail is 85 pound. Traffic, about 4,000 cars a year, includes grain, fertilizer, scrap, and forest products.

The line was built by the Wilmington & Weldon Railroad in 1887. It later became part of the Atlantic Coast Line. It was sold in 1985 to Nash County Railroad, a subsidiary of the Laurinburg & Southern. Shortline service started on November 4, 1985. Gulf & Ohio Railways acquired control of the company from Laurinburg & Southern interests on March 1, 1994.

Radio frequency: 160.980
Location of enginehouse: Rocky Mount, N. C.
Locomotives: 3

No.	Builder	Model	New	Builder No.	Rebuilt
2391	EMD	GP9	2/53	17779	
7913	EMD	GP8	5/53	18419	1977
8420	EMD	GP10	2/52	15851	1974

NASHVILLE & EASTERN RAILROAD CORP.

514 Knoxville Avenue
Lebanon, TN 37087

Reporting marks: NERR
Phone: 615-444-1434
Fax: 615-444-4682

Nashville & Eastern operates freight service from a connection with CSX near Nashville (Vine Hill) to Monterey, Tennessee. Short branch lines extend from Stone River to Old Hickory and from Carthage Junction to Carthage. A total of 131.11 miles are operated. Rail is predominantly 90 pound. The company runs a dinner train for a private operator. Freight traffic includes about 9,000 cars a year of chemicals, limestone, grain, and forest products.

The line was built by the Tennessee & Pacific Railroad, which was chartered in May 1866, and opened from Nashville to Lebanon in 1870. In 1877 the company was sold to the Nashville, Chattanooga & St. Louis.

The Nashville & Knoxville Railroad built the line from Lebanon to Cookesville in 1889. That company was merged with others to form the Tennessee Central Railroad (which also acquired the NC&StL branch) in May 1902. The Tennessee Central was abandoned in December 1968, and this portion of its line was sold to the Louisville & Nashville. The line was acquired by the Nashville & Eastern Railroad Authority in September 1986 and shortline service started September 15.

The operating company is controlled by William Drunsick.

Radio frequencies: 160.365, 160.560, 161.070
Location of enginehouse: Lebanon, Tenn.
Locomotives: 11

No.	Builder	Model	New	Builder No.	Rebuilt
5323	GE	U28B	11/66	36083	
5328	GE	U30B	12/71	38218	
5338	GE	U30B	11/72	38475	
5339	GE	U30B	11/72	38476	
5340	GE	U30B	11/72	38477	
5343	GE	U30B	11/72	38480	
5344	GE	U30B	11/72	38481	
5345	GE	U30B	11/72	38491	
5772	GE	U36B	7/70	37428	
8319	EMD	GP10	1/58	23856	1976
8463	EMD	GP10	12/50	12301	1976

Freight cars: 35 hopper cars

NEBKOTA RAILWAY, INC.

P. O. Box 506
Gordon, NE 69343

Reporting marks: NRI
Phone: 308-282-1550
Fax: 308-282-1550

Nebkota Railway operates freight service from Merriman, Nebraska, to Chadron, 73.5 miles, and from Chadron it operates over Chicago & North Western by trackage rights to Crawford (27.8 additional miles). Interchange is made with Chicago & North Western at Chadron, and with Burlington Northern at Crawford. Rail is 100 pound. Traffic includes grain, fertilizer, seed potatoes, hay, and aggregate — 1,500 cars a year.

The line is a short segment of Chicago & North Western's "Cowboy Line" from Fremont, Neb., to Deadwood, South Dakota. It was built in 1885 and 1886 by the Fremont, Elkhorn &

Missouri Valley Railroad, part of the Chicago & North Western system. On March 9, 1994, Chicago & North Western sold the Merriman-Chadron segment to the Nebkota Railway, which is controlled by shippers located along the line.
Radio frequency: 161.535
Location of enginehouse: Gordon, Neb.

Locomotives: 3

No.	Builder	Model	New	Builder No.
54	GMD	F9A	1958	A-1401
55	GMD	F9A	4/53	A-520
61	GMD	F9B	1/55	A-629

NEBRASKA CENTRAL RAILROAD CO.

2480 33rd Street
Columbus, NE 68602-0849

Reporting marks: NCRC
Phone: 402-562-6155
Fax: 402-562-7501

Nebraska Central operates 266 miles of former Union Pacific branch lines in northeastern Nebraska:
• Columbus through Oconee to Norfolk, 46.1 miles
• Oconee through Genoa to Albion, 34.6 miles
• Genoa to Spaulding, 44.5 miles
• Grand Island to Ord, 59.9 miles
• Central City to Brainard, 62.7 miles.

It connects with UP at Columbus, Grand Island, and Central City. UP has granted the company trackage rights between Central City and Grand Island, 22 miles. Rail is 131 to 133 pound. Traffic is predominantly grain (corn, soy, and milo) with some fertilizer and scrap iron — 33,000 cars a year.

The Columbus lines were built by the Omaha, Niobrara & Black Hills Railroad, chartered April 24, 1879. The line to Norfolk opened December 1, 1879, and the Spaulding line opened five years later. In 1887, the ON&BH was acquired by the Omaha & Republican Valley Railroad, which built the Ord and Brainard lines. The Brainard line opened from Valley Station to Stromsburg in January 1884, and the Ord branch was completed early in 1886. The Omaha & Republican Valley was controlled by Union Pacific, and was merged into UP in November 1898.

On June 27, 1993, UP leased the property to Nebraska Central, which is a subsidiary of Rio Grande Pacific Corp.
Radio frequencies: 161.190, 161.265
Location of enginehouses: Columbus and Grand Island, Neb.
Locomotives: 7

No.	Builder	Model	New	Builder No.
4200	EMD	GP38	8/66	32122
4201	EMD	GP38	8/66	32126
4202	EMD	GP38	8/66	32129
4201	EMD	GP38	8/66	32126
4202	EMD	GP38	8/66	32129
4203	EMD	GP38	12/69	35460
4204	EMD	GP38	9/66	32232

NEW BRUNSWICK SOUTHERN RAILWAY CO. LTD.

11 Gifford Road
P. O. Box 5666
Saint John, NB E2L 5B6
Canada

Reporting marks: NBSR
Phone: 506-635-2200
Fax: 506-635-2239

New Brunswick Southern operates from a connection with Eastern Maine Railroad at McAdam, New Brunswick, to a connection with Canadian National Railways at Saint John, 84.4 miles,and to St. Stephen, 33.9 miles. Rail is predominantly 100 pound.

Traffic is paper, forest products, chemicals, and general commodities. The road expects to handle about 20,000 cars a year.

The line is part of the former Canadian Pacific route between Montreal and Saint John, opened in 1889. The track within New Brunswick is owned by the New Brunswick Railway, which was leased to Canadian Pacific for 999 years in July 1890.

In September 1988 CP Rail turned over the operation of its lines east of Megantic, Quebec, to an affiliate, the Canadian Atlantic Railway, in September, 1988. The arrangement was not successful and CP abandoned the lines on December 31, 1994. The New Brunswick Railway, a subsidiary of J. D. Irving Ltd., took back its property, and formed the New Brunswick Southern to operate it. Shortline operations started on January 8, 1995.

Radio frequencies: 161.355, 160.185, 160.245
Enginehouse: Saint John, N. B.
Locomotives: 4 (additional power is leased from CP Rail)

No.	Builder	Model	New	Builder No.
4279	EMD	GP7	1952	16882
4280	EMD	GP7	1952	16860
4282	EMD	GP7	1952	16866
4463	EMD	GP7	1950	12921

NEW ENGLAND CENTRAL RAILROAD CO.

2 Federal Street
P. O. Box 1310
St. Albans, VT 05478

Reporting marks: NECR
Phone: 802-527-3411
Fax: 802-527-3482

New England Central provides freight service along its main route from New London, Connecticut, to East Alburg, Vermont, and on several short branch lines in Vermont, a total of 375 miles. Amtrak's *Vermonter* operates over the line between Palmer, Mass., and St. Albans, Vt. It connects with Canadian National at East Alburg; CP Rail at Rouses Point, New York; Conrail and Massachusetts Central at Palmer, Mass; Green Mountain at Bellows Falls, Vt.; Providence & Worcester at New London; ST Rail System (Boston & Maine) at Brattleboro and White River Junction, Vt.; Vermont Railway at Burlington, Vt.; and Washington County at Montpelier Junction, Vt. Traffic includes lumber, wood products, paper, cement, and general commodities — about 33,000 cars a year. Rail runs from 100 to 115 pounds.

New England Central took over the property of the Central Vermont Railway on February 4, 1995. The CV, a subsidiary of Canadian National Railways, was incorporated in Vermont on January 30, 1930.

New England Central is a subsidiary of RailTex.

Radio frequencies: 161.415, 160.935, 161.205
Location of enginehouses: St. Albans, Vt., Palmer, Mass., New London, Conn.
Locomotives: 20

NEW ENGLAND SOUTHERN RAILROAD CO.

8 Water Street
P. O. Box 2106
Concord, NH 03302

Reporting marks: NEGS
Phone: 603-228-8580
Fax: 603-228-9571

New England Southern operates freight service from a connection with ST Rail System (Boston & Maine) at Manchester, New Hampshire, to North Woodstock, 68 miles. A branch (part of the former Northern Railroad) runs 6.6 miles from Concord to Penacook. Rail is 85 to 112 pound. Traffic consists of about 2,500 cars a year of beer, wine, chemicals, clay, scrap metal, grain, paper, roofing material, salt, sand, and building materials. Seasonal excursion trains are operated over the line by other operators.

The Manchester-Concord portion of the line was built by the Concord Railroad, chartered in 1835 and opened in 1842. The line from Concord to Plymouth was part of the main line of the Boston, Concord & Montreal, opened in 1853.

The track from Plymouth to North Woodstock was built by the Pemigewasset Valley Railroad, which was chartered in 1874 and opened March 1, 1883. BC&M leased the PV and was in turn leased by the Concord, which became part of the Boston & Maine.

New England Southern began operations north of Concord in September 1982, as successor to the Goodwin Railroad, Wolfeboro Railroad, and North Stratford Railroad. Expansion to Manchester took place in August 1985. The track from Lincoln to Concord is owned by the state of New Hampshire, and from Concord to Manchester it is owned by the Boston & Maine. New England Southern is controlled by Peter M. Dearness.

Radio frequencies: 161.025, 160,395
Location of enginehouse: Concord, N. H.
Locomotives: 2

No.	Builder	Model	New	Builder No.
302	EMD	GP7	1/50	11690
503	EMD	GP18	2/60	25458

New England Southern 503, a GP18, rolls through the vegetation at Concord, New Hampshire, with a string of covered hoppers. Photo by Jim Shaw.

NEW HAMPSHIRE & VERMONT RAILROAD CO.

P. O. Box 1267
Trenton FL 32693

Reporting marks: NHVT
Phone: 904-463-1103
Fax: 904-463-1104

New Hampshire & Vermont RS-11 No. 405 stands at Morrisville, Vermont, on the Lamoille Valley, in October 1990. Photo by Jim Shaw.

The New Hampshire & Vermont operates freight service from a connection with the St. Lawrence & Atlantic Railroad at Groveton, New Hampshire, to Waumbek Junction and Woodsville, 60.3 miles. The railroad has trackage rights over ST Rail System (Boston & Maine) from Woodsville to White River Junction, Vermont, 40.5 miles, where interchange is made with the B&M. A branch line runs from Waumbek Junction to Berlin, 19.7 miles. Additional connections are made with Twin State Railroad at Whitefield and with Berlin Mills Railroad at Berlin. Rail ranges from 75 to 130 pound, and the load limit is restricted to 220,000 pounds into Berlin. As of 1995 most of the line from Berlin to White River Junction was out of service. Traffic includes about 1,000 cars a year of paper, related products, salt, and lumber.

The Woodsville-Groveton line was built by the White Mountain Railroad, which was chartered in 1848. It opened from Woodsville to Lancaster in 1870, and to Groveton in 1872. The Berlin branch was completed in July 1899. The company was leased by the Boston, Concord & Montreal in 1872, and reorganized as the Concord & Montreal in 1889. B&M absorbed the line in 1895.

Guilford entered into a lease-purchase agreement with the current operator effective November 21, 1989. New Hampshire & Vermont purchased the line on May 28, 1992, and established trackage rights from Woodsville to White River Junction on March 18, 1993. The line is owned by CSF Acquisitions, Inc. (Clyde S. Forbes), and is affiliated with Lamoille Valley Railroad and Twin State Railroad.

Radio frequencies: 160.230, 161.340
Location of enginehouse: Whitefield, N. H.
Locomotives: 3 (additional motive power is supplied by Lamoille Valley Railroad)

No.	Builder	Model	New	Builder No.
405	Alco	RS-11	6/61	83695
669	EMD	GP9	2/59	24821
3800	EMD	GP38	11/66	32667

NEW HAMPSHIRE CENTRAL RAILROAD, INC.

P. O. Box 1758
Meredith, NH 03253

Reporting marks: NHCR
Phone: 603-237-5245
Fax: 603-237-8472

New Hampshire Central operates freight service from a connection with the St. Lawrence & Atlantic Railroad at North Stratford, New Hampshire, to Columbia Bridge, 9.25 miles. Rail is 75 pound. Traffic is about 200 to 400 cars a year of railroad ballast, aggregate, logs, and lumber.

The line was built by the Upper Coos Railroad, which was chartered in October 1884. That company was leased to the Maine Central Railroad before it opened in May 1890 and was operated by MEC until the mid-1970s, when MEC abandoned the line and sold the property to the state of New Hampshire. The state leased the line to the North Stratford Railroad from May 1977 to April 1989, when service was once again abandoned. The New Hampshire Central, which is owned by Edward W. Jeffrey, leased the line from the state effective June 2, 1993.
Location of enginehouse: North Stratford, N. H.
Locomotives: 1 (a GE 44-tonner)

NEW HAMPSHIRE NORTHCOAST CORP.

P. O. Box 429
Ossipee, NH 03864

Reporting marks: NHN
Phone: 603-539-2789
Fax: 603-539-8060

New Hampshire Northcoast operates freight service from Ossipee, New Hampshire, to a connection with ST Rail System (Boston & Maine) at Dover, 41 miles. Rail is 112 pound. Traffic is primarily sand, gravel, and crushed stone moving in unit trains that amount to about 7,000 cars a year.

The line was built by the Great Falls & Conway Railroad, and opened into Conway in 1872. It came under the control of the Eastern Railroad, then the Boston & Maine, which operated it until the August 1985, when service was discontinued because of track conditions. New Hampshire Northcoast started service on May 27, 1986. The company is owned by Boston Sand & Gravel Co., which is affiliated with Ossippee Aggregates, Inc.
Radio frequencies: 160.275, 161.385
Location of enginehouse: Ossipee, N. H.
Locomotives: 6

No.	Builder	Model	New	Builder No.	Rebuilt
1755	EMD	GP9	5/57	23325	1979
1756	EMD	GP9	1956	21870	1979
1757	EMD	GP9	11/56	21888	1979
1758	EMD	GP9	11/56	21886	1979
1759	EMD	GP9	11/56	21898	1979
1760	EMD	GP9	10/55	20719	

New Hampshire Northcoast GP9s 1755 and 1757 lead a southbound Ossipee-Dover, New Hampshire, gravel train through Rochester in July 1991. Photo by Jack Armstrong.

NEW HOPE & IVYLAND RAILROAD CO.

P. O. Box 634
New Hope, PA 18938

Reporting marks: NHRR
Phone: 215-862-2332

The New Hope & Ivyland Railroad operates freight and excursion service from New Hope, Pennsylvania, to connections with Conrail and SEPTA at Warminster, 18 miles. Rail is 90 to 131 pound. Traffic is primarily excursions with limited but growing freight — currently under 200 cars a year.

The line was built by the Northeast Pennsylvania Railroad in 1888. That company was acquired by the Philadelphia & Reading (later the Reading Company).

The line was sold to the New Hope & Ivyland on July 4, 1965, following abandonment. Freight and excursion operations started in June 1966. The company filed for bankruptcy June 5, 1970, and was released from bankruptcy on June 30, 1979. The fixed assets, which were owned by the Bucks County Industrial Development Corporation, were sold to the Bucks County Railroad Preservation, and Restoration Corporation in October 1990.

The company is controlled by Robert Buzzard and others.

Radio frequency: 161.475
Location of enginehouse: New Hope, Pa.
Locomotives: 8

No.	Builder	Model	New	Builder No.
9	Alco	0-6-0	10/42	70402
11	Baldwin	VO660	11/45	72817
40	Baldwin	2-8-0	1925	58824
614	Lima	4-8-4	1948	
1513	Alco	RSC-2	5/49	76815
1553	MLW	4-6-0	1911	49878
3028	Alco	4-8-4	3/46	74383
9423	EMD	SW1	11/50	11217

NEW ORLEANS LOWER COAST RAILROAD CO., INC.

9387 Highway 23
P. O. Box 7133
Belle Chasse, LA 70037

Reporting marks: NOLR
Phone: 504-391-3167
Fax: 504-391-1534

New Orleans Lower Coast provides freight service from a connection with Union Pacific in Gouldsboro Yard in Gretna, a suburb of New Orleans, to Myrtle Grove, Louisiana, 24 miles. Rail is 112 pound. Traffic is predominantly petroleum products including oil, fuel additives, and chemicals. The road also carries inbound grain for export. Total traffic is about 4,000 cars a year.

The line is part of a railroad opened in 1891 by the New Orleans, Fort Jackson, and Grand Isle Railroad. That company was combined with the New Orleans Southern Railway in 1911 to form the New Orleans, Southern, and Grand Isle Railway, which was sold under foreclosure to the New Orleans & Lower Coast Railroad in September 1916. That company came under control of the Missouri Pacific 10 years later and was merged with MP in 1978.

Union Pacific sold the property to the current operator and shortline service began on March 17, 1991. New Orleans Lower Coast is a subsidiary of RailTex, Inc.

Radio frequencies: 160.635, 160.995
Location of enginehouse: Belle Chasse, La.
Locomotives: 2

No.	Builder	Model	New	Builder No.	Rebuilt
1237	EMD	SW9	12/53	18962	1974
2180	EMD	GP7U	10/52	17454	1980

NEW ORLEANS PUBLIC BELT RAILROAD

4822 Tchoupitoulas Street
P. O. Box 51658
New Orleans, LA 70151-1658

Reporting marks: NOPB
Phone: 504-896-7410
Fax: 504-896-7452

The company operates 124 miles of track (24 route miles) at New Orleans, Louisiana. It connects with Illinois Central, Kansas City Southern, Union Pacific, CSX, Norfolk Southern, and Southern Pacific. Rail is 80 to 115 pound. About 19,000 cars a year are handled.

The company was organized October 8, 1904, and became a common carrier in 1911. It is owned by the city of New Orleans and managed by the Public Belt Railroad Commission. The Commission owns and maintains the Huey P. Long Bridge across the Mississippi River at New Orleans.

Radio frequencies: 160.320, 160.530, 10525.0
Locomotives: 6

No.	Builder	Model	New	Builder No.
103	EMD	SW1001	8/71	37390
105	EMD	SW1001	8/71	37392
106	EMD	SW1001	8/71	37393
151	EMD	SW1500	8/71	7310-1
152	EMD	SW1500	8/71	7310-2
153	EMD	SW1500	8/71	4618-1

Freight cars: 397 boxcars

NEW YORK & LAKE ERIE RAILROAD

50 Commercial Street
Box 309
Gowanda, NY 14070

Reporting marks: NYLE
Phone: 716-532-5242
Fax: 716-532-9128

New York & Lake Erie operates freight, excursion, and dinner trains from a connection with Buffalo Southern at Gowanda, New York, to Waterboro, 25.7 miles, and from a connection with Conrail at Salamanca to Dayton, 24.4 miles. Total mileage is 50.1. Rail is 100 to 131 pound. Traffic includes grain, scrap metal, fertilizer, particleboard, paper, and other commodities — about 750 cars a year. Significant income comes from the excursion and dinner trains.

The Cattaraugus-Dayton line opened in 1851 as part of the Erie's original route from Jersey City to Dunkirk. Most of the line was not included in Conrail, and the property was sold to a local development authority. New York & Lake Erie operations started October 15, 1978, between Salamanca and Cattaraugus. The company expanded from Cattaraugus to Dayton in 1980 and also operated briefly to Buffalo until Buffalo Southern began operating from Buffalo to Gowanda.

The New York & Lake Erie is owned by Robert O. Dingman, Jr.
Radio frequencies: 161.355, 160.365
Location of enginehouse: Gowanda, N. Y.
Locomotives: 3

No.	Builder	Model	New	Builder No.
85	Alco	S-2	3/50	77060
1013	Alco	C-425	1/65	3400-07
6101	Alco	C-425	2/65	3403-02

Alco S-2 No. 75 heads through Collins, New York, with a two-car train on the New York & Lake Erie. Photo by Jim Shaw.

221

NEW YORK CROSS HARBOR RAILROAD TERMINAL CORP.

403 First Avenue
P. O. Box 182
Brooklyn, NY 11232

Reporting marks: NYCH
Phone: 718-788-3690
Fax: 718-788-4462

New York Cross Harbor is a terminal switching line in Brooklyn, New York, connecting with the Long Island Railroad, South Brooklyn Railroad, and Conrail (at Jersey City by car float). Rail is 100 and 120 pound. About 5,000 cars a year are carried. The company also operates an intermodal COFC/TOFC terminal in Brooklyn.

The company was formed in August 1983 as a consolidation and reorganization of the Brooklyn Eastern District Terminal and New York Dock Railroads. It is controlled by Robert Crawford and others.

Radio frequencies: 160.590, 156.650 (marine)
Locomotives: 6

No.	Builder	Model	New	Builder No.
11	Alco	S-4	10/51	79219
21	Alco	S-1	8/47	75351
22	Alco	S-1	10/47	75525
25	Alco	S-1	10/46	74962
58	EMD	NW2	6/47	4753
59	EMD	NW2	9/46	3645

Marine equipment: 2 tugboats, 4 car floats

NEW YORK, SUSQUEHANNA & WESTERN RAILWAY CO.

1 Railroad Avenue
Cooperstown, NY 13326

Reporting marks: NYSW
Phone: 607-547-2555
Fax: 607-547-9834

The New York, Susquehanna & Western operates 444 miles of line from Jersey City (Croxton), New Jersey, to Utica and Syracuse, New York. It uses its own line from Croxton to Sparta Junction, then runs over the former Lehigh & Hudson River Railway to Warwick, N. Y., 82.7 miles from Croxton. It has operating rights over Conrail for 179 miles between Warwick and Binghamton. The Susquehanna's bifurcated Northern Division extends from Binghamton to Utica, 96 miles; a 61.7-mile branch runs from Chenango Forks to Janesville, just south of Syracuse.

The Susquehanna operates short branch lines to Edgewater, Passaic, and Lodi, New Jersey. It connects with Conrail at Croxton and Passaic Junction, N. J., and Warwick, Binghamton, and Utica, N. Y.

Traffic includes chemicals, farm products, paper, general commodities, and containers amounting to about 17,500 cars a year. The company operates passenger service in the Syracuse area, and seasonal excursions operate from various points on the line.

Susquehanna's original line was built by the New Jersey Midland in the 1870s. It came under the control of the Erie in 1898, by which time it reached northwest into Pennsylvania coalfields. It entered bankruptcy in 1937 and emerged from Erie control in 1940. It enjoyed a period of prosperity until the mid-1950s, then gradually withered into bankruptcy. At the request of the state of New Jersey, Delaware Otsego system began operating the Susquehanna in 1980 and purchased it in 1982. The New York, Susquehanna & Western Railway was formed as a reorganization of the New York, Susquehanna & Western Railroad in April 1981.

The Syracuse branch of the Northern Division was built by the Syracuse & Binghampton Railroad in 1854, and the Utica line was built by the Utica, Chenango & Susquehanna Valley Railroad, opened in June 1868. Both lines came under the control of the Lackawanna about 1870. They were acquired from Conrail in 1982.

The company is a subsidiary of the Delaware Otsego System.

Radio frequencies: 160.485, 160.620, 161.295

Location of enginehouses: Little Ferry, N. J., and Binghamton, N. Y.

Locomotives: 26

No.	Builder	Model	New	Builder No.
17	GE	70-ton	1/54	32130
116	EMD	NW2	6/48	3169
120	EMD	SW9	1/53	17263
142	Tang Shan	2-8-2	5/89	
1800	EMD	GP18	9/62	27404
1802	EMD	GP18	9/62	27405
1804	EMD	GP18	9/62	27406
2010	Alco	C-420	12/67	3384-01

No.	Builder	Model	New	Builder No.	Rebuilt
2012	EMD	GP38	10/67	33318	
2400	EMD	E9A	7/54	19630	1973
2402	EMD	E9A	12/55	20533	1973
3000	Alco	C-430	12/67	3494-1	
3006	Alco	C-430	12/67	3494-6	
3612	EMD	SD45	8/70	36369	
3614	EMD	SD45	8/70	36374	
3618	EMD	SD45	8/71	37108	
3634	EMD	SD45	8/71	37150	
3636	EMD	F45	5/71	37182	
3638	EMD	F45	5/71	37184	
4002	GE	Dash 8-40B	6/88	4576	
4004	GE	Dash 8-40B	6/88	4577	
4006	GE	Dash 8-40B	6/88	4578	
4008	GE	Dash 8-40B	6/88	4579	
4050	EMD	SD70M	6/95	946531-23	
4052	EMD	SD70M	6/95	946531-24	
4054	EMD	SD70M	6/95	946531-25	

NEWBURGH & SOUTH SHORE RAILROAD CO.

4200 East 71st Street
Cleveland, OH 44105-5726

Reporting marks: NSR
Phone: 216-271-1183
Fax: 216-271-5304

This switching line operates 9.5 miles (3.2 route miles) of track in Cleveland, Ohio. It connects with Conrail, CSX, Norfolk Southern, Wheeling & Lake Erie, Cuyahoga Valley, and River Terminal. It handles 7,000 cars a year.

The Newburgh & South Shore Railway was abandoned February 22, 1986, and 2.2 miles of the railroad were sold to the Cuyahoga Valley Railway Co. The rest of the rails remained in place, and in July 1986 the United States Steel sold the company to the Chicago West Pullman Transportation Corporation, which restored service. The company is now part of OmniTRAX.

Radio frequency: 160.890

Locomotives: 2

No.	Builder	Model	New	Builder No.
1019	EMD	SW1001	7/71	37534
1021	EMD	SW1001	4/75	74669-1

Freight cars: 30 gondolas

NIMISHILLEN & TUSCARAWAS RAILWAY CO.

2633 8th Street N.W.
P. O. Box 24700
Canton, OH 44701-4700

Reporting marks: NTRY
Phone: 216-438-5821
Fax: 216-438-5866

Radio frequencies: 161.425, 160.695, 161.445, 161.295
Locomotives: 7

No.	Builder	Model
1203	EMD	SW1200
1208	EMD	SW1200
1210	EMD	SW1200
1211	EMD	SW1200
1250	EMD	SW1200
1283	EMD	SW1200
1285	EMD	SW1200

NTRY provides switching service on 24.7 miles of line on two separate line segments — one at Perry (Massillon), Ohio, and the other at Canton. It connects with Conrail, Wheeling & Lake Erie, and R. J. Corman at Massillon and with Conrail and Wheeling & Lake Erie at Canton. Traffic is about 35,000 cars a year.

The company acquired lines from the Mahoning Valley Railway and Republic Engineered Steel and started service on January 19, 1990. It is a subsidiary of Republic Engineered Steels.

NITTANY & BALD EAGLE RAILROAD CO.

P. O. Box 70
Bellefonte, PA 16823

Reporting marks: NBER
Phone: 814-355-4736
Fax: 814-355-8432

Nittany & Bald Eagle operates freight service between Conrail connections at Tyrone and Mill Hall, Pennsylvania, 63 miles, plus a 9-mile branch from Milesburg to Lemont and a short branch to Pleasant Gap. Rail is 85 to 152 pound with a predominant weight of 130 pound. Traffic includes limestone, lime, sand, lumber, grain, metals chemicals, and other commodities — 3,300 cars a year. Seasonal excursion trains are operated by the Bellefonte Historical Railroad Society.

Nittany & Bald Eagle's CF7 No. 2427 heads through Milesburg, Pennsylvania, with the daily freight. Photo by Jim Shaw.

The line was built in large part by the Bald Eagle Valley Railroad, which was chartered March 25, 1861, and opened December 7, 1864. The line was promptly leased to the Pennsylvania Railroad, and operated as part of its Philadelphia & Erie Division. It continued under Penn Central and Conrail management until August 1, 1984, when the Nittany & Bald Eagle leased it from its owner, the SEDA-COG Joint Rail Authority. The operating company is controlled by Richard D. Robey.

Radio frequency: 160.590
Location of enginehouse: Bellefonte (Coleville), Pa.
Locomotives: 3

No.	Builder	Model	New	Builder No.
1601	EMD	GP8	3/52	15460
1602	EMD	GP8	11/50	13000
2427	AT&SF	CF7	12/77	

NOBLES ROCK RAILROAD CO.

P. O. Box 623
Luverne, MN 56156-0332

Reporting marks: NRR
Phone: 507-283-4486
Fax: 507-283-8360

Nobels Rock Railroad operates freight service from a connection with Chicago & North Western at Agate (Worthington) to a connection with the Burlington Northern at Manley, Minnesota, 41.44 miles. Rail is 90 to 100 pound. Traffic is primarily grain and fertilizer, about 3,000 cars a year.

Chicago & North Western operated the line until 1988, when it was abandoned and sold to the Buffalo Ridge Regional Railroad Authority. It was reopened and operated by the Buffalo Ridge Railroad until April 1992, when it closed due to track conditions and lack of business. The line was rehabilitated and reopened by the current operator in July 1994.

The company is controlled by Rail Locomotives Transportation, Inc. of Fargo, North Dakota.

Radio frequency: 160.800
Location of enginehouse: Luverne, Minn.
Locomotives: 1

No.	Builder	Model	New	Builder No.
301	EMD	GP30	2/63	28172

NORFOLK & PORTSMOUTH BELT LINE RAILROAD CO.

1050 Virginia Avenue
P. O. Box 7547
Portsmouth, VA 23707

Reporting marks: NPB
Phone: 804-393-2622

The Norfolk & Portsmouth Belt Line is a switching line at Portsmouth, Virginia. It operates 29.7 miles of track and connects with Eastern Shore, CSX, and Norfolk Southern. About 85,000 cars are handled annually.

The company started operations in 1898, and is owned jointly by CSX and Norfolk Southern.

Radio frequencies: 160.905, 160.980
Locomotives: 6 (supplied by Norfolk Southern)

NORFOLK SOUTHERN'S THOROUGHBRED SHORT LINE PROGRAM

In the mid-1980s, after an unsuccessful attempt to expand its system by purchasing control of Conrail, Norfolk Southern recognized that it needed to reduce its system mileage. The task of developing a restructuring and spinoff program was assigned to Jim McClellan, NS's Director of Corporate Development.

Of a total system of 17,000 miles, a 1987 review showed 2,700 miles of low-density track. NS took the unprecedented step of writing down earnings by $620 million on property and work force (labor separation payments) in the third quarter of 1987 as the first step in restructuring.

Of the 2,700 miles of low-density line, 1,500 were clearly destined to be abandoned. The remaining 1,200 miles seemed to have shortline potential. Those lines generated annual operating revenue of nearly $60 million for NS, and a plan to retain as much of that income as possible was warranted. McClellan had investigated the spinoff programs of other Class 1 railroads, and he and his staff created their own, the Thoroughbred Short Line Program.

The most important element of Thoroughbred was that the lines were not for sale — they were to be leased to their new operators. The lessees could then concentrate on retaining and improving traffic rather than making mortgage payments. If they were successful in keeping traffic at pre-shortline levels, the new operators would receive credits on their lease, eliminating payments altogether. The leases were to run from 3 to 20 years. Generally after 3 years the operator could purchase the line at net liquidation value — the scrap price. If the line couldn't make it financially, service would be discontinued and the line would be abandoned and liquidated by NS.

A key element in the program is marketing and pricing support from NS. Shortline stations remain on NS's station list, and NS sets rates and solicits traffic in cooperation with the short line, which generally receives not a division of revenue but rather a fixed rate per car, typical of switching railroads. NS usually performs customer freight billing, so the short line has minimal accounting expenses.

Per diem relief is available to the shortline operator during the first five years of the program. Per diem charges (the daily rental charges for freight cars) can equal 25 to 40 percent of the shortline revenue on some shipments, so this represents a big savings. NS provides technical assistance in such areas as electronic data interchange.

Offering what amounted to a "no money down" program, NS's Corporate Development Department was contacted by more than 140 companies and individuals. NS decided early that proposals would be requested for specific lines from no more than three or four operators per segment. Preference was given to nearby shortline operators, but experience was the primary requirement, and many of those interested in the program but lacking experience were politely turned away. NS kept shippers located along the lines informed about the program but encouraged potential shortline operators to talk with customers as they prepared their proposals

In November 1988 the first lease was signed with the Virginia Southern Division of the North Carolina & Virginia Railroad, a RailTex property, to operate a 72-mile line from O&H Junction, North Carolina, to Burkeville, Virginia. Other leases followed, and 20 Thoroughbred leases covering 1,040 miles of track were made through April 1991, when the program was officially completed.

NS judged the Throughbred Short Line Program a success. According to NS Chief Executive Officer Arnold McKinnon, it produced a win-win-win situation: The involved shippers win when they retain their rail service; the new short lines win with profitable new business; and NS wins by retaining and enhancing its revenues. In most cases traffic was stabilized, and in several instances traffic increased for the first time in years. Smaller shippers often note the greatest improvements in service, according to McClellan.

While there are no plans to reactivate the program — NS prefers to manage and operate its own lines — changing traffic patterns on a particular route could lead to another Throughbred program in the future.

The railroads in the Thoroughbred Short Line Program are:
Aberdeen, Carolina & Western Railway
Carolina & Northwestern Railroad
Carolina Coastal Railway
Central Railroad Company of Indianapolis
Chattanooga & Chickamauga Railway
Chesapeake & Albemarle Railway
Commonwealth Railway
Great Walton Railroad
Indiana Hi-Rail Corporation
Indiana Rail Road
North Carolina & Virginia Railroad
Ogeechee Railway
Pickens Railroad
South Carolina Central Railroad
Yadkin Valley Railroad

NORTH CAROLINA & VIRGINIA RAILROAD CO., INC.

214 North Railroad Street
P. O. Box 1063
Ahoskie, NC 27910

Reporting marks: NCVA
Phone: 919-332-2778
Fax: 919-332-3325

North Carolina & Virginia Railroad provides freight service from a connection with CSX at Boykins, Virginia, to Tunis, North Carolina, 53.1 miles. Rail is 75, 85, and 100 pound. Traffic consists of 2,500 cars a year of forest products, particle board, chemicals, peanuts, grain, and other commodities.

The main line from Boykins to Kelford was built by the Roanoke & Tar River Railroad, which was chartered on March 5, 1885, and opened on October 1, 1887. The company was leased to the Seaboard & Roanoke Railroad prior to opening, and became part of the Seaboard Air Line. The line from Kelford to Tunis was built by the Norfolk & Carolina Railroad in 1898. It became part of Atlantic Coast Line's route from Rocky Mount, N. C., to Portsmouth, Virginia.

North Carolina & Virginia, which is a subsidiary of RailTex, Inc., bought the lines from CSX on November 1, 1987.

Radio frequency: 161.310
Location of enginehouse: Ahoskie, N. C.
Locomotives: 2

No.	Builder	Model	New	Builder No.
6244	EMD	GP9	8/57	23506
6515	EMD	GP9	5/57	22989

NORTH COAST RAILROAD

4 West Second Street
Eureka, CA 95502

Reporting marks: NCRR
Phone: 707-441-8055
Fax: 707-441-1324

North Coast Railroad operates freight service from a connection with the California Northern and California Western railroads at Willits, California, north through Eureka to Korblex, 156 miles. Branch lines extend from Alton to Carlotta, 5 miles, and from Arcata to Fairhaven, 9.4 miles. Rail ranges from 90 to 132 pound. Traffic is primarily lumber, and forest products — about 4,000 cars a year.

The north end of the road was built by the Eureka & Klamath Railroad, incorporated January 6, 1896. The south end was built by the Northwestern Pacific and opened about 1907. The E&K was absorbed in November 1914 by the NWP, which was owned jointly by Southern Pacific and Santa Fe (SP bought Santa Fe's interest in 1929).

In 1984 SP sold the portion of the NWP north of Willits to the Eureka Southern Railroad Co. In September 1988 the Eureka Southern acquired the Arcata & Mad River Railroad from Simpson Timber Co. for $30,000 and reopened it after a two-year closure. The line had been closed for two years. Eureka Southern went bankrupt, and its assets were sold to the North Coast Rail Authority for $5.25 million in April 1992. The Authority designated North Coast Railroad, an independent company, to operate the line, and service started on April 1, 1992.

Radio frequencies: 160.755, 161.520
Location of enginehouse: Eureka, Calif.
Locomotives: 7

No.	Builder	Model	New	Builder No.	Rebuilt
70	EMD	GP7	5/53	18418	
2872	EMD	GP9E	12/56	22897	1976
3190	EMD	GP9E	4/55	19980	1977
3779	EMD	GP9E	1/57	22922	1975
3786	EMD	GP9E	3/57	22945	1976
3804	EMD	GP9E	3/57	22943	1977
3857	EMD	GP9E	4/59	25139	1977

NORTH SHORE RAILROAD CO.

356 Priestley Avenue
Northumberland, PA 17857

Reporting marks: NSHR
Phone: 717-473-7949
Fax: 717-473-8432

North Shore operates freight service from a connection with Conrail at Northumberland, Pennsylvania, to Hicks Ferry, 43.5 miles. Rail is 101 to 130 pound. Annual traffic 2,500 cars a year is plastic, auto carpet, pet food, paper, wood products, potato starch, manufactured products, lumber, railroad cars, steel, and vegetable oil.

The line was part of the Lackawanna & Bloomsburg Railroad, which opened in April 1852, and it was acquired by the Delaware, Lackawanna & Western in June 1873.

North Shore, which is owned by Richard D. Robey and others, started operations August 1, 1984. The property is owned by SEDA-COG Joint Rail Authority.

Radio frequencies: 160.455, 160.725
Location of enginehouse: Northumberland, Pa.
Locomotives: 4

No.	Builder	Model	New	Builder No.
364, 365	EMD	SW8	12/50	13155, 13156
366	EMD	SW8	9/51	14490
446	EMD	SW9	2/53	16305

North Shore paints its engines in a scheme reminiscent of the Erie-Lackawanna, former owner of the line now operated by the NS. The train is at Bloomsburg, Pennsylvania, and ex-CR SW8 No. 365 is doing the honors. Photo by Jim Shaw.

NORTHAMPTON SWITCHING CO.

411 East 11th Street
Northampton, PA 18067

Reporting marks: NDCR
Phone: 610-262-7017

Northampton Switching operates a mile of switching track connecting with Conrail at Northampton, Pennsylvania. Traffic is salt transloading, paper, grain, glass, and newsprint. The company expect to handle up to 2,000 cars a year. The line was built originally by the Northampton & Bath Railroad. The NDC Railroad began service July 1, 1986. It was purchased by Edward J. Marakovits and the name was changed to Northampton Switching Company in January 1996.

Locomotives: 3

No.	Builder	Model	New	Builder No.	Rebuilt
51	Alco	S-6	7/41	62499	
99	Alco	RS-3M			5/79
101	Alco	S-6	2/56	81721	

NORTHEAST KANSAS & MISSOURI DIVISION, MID-MICHIGAN RAILROAD

P. O. Box 476
Hiawatha, KS 66434

Reporting marks: NEKM
Phone: 913-742-7944
Fax: 913-742-7957

Northeast Kansas & Missouri operates freight service from St. Joseph, Missouri, to Upland, Kansas, 107.7 miles. It connects with Union Pacific at St. Joseph, Hiawatha, Kan., and Marysville, Kan. Rail is 132 pound. The company also operates the Blue Rapids Railway from Marysville to Bestwall, 10.12 miles.

Traffic includes grain, food products, aggregate, chemicals, lumber, and steel — 6,000 cars a year.

The line was built by the St. Joseph & Denver City Railroad in the early 1860s. The property was sold under foreclosure in November 1875 to the St. Joseph & Pacific, and consolidated with the Kansas & Nebraska Railway in March 1877 to form the St. Joseph & Western Railroad. That line came under control of the Union Pacific in 1880. In 1885 the property was reorganized as the St. Joseph & Marysville Railroad, and consolidated with the Grand Island & Marysville to form the St. Joseph & Grand Island, a Union Pacific subsidiary.

SJ&GI sold the line to the Northeast Kansas & Missouri, a subsidiary of RailTex, Inc., on February 26, 1990. In July 1994 the company leased the Blue Rapids Railway.

Radio frequency: 160.815
Location of enginehouse: Hiawatha, Kan.
Locomotives: 2

No.	Builder	Model	New	Builder No.	Rebuilt
2167	EMD	GP7	10/52	17011	1979
2210	EMD	GP7	1/52	15798	1980

NORTHERN NEVADA RAILROAD CORP.

1100 Avenue A
P. O. Box 150150
East Ely, NV 89315-0150

Reporting marks: NN
Phone: 702-289-3000
Fax: 702-289-6313

The company operates the line of the former Nevada Northern Railway from Cobre, Nevada, through Ely to McGill, 150.5 miles. It connects with Southern Pacific at Cobre, and with Union Pacific at Shafter. Rail ranges from 60 to 115 pound. Traffic is copper concentrates, slag, crude oil, and general freight. White Pine Historical Foundation runs excursions over part of the line.

The railroad was built by the Nevada Northern Railway and opened on June 2, 1906. When the copper mines shut down in 1983, the railroad closed. It was eventually sold to the Los Angeles Department of Water & Power, which leased it to Northern Nevada, an independent company. Freight service resumed in January 1995.

Radio frequencies: 161.370, 160.260
Location of enginehouse: East Ely, Nev.
Locomotives: 4

No.	Builder	Model	New	Builder No.
12	GE	70-ton	3/52	31282
13	GE	70-ton	8/50	30447
24, 25	Alco	MRS-1		

NORTHERN OHIO & WESTERN RAILWAY, LTD.

729 North County Road 11
Tiffin, OH 44883

Reporting marks: NOW
Phone: 419-448-8896
Fax: 419-448-8898

Northern Ohio & Western operates freight service from a connection with CSX at Tiffin, Ohio, to a connection with Conrail at Woodville, 25.5 miles. Interchange is also made with Norfolk Southern at Maple Grove. Rail is 132 pound. Traffic includes lime, feldspar, clay, and presswood.

The line was built by the Toledo, Tiffin & Eastern Railroad, which opened May 1, 1873. It was reorganized under foreclosure as the Northern Ohio Railroad in 1876, and leased to the Pennsylvania Railroad in 1879.

Indiana Hi-Rail started shortline service on the line in 1990 when it was purchased from Conrail by the Sandusky County/Seneca County/Tiffin Port Authority. The authority leased it to OmniTRAX effective May 16, 1995.

Location of enginehouse: Tiffin, Ohio
Locomotives: 1

No.	Builder	Model	New	Builder No.
4497	EMD	GP9	7/59	23662

NORTHWESTERN OKLAHOMA RAILROAD CO.

North 15th and Dead End
P. O. Box 1131
Woodward, OK 73801

Reporting marks: NOKL
Phone: 405-256-7601
Fax: 405-256-7701

Northwestern Oklahoma operates a 4.8-mile switching line at Woodward, Oklahoma. It interchanges with Santa Fe. Rail is 60 pound. Traffic includes drilling mud, propane, sand, and tank cars moving to a car repair facility — under 500 cars a year.

This railroad is part of the 304-mile Wichita Falls & Northwestern Railway, opened in 1912. It was acquired and operated as a subsidiary of the Missouri-Kansas-Texas until it was abandoned west of Altus, Okla., in 1972. Northwestern Oklahoma began operations in January 1973. It is owned by Interail, Inc. (Garvey International).

Location of enginehouse: Woodward, Okla.
Locomotives: 1

No.	Builder	Model	New	Builder No.
101	GE	65-ton	5/42	15267

Freight cars: 1,895

OAKLAND TERMINAL RAILWAY

2001 Engineers Road
Oakland, CA 94607

Reporting marks: OTR
Phone: 510-832-8464
Fax: 510-231-2628

Oakland Terminal operates 10 miles of switching track in Oakland, California, connecting with the Santa Fe, Southern Pacific, and Union Pacific. Rail is 90 to 112 pound. About 1,000 cars a year are handled.

The company was organized in 1943 under the joint ownership of the Santa Fe and the Western Pacific to take over the freight operations of the Oakland Terminal Railroad, a subsidiary of the Key System, a street and interurban railway connecting Oakland and Berkeley with San Francisco via the Bay Bridge. WP's share of the Oakland Terminal is now owned by Union Pacific.

Radio frequency: 160.935
Locomotives: 1

No.	Builder	Model	New	Builder No.	Rebuilt
97	EMD	GP7	12/52	17701	1980

OGEECHEE RAILWAY CO.

723 Dover Road
Route 5, Box 172B
Sylvania, GA 30467

Reporting marks: OGEE
Phone: 912-863-7565
Fax: 912-863-7028

The Ogeechee operates four separate line segments in Georgia:
• from a Norfolk Southern connection at Dover to Metter, 29.2 miles
• from the Norfolk Southern at Ardmore to Sylvania, 21.1 miles
• from Hawkinsville to Cochran, 9.53 miles
• from Roberta through Fort Valley to Perry, 32 miles

Rail ranges from 65 to 100 pound. About 6,000 cars a year of lumber, pulpwood, wood chips, fertilizer, soybeans, scrap, and aggregates make up the road's traffic.

The Hawkinsville and Fort Valley lines are former Southern Railway trackage. The Metter line was a Central of Georgia branch, and the Sylvania line was part of the Savannah & Atlanta main line. They are leased from Southern Railway under Norfolk Southern's Throughbred Shortline Program.

Ogeechee service started June 20, 1989 on the Metter and Sylvania lines. Service on the Perry line started April 15, 1991.

The Ogeechee Railway is controlled by David P. Bodiford.
Radio frequencies: 160.230, 161.280
Location of enginehouses: Dover, Sylvania, Fort Valley, and Cochran, Ga.

Locomotives: 4

No.	Builder	Model	New	Builder No.
1001, 1002	GMD	SW8	6/51	A-235, A-233
1551	EMD	GP7	6/51	13364
6707	EMD	SW8	11/52	16225

Ogeechee SW8 No. 102, "The Georgia Peach," awaits assignment at Fort Valley, Georgia, in December 1992. Photo by Jim Shaw.

OHI-RAIL CORP.

6200 Salineville Road, N.E.
P. O. Box 75
Mechanicstown, OH 44651

Reporting marks: OHIC
Phone: 216-738-6735

Ohi-Rail operates freight service from a connection with Conrail at Bayard, Ohio, through Minerva to a connection with the Wheeling & Lake Erie at Hopedale, 34 miles. There is a second W&LE connection at Minerva Junction. Rail is predominantly 105 pound. Traffic includes brick, machinery, solid waste, lumber, and wallboard — under 500 cars a year.

Ohi-Rail started service July 30, 1982, on this former Conrail line, which comprises parts of New York Central's Alliance branch, and Pennsylvania's Tuscarawas branch. The track south of Minerva yard is owned by the state of Ohio and leased to the railroad. Ohi-Rail is controlled by Mike Carapellotti, Tom Barnett, and others.

Radio frequency: 160.845
Location of enginehouses: Minerva and Mechanicstown, Ohio
Locomotives: 2

No.	Builder	Model	New	Builder No.
101	Alco	S-2	10/45	74336
102	Alco	S-2	6/46	74482

OHIO & PENNSYLVANIA RAILROAD CO.

136 South Fifth Street
Coshocton, OH 43812

Reporting marks: OHPA
Phone: 614-622-8092
Fax: 614-622-8097

Ohio & Pennsylvania provides freight service from Darlington, Pennsylvania, to Youngstown and Struthers (Gateway Yard), Ohio, 38.5 miles, and from Negley, Ohio, to Smith's Ferry, Pa., 13 miles. Interchange is made with CSX and Conrail at Youngstown. Rail ranges from 90 to 132 pound. Traffic includes under 500 cars a year of pipe, lumber, pulpboard, scrap paper, brick, and railcar parts.

The line from Struthers to Youngstown is a former Pittsburgh & Lake Erie line. The other lines were acquired from the Youngstown & Southern. The north end of the line was built by the Youngstown & Southern Railroad, which was incorporated in 1905 (from 1916 to 1944 the name of the company was Youngstown & Suburban).

The south end of the line, from Darlington to Lisbon, was built by the Pittsburgh, Lisbon & Western Railroad, incorporated in 1896. It was absorbed by the Y&S on January 1, 1945. The Pittsburgh & Lake Erie controlled the company from 1946 until the property was leased to the PL&W Railroad on May 1, 1993. Ohio & Pennsylvania Railroad took over operation under a lease-purchase agreement on June 14, 1995. The Ohio & Pennsylvania is part of the Ohio Central Railroad System (Jerry J. Jacobson).

Location of enginehouse: Negley, Ohio
Locomotives: 2

No.	Builder	Model	New	Builder No.
71	EMD	SW7	11/50	13020
91	EMD	GP9	4/57	22468

OHIO CENTRAL RAILROAD CO.

136 South Fifth Street
Coshocton, OH 43812

Reporting marks: OHCR
Phone: 614-622-8092
Fax: 614-622-8097

Radio frequencies: 160.215, 160.845
Location of enginehouse: Coshocton, Ohio
Locomotives: 14

No.	Builder	Model	New	Builder No.
12	Alco	S-1	5/50	77487
13	Alco	2-8-0	1/20	61579
52	EMD	SW9	4/53	12866
63	Alco	S-2	1948	76163
64	Alco	S-1		
94	EMD	GP9	1/58	24378
95	Alco	S-4	8/51	78827
99	EMD	GP9	9/56	22243
1551	MLW	4-6-0	1912	60778
1663	Alco	S-2	9/48	76163
1695	Alco	S-4		
5407	EMD	GP8	8/53	18635
5408	EMD	GP8	12/50	12008
6325	Alco	4-8-4	2/42	69631

Ohio Central operates freight service from a connection with CSX and Ohio Southern at Zanesville, Ohio, to a connection with Wheeling & Lake Erie near Brewster, 70.6 miles. Additional connections are made with Columbus & Ohio River at Morgan Run (Coshocton) and with CSX at Warwick. Rail is 90 and 110 pound. Traffic includes coiled steel, scrap, coke, coal, brick, paper, lumber, and plastic — 6,400 cars a year. Seasonal excursions run between Sugar Creek and Baltic.

The line was built in part by the Connotton Valley & Straightsville Railroad, incorporated June 20, 1881. By 1883 the line was open from Brewster to Coshocton. In May 1885 the company was reorganized as the Cleveland & Canton Railroad, and three years later the 3-foot gauge line was relaid to standard gauge. The affiliated Coshocton & Southern Railroad opened a line from Coshocton to Zanesville on June 12, 1889. It was reorganized as the Cleveland, Canton & Southern in May 1892 and came under control of the Wheeling & Lake Erie in August 1899. Wheeling & Lake Erie became part of the Nickel Plate System in 1949, and NKP became part of the Norfolk & Western in 1964. The line was sold by Norfolk Southern to Ohio Central and started April 10, 1988.

The company is part of the Ohio Central Railroad System (Jerry J. Jacobson).

Ohio Central 99, a GP9, and 52, an SW9, lead a freight train through Pear, Ohio. Photo by Jim Shaw.

OHIO SOUTHERN RAILROAD CO.

136 South Fifth Street
Coshocton, OH 43812

Reporting marks: OSRR
Phone: 614-622-8092
Fax: 614-622-8097

Ohio Southern operates freight service from a connection with Conrail at New Lexington, Ohio, to connections with CSX and Ohio Central at Zanesville, with a branch from "FS" to Glass Rock, 31.7 miles total. Rail is 85, 105, and 131 pound. The railroad's annual traffic is under 500 cars a year of clay, silica sand, cement, and coal.

The lines are former Conrail track (part Pennsylvania Railroad and part New York Central) acquired by the state of Ohio in 1982. Operations were conducted by Moxahala Valley Railroad starting in March 1983, then turned over to Ohio Southern on September 20, 1986. The company is part of the Ohio Central Railroad System (Jerry J. Jacobson).

Radio frequency: 160.845
Locomotives: 1 (pooled with Ohio Central)

No.	Builder	Model	New	Builder No.
70	EMD	GP7	4/53	17983

OIL CREEK & TITUSVILLE LINES, INC.

50 Commercial Street
P. O. Box 309
Gowanda, NY 14010

Reporting marks: OCTL
Phone: 716-532-5242

Oil Creek & Titusville operates freight and excursion service from a connection with Conrail near Rouseville, Pennsylvania, to Titusville, 16.5 miles. Rail ranges from 80 to 140 pound. Freight traffic includes lumber, plastic, and wax — under 300 cars a year. The excursions are sponsored by the Oil Creek Railway Historical Society.

The line was part of the main line of the Buffalo, New York & Philadelphia Railroad in the 1880s. It was reorganized as the Western New York & Pennsylvania in 1887, and acquired by the Pennsylvania Railroad in August 1900. Titusville industrial trackage was originally part of the Dunkirk, Allegheny Valley &

Pittsburgh. The lines were acquired from Conrail in 1986 by the Oil Creek Railway Historical Society, Inc. Excursions started July 18, 1986, and the company secured freight operating agreements with Conrail effective September 25, 1986. The operating company is owned by Robert O. Dingman, Jr.

On December 2, 1995, Oil Creek & Titusville began operation on Conrail's former Erie main line between Meadville and Corry, Pa. Traffic is primarily sand; the company expects to move about 250 cars a year on that line. Rail is 115 and 131 pound. The line is owned by the Meadville Rail Authority.

Radio frequency: 160.920
Location of enginehouse: Titusville, Pa.
Locomotives: 1

No.	Builder	Model	New	Builder No.
75	Alco	S-2	3/47	74973

OLD AUGUSTA RAILROAD CO.

Buck Creek Road
P. O. Box 329
New Augusta, MS 39462

Reporting marks: OAR
Phone: 601-964-8411
Fax: 601-964-3227

The Old Augusta Railroad operates freight service from a connection with Illinois Central at New Augusta, Mississippi, to Augusta, 2.5 miles. Rail is 90 pound. Traffic is paper products, pulp, and lumber — more than 10,000 cars a year.

The line was built between August 1982 and early 1983. The

ICC approved common carrier status February 23, 1983. The company is owned by Leaf Forest Products (Georgia Pacific Corp.).
Radio frequencies: 160.425, 160.815
Location of enginehouse: Augusta, Miss.
Locomotives: 2

No.	Builder	Model	New	Builder No.
100	EMD	NW2	7/46	3609
200	EMD	MP15	12/74	74641-10

Freight cars: 195 boxcars

It takes all the motive power on Old Augusta's roster to move a long freight train over the concrete-pile trestle spanning the Leaf River. Photo by Louis Saillard.

OMAHA, LINCOLN, AND BEATRICE RAILWAY CO.

1815 Y Street
P. O. Box 80268
Lincoln, NE 68501

Reporting marks: OLB
Phone: 402-476-1212
Fax: 402-476-3310

The Omaha, Lincoln, and Beatrice is a switching road with 4.67 miles of track (2.5 route miles) at Lincoln, Nebraska. It connects with the Burlington Northern and Union Pacific. It handles about 8,000 cars of sand, grain, and cement annually. The company was organized in 1913 as an electric road, and is currently owned by Nebco, Inc.

Radio frequency: 160.740
Locomotives: 3

No.	Builder	Model	New	Builder No.
47	Republic	RL-1500	1990	
101	GE	44-ton	12/50	30849
102	GE	70-ton	10/51	31170

Freight cars: 166 hopper cars

OL&B "Big Red Line" GE 70-ton switcher switches aggregate cars at Lincoln, Nebraska. Photo by Jim Shaw.

ONTARIO CENTRAL RAILROAD CORP.

280 Maple Avenue
Victor, NY 14564

Reporting marks: ONCT
Phone: 716-924-2127
Fax: 716-924-7906

Ontario Central operates freight service from a connection with Finger Lakes Railroad at Shortsville, New York, to West Victor, 13.3 miles. Rail is 136 pound. About 120 cars a year of lumber, feldspar, sand, and clay make up the road's traffic.

The line is a short section of the former Lehigh Valley main line opened in the 1892. Ontario County purchased the property from Conrail, and Ontario Central, which is controlled by local shippers, started service on October 1, 1979.

Radio frequency: 161.370
Location of enginehouse: Victor, N. Y.
Locomotives: 1

No.	Builder	Model	New	Builder No.
86	Alco	RS-36	2/62	83697

ONTARIO MIDLAND RAILROAD CORP.

48 Beldon Avenue
P. O. Box 248
Sodus, NY 14551

Reporting marks: OMID
Phone: 315-483-6914
Fax: 315-483-6814

Ontario Midland Railroad Corp. operates freight service from a connection with Conrail at Newark, New York, to Wallington, 12 miles, and from West Webster to Wolcott, 44 miles. Rail ranges from 90 to 130 pounds. Traffic includes food products, lumber, fertilizer, pulpboard, and chemicals — about 850 cars a year. The Rochester Chapter of the National Railway Historical Society operates seasonal excursions from Sodus to Newark.

The Sodus Point line was built by the Sodus Point & Southern Railroad, which was chartered in 1852 but not opened until 1872. In 1875 it was reorganized as the Ontario Southern, and seven years later as the Sodus Bay & Southern. In 1884 it was sold to the Northern Central Railroad (Pennsylvania Railroad).

The Webster line was built by the Lake Ontario Shore Railroad, which was chartered in 1858. That line was sold to the Rome, Watertown & Ogdensburg in 1875, and the following year it became part of a through route from Lewiston, near Niagara Falls, to Oswego. RW&O became part of the New York Central.

Ontario Midland service started October 1, 1979. The fixed property is owned by Wayne and Monroe counties, and the operating company is controlled by shippers located along the line.
Radio frequency: 161.370
Location of enginehouse: Sodus, N. Y.
Locomotives: 2

No.	Builder	Model	New	Builder No.
36	Alco	RS-11	12/57	82638
40	Alco	RS-36	3/62	84108

ONTARIO NORTHLAND RAILWAY

555 Oak Street, East
North Bay, ON P1B 8L3
Canada

Reporting Marks: ONT
Phone: 705-472-4500
Fax: 705-472-5598

Ontario Northland Railway operates freight, TOFC, and passenger service on its main line from North Bay, Ontario, to Moosonee, 439 miles. There are several branch lines
• from Swastika to Noranda, Quebec, 58 miles
• from Iroquois Falls through Porquis to Kidd, 19 miles
• from Cochrane to Hearst, 129 miles, a line acquired from Canadian National in August 1993

Traffic consists of paper, forest products, iron ore, and other minerals, about 42,000 cars a year

The railroad was incorporated as the Temiskaming & Northern Ontario Railroad on March 17, 1902. Its name was changed to Ontario Northland Railway in 1946. The railway is owned by the Province of Ontario and operated by the Ontario Northland Transportation Commission.
Radio frequencies: 161.265/160.545, 160.995
Enginehouse: North Bay, Ont.
Locomotives: 33

No.	Builder	Model	New	Builder No.	No.	Builder	Model	New	Builder No.
1501	GMD	FP7A	1951	A-174	1987	GMD	FP7A	1952	A-381
1509	GMD	FP7A	1952	A-380	2000	GMD	FP7A	1951	A-176
1521	GMD	FP7A	1953	A-532	73B	EMD	F7B	1950	10339
1600-1605	GMD	GP9	1956-1957		84B	EMD	F3B	1949	6318
1730-1737	GMD	SD40-2	1973-1974		121B	EMD	F7B	1953	18216
1800-1809	GMD	GP38-2	1974, 1982, 1984		126C	EMD	F9B	1955	20611
1984, 1985	GMD	FP7A	1951	A-530, A-529					

Freight cars: 592

ORANGE PORT TERMINAL RAILWAY

9221 Northridge
Orange, TX 77632

Reporting marks: OPT
Phone: 409-886-8562

Orange Port Terminal Railway is a switching road with 1.8 miles of former Southern Pacific track at Orange, Texas. It connects with SP and is operated by Gulf Coast Rail Service (Russell A. Peterson, Larry Locke, and others).

Locomotives: 2

No.	Builder	Model	New	Builder No.
2450	EMD	SW1500	9/67	33141
3816	EMD	GP9	3/59	25153

OSAGE RAILROAD

1604 South Spruce Street
Coffeyville, KS 67337

Reporting marks: ORR
Phone: 316-251-3600

The Osage Railroad provides freight service from a connection with Burlington Northern and Union Pacific at Tulsa, Oklahoma, to Barnsdall, 35 miles. Rail is 90 pound. Traffic is predominantly refinery products — 500 cars a year.

The line is part of the route of the Midland Valley Railroad, which was incorporated in 1903 and ran between Wichita, Kansas, and Fort Smith, Arkansas. MV was acquired by Texas & Pacific in 1964, and merged into that company three years later. Shortline operations started August 20, 1990.

The Osage Railroad is affiliated with the Southeast Kansas Railroad.

Locomotives: 1

No.	Builder	Model	New
1000	AT&SF	CF7	1971

OTTER TAIL VALLEY RAILROAD CO., INC.

200 North Mill Street
Fergus Falls, MN 56537

Reporting marks: OTVR
Phone: 218-736-6073
Fax: 218-736-7636

GP18 No. 194 pulls a short train on the Otter Tail Valley Railroad at Brandon, Minnesota, in June 1990. Photo by Jim Shaw.

The Otter Tail Valley Railroad operates freight service from Fergus Falls, Minnesota, to Moorhead, 55 miles, connecting with Burlington Northern at Dilworth, near Moorhead. A 12-mile branch runs from Fergus Falls to Foxhome. Rail is 112 to 115 pound. Traffic includes coal, grain, and agricultural chemicals, and amounts to about 5,000 cars a year.

The line is part of the former Great Northern main line between St. Cloud and Fargo. It was acquired from Burlington Northern, and shortline service started October 27, 1986. Otter Tail Valley abandoned a 96-mile portion of the line from Fergus Falls to Avon in February 1991. The company is independent.

Radio frequency: 160.425
Location of enginehouse: Fergus Falls, Minn.
Locomotives: 4

No.	Builder	Model	New	Builder No.
181	EMD	GP18	9/63	27774
189	EMD	GP18	9/63	27782
192	EMD	GP18	10/63	27785
194	EMD	GP18	10/63	27787

OUACHITA RAILROAD CO.

730 South Washington
El Dorado, AR 71730

Reporting marks: OUCH
Phone: 501-663-7044
Fax: 501-663-7048

Ouachita Railroad operates freight service from a connection with Union Pacific at El Dorado, Arkansas, to Lille, Louisiana, 26.2 miles. Rail is 90 pound. Traffic includes chemicals, lumber, and particle board — 2,000 cars a year.

The line is a former Rock Island branch previously operated by the South Central Arkansas Railroad and the East Camden & Highland Railroad. On November 10, 1990, the East Camden & Highland sold it to Arkansas Short Line Railroads, Inc. (William K. Robbins, Jr.)

Radio frequencies: 161.295, 161.175
Location of enginehouse: El Dorado, Ark.
Locomotives: 2

No.	Builder	Model	New	Builder No.
63	EMD	SW9	5/53	18298
64	EMD	NW2	5/39	868

Freight cars: 70 boxcars

OWEGO & HARFORD RAILWAY, INC.

701 Wyoming Avenue
Scranton, PA 18509

Reporting marks: OHRY
Phone: 603-542-2756

The Owego & Harford Railway provides freight service from a connection with Conrail and CP Rail System (Delaware & Hudson) at Owego, New York, to North Harford, 27.6 miles. Rail is 100 pound. Traffic includes LP gas, logs, aggregate, and paper scrap amounting to about 800 cars a year. The affiliated Tioga Scenic Railroad operates seasonal excursion trains over the line.

The line was built by the Southern Central Railroad in 1874. It became part of the Lehigh Valley by the 1880s. The property was sold to the Tioga County Industrial Development Agency by Conrail in April 1987. Tioga Central Railroad was chosen to run the line, and shortline service started on April 14, 1987. In 1992, the agency chose chose the current company to operate the line. It started service on May 1, 1992. The railroad is controlled by Steven C. May, who also controls the Luzerne & Susquehanna Railway.

Radio frequency: 161.310
Location of enginehouse: Owego, N. Y.
Locomotives: 1

No.	Builder	Model	New	Builder No.
151	GMD	GP9	4/56	A-930

Freight cars: 10 boxcars

PADUCAH & LOUISVILLE RAILWAY, INC.

1500 Kentucky Avenue
Paducah, KY 42001

Reporting marks: PAL
Phone: 502-444-4300
Fax: 502-444-4388

Paducah & Louisville operates a freight line from Paducah, Kentucky, to Louisville, 225 miles, with branch lines from Dawson Springs to Central City (37 miles), and from Kevil through Paducah to Clayburn (28 miles). A total of 309 miles are operated. It connects with Burlington Northern, CSX, Illinois Central, CP Rail System, Norfolk Southern, and several short lines.

Traffic, primarily coal and chemicals, is about 181,000 cars a year. The railroad serves rail-river transfer stations at Jessup, Grand River, and Paducah.

The line was acquired from Illinois Central Gulf by CG&T Industries, Inc. (Jim R. Smith and David W. Reed) for $70 million in August 1986. First National Bank of Boston provided financing assistance. Service started August 27, 1986.

The company was sold to Rail Holdings, Inc./First Chicago Corporation on November 18, 1988. On May 26, 1995, an agreement was made to sell the company to Four Rivers Transportation, Inc., which is controlled by P&L management (CSX will have a minority interest). No changes are expected.

Radio frequencies: 160.740 (road), 160.695, 161.325
Principal shop: Paducah, Ky.
Locomotives: 73 (11 SW9/13/14, 62 GP7/8/10/30/35)
Freight cars: 1,146

PALOUSE RIVER RAILWAY

709 North Tenth Street
Walla Walla, WA 99362

Reporting marks: BLMR
Phone: 509-522-1464

The Palouse River Railway provides freight service from a connection with Union Pacific at Hooper Junction, Washington, through Colfax to Moscow, Idaho, 81 miles. A branch runs from Winona, Wash., to Thorton, 28.5 miles. Total mileage is 112.8. Traffic includes about 3,000 cars a year of grain and coal.

These lines were built in part by the Walla Walla & Columbia River and acquired by the Oregon Railway & Navigation Co. during the late 1800s. The line from Colfax to Moscow was built by the Columbia & Palouse Railroad and opened in 1885. The lines were purchased from Union Pacific, and shortline service began on November 20, 1992. The Palouse River Railway is controlled by Charles and Kaye Webb and is operated in conjunction with the Blue Mountain Railroad.
Radio frequency: 160.785
Location of enginehouse: Colfax, Wash.
Locomotives: 2

No.	Builder	Model	New	Builder No.
792	EMD	GP35	3/65	30217
799	EMD	GP35	4/65	30226

PANHANDLE & NORTHERN RAILROAD CO.

100 East Grand
Borger, TX 79007

Reporting marks: PNR
Phone: 806-273-3513
Fax: 806-273-2708

Panhandle & Northern operates freight service from Borger, Texas, to a connection with the Santa Fe at Panhandle, 31.27 miles. Rail is 112 to 115 pound. Traffic is primarily petroleum products, and carbon black, LP gas, scrap, grain, and fertilizer — about 15,000 cars a year. The line was built by the Panhandle & Santa Fe Railroad in 1926. It became part of the Santa Fe system, and was sold to the current operator on November 15, 1993. The Panhandle & Northern is a subsidiary of OmniTRAX.
Radio frequency: 161.085

Location of enginehouse: Borger, Texas
Locomotives: 10

No.	Builder	Model	New	Builder No.	Rebuilt
2066	EMD	GP7	1/52	15810	1974
2067	EMD	GP7	12/53	18910	1974
2069	EMD	GP7	12/52	17643	1974
4284	EMD	GP7	4/51	14309	
4433	EMD	GP7	1953	18476	
4434	EMD	GP7	1952	15475	
4435	EMD	GP7	1953	18487	
4482	EMD	GP7	1951	14307	
4484	EMD	GP7	1953	18250	
4547	EMD	GP9	1957	23566	

PARR TERMINAL RAILROAD

402 Wright Avenue
P. O. Box 5297
Richmond, CA 94804

Reporting marks: PRT
Phone: 510-232-4422
Fax: 510-236-9235

The Parr Terminal is a switching line with 1.9 miles of track at Richmond, California. It connects with Santa Fe and Southern Pacific. Traffic is about 3,250 cars a year.

The railroad was incorporated in July 1950 to take over the private railroad of the Parr-Richmond Industrial Corp. It is owned by Levin-Richmond Terminal Corp.

Radio frequencies: 469.525, 469.875
Locomotives: 3

No.	Builder	Model	New	Builder No.
1195	EMD	SW900	6/54	19645
1402	EMD	NW2	6/49	7314
2285	EMD	SW1200	11/65	30252

PATAPSCO & BACK RIVERS RAILROAD CO.

Sparrows Point Boulevard
P. O. Box 9166
Baltimore, MD 21222

Reporting marks: PBR
Phone: 301-388-7937

The Patapsco & Back Rivers is a switching line with 97 miles of track at Sparrows Point (Baltimore), Maryland. It connects with Conrail at Sparrows Point and with CSX at Bear Creek Junction. Rail is 115 pound. It handles about 35,000 cars a year. The railroad started operations in 1918 and is owned by Bethlehem Steel Company.

Radio frequencies: 160.590, 161.520
Locomotives: 21

No.	Builder	Model
107-109	EMD	SW1001
116, 121, 122	EMD	SW7
112-115, 117, 123, 124	EMD	SW9
128, 130, 132, 133, 135	EMD	SW1200

Freight cars: 175 gondolas

PEARL RIVER VALLEY RAILROAD CO.

1801 Goodyear Boulevard
P. O. Box 190
Picayune, MS 39466

Reporting marks: PRV
Phone: 601-798-6961
Fax: 601-798-8415

Pearl River Valley operates freight service from a connection with Norfolk Southern at Nicholson, Mississippi, to Goodyear, 4.69

Pearl River Valley No. 101 works the Norfolk Southern interchange at Nicholson, Mississippi. Photo by Warren Calloway.

miles. Rail is 85 pound. Traffic is forest products, chemicals, and miscellaneous commodities — less than 500 cars a year.

The company was incorporated May 22, 1917, to build a railroad from Nicholson to Columbia. It was opened as far as Crosby, 25.34 miles, on December 31, 1924. It is owned by the Gammill family.

Radio frequencies: 466.450/461.450, 466.700/461.700
Location of enginehouse: Picayune, Miss.
Locomotives: 1

No.	Builder	Model	New	Builder No.
101	GE	65-ton	9/49	30041

PECOS VALLEY SOUTHERN RAILWAY CO.

1626 West Third Street
P. O. Box 349
Pecos, TX 79772

Reporting marks: PVS
Phone: 915-445-2487
Fax: 915-445-2488

Pecos Valley Southern operates freight service from a connection with the Union Pacific at Pecos, Texas, to Saragosa, 29.3 miles. Rail ranges from 56 to 110 pound. Traffic amounts to about 2,000 cars a year of sand, gravel, and barite ore.

The company was incorporated May 28, 1909, and the railroad opened from Pecos to Toyahvale, 40.1 miles, on May 1, 1910. The company was controlled and operated by the Texas & Pacific Railroad from 1927 to 1946. Passenger service ended in the late 1940s, and the line was cut back from Toyahvale to Saragosa in 1971. Trans-Pecos Materials, Inc. owns the company.

Radio frequency: 161.100
Location of enginehouse: Pecos, Texas
Locomotives: 2

No.	Builder	Model	New	Builder No.
7	GE	70-ton	7/49	30181
9	EMD	SW900M	5/57	23538

PEE DEE RIVER RAILWAY DIVISION, ABERDEEN & ROCKFISH RAILROAD

101 East Main Street
P. O. Box 917
Aberdeen, NC 28315

Reporting marks: PDRR
Phone: 910-944-2341

The Pee Dee River Railway operates freight service from a CSX connection at McColl, South Carolina, to Marlboro, 16.79 miles. A

Pee Dee River's blue-and-white CF7 No. 2486 and Aberdeen & Rockfish GP7U No. 210 leave the Willamette paper mill at Marlboro, South Carolina, bound for the CSX connection at Clio. Photo by Jim Shaw.

2-mile spur runs from Bennettsville to Breeden. Mainline rail is 85 to 100 pound. Approximately 8,500 cars a year of wood chips, paper, chemicals, grain, fertilizer, and aggregates make up the road's traffic.

The line was built by the South Carolina Pacific Railway, which was chartered February 9, 1882. When it opened, it was leased to the Cape Fear & Yadkin Valley and subsequently to the Atlantic Coast Line. It was merged into Seaboard System in May 1984. The line was abandoned by CSX, and sold to Marlboro County in 1987. Pee Dee River Railway service started October 1, 1987. It is a division of the Aberdeen & Rockfish Railroad.

Radio frequencies: 161.310, 161.280
Location of enginehouse: Bennettsville, S. C.
Locomotives: 2 (pooled with Aberdeen & Rockfish)

No.	Builder	Model	New	Builder No.
2486	AT&SF	CF7	1/75	
5081	EMD	SW9	4/52	11714

Freight cars: 51 boxcars

PEND OREILLE VALLEY RAILROAD

1981 Black Road
Usk, WA 99180

Reporting marks: POVA
Phone: 509-445-1750
Fax: 509-445-1522

Pend Oreille Valley operates freight service from Metaline Falls, Washington, to a connection with the Burlington Northern at Newport, 61.5 miles. Rail is 75 to 100 pound. Traffic is wood chips, lumber, newsprint, and chemicals — about 3,000 cars a year.

The line was built by the Idaho & Washington Northern Railroad between 1907 and 1910. The Milwaukee Road obtained control of the line by 1916. When the Milwaukee Road abandoned its western lines, the Metaline Falls-Newport line was sold to the Port of Pend Oreille. Shortline service started on October 1, 1979, under the management of Kyle Railways, which continued until 1984.

The Pend Oreille Valley Railroad is owned and operated by the Port of Pend Oreille.

Radio frequencies: 160.415, 160.500
Location of enginehouse: Usk, Wash.
Locomotives: 2

No.	Builder	Model	New	Builder No.
101	EMD	GP9	6/55	20307
102	EMD	GP9	2/57	22718

Pend Oreille Valley GP9 No. 102 passes through Lost Creek, Washington, in June 1990. Photo by Jim Shaw.

PENINSULA TERMINAL CO.

2416 North Marine Drive, Suite 226
Portland, OR 97217

Reporting marks: PT
Phone: 503-285-5023
Fax: 503-285-6154

Peninsula Terminal operates 2.23 miles of track at North Portland, Oregon, connecting with Burlington Northern, Union Pacific, and Southern Pacific (via BN or UP). Rail is 70 to 90 pound. It carries about 1,200 cars a year.

The railroad was incorporated in 1916, and was leased to the Union Pacific and Spokane, Portland & Seattle until 1931. It was acquired by Kess Railway Group on July 1, 1994.

Radio frequency: 457.775
Locomotives: 3

No.	Builder	Model	New	Builder No.
3	GE	70-ton	3/56	32510
20	GE	70-ton	7/49	30176
50	GE	70-ton	3/52	31283

PEORIA & PEKIN UNION RAILWAY CO.

101 Wesley Road
Creve Coeur, IL 61611

Reporting marks: PPU
Phone: 309-694-8600
Fax: 309-694-8623

The Peoria & Pekin Union is a switching line operating 130 miles of track (12 route miles) at Peoria, Illinois for freight, TOFC, and COFC service. It connects with Burlington Northern, Chicago & Illinois Midland, Chicago & North Western, Conrail, Iowa Interstate, Illinois Central, Keokuk Junction, Norfolk Southern, and Toledo, Peoria & Western. The railroad handles more than 150,000 cars a year. The company was incorporated on September 28, 1880, and is owned by Illinois Central, Conrail, Norfolk Southern, and Chicago & North Western. In 1985 the company began operating the Peoria, Peoria Heights & Western Railroad, a short section of former Rock Island track at Peoria Heights.

Radio frequencies: 160.470, 160.500, 160.530, 160.545
Locomotives: 7

No.	Builder	Model	New	Builder No.	Rebuilt
601	EMD	NW2	10/47	5535	1975
602	EMD	SW7	8/50	10088	1977
608	EMD	NW2	6/48	5598	1981
609	EMD	SW1200	5/65	30307	
700	EMD	SW10	12/50	11674	1992
701	EMD	SW10			1993
800	PLW*	SC15A-3	12/94		

*Peoria Locomotive Works

Freight cars: 50 flatcars, 30 covered hoppers, 20 boxcars, 280 gondolas

PHILADELPHIA, BETHLEHEM & NEW ENGLAND RAILROAD CO.

1744 East Fourth Street
Bethlehem, PA 18015

Reporting marks: PBNE
Phone: 215-694-4638

The Philadelphia, Bethlehem, and New England is a switching line at Bethlehem, Pennsylvania. It operates 56 miles of track and connects with Conrail and CP Rail System (Delaware & Hudson). Rail is 115 pound. It handles about 60,000 cars a year.

The company was incorporated in 1910 and began operations in 1912. It is owned by Bethlehem Steel Co.

Radio frequencies: 160.215, 160.575, 161.280, 161.565

Locomotives: 24 (plus 5 slugs)

No.	Builder	Model
10-14		Slug
21-28	EMD	NW2
31-34	EMD	SW7
35-38	EMD	SW9
39-43	EMD	SW1200
50, 51	EMD	SW900M
90	EMD	SW7

Freight cars: 125 flatcars, 169 gondolas

PICKENS RAILROAD CO.

402 Cedar Rock Street
P. O. Box 216
Pickens, SC 29671

Reporting marks: PICK
Phone: 864-878-3581
Fax: 864-878-3582

The Pickens operates freight service from a connection with the Norfolk Southern at Easley, South Carolina, to Pickens, 9.9 miles, and from Belton to Honea Path, 16 miles. Rail is 85 to 100 pound on the Easley-Pickens line and 85 pound on the Belton-Honea Path line. Traffic is transportation equipment, cotton, lumber, paper, and fertilizer, amounting to about 700 cars a year.

The company was chartered May 10, 1892, to build a 19-mile line from Easley to Olenoy Gap via Pickens. The line was opened to Pickens in May 1898, and never extended. Passenger service ended in 1928. The Belton line (part of the old Blue Ridge Railway) was leased to the Pickens Railroad under NS's Throughbred Shortline Program on April 11, 1990.

Emergent Group and its predecessor, National Railway Utilization Corporation, have controlled the company since 1973.

Radio frequency: 161.280
Location of enginehouses: Pickens, and Anderson, S. C.
Locomotives: 2

No.	Builder	Model	New	Builder No.
2	BLW	VO-660	11/46	72824
5	BLW	S-8	2/51	73658

PIGEON RIVER RAILROAD CO.

Railroad Street
P. O. Box 123
South Milford, IN 46786

Reporting marks: PGRV
Phone: 219-351-2421

Pigeon River Railroad operates freight service from South Milford, Indiana, to Ashley-Hudson, Ohio, 9.3 miles, then by trackage rights over the Indiana Northeastern to Montpelier, Ohio, where it connects with Norfolk Southern. Rail is 100 pound. Traffic is grain, and agriculture-related — 500 cars a year.

The line was built about 1893 as part of Wabash's Chicago to Detroit route. It was acquired in 1985 following abandonment by Norfolk & Western. Service started November 18, 1985, and 5 miles from South Milford to Wolcottville was abandoned in Sept. 1991. The Pigeon River Railroad was acquired by the Indiana Northeastern in 1992 and is now operated as part of that line. The two roads are owned by the South Milford Grain Company.

Radio frequency: 461.825
Location of enginehouse: South Milford, Ind.
Locomotives: 1

No.	Builder	Model	New	Builder No.
47	EMD	GP7	4/52	16205

PINE BELT SOUTHERN RAILROAD CO., INC.

P. O. Box 1317
Shelbyville, TN 37160

Reporting marks: PBRR
Phone: 615-684-7376

Pine Belt Southern provides freight service from Hurtsboro, Alabama, to a connection with Norfolk Southern at Nuckols, 25 miles. Rail is 100 pound. Traffic, primarily sand and logs, is expected to be about 2,500 cars a year.

The line is part of a route from Columbus, Georgia, to Troy, Ala., that was completed in 1879 by the Mobile & Girard Railroad. It was leased to the Central of Georgia in 1886.

Norfolk Southern sold the line to Pine Belt Southern and shortline service started July 29, 1995.

The company, which is owned by Richard Abernathy, acquired a second ex-Central of Georgia line, from Roanoke Junction to Lafayette, Ala., on January 8, 1996.

Location of enginehouse: Hurtsboro and Lafayette, Ala.
Locomotives: 2

No.	Builder	Model	New	Builder No.
2676	EMD	GP35	3/65	29931
3986	GE	B23-7	1/79	41995

PIONEER VALLEY RAILROAD CO., INC.

One Depot Street
P. O. Box 995
Westfield, MA 01086

Reporting marks: PVRR
Phone: 413-568-3331
Fax: 413-568-6941

Pioneer Valley operates freight service from a connection with Conrail at Westfield, Massachusetts, to a connection with the Boston & Maine at Holyoke, 10.2 miles. A branch runs from Westfield through Easthampton to Mount Tom, 16 miles. Additional switching track at Westfield covers 2 miles, and at Holyoke, 2.4 miles. The Holyoke main line is 107 pound rail while the Easthampton branch is 80 pound. Traffic includes lumber, plastics, trap rock, manufactured products, and other commodities — about 2,500 cars a year. The Heritage Park Railroad operates excursions over part of the line.

Rail service was first provided between Holyoke and Westfield by the Holyoke & Westfield Railroad, chartered in 1870 and opened in October 1871. In 1879 the company was leased to the New Haven & Northampton, and came under control of the New Haven. The Westfield-Easthampton line was also part of the New Haven; the Easthampton and Mount Tom portion of the line was a Boston & Maine Branch. Conrail acquired the two former New Haven lines in 1976 and operated them until July 1982, when they were sold to the Pioneer Valley Railroad, which is owned by Pinsly Railroad Company. The B&M branch was also acquired in 1982.

Radio frequencies: 160.335, 161.085
Location of enginehouse: Westfield, Mass.
Locomotives: 5

No.	Builder	Model	New	Builder No.
106	Alco	S-2	10/49	77140
2558	AT&SF	CF7	8/73	
2565	AT&SF	CF7	6/73	
2597	AT&SF	CF7	10/72	
2647	AT&SF	CF7	8/70	

A pair of CF7s wearing Pinsly red and black pull a train on the Pioneer Valley Railroad at Holyoke, Massachusetts. Photo by Jim Shaw.

PITTSBURG & SHAWMUT RAILROAD CO.

One Glade Park East
RD 8, Box 45
Kittanning, PA 16201

Reporting marks: PS
Phone: 412-543-0201
Fax: 412-543-2042

Pittsburg & Shawmut operates freight service from Freeport Junction, Pennsylvania to Brockway, 88 miles, with short branches to Dellwood, Conifer, Widnoon, and West Mosgrove. It connects with Conrail at Freeport Junction, with Buffalo & Pittsburgh at Dellwood and West Mosgrove, and with Mountain Laurel at Brookville. Rail is 100 and 131 pound. Traffic is 17,000 cars a year of outbound coal, and general commodities.

The Brookville & Mahoning Railroad opened from Brookville to Brockway, 21 miles, in 1908. The present name was adopted January 3, 1910, and the entire railroad was opened on January 2, 1917. From 1908 to 1916, the railroad was leased by Pittsburg, Shawmut & Northern.

The Pittsburg & Shawmut also operates the affiliated Red Bank and Mountain Laurel railroads. The Arthur T. Walker Estate Corporation has direct control of the company (the Dumaine interests have indirect control).

Radio frequencies: 160.740, 161.160
Location of enginehouse: Brookville, Pa.
Locomotives: 11

No.	Builder	Model	New	Builder No.
10	EMD	GP7	6/53	18521
11	EMD	GP7	3/51	A154
1774	EMD	SW9	10/53	18862
1775	EMD	SW9	10/53	18860
1776	EMD	SW9	11/53	19043
1816	EMD	SW9	11/53	18968
1851	EMD	SW9	11/53	18965
1865	EMD	SW9	11/53	18966
1866	EMD	SW9	10/53	18861
1891	EMD	SW9	10/53	18863
1949	EMD	SW9	11/53	18967

Freight cars: 710 hopper cars

PITTSBURGH, ALLEGHENY & MCKEES ROCKS RAILROAD CO.

180 Nichol Avenue
McKees Rocks, PA 15136

Reporting marks: PAM
Phone: 412-331-3555
Fax: 412-331-0746

The Pittsburgh, Allegheny & McKees Rocks is a switching road with 5 miles of track at McKees Rocks, Pennsylvania. It connects with Conrail. Rail is 85, 90, and 105 pound. Traffic is under 500 cars a year of steel and chemicals.

The company was incorporated September 25, 1899, as a consolidation of the Pittsburgh & Allegheny Railroad, the McKees Rocks Railroad, and the North Shore Terminal Railroad. It is now owned by McKees Rocks Industrial Enterprises.
Radio frequency: 160.425
Locomotives: 2

No.	Builder	Model	New	Builder No.
17	GE	70-ton	9/50	30445
20	GE	70-ton	10/51	31168

PL&W RAILROAD, INC. — *See Ohio & Pennsylvania Railroad.*

PLAINVIEW TERMINAL CO.

211 South Sixth Street
Brownfield, TX 79316

Reporting marks: PTC
Phone: 806-637-6954

Plainview Terminal is a switching road with 4.5 miles of track at Plainview, Texas. It connects with the Santa Fe. It is a RailAmerica subsidiary and acquired its property and equipment from the Floydada & Plainview Railroad on November 1, 1995.
Locomotives: 1 (pooled with the West Texas & Lubbock Railroad)

POINT COMFORT & NORTHERN RAILWAY CO.

Jackson Street and FM 616
P. O. Box 238
Lolita, TX 77971

Reporting marks: PCN
Phone: 512-874-4466
Fax: 512-874-4519

The Point Comfort & Northern operates freight service from a connection with the Union Pacific at Lolita, Texas, to Point Comfort, 12.71 miles. Rail is 115 pound. Traffic is aluminum and chemicals — more than 20,000 cars a year.

The railroad was incorporated April 29, 1948, and opened a short time later. Aluminum Company of America has always owned the railroad.
Radio frequency: 160.500

Location of enginehouse: Lolita, Texas
Locomotives: 8

No.	Builder	Model	New	Builder No.
12, 13	EMD	MP15	11/74	74622-2, 74622-3
14, 15	EMD	MP15DC	11/80	796384-1, 796384-2

No.	Builder	Model	New	Builder No.
16	EMD	GP38	10/69	35425
3000	EMD	GP40	12/65	30937
3726, 3731	EMD	GP38	3/69	34849, 34854

Freight cars: 437 covered hoppers

PORT BIENVILLE RAILROAD

P. O. Box 2267
Bay St. Louis, MS 39521

Reporting marks: PBVR
Phone: 601-467-9231
Fax: 601-467-9341

The Port Bienville Railroad operates freight and TOFC service from a connection with CSX at Ansley, Mississippi, to Port Bienville, 9 miles. Rail is 85 pound. Traffic is primarily chemicals — 1,000 cars a year.

This is a new line built in connection with Port Bienville in 1973. The railroad is owned, and operated by the Hancock County Port & Harbor Commission, Bay St. Louis.

Radio frequency: 160.695
Location of enginehouse: Port Bienville, Miss.
Locomotives: 2 engines

No.	Builder	Model	New	Builder No.	Rebuilt
140	EMD	SW9	2/51	13135	
1790	EMD	GP16	9/52	17375	1981

Port Bienville's SW1 No. 522, no longer on the roster, pulls a cut of covered hoppers out of Port Bienville, Mississippi. Photo by Jim Shaw.

PORT JERSEY RAILROAD

203 Port Jersey Boulevard
Jersey City, NJ 07305

Reporting marks: PJR
Phone: 201-434-8373
Fax: 201-434-8242

Port Jersey operates a 2.2 mile switching line between Conrail's Greenville Yards and Jersey City, New Jersey. Traffic is primarily food products, about 2,500 cars a year. The railroad started operations in 1970 and is independent.

Locomotives: 1

No.	Builder	Model	New	Builder No.
1197	EMD	SW1200	3/63	27865

PORTLAND & WESTERN RAILROAD, INC.

110 West Tenth Avenue
Albany, OR 97321

Reporting marks: PNWR
Phone: 503-924-6565
Fax: 503-924-6580

The Portland & Western provides freight service on three former Southern Pacific lines near Portland, Oregon, that it leased in August 1995:
• Willsburg Junction to Schefflin, 28.9 miles
• Hillsboro to Seghers, 9.5 miles
• Cook to Newberg, 14.3 miles
    It also operates on three former Burlington Northern lines:
• Salem to Greton, 37.7 miles
• Bendemeer to Banks, 11.8 miles
• BN Junction (at Hillsboro) to Forest Grove, 5.4 miles
    It connects with Southern Pacific and Burlington Northern at Brooklyn Yard in Portland, with BN at Salem, with Willamette & Pacific at Newberg, and with Port of Tillamook Bay at Schefflin. Total mileage is 113.8. Rail is mostly 90 pound. The company expects to move about 9,000 cars a year of forest products, agricultural products, salt, foodstuffs, scrap steel, and general commodities, plus cars moving to and from the Port of Tillamook Bay Railroad.

Portland & Western began service on the ex-SP lines on September 1, 1995, and on the ex-BN lines on October 1, 1995. It is a subsidiary of Genesee & Wyoming Industries and is operated in conjunction with the Willamette & Pacific.

Locomotives: 2 (pooled with Willamette & Pacific)

No.	Builder	Model	New	Builder No.
1851	EMD	SD9	4/54	19449
1853	EMD	SD9	1/53	17157

PORT OF PALM BEACH DISTRICT RAILWAY

4 East Port Road
P. O. Box 9935
Riviera Beach, FL 33419

Reporting marks: PPBD
Phone: 407-842-4201
Fax: 407-842-4240

The Port of Palm Beach District Railway is an industrial switching line operating 4.2 miles of track in the Riviera Beach area of Palm Beach, Florida. Traffic is about 2,000 cars a year.

Locomotives: 2

No.	Builder	Model	New	Builder No.	Rebuilt
238	EMD	SW1	9/41	1396	
1311	EMD	SW13	7/45	3280	1975

PORT OF TILLAMOOK BAY RAILROAD

4000 Blimp Boulevard
Tillamook, OR 97141

Reporting marks: POTB
Phone: 503-842-2413
Fax: 503-842-3680

The Port of Tillamook Bay Railroad provides freight service on 94.4 miles of track from Tillamook, Oregon, to a connection with Southern Pacific (via the Portland & Western) at Hillsboro. The railroad connects with Burlington Northern (via the Portland & Western) at North Plains by trackage rights from Banks and with Portland & Western at Schefflin. Rail is 75 to 132 pound. About 5,000 cars a year of lumber, forest products, aggregate, and grain make up the road's traffic. *Spirit of Oregon* dinner trains and *Oregon Coastline Express* seasonal excursion trains operate on this line.

The railroad was formed in 1952 to acquire and develop a former United States Navy switching line built in 1943 at Tillamook Naval Blimp Base. In May 1986 the company was granted trackage rights over Southern Pacific's line to Hillsboro.

That line was built by the Pacific Railway & Navigation Company between 1906 and 1911 and became part of Southern Pacific in 1915. The line from Tillamook to Shefflin, 5 miles from Hillsboro, was purchased by the state of Oregon and the Port of Tillamook Bay Railroad on February 1, 1990. Operation between Shefflin, Hillsboro, and Banks is by trackage rights over Southern Pacific. The railroad is owned and operated by the Port of Tillamook Bay.

Radio frequencies: 161.055, 160.305, 161.070
Location of enginehouse: Tillamook and Banks, Ore.
Locomotives: 8 engines

No.	Builder	Model	New	Builder No.
101	EMD	GP9		
3771	EMD	GP9	12/56	22900
4368	EMD	SD9	4/55	20203
4381	EMD	SD9	3/55	19945
4405	EMD	SD9	4/55	19986
4406	EMD	SD9	4/55	19983
4414	EMD	SD9	4/56	21314
4432	EMD	SD9	3/55	19955

Three Port of Tillamook Bay SD9s pull a train along a Pacific Ocean inlet at Wheeler, Oregon, in September 1991. Photo by Jim Shaw.

PORT RAILROADS, INC.

221 North F Street
P. O. Box 937
Exeter, CA 93221

Reporting marks: PRI
Phone: 209-592-1172
Fax: 209-592-6308

Port Railroads operates two separate divisions. The West Side line runs from a Southern Pacific connection at Fresno, California, to Oxalis, 47.8 miles, with a branch from Ingle to Burrell, 25.2 miles. The Buttonwillow line runs from an SP connection at Kern Junction, near Bakersfield, to Buttonwillow, 32.7 miles. Rail is 90 to 110 pound. Traffic includes fertilizer, grain, food products (tomato paste, corn oil, sugar), lumber, paper, LP gas, scrap, and general commodities — about 8,000 cars a year.

The Oxalis line opened prior to 1890, and the Buttonwillow line was built after 1910. Both were built and operated by the Southern Pacific until they were sold to the Port Railroads. Short-line service started March 13, 1994. The company is affiliated with Kyle Railways and is operated in conjunction with the San Joaquin Valley Railroad, which provides the locomotives.
Radio frequency: 160.365
Location of enginehouses: Fresno and Bakersfield, Calif.

PORT ROYAL RAILROAD

3127 Depot Road
Beaufort, SC 29902

Reporting marks: PRYL
Phone: 803-524-5752
Fax: 803-524-4048

Port Royal Railroad operates freight service from Port Royal to a CSX connection at Yemassee, South Carolina, 26 miles. Rail ranges from 80 to 115 pound. Traffic includes clay slurry, paper, beer, lumber, aggregates, and various export and import shipments moving through Port Royal — about 2,000 cars a year.

The line was built by the Port Royal Railroad in the 1870s. It was consolidated with the Port Royal & Augusta Railroad in September 1896 to form the Charlestown & Western Carolina Railway. In 1959, the C&WC was merged into the Atlantic Coast Line, which later became the Seaboard Coast Line, then Seaboard System. Seaboard abandoned this line, and Port Royal operations started May 13, 1985.

The railroad is a facility of the South Carolina Public Railways Commission.
Radio frequency: 160.980
Location of enginehouse: Port Royal, S. C.
Locomotives: 3

No.	Builder	Model	New	Builder No.
6152	EMD	GP9	11/56	22060
6155	EMD	GP9	11/56	22063
6554	EMD	GP9	6/57	23028

PORT TERMINAL RAILROAD OF SOUTH CAROLINA

540 East Bay Street
P. O. Box 279
Charleston, SC 29402

Reporting marks: PTSC
Phone: 803-727-2067
Fax: 803-727-2005

Radio frequency: 160.980
Locomotives: 5

No.	Builder	Model	New	Builder No.
1001	EMD	SW1001	3/75	74670-1
1002	Alco	S-4	4/53	80458
1003	Alco	S-2	9/46	74792
5105	Alco	S-4	8/53	80629
6513	EMD	GP9	5/57	22987

Port Terminal Railroad of South Carolina is a switching road operating 10 miles of track at North Charleston. It connects with CSX and handles about 10,000 cars a year. Rail is 85 pound. The railroad began operations in 1956 and is owned by the South Carolina Public Railways Commission.

PORT UTILITIES COMMISSION OF CHARLESTON, S. C.

540 East Bay Street
P. O. Box 279
Charleston, SC 29402

Reporting marks: PUCC
Phone: 803-727-2067
Fax: 803-727-2005

The Port Utilities Commission operates 12 miles of track at Charleston, South Carolina. It connects with CSX and Norfolk Southern. The commission switches about 6,500 cars a year. Rail is 100 pound.

The line began operations in 1922. It is operated by the South Carolina Public Railways Commission, and it uses locomotives of the Port Terminal Railroad of South Carolina.

Radio frequency: 160.980

POSEYVILLE & OWENSVILLE RAILROAD CO., INC.

Reporting marks: POR

The Poseyville & Owensville owns an 11-mile line from Poseyville (Cynthiana), Indiana, to a connection with Norfolk Southern at Owensville. Traffic includes grain and agricultural products moving to and from a barge transfer on the Ohio River.

The line was built by the Evansville & Terre Haute Railroad and later became the Mount Vernon branch of the Chicago & Eastern Illinois.

Louisville & Nashville acquired C&EI's Evansville line from the Missouri Pacific in 1969 and sold a portion of the branch to the P&O in April 1987.

The P&O is owned by Merchants Management Corp. (in bankruptcy) and is operated by Indiana Hi-Rail.

PRESCOTT & NORTHWESTERN RAILROAD CO.

212 West Chestnut Street
P. O. Box 747
Prescott, AR 71857

Reporting marks: PNW
Phone: 501-887-3103
Fax: 501-887-2861

Prescott & Northwestern GE 70-tonner No. 24 switches wood chip hoppers on the interchange track near Prescott, Arkansas. Photo by Jim Shaw.

The Prescott & Northwestern operates 5 miles of switching track at Prescott, Arkansas, connecting with Union Pacific. Rail is 56 to 85 pound. The line's traffic comprises about 4,000 cars a year of forest products.

The railroad was chartered in October 1890 and reorganized under the same name on January 2, 1892. It opened a 32-mile line to the peach orchards in Highland in 1903. It proposed extensions west from Highland to De Queen and south from Prescott to Magnolia but built neither. It carried passengers until 1945, and it abandoned its line from Prescott to Highland in November 1994. Potlatch Corporation acquired the company in July 1966.

Location of enginehouse: Prescott, Ark.

Locomotives: 3

No.	Builder	Model	New	Builder No.
23	GE	70-ton	6/54	32200
24	GE	70-ton	4/55	32283
25	GE	70-ton	7/56	32595

PROVIDENCE & WORCESTER RAILROAD CO.

75 Hammond Street
P. O. Box 16551
Worcester, MA 01601

Reporting marks: PW
Phone: 508-775-4000
Fax: 508-795-0748

The Providence & Worcester provides freight service in Rhode Island, Massachusetts, and Connecticut on 470 miles of routes, 174 miles of which it owns:
• Providence, R. I., through Worcester, Mass., to Gardner, 70 miles
• Groton, Conn., to Worcester, 75 miles

• Pawtucket, R. I., to New Haven, Conn., 117.4 miles, on Amtrak's Shore Line
• Valley Falls, R. I., to East Providence, 6 miles
• Plainfield to Willimantic, Conn., 23 miles
• New Haven to South Norwalk and Danbury, Conn.

Principal interchanges are with Conrail at Worcester, New England Central at New London, Conn., and ST Rail System (Boston & Maine) at Gardner.

Traffic includes a wide range of general commodities — more than 28,000 freight cars and 45,000 containers a year.

The Providence & Worcester was chartered November 25, 1845. A portion of the line was laid on the bank of the Blackstone Canal, and the railroad opened from Providence to Worcester on October 25, 1847. The company was leased to the New York, Providence & Boston Railroad in 1889, and in turn to the New York, New Haven & Hartford the following year.

When the New Haven was absorbed by Penn Central in November 1968, Penn Central would not accept the P&W's lease, and the P&W chose to resume independent operations. On February 3, 1973, P&W began running its own trains.

P&W purchased Boston & Maine's Worcester-Gardner line in October 1974, and in 1976 acquired Conrail's New London-Worcester line. It added several short Conrail branch lines to its map in 1976, 1980, and 1982, and acquired two of Rhode Island's short lines — the Warwick Railway on August 14, 1979 (merged into P&W January 1, 1984) and the Moshassuck Valley Railroad on September 1, 1981.

In 1982 P&W took over all CR freight operations in Rhode Island plus CR's operating rights on Amtrak from the Massachusetts-Rhode Island line to Old Saybrook, Conn. In 1991 P&W took over CR freight operations from Old Saybrook to East Haven. In 1993, P&W acquired the assets of the affiliated Connecticut Rail Systems, Inc., and its freight rights from Durham, Conn., through New Haven to Danbury. The P&W is controlled by Robert Eder.

Radio frequencies: 161.100 (yard), 160.650 (road)

Location of enginehouses: Worcester, Mass., Valley Falls, R. I., New Haven and Plainfield, Conn.

Locomotives: 21

No.	Builder	Model	New	Builder No.
1702	EMD	GP9	11/57	24237
1201	EMD	SW7	1/50	8136
1202	EMD	SW7	1/50	9451
1801	GE	U18B	10/76	41482
2006	EMD	GP38	2/80	796301-1
2007	EMD	GP38	11/80	796356-1
2008	EMD	GP38	11/80	796356-2
2009	EMD	GP38	9/82	827002-1
2010	EMD	GP38	10/69	35423
2011	EMD	GP38	10/69	35437
2201	GE	B23-7	3/78	41740
2202	GE	U23B	5/77	41587
2203	GE	U23B	6/77	41593
2204	GE	U23B	6/77	41590
2205	GE	U23B	5/77	41585
2206	GE	U23B	6/77	41592
2207	GE	U23B	5/77	41589
2208	GE	U23B	6/77	41591
2209	GE	U23B	2/75	40124
2210	GE	U23B	2/75	40139
2211	GE	U23B	2/73	38766

Freight cars: 37 gondolas, 2 flatcars

QUEBEC NORTH SHORE & LABRADOR RAILWAY CO.

100 Retty Street
P. O. Box 1000
Sept-Îles, PQ G4R 4L5
Canada

Reporting marks: QNSL
Phone: 418-968-7495
Fax: 418-968-7451

The Quebec North Shore & Labrador operates freight, TOFC, and passenger service from the port at Sept-Îles, Quebec, to Schefferville, Newfoundland, 353.2 miles. A branch extends from Ross Bay Junction to Carol Lake, Nfld., 36.6 miles. A connection is made with the 22-mile Arnaud Railway at Arnaud Junction, and with the Wabush Lake Railway at Wabush Lake on the Carol Lake branch. Rail is 136 pound. Traffic is primarily iron ore plus a limited amount of general commodities. The QNS&L carries more than 240,000 cars a year. The company has petitioned to end passenger service.

Construction of the railroad started in 1949, and the road was completed in 1952. It was built and is controlled by Iron Ore Company of Canada

Radio frequencies: 159.910, 160.335, 159.930, 160.215
Enginehouse: Sept-Îles, Que.

Locomotives: 52 plus 6 RDCs

No.	Builder	Model	New	Builder No.
155	GMD	GP9	1956	A-934
200-203	GMD	SD-40	1968	A-2328–A-2331
220	GMD	SD-40	1971	A-2557
221-264*	GMD	SD40-2	1972-1975	
301-318	GMD	SD40-2	1994	
401-403	GE	Dash 8-40CM	1994	47637-47639

* 25 units in service
Freight cars: 332

QUEBEC RAILWAY CORP. (CHARLEVOIX RAILWAY)

1245 Sherbrooke West, Suite 1415
Montreal, PQ H3C 1G2
Clermont, PQ
Canada

Reporting marks: QRC
Phone: 514-982-9944
Phone: 418-439-5122

Charlevoix Railway operates freight service from a connection with Canadian National at Limoilou (Quebec City) to Clermont, Quebec, 92.1 miles. Rail ranges from 85 to 130 pounds. Traffic includes wood chips, paper, clay, and cement — about 7,000 cars a year are expected. A separate company operates passenger excursions over part of the line.

The line was built in part by the Quebec, Montmorency & Charlevoix Railway in the 1890s. That company was reorganized as Quebec Railway Light & Power Co., and later became CN's Murray Bay subdivision. CN sold the line to the Quebec Railway Corporation, which started service December 1, 1994, under the name Charlevoix Railway. Quebec Railway Corporation is an independent company that plans to operate a number of short lines in Quebec.

Radio frequency:
Enginehouse: Clermont, Que.
Locomotives: 2

No.	Builder	Model	New	Builder No.
1303	GMD	SW1200	1958	A-1372
1330	GMD	SW1200	1958	A-1567

QUINCY RAILROAD CO.

Lee Road
P. O. Box 420
Quincy, CA 95971
P. O. Box 820
Susanville, CA 96130

Reporting marks: QRR
Phone: 916-283-2820

Phone: 916-257-2158

The Quincy Railroad operates freight service from a connection with the Union Pacific at Quincy Junction, California, to Bell Lane, on the outskirts of Quincy, 3.27 miles. Rail is 45 to 75 pound, and the load limit is 225,000 pounds. The company also operates a line from a Southern Pacific connection at Wendel to

Susanville, 23.3 miles. Traffic is 1,000 cars a year of outbound lumber and forest products.

The company was incorporated as the Quincy & Eastern Railway in July 1909, and reorganized three months later as the Quincy Western Railway. The railroad opened June 14, 1910, and reorganized as the Quincy Railroad on November 9, 1917. Passenger service ended in the 1950s.

On May 7, 1986, the company took over operation of a Southern Pacific branch line from Wendel to the site of a Sierra Pacific sawmill at Susanville. Sierra Pacific Industries owns the company.

Location of enginehouses: Quincy and Susanville, Calif.

Locomotives: 2

No.	Builder	Model	New	Builder No.
4	Alco	S-1	4/42	69685
1100	EMD	SW8	11/50	13549

Quincy Alco S-2 No. 4 pulls a train of wrapped lumber near Quincy, California. Photo by Jim Shaw.

QUINCY BAY TERMINAL CO.

8 Water Street
Concord, NH 03302

Reporting marks: QBT
Phone: 603-226-3395
Fax: 603-228-9571

Quincy Bay Terminal operates freight service from a Conrail connection at Braintree, Massachusetts, to Quincy Point, 5 miles. Rail is 131 pound. Traffic, which amounts to about 1,000 cars a year, consists primarily of pelletized sewage sludge, construction materials, steel plate, and oils used in soap manufacture.

The rail line is owned by the Fore River Railroad, which in turn is owned by the Massachusetts Water Resources Authority. The Fore River Railroad was incorporated on January 16, 1919,

to operate a private industrial railroad built a few years earlier.

Quincy Bay Terminal started service February 1, 1992, following cancellation of the previous operator's lease. The operating company is owned by Peter Dearness and Richard Currier, and is affiliated with the New England Southern Railroad.

Radio frequency: 160.215

Location of enginehouse: Quincy, Mass.

Locomotives: 3

No.	Builder	Model	New	Builder No.
17	Alco	S-6	11/56	82285
18	Alco	S-4	9/50	78239
19	Alco	S-4	9/50	78032

RAILROAD SWITCHING SERVICE OF MISSOURI

103 North Oak Street
P. O. Box 99
O'Fallon, IL 62269

Reporting marks: RSM
Phone: 618-632-4400
Fax: 618-632-4562

Railroad Switching Service of Missouri provides switching service on 1.89 miles of former Norfolk & Western (ex-Illinois Terminal) trackage at St. Louis, Missouri, acquired in July 1989. Traffic is under 500 cars a year. The track was purchased by the city of St. Louis in July 1989. The operating company is affiliated with Ironhorse Resources, Inc. RSM also operates the Bi-State Development Agency Railroad.

Locomotives: 1

No.	Builder	Model	New	Builder No.
1209	EMD	SW9	10/52	16834

RAILWAY ASSOCIATION OF CANADA

800 Rene-Levesque Boulevard West, Suite 1105
Montreal, PQ H3B 1X9
Canada

Phone: 514-879-8555
Fax: 514-879-1522

The Railway Association of Canada was founded in 1917 for the purpose of coordinating railway activities during World War I. Today the association works to establish continent-wide operating standards in cooperation with the Association of American Railroads. The association also represents its members in a broad range of political activity and serves as a reference source for information about Canadian railways. The association coordinates Operation Life Saver grade crossing safety programs throughout Canada.

RARUS RAILWAY CO.

300 West Commercial Avenue
P. O. Box 1070
Anaconda, MT 59711

Reporting marks: RARW
Phone: 406-563-2851
Fax: 406-563-7121

Rarus Railway operates freight service from a connection with Montana Western at Butte, Montana, to Anaconda, 25.7 miles. It connects with Montana Western and Union Pacific at Silver Bow. Rail is 115 pound. Annual traffic includes about 5,000 cars a year of scrap, copper slag, copper concentrates, and general commodities.

Rarus Railway took over the Butte, Anaconda & Pacific Railway on May 1, 1985. The line was built by the BA&P in the 1890s. It was electrified from 1913 to 1967, and passengers were carried until April 1955. The BA&P property was transferred to the state of Montana in 1985, and subsequently purchased by Rarus from the state in 1990. The railroad is privately held.

Radio frequencies: 160.320, 160.380
Location of enginehouse: Anaconda, Mont.
Locomotives: 8

No.	Builder	Model	New	Builder No.
102	EMD	GP7	4/52	17051
103	EMD	GP7	6/53	18408
104, 105	EMD	GP9	3/57	22823, 22824
106, 107	EMD	GP9	3/57	23355, 23356
301	EMD	GP7	12/53	19031
302	EMD	GP9	12/56	22705

Freight cars: 36 gondolas

Rarus GP9s 106 and 103 pull a four-car train through Ramsey, Montana, in September 1991. Photo by Jim Shaw.

READING, BLUE MOUNTAIN & NORTHERN RAILROAD CO.

P. O. Box 218
Port Clinton, PA 19579

Reporting marks: RBMN
Phone: 610-562-2100

Reading, Blue Mountain & Northern operates freight service from a connection with Conrail at Reading, Pennsylvania, to Port Clinton (21 miles), from Port Clinton to Pottsville, and Good Springs (47 miles), and from Port Clinton to Locust Summit, PA (40 miles). Total mileage operated is 124. Traffic is predominantly coal but the road also carries lumber, chemicals, cardboard, and agricultural products — about 8,000 cars a year in all. The railroad also operates excursion trains.

These lines were leased by the Philadelphia & Reading from the Mahanoy & Shamokin, Mine Hill & Schulykill Haven, and Lebanon & Tremont among others. P&R became the Reading, and these branches were included in Conrail in 1976.

Conrail sold to lines to the Reading, Blue Mountain & Northern, which began operation December 15, 1990.

The company is part of the Reading & Northern System owned by Andrew M. Muller, Jr.

On July 1, 1995 the Reading, Blue Mountain & Northern absorbed the operations of the affiliated Blue Mountain & Reading.

The Blue Mountain & Reading ran from a connection with Conrail at Temple, Pennsylvania, to Hamburg, 13 miles. The track is owned by the commonwealth of Pennsylvania. It runs regular passenger excursions over its Hamburg line as well as occasional trips on the other lines.

Freight traffic includes about 1,500 cars a year of brick, lumber, and miscellaneous commodities.

The Hamburg line was built by the Pennsylvania Railroad as part of its Schuylkill Division between 1884 and 1886. Conrail discontinued service June 15, 1982. The Pennsylvania Department of Transportation designated Blue Mountain & Reading to provide service, which started September 10, 1983. The company also ran three lines owned by the commonwealth of Pennsylvania

at Kutztown, Boyertown, and Pennsburg from 1988 to June 1995, when the lease was turned over to East Penn Railways.
Radio frequencies: 161.250, 161.370, 161.310, 160.470, 160.770
Location of enginehouses: Port Clinton, South Hamburg, and West Cressona, Pa.
Locomotives: 18

No.	Builder	Model	New	Builder No.
425	Baldwin	4-6-2	1/28	60339
800	EMD	SW8	6/52	15730
801	EMD	SW8M	12/52	16973
802	EMD	SW8M	12/50	13154
803	EMD	SW8M	9/51	14495
1000	EMD	NW2	1/48	5138
1032	EMD	NW2	9/46	3652
1200	EMD	NW2	1/48	6422
1201	EMD	SW7	1/51	9956
1201	EMD	SW7	1/51	9956
1501, 1502	AT&SF	CF7	1977	
2102	Reading	4-8-4	10/45	
2397	GE	U23B	5/77	41564
2398	GE	U23B	5/77	41588
2399	GE	U23B	5/77	41586
5706	EMD	E8	10/52	16775
5898	EMD	E8	3/51	13113

RED BANK RAILROAD

One Glade Park East
RD 8, Box 45
Kittanning, PA 16201

Reporting marks: RBKR
Phone: 412-543-0201
Fax: 412-543-2042

Red Bank Railroad operates freight service from a connection with the affiliated Mountain Laurel Railroad at Lawsonham, Pennsylvania, to Sligo, 10 miles. Rail is 115 pound. Traffic is primarily coal.

This is a former Pennsylvania Railroad line sold by Conrail. The property is owned by Shannon Transport Inc. (C&K Coal Co.), and the operating company is a subsidiary of the Arthur T. Walker Estate Corp. (Dumaine interests). Shortline service started July 18, 1990.
Radio frequency: 161.160
Locomotives: supplied by the Pittsburg & Shawmut Railroad.

RED RIVER VALLEY & WESTERN RAILROAD CO.

116 South Fourth Street
P. O. Box 608
Wahpeton, ND 58074

Reporting marks: RRVW
Phone: 701-642-8257
Fax: 701-642-3534

Red River Valley & Western operates 687 miles of track from Breckenridge, Minnesota, throughout southeast North Dakota.

Traffic is farm and agriculture related — about 22,500 cars a year. The principal lines are:
• from Breckenridge west to Wahpeton, N. D. (1 mile), then northwest through Davenport to Casselton, then southwest to Marion
• from Wahpeton west to Oakes, then north through La Moure, Jamestown, and Carrington to Minnewaukan

• from Horace southwest through Davenport and La Moure to Edgeley

Branch lines run:
• from Pingree west to Regan
• from Carrington west to Turtle Lake
• from Oberon west to Esmond.

Principal connections are with CP Rail System (Soo Line) at Oakes and Carrington, and with Burlington Northern at Breckenridge, Casselton, Jamestown, and New Rockford. Traffic includes grain, sugar, and coal — 24,000 cars a year.

The lines were acquired from Burlington Northern, and for the most part they consist of former Northern Pacific lines except for the Wahpeton-Casselton line, which was part of the Great Northern. Red River Valley & Western began service July 19, 1987. It abandoned an 8.7-mile stretch of line between Alice and Lucca in August 1993.

The company is controlled by Kent Shoemaker, Douglas Head, and Charles Clay.

Radio frequencies: 160.365, 160.440, 161.295
Employees: 75
Location of enginehouses: Breckenridge and Carrington, Minn.
Locomotives: 10

No.	Builder	Model	New
300-309	AT&SF	CF7	1970-1977

RED SPRINGS & NORTHERN RAILROAD CO.

P. O. Box 1929
Laurinburg, NC 28352

Reporting marks: RSNR
Phone: 919-276-0786

The Red Springs & Northern operates freight service from Red Springs, North Carolina, to a connection with CSX at Parkton, 12.5 miles. Rail is 70 to 85 pound. Traffic consists of 500 cars a year of pulpwood and fertilizer.

The line was built as part of the Cape Fear & Yadkin Valley Railroad, acquired in 1899 in part by Atlantic Coast Line.

Seaboard System sold it in 1984 to Advancement, Inc., a local industrial development group, which leased the line to the Red Springs & Northern, and service started August 1, 1984. The company is affiliated with the Laurinburg & Southern Railway.

Radio frequency: 160.980
Location of enginehouse: Red Springs, N. C.
Locomotives: 1

No.	Builder	Model	New	Builder No.
104	GE	70-ton	9/50	30458

REDMONT RAILWAY CO, INC.

201 19th Street
North Columbus, MS 39701

Reporting marks: RRC
Phone: 601-327-8664

The Redmont Railway operates freight service from a connection with Norfolk Southern at Corinth, Mississippi, to Red Bay, Alabama, 41.5 miles. Rail is 112 pound. Traffic includes logs and grain — 1,400 cars a year.

The line was part of an Illinois Central secondary main line between Birmingham, Alabama, and Jackson, Tennessee. IC sold it to the Southern Railway in 1986. Norfolk Southern sold this portion to the Mississippi-Alabama Railroad Authority, which leased it to the Redmont Railway. Shortline service started February 18, 1995.

Redmont is a subsidiary of CAGY Industries, and an affiliate of the Columbus & Greenville Railroad.

Location of enginehouse: Red Bay, Ala.
Locomotives: 1

No.	Builder	Model	New
101	AT&SF	CF7	1973

REGIONAL RAILROADS OF AMERICA

122 C Street, N. W., Suite 850
Washington, DC 20001

Phone: 202-638-7790
Fax: 202-638-1045

In the mid-1980s several Class 2 and regional railroads formed Regional Railroads of America to lobby Congress on issues affecting medium-size and small railroads. These issues included the federal railroad retirement and unemployment program, the Federal Employers Liability Act, and labor protection responsibilities during the sale and abandonment of railroads. The group works to educate legislators and the public on the emerging role of regional and feeder railroads.

Approximately 125 railroads are members. Associate memberships are available for interested suppliers and others.

RIO VALLEY SWITCHING CO.

3600 Formosa Street
Building N, Suite 6
McAllen, TX 78503

Reporting marks: RVSC
Phone: 210-971-9111

Rio Valley Switching operates freight service from a connection with Union Pacific at Harlingen, Texas, to a connection with Border Pacific at Mission, 41 miles. A branch runs from Mission to Hidalgo, 8.1 miles.

Traffic includes paper, foodstuffs, and agricultural products totaling about 4,500 cars a year.

This former Missouri Pacific branch line was leased to Rio Valley Railroad on March 7, 1993. On August 30, 1994, the name was changed to Rio Valley Switching Co. The railroad is affiliated with Ironhorse Resources.

Location of enginehouse: McAllen, Texas
Locomotives: 2

No.	Builder	Model	New	Builder No.
1233	EMD	SW1200	7/64	29446
1705	EMD	GP16	12/50	12302

RIVER TERMINAL RAILWAY CO.

3060 Eggers Avenue
Cleveland, OH 44127

Reporting marks: RT
Phone: 216-429-6550
Fax: 216-429-6555

River Terminal Railway is a switching line with 35.48 miles of track at Cleveland, Ohio. It connects with Conrail, CSX, Norfolk Southern, Cuyahoga Valley, Newburgh & South Shore, and Wheeling & Lake Erie. Traffic includes hot metal, slabs, coils, coke, and ore. The road handles about 28,000 cars a year. The company was incorporated December 8, 1909, and is owned by LTV Steel Co., Inc.
Radio frequency: 161.370
Locomotives: 12

No.	Builder	Model	New	Builder No.
92	EMD	SW900	1955	20956
98	EMD	SW900	1955	21472
100	EMD	SW900	1959	24486
101	EMD	SW1001	1968	34109
102	EMD	SW1001	1968	34110
103	EMD	SW1001	1975	74657-1
104	EMD	SW1001	1975	74657-2
105	EMD	SW1001	1976	766009-1
106	EMD	SW1001	1976	766009-2
107	EMD	SW1001	1978	776072-1
108	EMD	SW1001	1978	786155-1
109	EMD	SW1001	1975	756054-1

R. J. CORMAN RAILROAD CORP.

602 North Third Avenue
P. O. Box 279
Bardstown, KY 40004

Reporting marks: RJCR
Phone: 505-348-7444
Fax: 505-348-1118

R. J. Corman operates freight service from a connection with CSX at Bardstown Junction to Bardstown, Kentucky, 20 miles. *My Old Kentucky Dinner Train* operates over this line. Rail is 110 pound. Traffic includes general commodities — 700 cars a year.

The line was built by the Bardstown & Louisville Railroad in 1860. That company was acquired by the Louisville & Nashville in 1864, and in 1888 the L&N extended the line from Bardstown through Wickland to Springfield. R. J. Corman acquired the line from CSX in late January 1987. The company is owned by R. J. Corman.
Radio frequencies: 160.845, 161.235
Location of enginehouse: Bardstown, Ky.
Locomotives: 6

No.	Builder	Model	New	Builder No.
1940	EMD	F7A	11/50	12337
1941	EMD	F7A	12/50	12344
9001	EMD	GP9	11/55	20865
9002	EMD	GP9	6/56	21707
9005	EMD	GP9	10/56	22253
9009	EMD	GP9	5/57	22997

R. J. CORMAN RAILROAD. CO. — CLEVELAND LINE

Route 5, Box 498
Dover, OH 44622

Reporting marks: RJCL
Phone: 216-364-4567

R. J. Corman's Cleveland line operates freight service from a connection with CSX at Warwick, Ohio, to connections with Conrail at Massillon and with Ohio Central at Urichsville. The line is 49.7 miles long. Rail is 131 pound. Traffic includes about 2,700 cars a year of chemicals, plastic, steel, paper, and lumber.

The line was built by the Lake Shore & Tuscarawas Valley Railway, which was chartered July 2, 1870, and completed to Urichsville on August 18, 1873. The company was reorganized as the Cleveland, Tuscarawas Valley & Wheeling two years later, and as the Cleveland, Lorain & Wheeling in 1883. It came under control of the Baltimore & Ohio in July 1909. CSX sold the line to R. J. Corman, who started service December 1, 1990. The company is controlled by R. J. Corman.

Radio frequencies: 160.455, 161.385
Location of enginehouse: Dover, Ohio
Locomotives: 2

No.	Builder	Model	New	Builder No.
9003	EMD	GP9	12/55	21183
9004	EMD	GP9	8/56	22213

R. J. CORMAN RAILROAD CO. — MEMPHIS LINE

145 East First Street
P. O. Box 337
Guthrie, KY 42234

Reporting Marks: RJCM
Phone: 502-483-9000
Fax: 502-483-9009

R. J. Corman's Memphis line operates freight service from Zinc, Tennessee, through Guthrie to South Union (Memphis Junction), Kentucky, 92 miles. It connects with CSX at Guthrie and Memphis Junction. Rail is 100 pound. Traffic includes about 15,000 cars a year of grain, fertilizer, lumber, pulpwood, paper, chemicals, plastic, and minerals (alumina and zinc).

The line was built as part of the Louisville & Nashville's Memphis branch about 1861. CSX sold the line to R. J. Corman, which started service on August 29, 1987.

Location of enginehouse: Guthrie, Ky.
Locomotives: 9

No.	Builder	Model	New	Builder No.	Rebuilt
1601	EMD	GP16	5/50	11144	1981
1602	EMD	GP16	12/51	14983	1980
1603	EMD	GP16	9/52	17391	1980
1604	EMD	GP16	2/51	13930	1980
1605	EMD	GP16	11/51	14968	1980
1607	EMD	GP16	2/51	13906	1981
1608	EMD	GP16	5/51	13949	1980
9006	EMD	GP9	5/57	22995	
9008	EMD	GP9	2/58	24370	

Freight cars: 229 boxcars, 16 gondolas, 6 flatcars

R. J. CORMAN RAILROAD CO. — WESTERN OHIO LINE

304 South Ash Street
St. Marys, OH 45885

Reporting marks: RJCW
Phone: 419-394-1158

R. J. Corman's Western Ohio line operates freight service from South Lima to St. Marys and Fort Recovery, Ohio, 41.5 miles, and from St. Marys to Minster, 10 miles. It connects with Norfolk

Southern, and CSX at Lima. Rail is 85 and 112 pound. Traffic includes steel, grain, fertilizer, plastic, lumber, and bicycles — about 1,000 cars a year.

The Fremont & Indiana Railroad started to build a rail line from Lima to St. Marys in 1857. Construction went slowly, and the line was opened in July 24, 1873 — by the Lake Erie & Louisville Railway. The Minster branch was completed on January 28, 1878.

The line from St. Marys to Fort Recovery was built by the Indianapolis & Sandusky Railroad in 1879. That company, and the Lake Erie & Louisville were consolidated with other lines to become the Lake Erie & Western late in 1879. After more than two decades of control by New York Central interests, LE&W became part of the Nickel Plate system in 1922 — later part of Norfolk & Western, then Norfolk Southern.

The Minster branch is owned by the Western Ohio Rail Authority, and portions of the main line are being acquired and leased from Norfolk Southern. R. J. Corman began operations on August 23, 1993. The company is owned by R. J. Corman.
Radio frequencies: 160.455, 161.385
Location of enginehouse: St. Marys, Ohio
Locomotives: 3

No.	Builder	Model	New	Builder No.	Rebuilt
1606	EMD	GP16	8/60	26116	1980
9007	EMD	GP9	6/57	23007	
9010	EMD	GP9	2/58	24376	

ROBERVAL & SAGUENAY RAILWAY CO.

P. O. Box 1277
Jonquiere, PQ G7S 4K8
Canada

Reporting marks: RS
Phone: 418-699-3846

Roberval & Saguenay provides freight service from a Canadian National connection at Arvida (Jonquiere), Quebec, to Port Alfred and Bagotville, 18.2 miles, and over a separate line from a connection with CN near Saguenay Power to Alma, 10 miles. A total of 55 miles are operated. Rail is 100 and 115 pound.

Traffic includes bauxite, alumina, coke, chemicals, paper, forest products, and aluminum. Interchange traffic with CN is about 15,000 cars a year, but most of the road's traffic is local, moving between the port and local industries.

The company was incorporated March 24, 1911. It is a subsidiary of the Aluminum Company of Canada (ALCAN).
Radio frequencies: 160.185/161.145, 159.945, 160.020
Location of enginehouse: Arvida, Que.

Locomotives: 13

No.	Builder	Model	New	Builder No.
24	MLW	RS-18	1960	83278
25	MLW	RS-18	1965	84871
26	MLW	M-420	1972	M6051-01
27	MLW	M-420	1972	M6051-02
33	Alco	C-420	1964	84780
36	Alco	C-420	1964	84787
40	Alco	C-420	1964	84728
41	Alco	C-420	1964	84782
50	GE	B23-S7	1990	37528
51	GE	B23-S7	1990	37529
52	GE	B23-S7	1991	41531
2000	GE	B23-S7	1989	38409
2002	GE	B23-S7	1989	38403

Freight cars: 93 covered hoppers (plus non-interchange cars)

ROCHESTER & SOUTHERN RAILROAD, INC.

1372 Brooks Avenue
Rochester, NY 14624

Reporting marks: RSR
Phone: 716-328-5190
Fax: 716-328-6359

Rochester & Southern operates freight service from a connection with Conrail at Rochester, New York, to a connection with CP Rail System (Delaware & Hudson) at Silver Springs, 50 miles. The affiliated Genesee & Wyoming Railroad connects with the line at P& L Junction and has trackage rights from there to Rochester and Silver Springs. Rail is 120 to 131 pound. Traffic includes coal, salt, chemicals, lumber, and auto parts — 5,000 cars a year.

The line was built by the Rochester & State Line Railroad, which was incorporated October 6, 1869, and opened between Rochester and Salamanca on January 28, 1878. The company was reorganized January 20, 1881, as the Rochester & Pittsburgh Railroad, and in 1886 became part of the Buffalo, Rochester & Pittsburgh Railway. Baltimore & Ohio purchased the BR&P at the beginning of 1932.

Genesee & Wyoming Industries purchased the Rochester-Silver Springs line from CSX in 1985, and Rochester & Southern, a GWI subsidiary, started service July 21, 1986.

Radio frequencies: 160.770 (road), 161.100 (yard), 161.445
Location of enginehouse: Rochester, N. Y.
Locomotives: 3 (pooled with GWI railroads)

No.	Builder	Model	New	Builder No.
107	EMD	SW1200	12/64	29640
108	EMD	SW1200	12/64	29639
879	EMD	GP9	7/59	24888

Freight cars: 121 hopper cars

ROCKDALE, SANDOW & SOUTHERN RAILROAD CO.

Highway 79 West
P. O. Box 387
Rockdale, TX 76567

Reporting marks: RSS
Phone: 512-446-3478
Fax: 512-446-3470

Rockdale, Sandow & Southern operates freight service from a connection with the Union Pacific at Marjorie, Texas, to Sandow, 5.87 miles. Rail is 115 pound. Traffic consists of 12,000 cars a year of minerals.

The company was incorporated June 15, 1923, to operate a private railroad purchased from the Standard Coal Co. on January 1, 1923. Common carrier service began in March 1952. The railroad is owned by the Aluminum Company of America.

Radio frequencies: 160.500, 160.575
Location of enginehouse: Rockdale, Texas
Locomotives: 3

No.	Builder	Model	New	Builder No.
13-15	EMD	MP15	11/74	74620-1–74620-3

Freight cars: 124 gondolas

ROSCOE, SNYDER, & PACIFIC RAILWAY CO.

111 Cypress Street
P. O. Box 68
Roscoe, TX 79545

Reporting marks: RSP
Phone: 915-766-3394

Roscoe, Snyder, & Pacific operates switching service on 1.5 miles of track at Roscoe, Texas. It connects with Union Pacific. Rail is 90 pound.

The company was incorporated August 31, 1906, to construct a railroad from Roscoe to the New Mexico state line near Portales, 230 miles. The line was opened to Snyder, 30 miles, in 1908 and extended to Fluvanna, 49.65 miles, in September 1909.

The line was abandoned between Snyder and Fluvanna prior to 1945, and passenger service ended in 1953. The line was abandoned between Roscoe and Snyder in 1984 because of deregulation, which made it impossible for the company to compete for overhead traffic.

The company is owned by RSP Holding Corp.

Radio frequency: 160.365
Location of enginehouse: Roscoe, Texas
Locomotives: 1

No.	Builder	Model	New	Builder No.	Rebuilt
600	EMD	SW1500	6/70	36657	

SABINE RIVER & NORTHERN RAILROAD CO.

Old Highway 87 North
P. O. Box 5000
Orange, TX 77632

Reporting marks: SRN
Phone: 409-746-2453
Fax: 409-746-2897

The Sabine River & Northern operates freight service from Bessmay to Echo and Evadale, Texas, 40 miles. It connects with the Santa Fe, Kansas City Southern, Southern Pacific, and Union Pacific. Rail is 85, 100, and 115 pound. Traffic is pulp and paper products — about 20,000 cars a year.

The company was incorporated April 20, 1965, and the railroad opened from Mauriceville to Bessmay in April 1966. Part of the line was built on the grade of the abandoned Orange &

Northwestern Railroad. The Sabine River & Northern is owned by Inland Container Inc.

Radio frequencies: 161.455, 160.695
Location of enginehouse: Mulford, Texas
Locomotives: 5

No.	Builder	Model	New	Builder No.
1505	EMD	GP7	5/53	18409
1506	EMD	GP7	5/53	18413
1757	EMD	GP9	12/55	20841
1759	EMD	GP9	3/50	11119
17510	EMD	GP9	3/50	11120

Freight cars: 2,083 boxcars

SAGINAW VALLEY RAILWAY CO., INC.

3720 East Washington Road
Saginaw, MI 48601

Reporting marks: SGVY
Phone: 517-754-2500

Saginaw Valley Railway owns a 9.6-mile line from a connection with the Huron & Eastern at Denmark Junction, Michigan, to a connection with the Central Michigan at Harger. Rail is 100 pound. Traffic, which amounts to about 1,200 cars a year, includes grain and lumber plus overhead traffic moving between the Huron & Eastern and the Central Michigan.

The company is controlled by RailAmerica and is affiliated with the Huron & Eastern, which supplies motive power and equipment.

ST. LAWRENCE & ATLANTIC RAILROAD CO.

416 Lewiston Junction Road
Auburn, ME 04211

Reporting marks: SLR
Phone: 207-782-5680
Fax: 207-782-5857

The St. Lawrence & Atlantic operates freight service from Portland (East Deering), Maine, to Norton, Vermont, 164 miles. Branches run to Norway (1 mile), and Lewiston, Maine (3.3 miles). The road connects with Canadian National at Island Pond, Vt., ST Rail System (Maine Central) at Portland, Yarmouth Junction, and Danville Junction, Maine, New Hampshire & Vermont at Groveton, New Hampshire, Berlin Mills Railway at Berlin, N. H., and New Hampshire Central at North Stratford, N. H.

Rail is 100 to 132 pound. Traffic includes paper, woodpulp, chemicals, feed, lumber, salt, and building products — about 18,000 cars a year. A dedicated intermodal service operates daily between Auburn, Maine, and Chicago in cooperation with Canadian National Railways.

The line was built by the Atlantic & St. Lawrence Railroad between 1846 and 1853. Upon completion it was leased for 999 years to the Grand Trunk Railway and subsequently became part of the Canadian National system. The Lewiston branch is owned by the Lewiston-Auburn Railroad (chartered in 1874) and leased to the St. Lawrence & Atlantic.

The St. Lawrence & Atlantic bought the lines from CN on May 19, 1989, for $12 million. It is a subsidiary of Emons Transportation Group, Inc., of York, Pennsylvania.

Radio frequencies: 160.815, 160.965
Location of enginehouse: Lewiston Junction, Maine
Locomotives: 9

No.	Builder	Model	New	Builder No.
1758	EMD	GP9	4/52	19522
1760	EMD	GP9	5/56	21449
1762	EMD	GP9	5/56	21452
1764	EMD	GP9	5/56	214454
1766	EMD	GP9	5/56	21455
1768	EMD	GP9	5/56	21457
3702	EMD	GP40		
3707	EMD	GP40		
3733	EMD	GP40		

Freight cars: 1,462 boxcars, 98 flatcars

ST. LAWRENCE & RAQUETTE RIVER RAILROAD

50 Commercial Street
Box 309
Gowanda, NY 14070

Reporting marks: SLRR
Phone: 716-532-5242
Fax: 716-532-9128

The St. Lawrence & Raquette River operates freight service from Norfolk, New York, south to Norwood, where it connects with Conrail, then west to Ogdensburg, 31.2 miles. Rail is 70 to 90 pound. Under 1,000 cars a year of salt, lumber, recyclables, paper, ore, clay slurry, and lubricating oils constitute the road's traffic.

The line from Norfolk to Norwood was built by the Norwood & St. Lawrence Railroad. It opened on January 21, 1909, and that same day the company was consolidated with the Raymondville & Waddington Railroad. The company's owner, St. Regis Paper Co., gave the railroad to the Ogdensburg Bridge & Port Authority on December 26, 1974.

The Norwood-Ogdensburg line was built in part by the Northern Railroad as early as 1850. The line later became part of the Ogdensburg & Lake Champlain, then the Rutland. In 1965, 3 years after the abandonment of the Rutland, the Ogdensburg Bridge & Port Authority purchased the segment of track from Norwood to Ogdensburg. OB&PA leased this line to the Ogdensburg & Norwood Railroad, then to the St. Lawrence Railroad until April 1, 1990, when the lease was assigned by OB&PA to the present operator. The St. Lawrence & Raquette River is owned by Robert O. Dingman, Jr.

Radio frequencies: 161.160 (road), 160.260 (yard)
Location of enginehouse: Norfolk, N. Y.
Locomotives: 3

No.	Builder	Model	New	Builder No.
10	GE	70-ton	4/56	32567
12	EMD	SW9	9/51	14929
14	EMD	SW900	11/59	23457

ST. MARIES RIVER RAILROAD CO.

318 North 10th Street
P. O. Box 619
St. Maries, ID 83861

Reporting marks: STMA
Phone: 208-245-4531
Fax: 208-245-5373

The St. Maries River Railroad operates freight service from a connection with Burlington Northern at Bovill, Idaho, to a connection with Union Pacific at Plummer, 71 miles. Rail includes 75, 90, 100, 112, 115, and 132 pound sections.

Two of St. Maries River Railroad's three GP9s power a work train along the Idaho short line. Photo by Jim Shaw.

Traffic includes logs, plywood, forest products, and sand — 11,500 cars a year.

From Plummer to St. Maries the line is part of the former Milwaukee Road main line; from St. Maries to Bovill it is the former Elk River branch of the Milwaukee Road. The lines were acquired when the Milwaukee Road discontinued operation of its western lines in 1980. The St. Maries River Railroad, which is owned by Potlatch Forests, Inc., started service May 23, 1980.

Radio frequencies: 160.275, 161.055

Location of enginehouse: St. Maries, Idaho
Locomotives: 5

No.	Builder	Model	New	Builder No.	Rebuilt
101	EMD	GP9	4/59	25287	12/80
102	EMD	GP9	5/59	25296	12/80
103	EMD	GP9	6/59	25317	1/80
501	EMD	SW1200	12/54	20053	6/81
502	EMD	SW1200	1/54	18762	7/81

Freight cars: 142 boxcars, 493 flatcars

ST. MARYS RAILROAD CO.

1000 Osborne Street
P. O. Box 520
St. Marys, GA 31558

Reporting marks: SM
Phone: 912-882-5276
Fax: 912-882-7944

St. Marys Railroad operates freight service from St. Marys, Georgia, to a connection with CSX at Kingsland, 10.75 miles. The railroad also operates a 3-mile branch to Kings Bay Naval Station. Rail is 90 to 100 pound. Traffic includes 10,000 cars a year of pulp, chemicals, paper products, and general commodities.

The St. Marys & Kingsland Railroad was incorporated October 24, 1906, and reorganized in March 1911 as the Atlantic, Waycross & Northern Railroad, with the goal of extending the line more than 200 miles beyond Kingsland to Fort Valley. The extension was never built, and the company was reorganized January 11, 1924, as the St. Marys Railroad. Passenger service ended in 1950. The company has been owned by the Gilman Paper Company since 1939.

Radio frequencies: 160.620, 160.560
Location of enginehouse: St. Marys, Ga.
Locomotives: 3

No.	Builder	Model	New	Builder No.
503	EMD	SW1500	6/71	37068
504	EMD	MP15DC	10/74	74645-1
505	EMD	MP15DC	5/76	756156-1

Freight cars: 910 boxcars, 60 bulkhead flatcars

SALT LAKE CITY SOUTHERN RAILROAD CO., INC.

5330 South Riley Lane, #B
Murray, UT 84107

Reporting marks: SL
Phone: 801-261-5482
Fax: 801-261-5483

Salt Lake City Southern operates a line owned by Utah Transit Authority from Salt Lake City south to Mount, Utah, 25 miles. Interchange is made with Union Pacific at Salt Lake City, and with Denver & Rio Grande Western (Southern Pacific) at Murray.

Traffic includes cement, animal feed, grain, lumber, and furniture — about 2,300 cars a year.

The line is part of Union Pacific's Provo Subdivision. UP now runs its Provo-Salt Lake City trains over the D&RGW, making the line excess. Salt Lake City Southern, which is a subsidiary of RailTex, started service April 19, 1993.

Radio frequency: 160.815
Location of enginehouse: Murray, Utah
Locomotives: 1

No.	Builder	Model	New	Builder No.
2207	EMD	GP7U	1/51	13185

SALT LAKE, GARFIELD & WESTERN RAILWAY CO.

1200 West North Temple
P. O. Box 16047
Salt Lake City, UT 84116

Reporting marks: SLGW
Phone: 801-322-3429
Fax: 801-355-4814

The Salt Lake, Garfield & Western operates freight and TOFC service from a connection with the Denver & Rio Grande Western (Southern Pacific) and Union Pacific at Salt Lake City to City Limits, Utah, 10 miles. Rail is 100 pound. Traffic consists of under 500 cars a year of plastics, food, forest products, furniture, and general commodities.

The Salt Lake & Los Angeles Railway was incorporated September 21, 1891, and opened in February 1892 between Salt Lake City and the shore of the Great Salt Lake, where a large amusement pavilion was constructed. The present name was adopted October 28, 1916. The line was electrified in 1919 using standard interurban technology. Electric operation ended in 1951, and regular passenger service ended in 1958.

Hogle Group IC owns the company.

Radio frequencies: 160.305, 161.070
Location of enginehouse: Salt Lake City, Utah
Locomotives: 2 engines

No.	Builder	Model	New	Builder No.
D-4	Alco	S-6	5/55	81290
D-5	GE	65-ton	2/43	15889

GE 65-tonner No. D-5 on the "Saltair Route" at Salt Lake City, Utah. Photo by Jim Shaw.

SAN DIEGO & IMPERIAL VALLEY RAILROAD CO.

743 Imperial Avenue
San Diego, CA 92101

Reporting marks: SDIV
Phone: 619-239-7348
Fax: 619-239-7128

San Diego & Imperial Valley operates freight service from San Diego, California, northeast 18 miles to El Cajon and 130 miles to Plaster City (45 miles of that line are in Mexico, and the portion of the line east of Jacumba, Calif., is out of service). Rail is 90 pound. Traffic includes lumber, steel, plastic, ethafoam, LP gas, pulpwood, grain, scrap, and general merchandise — about 3,500 cars a year. The San Diego Trolley operates on the same line between San Diego and San Ysidro.

The San Diego & Arizona Railway was incorporated December 15, 1906, and opened between San Diego and El Centro on December 1, 1919. The company was reorganized as the San Diego & Arizona Eastern in 1932, a Southern Pacific subsidiary.

In September 1976 a tropical storm washed out the railroad in 89 locations. SP suspended service and applied to abandon the line. Most of the U. S. part of the line west of Plaster City was purchased by the San Diego Metropolitan Transit Development Board in 1979. Kyle Railways provided freight service for nearly five years as the San Diego & Arizona Eastern Transportation Co. before seeking release from its contract. On October 14, 1984, the San Diego & Imperial Valley Railroad took over operations. It is a subsidiary of RailTex, Inc.

Radio frequencies: 160.455, 161.505
Location of enginehouse: San Ysidro, Calif.
Locomotives: 5

No.	Builder	Model	New	Builder No.	Rebuilt
2151	EMD	GP7	11/53	18888	1979
2162	EMD	GP7	1/51	13188	1979
2168	EMD	GP7	10/52	17455	1979
5537	EMD	GP38			
5911	EMD	GP9	5/55	20523	

SAN JOAQUIN VALLEY RAILROAD CO.

221 North F Street
P. O. Box 937
Exeter, CA 93221

Reporting marks: SJVR
Phone: 209-592-1857
Fax: 209-592-1859

The San Joaquin Valley Railroad provides freight service on several lines in central California:
• from Fresno southeast through Exeter to Famoso, 89.2 miles
• from Exeter west through Goshen Junction to Huron and Stratford
• from Cameo to Clovis, 6.4 miles
• from Magunden to Arvin, 16 miles
• from Oil Junction to Maltha, 3 miles.

It connects with Southern Pacific at Fresno, Cameo, Magunden, and Oil Junction. Total mileage is 207. Traffic includes lumber, forest products, sugar beets, food, agricultural products, and hazardous materials and amounts to about 15,000 cars a year.

The company started taking over several Southern Pacific branch lines on January 2, 1992. The first line was from Reedley through Exeter to Terra Bella and from Exeter to Goshen Junction. On January 14, 1992, the company expanded its operation from Goshen Junction to Huron and Stratford, and on December 21, 1992, service began on the balance of the lines, which had been operated jointly by SP and Santa Fe. The San Joaquin Valley Railroad is a subsidiary of Kyle Railways, Inc.

Radio frequency: 160.365
Location of enginehouse: Exeter, Calif.
Locomotives: 14

No.	Builder	Model	New	Builder No.	Rebuilt
101	EMD	GP9	1/54	19110	1980
103	EMD	GP9	8/60	26073	1980
104	EMD	GP9	7/57	23665	1980
1751	EMD	GP9	5/55	19968	1970
1754	EMD	GP9	5/54	19477	1972
1755	EMD	GP9	4/56	21359	1974
1825	EMD	GP28	3/64	28938	
1826	EMD	GP28	3/64	28939	
2035	EMD	GP20	3/62	27102	1974
2037	EMD	GP20	2/62	27099	1977
2038	EMD	GP20	3/62	27106	1977
2041	EMD	GP20	2/62	27089	1978
2042	EMD	GP20	1/61	26313	1975
2043	EMD	GP20	12/61	26943	1977

SAN LUIS CENTRAL RAILROAD CO.

2899 Sherman Avenue
P. O. Box 108
Monte Vista, CO 81144

Reporting marks: SLC
Phone: 719-852-2681
Fax: 719-852-5198

The San Luis Central operates freight service from a connection with the Denver & Rio Grande Western (Southern Pacific) at Monte Vista, Colorado, to Center, 13 miles. Rail is 56 pound. Traffic includes grain, potatoes, and fertilizer — about 2,800 cars a year.

The company was incorporated February 19, 1913. The first portion of the line opened in September 1913 to haul sugar beets to a processing mill located on the line. Beet-growing did not prove popular with local farmers, and the facility closed. The farmers turned to other crops such as potatoes, barley, wheat, peas, and lettuce. Passenger service ended in 1937.

Pea Vine Corporation acquired the entire capital stock from the estate of the railroad's founder in 1969.

Radio frequency: 160.680
Location of enginehouse: Monte Vista, Colo.
Locomotives: 2

No.	Builder	Model	New	Builder No.	Rebuilt
70	EMD	SW8	10/52	17067	
71	GE	70-ton	1/55	32280	1985

Freight cars: 830

San Luis Central SW8 No. 70 arrives in Monte Vista, Colorado, with cars for the Rio Grande in October 1992. Photo by Jim Shaw.

SAN MANUEL ARIZONA RAILROAD CO.

200 South Redington Road
P. O. Box M
San Manuel, AZ 85631

Reporting marks: SMA
Phone: 602-385-3619
Fax: 602-385-3623

Radio frequency: 161.460
Location of enginehouse: San Manuel, Ariz.
Locomotives: 6

No.	Builder	Model	New	Builder No.
10	Alco	RS-3	7/51	78935
13	Alco	RS-3	10/51	79244
16	EMD	GP38-2	10/74	74631-1
17	EMD	GP38-2	10/74	74631-2
18	EMD	GP38	9/70	36686
19	EMD	GP38	5/77	786058-4

The San Manuel Arizona operates freight service from a connection with the Copper Basin Railroad (and by haulage agreement, Southern Pacific) at Hayden, Arizona, to San Manuel, 29.4 miles. Rail is 90 pound. Traffic consists of minerals, sulfuric acid, ore, and concentrates. The line moves about 9,000 cars a year, a little over half of those in interchange service.

The company was incorporated September 29, 1953, to build a railroad, which opened in 1955. Magma Copper Company owns the railroad.

San Manuel Arizona GP38-2s No. 16 and 17 pull a train through the Arizona desert near Mammoth. Photo by Jim Shaw.

SAN PEDRO & SOUTHWESTERN RAILWAY CO.

330 East Fourth Street
P. O. Box 1420
Benson, AZ 85602

Reporting marks: SWKR
Phone: 602-586-2266
Fax: 602-586-2999

The San Pedro & Southwestern operates from a connection with Southern Pacific at Benson, Arizona, to Douglas, 79.3 miles, with a 5.6-mile branch to Bisbee. A planned interchange with National Railways of Mexico will be made at Douglas or Naco.

Most traffic is generated at Curtiss and consists largely of chemicals used in manufacture of fertilizer and other nitrogen products — 2,000 cars a year. Excursion are operated through the scenic San Pedro River area.

The line between Benson and Bisbee was opened in 1889 by the Arizona & Southeastern. That company was acquired by the El Paso & Southwestern and extended east through Douglas to El Paso in 1902. The EP&SW was leased by Southern Pacific in 1924 and merged into Southern Pacific in 1955.

On June 15, 1992, Southern Pacific sold the property to the San Pedro & Southwestern Railway, which has contracted with SWKR Operating Company, Inc. (a subsidiary of Kyle Railways), to provide service.

Radio frequencies: 160.440, 161.520, 160.935
Location of enginehouse: Benson, Ariz.
Locomotives: 1

No.	Builder	Model	New	Builder No.
2039	EMD	GP20	2/61	26574

SAND SPRINGS RAILWAY CO.

216 North McKinley
P. O. Box 128
Sand Springs, OK 74063

Reporting marks: SS
Phone: 918-245-8625
Fax: 918-245-8684

The Sand Springs Railway operates freight service from Tulsa, Oklahoma, to Sand Springs, 5 miles. It connects with the Santa Fe, Burlington Northern, and Union Pacific. Rail is 75 to 110 pound. Traffic includes steel, raw materials for glass pulpboard, scrap iron, and other commodities amounting to about 11,000 cars a year.

The company was incorporated February 6, 1911, by Charles Page to serve the Sand Springs Home, an institution for widows and orphans and one of Page's philanthropies. It was opened later that year from Tulsa to Sand Springs, 8.6 miles. The railroad was operated by electricity until 1955, when it discontinued passenger service and dieselized.

The Sand Springs Home sold the railroad to HMK of Oklahoma, Inc., in 1987. The railroad acquired some switching track at Sand Springs from the Missouri-Kansas-Texas in 1988.

Radio frequency: 160.230
Location of enginehouse: Sand Springs, Okla.
Locomotives: 3

No.	Builder	Model	New	Builder No.
100	EMD	SW900	2/56	20891
101	EMD	SW900	2/56	20892
102	EMD	SW900	1/57	23782

Freight cars: 20 gondolas, 2 flatcars

SANDERSVILLE RAILROAD CO.

206 North Smith Street
P. O. Box 269
Sandersville, GA 31082

Reporting marks: SAN
Phone: 912-552-5151
Fax: 912-552-1118

The Sandersville Railroad operates freight service from a connection with Norfolk Southern at Tennille, Georgia, to Kaolin, 9.1 miles. Rail is 90 to 132 pound. Traffic consists of about 36,000 cars a year of kaolin, wood chips, lumber, and general commodities.

The company was incorporated September 18, 1893, and built 4 miles of track from Tennille to Sandersville. It was extended to Kaolin in 1957. The Tarbutton family controls the company.
Radio frequencies: 160.335, 160.560, 160.860, 161.325

Location of enginehouse: Sandersville, Ga.
Locomotives: 5 plus 2 slugs

No.	Builder	Model	New	Builder No.
90		Slug	3/80	
91		Slug	1966	
100	EMD	SW1500	12/67	33487
200	EMD	SW1200	12/64	29888
300	EMD	SW1500	5/70	36484
400	EMD	SW1500	2/70	35827
500	EMD	SW1500	4/69	34435

Freight cars: 144 boxcars, 242 covered hoppers, 70 wood-chip hopper cars

---

SANTA CRUZ, BIG TREES & PACIFIC RAILWAY CO.

Graham Hill Road
P. O. Box G-1
Felton, CA 95018

Reporting marks: SCBG
Phone: 408-335-1171
Fax: 408-335-3509

The Santa Cruz, Big Trees & Pacific operates excursion trains and limited freight service from a connection with Southern Pacific at Santa Cruz, California, to Olympia, 8.8 miles. Rail ranges from 90 to 136 pound.

The chief item of freight traffic is lumber, less than 500 cars a year. Most revenue comes from excursion trains.

The line was built to 3-foot gauge by the Santa Cruz & Felton Railroad, which was chartered in August 1874 and opened the following year. The company was acquired in 1880 by the South

The Santa Cruz, Big Trees & Pacific still operates this 1942-vintage Whitcomb 45-tonner. Photo by Jim Shaw.

Pacific Coast Railway, which came under Southern Pacific control by 1885. The road was relaid to standard gauge in 1906 and 1907.

SP sold the line to the present operator in September 1985. Passenger service started in 1985, and freight service resumed in 1990. The company is controlled by Georgiana P. Clark.

Radio frequency: 160.995

Location of enginehouse: Felton, Calif.
Locomotives: 3

No.	Builder	Model	New	Builder No.
20	Whitcomb	55-ton	12/42	60208
2600	AT&SF	CF7	10/72	
2641	AT&SF	CF7	2/71	

SANTA FE SOUTHERN RAILWAY, INC.

410 South Guadalupe
Santa Fe, NM 87501

Reporting marks: SFS
Phone: 505-989-8600
Fax: 505-983-7620

The Santa Fe Southern Railway operates freight and excursion service from a connection with the Santa Fe at Lamy, New Mexico, to Santa Fe, 18 miles. Rail is 85 to 112 pound. Traffic amounts to about 500 cars a year of beer, volcanic cinders, and pumice.

The line was built by the New Mexico & Southern Pacific Railroad, which was chartered in 1878. It opened on February 16, 1880, and it was leased to the Atchison, Topeka & Santa Fe by 1884. Santa Fe sold the line on March 13, 1992. The company is controlled by Bob Sarr, and six other investors.

Radio frequency: 160.290
Location of enginehouse: Santa Fe, N. M.
Locomotives: 2

No.	Builder	Model	New	Builder No.
92	EMD	GP7	7/53	18566
93	EMD	GP16	8/52	17242

Santa Fe Southern operates over the former Atchison, Topeka & Santa Fe branch into Santa Fe, the capital city of New Mexico. GP7 No. 92 is shown near Santa Fe in October 1992. Photo by Jim Shaw.

SANTA MARIA VALLEY RAILROAD CO.

625 South McClelland Street
P. O. Box 340
Santa Maria, CA 93456

Reporting marks: SMV
Phone: 805-922-7941
Fax: 805-928-9615

The Santa Maria Valley Railroad operates freight service from Santa Maria, California, to a connection with Southern Pacific at Guadalupe, 14.8 miles. The railroad has several short branch lines. Rail is 75 to 90 pound. Traffic includes sugar, asphalt, beer, plastic, lumber, and food products — about 2,000 cars a year.

The railroad was incorporated July 14, 1911, as the Santa Maria Valley Railway and reorganized under the present name in 1926. Passenger service was never operated. The line was abandoned between Gates and Roadamite in 1950.

The company is owned by the G. Allan Hancock Estate and the Marion Mullin Charitable Trust.

Radio frequencies: 160.770 (road), 161.175 (yard)
Location of enginehouse: Santa Maria, Calif.
Locomotives: 3

No.	Builder	Model	New	Builder No.
70	GE	70-ton	1/50	30381
80	GE	70-ton	12/53	32207
1801	EMD	GP9	6/59	25314

SAVANNAH STATE DOCKS RAILROAD CO.

U. S. Highway 17 North
P. O. Box 2406
Savannah, GA 31402

Reporting marks: SSDK
Phone: 912-964-3987
Fax: 912-964-3969

The Savannah State Docks Railroad is a switching line operating 30 miles of track at Savannah and Port Wentworth, Georgia. It connects with CSX and Norfolk Southern and handles about 36,000 cars a year. Rail is 85 and 100 pound. The railroad began operations in 1952 and is owned by the Georgia Port Authority.

Radio frequency: 158.805
Location of enginehouse: Savannah, Ga.
Locomotives: 3

No.	Builder	Model	New	Builder No.
1001	EMD	SW1001	4/78	776103-1
1002	EMD	SW1001	4/78	776103-2
8237	EMD	GP7	1/51	14569

SEMINOLE GULF RAILWAY, LP

4110 Centerpoint Drive, Suite 207
Fort Myers, FL 33916

Reporting marks: SGLR
Phone: 813-275-6060
Fax: 813-275-0581

Seminole Gulf operates two separate line segments in southwest Florida. One runs from a connection with CSX at Arcadia to North Naples (Vanderbilt Beach), 78 miles, and the other extends from a CSX connection at Oneco to Venice, 30 miles. Branch lines bring the total mileage to 118. Rail is 75 to 112 pound. Annual traffic includes about 6,000 cars a year of stone, forest products, building materials, newsprint, LP gas, plastic, food products, and paper products. Seminole Gulf also operates excursion and dinner trains.

Both routes were built about 1900 — the Venice line is a

mixture of trackage from both Seaboard Air Line and Atlantic Coast Line, and the Vanderbilt Beach line is primarily ACL. CSX sold the lines to Seminole Gulf and shortline service started November 14, 1987. The company is controlled by Gordon H. Fay, G. Bartholomew, and others.

Radio frequencies: 160.710, 161.235, 161.550
Location of enginehouse: Fort Myers and Oneco, Fla.
Locomotives: 7

No.	Builder	Model	New	Builder No.
571	EMD	GP9	2/58	24377
572	EMD	GP9	6/57	23372
573	EMD	GP9	4/56	21532
575	EMD	GP9	3/56	21492
576	EMD	GP9	10/56	22420
577	EMD	GP9	10/56	22423
578	EMD	GP10	12/57	23827

Freight cars: 16 boxcars

Seminole Gulf GP9s 572 and 571 pull the daily freight on the Fort Myers subdivision at Punta Gorda, Florida. Photo by Jim Shaw.

SEMO PORT RAILROAD, INC.

2110 Main Street
Scott City, MO 63780

Reporting marks: SE
Phone: 314-264-4045
Fax: 314-264-2727

Semo Port Railroad operates from a connection with the Burlington Northern at Rush Junction (Cape Girardeau), Missouri, to connections with Union Pacific and Southern Pacific at Capedeau Junction, 5.8 miles. Rail is 112 to 133 pound.

The Port Authority is developing a Mississippi River port near Cape Girardeau, and the rail line will give aggregate and grain shippers competitive rail access. The line was built in 1929 by the Missouri Pacific. It was acquired by the the Southeast Missouri Regional Port Authority on October 28, 1994. The railroad is a subsidiary of the port authority and is being operated under contract by Respondek Railroad Corp. Service started December 3, 1994.

Location of enginehouse: Scott City, Mo.
Locomotives: 1

No.	Builder	Model	New	Builder No.
1823	EMD	GP7L	8/51	15693

SEQUATCHIE VALLEY RAILROAD

P. O. Box 1317
Shelbyville, TN 37160

Reporting marks: SQVR
Phone: 615-684-7376

The Sequatchie Valley Railroad operates freight service from a CSX connection at Bridgeport, Alabama, to Dunlap, Tennessee, 37 miles. Rail is 90 pound, and the load limit is 220,000 pounds. Traffic includes about 4,000 cars a year of coal and plastic.

The line was built in the 1890s by the Sequatchie Valley Railroad and leased by the Nashville, Chattanooga & St. Louis by 1893. In early 1986 Seaboard System sold the line to G. R. Abernathy, and shortline service started on May 20, 1986.
Radio frequencies: 154.600, 464.7, 469.7

Location of enginehouse: South Pittsburg, Tenn.
Locomotives: 8

No.	Builder	Model	New	Builder No.
600	EMD	FP7A	6/50	10323
1201	EMD	SW1200	11/55	20666
1488	EMD	SW1200	12/55	20675
1507	EMD	F7B	12/53	19047
1534	EMD	SD35	10/65	31167
1686	EMD	NW2	1/48	5130
1819	GE	U18B		
2561	EMD	GP30	10/62	27432

Sequatchie Valley's ex-Conrail NW2 No. 1686 pulls through Jasper, Tennessee, with a long cut of empty coal cars. Photo by Jim Shaw.

SF&L RAILWAY, INC.

P. O. Box 26421
Salt Lake City, UT 84126

Reporting marks: SFAL
Phone: 801-972-8330

The company, which is affiliated with principals of A&K Materials, has acquired a Missouri Pacific branch line between Hillsboro and Italy, Texas, 18.5 miles. Operations appear unlikely.

SHAMOKIN VALLEY RAILROAD CO.

356 Priestley Avenue
Northumberland, PA 17857

Reporting marks: SVRR
Phone: 717-473-7949

Shamokin Valley Railroad provides freight service over 25 miles of track from a connection with Conrail at Sunbury, Pennsylvania, to Mount Carmel Junction. It connects with the Reading, Blue Mountain & Northern at Locust Summit by trackage rights. Rail ranges from 90 to 152 pound. Traffic includes outbound coal, and grain, woodpulp, lumber, truck chassis, coke, and graphite — under 600 cars a year.

The east end of the main line was built in part by the Mahanoy & Broad Mountain Railroad (chartered 1859). That company and several others were consolidated on July 27, 1870, to become the Mahanoy & Shamokin Railroad, which was merged into the Philadelphia & Reading the following year. The west end of the main line is a consolidation of trackage built by the Shamokin, Sunbury & Lewisburg Railroad, chartered February 16, 1882, and trackage built as the Shamokin Division of the Northern Central in the 1850s. The SS&L became part of the Reading, and the Northern Central became part of the Pennsylvania Railroad.

Conrail operated this line until December 1988, when it was sold to SEDA-COG Joint Rail Authority. Shortline service started December 13, 1988. The operating company is owned by Richard Robey.

Radio frequency: 160.455
Location of enginehouse: Northumberland, Pa.
Locomotives: pooled with North Shore Railroad

SHENANDOAH VALLEY RAILROAD CO.

P. O. Box 1800
Harrisonburg, VA 22801

Reporting marks: SV
Phone: 703-568-1800

Shenandoah Valley owns a line from a CSX connection at Staunton, Virginia, to a connection with the Chesapeake Western (Norfolk Southern) at Pleasant Valley, 20.2 miles. Rail is 80 pound. Traffic consists of under 500 cars a year of feed ingredients, fertilizer, and LP gas.

The line is the south end of the Chesapeake Western Railway, which was purchased by the Greater Shenandoah Valley Development Company early in 1993. The company has contracted with Buckingham Branch Railroad to operate the line. The first train operated on August 23, 1994.

Location of enginehouse: Verona, Va.
Locomotives: pooled with Buckingham Branch Railroad

SIDNEY & LOWE RAILROAD, INC.

201 Huntsman Street
P. O. Box 296
Sidney, NE 69162

Reporting marks: SLGG
Phone: 308-254-4938
Fax: 308-254-2999

The Sidney & Lowe Railroad is a switching line with 12 miles of track at Sidney, Nebraska. It connects with Burlington Northern at Huntsman and with Union Pacific at Brownson. Rail is 90 to 112 pound. It handles nearly 1,500 cars a year.

The company was incorporated in 1980 to provide rail service for an industrial area being developed near the U. S. Army Big Sioux Depot. The ICC approved common carrier service on July 29, 1982. The company was owned by the Glover Group until November 25, 1995, when it was acquired by Progress Rail Services Corporation.

Radio frequencies: 463.325, 468.325
Locomotives: 2

No.	Builder	Model	New	Builder No.	Rebuilt
7	EMD	GP10	1/57	22328	1973, 1990
8	EMD	GP10	4/53	18050	1973, 1990

SIERRA RAILROAD CO.

13645 Tuolumne Road
Sonora, CA 95370

Reporting marks: SERA
Phone: 209-532-3685
Fax: 209-532-7883

The Sierra Railroad operates freight service from a connection with the Santa Fe and Southern Pacific at Oakdale, California, to Standard, 49 miles. Rail is 90 to 110 pound. Traffic includes lumber, forest products, and other general commodities — under

The new owners of the Sierra Railroad have leased the line's Baldwin switchers, which will soon be replaced by EMD power. Scenes like this one at Keystone, California, will no longer take place. Photo by Jim Shaw.

1,000 cars a year. Excursion trains are operated over the line by Railtown 1897 State Historic Park.

The Sierra Railway Company of California was incorporated in 1897 and opened for traffic that year. The Sierra Railroad was incorporated July 10, 1935, to purchase the assets of the Sierra Railway. Regular passenger service ended on September 1, 1938.

Sierra Pacific Coast Railways, Inc., an investment group, acquired control in March 1995.

Radio frequencies: 160.590
Location of enginehouse: Oakdale, Calif.
Locomotives: 3

No.	Builder	Model	New	Builder No.	Rebuilt
40	BLW	S-12	2/55	76092	
42	BLW	S-12	2/55	76093	
44	BLW	S-12	7/51	75140	
46	EMD	GP9	1/57	22913	1975

SISSETON MILBANK RAILROAD, INC.

405 West Milbank Avenue
Milbank, SD 57252

Reporting marks: SMRR
Phone: 605-432-6912
Fax: 605-432-9318

The Sisseton Milbank Railroad operates a line from Sisseton, South Dakota, to a connection with Burlington Northern and CP Rail System (Soo Line) at Milbank, 38 miles. Rail ranges from 56 to 90 pound. Traffic is about 1,200 cars a year of grain and agricultural products. Occasional excursion trains are operated in cooperation with the Milbank Chamber of Commerce.

The line was built by the Milwaukee Road between 1880 and 1893. The property was purchased by SLA Property Management in June 1982 and was operated by Dakota Rail until July 18, 1987, when Sisseton Southern Railway was given the operating contract. SLA Property Management formed the Sissteon Milbank Railroad to assume operations effective July 1, 1989.

Radio frequencies: 461.95, 466.95
Location of enginehouse: Milbank, S. D.
Locomotives: 1

No.	Builder	Model	New	Builder No.
627	EMD	SW1200	11/54	20057

Freight cars: 107 covered hoppers

SMS RAIL SERVICE, INC.

P. O. Box 711
Bridgeport, NJ 08014

Reporting marks: SMS
Phone: 609-467-2121
Fax: 609-467-4800

The company leases and operates 4.5 miles of switching track at the Pureland Industrial Complex between Nortonville and Bridgeport, New Jersey. It interchanges with Conrail. Rail ranges from 100 to 130 pounds. Traffic includes paper products and chemicals — about 1,100 cars a year. Service started June 1, 1994. The company is controlled by Jeffery L. Sutch and Leonard J. Smolsky.

Locomotives: 4

No.	Builder	Model	New	Builder No.
17	BLW	S-12	1952	75704
1293	BLW	DS-4-4-1000	2/47	72840
1494	BLW	DS-4-4-1000	4/49	74119
1842	BLW	S-12	11/52	75704

SOMERSET RAILROAD CORP.

7725 Lake Road
Barker, NY 14012

Reporting marks: SOM
Phone: 716-795-9501

Somerset Railroad operates freight service from a connection with Conrail near Lockport, New York, to a New York State Electric & Gas Corporation power plant near West Somerset, 15.59 miles. Rail is 119 to 136 pound. Traffic is coal in unit trains and limestone, about 15,000 cars a year. The railroad was opened in November 1983. It is owned by New York State Electric & Gas and operated by Conrail.

Radio frequencies: 160.380, 161.040
Locomotives: supplied by Conrail
Freight cars: 428 rotary-dump gondolas

SOUTH BRANCH VALLEY RAILROAD

South Fork Road
P. O. Box 470
Moorefield, WV 26836

Reporting marks: SBVR
Phone: 304-538-2305
Fax: 304-538-7474

South Branch Valley Railroad operates freight service from a connection with CSX at Green Spring, West Virginia, to Petersburg, 52.4 miles. Rail is 85, 100, and 132 pound. Traffic includes poultry feed, liquid carbon dioxide, plastic, limestone, and other commodities — about 3,500 cars a year. The railroad also operates seasonal "Potomac Eagle" excursion trains.

The South Branch Railroad opened a line from Green Springs to Romney on September 1, 1884. The company was affiliated with and operated by the Baltimore & Ohio. In 1914 the Hampshire Southern opened its line from Romney Junction to Petersburg, 34 miles, and was purchased by the B&O. The state of West Virginia acquired the line from the B&O in 1978. South Branch Valley began service on October 15, 1978.

The company is owned and operated by the West Virginia State Rail Authority.

Radio frequency: 800 MHZ
Location of enginehouse: Moorefield, W. Va.
Locomotives: 9

No.	Builder	Model	New	Builder No.	Rebuilt
2001	EMD	GP9	7/56	21833	
6135	EMD	GP9	9/56	22043	
6240	EMD	GP9	8/57	23502	
6352	EMD	GP10	7/56	21849	1978
6447	EMD	GP10	2/58	21835	1978
6506	EMD	GP9	10/56	22250	
6600	EMD	GP9	4/55	20417	
6604*	EMD	GP9	4/55	20421	
7172	EMD	BL2	10/48	5922	

*lettered B&O

286

SOUTH BROOKLYN RAILWAY CO.

990 Third Avenue
Brooklyn, NY 11232

Reporting marks: SBK
Phone: 718-788-1799
Fax: 718-832-0635

The South Brooklyn Railway operates 1.5 miles of switching track at Brooklyn, New York. It connects with the New York Cross Harbor Railroad and Conrail (via New York Cross Harbor). It handles less than 500 cars a year. Rail is 100 pound.

The company was formed in 1907 as successor to the Brooklyn Heights Railroad. It is owned by the city of New York and operated by the New York City Transit Authority.
Radio frequencies: 158.775, 160.845, 161.505,
Locomotives: 2

No.	Builder	Model	New	Builder No.
N-1	GE	50-ton	10/74	38946
N-2	GE	50-ton	10/74	38947

SOUTH BUFFALO RAILWAY CO.

2600 Hamburg Turnpike
Lackawanna, NY 14218

Reporting marks: SB
Phone: 716-821-3631
Fax: 716-821-3687

South Buffalo is a switching line operating 61 miles of track at Lackawanna, New York. It connects with Buffalo & Pittsburgh, Conrail, CSX, CP Rail System (Delaware & Hudson), and Norfolk Southern. It handles about 60,000 cars a year. The railroad started operation in 1901. It is owned by Bethlehem Steel Company.
Radio frequencies: 161.190, 161.280
Locomotives: 20
Freight cars: 97 gondolas

SOUTH CAROLINA CENTRAL RAILROAD CO., INC.

101 South Fourth Street
P. O. Box 490
Hartsville, SC 29550

Reporting marks: SCRF
Phone: 803-332-7584
Fax: 803-332-1222

South Carolina Central Railroad operates two separate lines in South Carolina. One extends from a CSX connection at Florence to Bishopville, 42.4 miles. Rail is 70 to 132 pound. The other extends from a CSX connection at Cheraw to Society Hill, 13 miles. Rail is predominantly 85 pound. Traffic includes paper, forest products, grain, steel, scrap, food products, coal, chemicals, and automobiles — about 24,000 cars a year.

The lines are former Seaboard Air Line track, except for the Florence-Hartsville portion, which was an Atlantic Coast Line branch. CSX sold the lines to South Carolina Central in December 1987. Shortline service started on December 1, 1987. South Carolina Central is a subsidiary of RailTex.

Radio frequency: 161.175
Location of enginehouses: Hartsville and Cheraw, S. C.
Locomotives: 6

No.	Builder	Model	New	Builder No.
5905	EMD	GP9	12/54	20187
6097	EMD	GP9	1956	22098
6187	EMD	GP9	11/56	22570
6439	EMD	GP9	5/55	20443
6550	EMD	GP9	1957	23024
6555	EMD	GP9	1957	23029

South Carolina Central's home-chopped GP9 No. 5905 switches at Floyd, South Carolina, in March 1991. Photo by Jim Shaw.

SOUTH CENTRAL FLORIDA EXPRESS, INC.

P. O. Box 129
Clewiston, FL 33440

Reporting marks: SCXF
Phone: 813-983-3163
Fax: 813-983-6773

South Central Florida Express operates freight service from a CSX interchange at Sebring, Florida, to a connection with Florida East Coast at Lake Harbor, 82.2 miles. Rail is 85 pound. Traffic includes sugar cane, refined sugar, molasses, pulpwood, paper, lumber, fertilizer, and LP gas. It totals about 40,000 cars a year (about 75 percent of that is sugar cane moving locally).

The portion of the line between Sebring and Palmdale was built by the Atlantic Coast Line between 1915 and 1920. The line between Palmdale and Clewiston was built in part by the Moore Haven & Clewiston Railway. That company was chartered in 1921 and acquired by ACL in June 1925.

CSX sold the line to the South Central Florida Railroad on June 2, 1990. South Central Florida Express, an affiliate of United States Sugar Corporation, acquired the line on September 17, 1994.

Radio frequencies: 160.830, 161.250
Location of enginehouse: Clewiston, Fla.
Locomotives: 9

No.	Builder	Model	New	Builder No.	Rebuilt
9010	EMD	GP7	5/53	18416	
9011	EMD	GP7	1/52	15943	
9012	EMD	GP7	1/52	15944	1976
9013	EMD	GP8	5/54	18814	1976
9014	EMD	GP8	4/53	17980	1976
9015	EMD	GP8	4/53	18049	1976
9016	EMD	GP16	6/51	13878	1980
9017	EMD	GP16	12/51	15946	1980
9018	EMD	GP7U	5/51	13199	1978

Freight cars: 56 boxcars

SOUTH CENTRAL TENNESSEE RAILROAD CO. INC.

P. O. Box 259
Centerville, TN, 37033`

Reporting marks: SCTR
Phone: 615-729-4227

The South Central Tennessee Railroad operates freight service from a connection with CSX at Colesburg, Tennessee, to Hohenwald, 50.5 miles. Rail is 80 to 100 pound. Traffic includes wood chips, cross ties, carbon black, paper, and plastic resin — more than 3,700 cars a year.

The line was built by the Nashville, Chattanooga & St. Louis between 1879 and 1884. Seaboard System sold the line to the South Central Tennessee Railroad Authority, which started service July 1, 1978. RailAmerica acquired the railroad from Kyle Railways on February 1, 1995, and operates the line under a lease-purchase agreement.

Radio frequency: 161.355
Location of enginehouse: Watson, Tenn.
Locomotives: 3

No.	Builder	Model	New	Builder No.	Rebuilt
121	EMD	SW1200	6/56	21471	
2062	EMD	GP7	1/52	15808	1973
2070	EMD	GP7	9/52	16993	1974

Freight cars: 78 wood-chip hopper cars

SOUTH KANSAS & OKLAHOMA RAILROAD INC.

1230 South Walnut Street
Coffeyville, KS 67337

Reporting marks: SKOL
Phone: 316-251-3600

The South Kansas & Oklahoma operates freight service on several former Santa Fe lines:
• from Tulsa, Oklahoma, north through Bartlesville, Okla., and Independence and Chanute, Kansas, to Iola, 147 miles
• from Chanute southwest to Winfield and Wellington, Kan., 139 miles
• from Cherryvale, Kan., to Coffeyville, 18.7 miles
• from Owasso to the Port of Catoosa (Tulsa Port Authority), 8 miles.

It connects with the Santa Fe at Winfield and Wellington, with Burlington Northern at Tulsa and Cherryvale, with the affiliated Southeast Kansas Railroad at Coffeyville, and with Union Pacific at Tulsa, Wellington, and Coffeyville.

Total mileage owned and operated is 296. Rail is 100 to 132 pound. Traffic includes grain, flour, cement, and aggregate. About 14,000 cars a year are handled.

The Iola line was built by the Southern Kansas Railway in the late 1870s; it was leased to Santa Fe before the turn of the century. The Tulsa line was completed in 1905, the Wellington line in the 1880s, and the Catoosa branch in 1968.

On December 28, 1990, Santa Fe sold the lines to the South Kansas & Oklahoma, which is a subsidiary of WATCO.

Radio frequency: 160.785
Location of enginehouses: Coffeyville, Winfield, and Chanute, Kan.

Locomotives: 17

No.	Builder	Model	New	Builder No.	Rebuilt
2174	EMD	GP7	2/52	15820	10/79
2178	EMD	GP7	9/52	17006	12/79
2184	EMD	GP7	9/52	16980	2/80
2186	EMD	GP7	4/53	17018	3/80
2187	EMD	GP7	12/52	17639	3/80
2188	EMD	GP7	9/52	16994	4/80
2191	EMD	GP7	3/53	17017	4/80
2211	EMD	GP30	3/63	28119	
4101	EMD	GP30	5/62	27789	

No.	Builder	Model	New	Builder No.
4103	EMD	GP30	5/62	27791
4107	EMD	GP30	5/62	27795
4109	EMD	GP30	5/62	27797
4111	EMD	GP30	7/63	28389
4112	EMD	GP30	7/63	28390
4114	EMD	GP30	7/63	28392
4115	EMD	GP30	7/63	28393
411x	EMD	GP30	7/63	28395

Freight cars: 43 covered hoppers

SOUTH ORIENT RAILROAD CO., LTD.

3811 Turtle Creek Boulevard, Suite 380
Dallas, TX 75219

Reporting marks: SO
Phone: 214-528-2888
Fax: 214-528-0770

The South Orient operates freight, TOFC, and COFC service from San Angelo, Texas, to Presidio, 406 miles. Principal connections are with the Santa Fe at San Angelo Junction (and via Santa Fe with Cen-Tex at Ricker for Fort Worth traffic), with Southern Pacific at Alpine, and with National Railways of Mexico at Presidio. Rail is 70, 90, and 115 pound.

Traffic is primarily grain, agricultural products, and manufactured commodities. There is substantial potential for international traffic moving from and to the Chihuahua region and the port of Topolobampo in Mexico. The road expects to handle more than 2,000 cars a year.

The line from San Angelo to Alpine was built during the first two decades of the 20th century by the Kansas City, Mexico & Orient Railway, which was intended to connect Kansas City with a new port on the Gulf of California. The KCM&O wandered in and out of receivership and reorganization. The Santa Fe bought it in 1928 partly for access to the area it served and partly to keep other roads from getting it. Santa Fe extended the line from Alpine to a connection with the Mexican portion of the KCM&O at Presidio in 1930.

The line was purchased from Santa Fe for $5.5 million. It is owned jointly by Dallas investors, and the South Orient Rural Railroad Transportation District of the state of Texas. The operating company is run by Texas Train Management. Shortline service started January 2, 1992.

Radio frequencies: 160.440, 161.490
Location of enginehouse: San Angelo and Alpine, Texas
Locomotives: 7 (also used on Cen-Tex Railroad)

No.	Builder	Model	New	Builder No.
1	Alco	S-4	10/46	74803
101	EMD	GP7	1952	16864
102	EMD	GP7	1952	16867
103	EMD	GP7	8/50	9228
104	EMD	GP7	3/51	12931
105	EMD	GP7	8/51	13307
106	EMD	GP7	4/51	12937

SOUTH PLAINS LAMESA RAILROAD LTD.

P. O. Box 1263
Lamesa, TX 79331

Reporting marks: SLAL
Phone: 806-872-6766
Fax: 806-872-6792

The South Plains Lamesa Railroad operates from a connection with the Santa Fe at Slayton, Texas, to Lamesa, 54.5 miles. Rail is 90 pound. Traffic is primarily grain, fertilizer, and cotton — 1,000 cars a year.

The line was built by the Pecos & Northern Texas Railway in 1910 and became part of the Santa Fe soon after it was built. Santa Fe sold the line to South Plains Lamesa on October 15, 1993. The company is owned by Larry Wisener.
Location of enginehouse: Lamesa, Texas
Locomotives: 1

No.	Builder	Model	New	Builder No.
1555	EMD	GP7	3/53	17869

SOUTHEAST KANSAS RAILROAD CO.

1230 South Walnut Street
Coffeyville, KS 67337

Reporting marks: SEKR
Phone: 316-251-3600

Southeast Kansas Railroad operates a line from Bartlesville, Oklahoma, through Coffeyville, Kansas, to Nassau Junction, Missouri, 133.8 miles. It connects with the South Kansas & Oklahoma at Bartlesville and Coffeyville; with Union Pacific at Coffeyville and Chetopa, Kan.; with Burlington Northern at Cherokee, Kan.; with Kansas City Southern at Pittsburg, Kan.; and with Missouri & Northern Arkansas at Nassau Junction. About 5,000 cars a year of grain, coal, coke, sand, lumber, plastic, paper products, and resin make up the road's traffic.

The line is a former Missouri Pacific branch. MP sold the Coffeyville-Nassau Junction line and shortline service started April 13, 1987. The line from Coffeyville to Bartlesville was acquired in 1994. The company is controlled by C. R. Webb of Coffeyville.

Radio frequencies: 160.785, 160.845
Location of enginehouse: Coffeyville, Kan.
Locomotives: 10

No.	Builder	Model	New	Builder No.	Rebuilt
102	EMD	GP7	1/51	12060	
103	EMD	GP7	1/51	12061	
106	EMD	GP7	2/51	12064	
117	EMD	GP7	11/51	14994	
123	EMD	GP7	12/52	17085	
142	Alco	RS-3M	6/51	78893	1959
143	Alco	RS-3M	6/51	78894	1959
1002	AT&SF	CF7	1971		
1003	AT&SF	CF7	1973		
1274	EMD	SW10	7/52	16680	

SOUTHEASTERN INTERNATIONAL CORP.

c/o Houston & Gulf Coast
    Railroad Services
3203 Areba Street
Houston, TX 77091

Reporting marks: SEI
Phone: 713-682-8458

Southeastern International operates freight service on two separate former Santa Fe lines in Texas:
• from a Santa Fe connection at Fannett to Stowell, southwest of Beaumont, 12 miles

• from a Santa Fe connection at Cane Junction to Wharton, southwest of Houston, 13 miles

Rail is 70 and 90 pound. The company expects to move less than 500 cars a year of grain, fertilizer, and limestone.

The lines were acquired by Southeastern International and are operated by Houston & Gulf Coast Railroad Services. Operation began on July 6, 1995.

Locomotives: leased from Santa Fe as needed

SOUTHERN ALABAMA RAILROAD CO., INC.

P. O. Box 1317
Shelbyville, TN 37610

Reporting marks: SUAB
Phone: 615-684-7376

The Southern Alabama Railroad operates freight service from a connection with CSX at Troy, Alabama, to Goshen, 16 miles. Rail is 85 pound. Traffic includes poultry feed, plastic, vegetable oil, and food products — 2,500 cars a year.

The line was built by the Mobile & Girard Railroad, which opened a line from Troy to Columbus, Georgia, in 1870, It was not extended from Troy through Goshen until after the company had been leased by the Central Railroad & Banking Company of Georgia. It was completed to Searight in 1891.

The property was sold by Norfolk Southern to the current operator, and shortline service started on October 31, 1988. The company is controlled by Richard Abernathy.

Radio frequency: 154.600
Location of enginehouse: Troy, Ala.
Locomotives: 3

No.	Builder	Model	New	Builder No.	Rebuilt
9	EMD	SW600	6/54	19301	
7013	EMD	SW9	6/52	11168	
9424	EMD	SW14	12/50	11672	1980

SOUTHERN INDIANA RAILWAY, INC.

P. O. Box 132
Sellersburg, IN 47172

Reporting marks: SIND
Phone: 812-246-2716

The Southern Indiana operates freight service from a connection with CSX at Watson, Indiana, to Speed, 5.45 miles. Rail is 105 to 132 pound. Traffic is cement, nearly 3,000 cars a year. The company was incorporated August 5, 1939, to acquire and operate a portion of the Indiana Railroad. The Southern Indiana is the last operating segment of that interurban line. The company is owned by W. L. Elder and others.

Radio frequency: 27.395
Location of enginehouse: Speed, Ind.
Locomotives: 3

No.	Builder	Model	New	Builder No.
100	GE	65-ton	4/47	28657
101	GE	65-ton	11/46	28474
102	GE	80-ton	1952	31805

Southern Indiana GE 65-tonner No. 101 pulls a train through a daisy field near New Watson, Indiana. Photo by Jim Shaw.

SOUTHERN RAILROAD CO. OF NEW JERSEY

P. O. Box 122
Willingboro, NJ 08046

Reporting marks: SRNJ
Phone: 609-871-8699
Fax: 609-871-7432

The Southern Railroad of New Jersey operates freight service from a connection with Conrail at Winslow Junction, New Jersey, to Griff, near Alantic City, 28.8 miles, on track owned by NJ Transit. In addition the company owns and operates several branch lines:
• Pleasantville to Linwood, 3.9 miles
• Winslow Junction to Vineland, 15.5 miles
• Tuckahoe to Rio Grande (near Cape May), 20.7 miles

In May 1995, SRNJ took over the former West Jersey Railroad line from a Conrail connection at West Swedesboro to Salem and Port Salem, 18 miles.

Rail ranges from 85 to 130 pound. Traffic includes building materials, aggregates, newsprint, recyclables, frozen food, produce, and nonmetallic minerals, under 1,500 cars a year.

The lines are all former Conrail track that was previously part of the Pennsylvania-Reading Seashore Lines, except for the Vineland branch, which is ex-Central of New Jersey. Shore Fast Line started service to Linwood in May 1983, to Atlantic City in August 1983, to Vineland on July 1, 1987, and to Rio Grande in July 1990. Southern Railroad of New Jersey acquired the assets of Shore Fast Line on December 9, 1991. The company is a subsidiary of JP Rail Inc. (Joe Petaccio).

Radio frequencies: 160.335, 161.385
Location of enginehouse: Winslow Junction, N. J.
Locomotives: 6

No.	Builder	Model	New	Builder No.
100	EMD	GP9	6/56	21703
101	EMD	GP9	1/59	25055
414	Alco	C420	1964	3385-11
727	EMD	F7A	2/53	17911
728	EMD	F7A	2/53	17912
1548	Alco	RS-3M	1953	

SOUTHERN RAILWAY OF BRITISH COLUMBIA

2102 River Drive
New Westminster, BC V3M 6S3
Canada

Reporting marks: SRY
Phone: 604-521-1966
Fax: 604-526-0914

Southern Railway of British Columbia operates freight and TOFC service from New Westminster, British Columbia, to Chilliwack, 63.8 miles. Branch lines extend from New Westminster to McKay, 5.7 miles, and Annacis, 4.5 miles. The principal interchange is at New Westminster with Canadian National, CP Rail, BC Rail, and Burlington Northern. Rail ranges from 85 to 115 pound. Annual traffic consists of about 45,000 cars of automobiles, lumber, and grain.

The British Columbia Electric Railway was formed in 1905, and it completed a line to Chilliwack in 1910. Passenger service on that line ceased in 1950. BCE became British Columbia Hydro Railway in 1961; in 1988 it was sold to Itel Rail Corporation, which reorganized the railroad as Southern Railway of British Columbia. The company is controlled indirectly by Dennis Washington, owner of the Washington Central Railroad.

Radio frequencies: 160.275, 160.545, 160.605
Enginehouse: New Westminster, B. C.
Locomotives: 19

No.	Builder	Model	New	Builder No.
151	EMD	MP15	1975	75626-1
152	EMD	MP15	1975	75626-2
153	EMD	MP15	1975	75626-3
381	EMD	SD38	1971	37816
382	EMD	SD38	1972	71606-1
383	EMD	SD38	1972	71606-2
384	EMD	SD38	1974	74614-1
900-911	GMD	SW900	1955-1969	

Freight cars: 167 boxcars, 97 center-beam flatcars

SOUTHERN SWITCHING CO.

300 South Swenson
P. O. Box 272
Stamford, TX 79553

Reporting marks: SSC
Phone: 915-773-2090
Fax: 915-773-2857

Southern Switching Company operates freight service from a connection with Union Pacific at Abilene, Texas, to Lanius, 10 miles. Burlington Northern at Wichita Falls, Texas, 149. Rail is 75 pound. Traffic includes lumber, chemicals, wallboard, and grain; the company expects to move about 3,000 cars a year.

The line was built by the Wichita Valley Railroad, which was chartered in 1890. WV came under control of the Burlington system in 1907 and was merged into the Fort Worth & Denver in 1952.

Shortline service started May 16, 1994, on the entire 149 miles of the line between Wichita Falls and Abilene. Abandonment of service between Wichita Falls and Lanius, 139 miles, was approved in June 1995.

The track is owned by Lone Star Railroad, Inc., and both Lone Star and Southern Switching are controlled by Gregory B. Cundiff, owner of three other shortlines.

Location of enginehouse: Abilene, Texas
Locomotives: 3

No.	Builder	Model	New	Builder No.	Rebuilt
705	EMD	GP7	2/53	17926	
1729	EMD	GP16	10/56	22633	1981
3361	EMD	GP9	4/56	21374	

SOUTHWESTERN PENNSYLVANIA RAILROAD CO.

304 North Third Street
Youngwood, PA 15697

Reporting marks: SWP
Phone: 412-582-5652
Fax: 412-439-9543

The Southwestern Pennsylvania Railroad operates freight service from Greensburg, Pennsylvania, to Uniontown, 65 miles. It connects with Conrail at Greensburg and with CSX at Connellsville. Rail ranges from 90 to 131 pound. Traffic includes paper, lumber, and building materials, and coal. The railroad expects to move about 1,000 cars in its first year of operation.

The Greensburg-Connellsville portion of the railroad is a former Pennsylvania Railroad branch. The line south of Connellsville was CSX's Mount Pleasant subdivision (formerly a Baltimore & Ohio branch)

The lines were acquired in 1995 by Fayette and Westmoreland counties; they were then leased to the Southwestern Pennsylvania Railroad. Shortline service started on June 29, 1995. The company is controlled by Phillip C. Larson, Russell Peterson, and Dennis E. Larson.
Radio frequency: 160.425
Location of enginehouse: Everson, Pa.
Locomotives: 2

No.	Builder	Model	New	Builder No.
1606	GMD	GP7	12/51	A271
1706	EMD	GP16	8/51	14954 1980

SOUTHWESTERN RAILROAD CO., INC.

2 North Main Street
Perryton, TX 79070
310 Diaz Avenue
P O. Box 126
Hurley, NM 88043

Reporting marks: SW
Phone (Texas): 806-435-2322
Phone (New Mexico): 505-537-2505
Fax: 505-537-2624

Southwestern Railroad operates two divisions. The Texas Division runs from a Santa Fe connection at Shattuck, Oklahoma, to Spearman, Texas, 84 miles. Rail is 85 to 90 pound. Traffic on the Texas Division consists of about 3,000 cars a year of grain and agricultural products

The New Mexico division is a cluster of lines running from a connection with the Santa Fe at Peruhill (near Black Mountain siding) to Tyrone, Fierro, and Santa Rita, a total of 54 miles. The New Mexico division carries 8,000 cars a year of copper ore, concentrates, and chemicals.

The Texas division was built from Shattuck to Spearman by the North Texas & Santa Fe Railroad between 1917 and 1920. It was extended to Morse in 1931. The New Mexico division includes Santa Fe lines opened in the 1880s as well as a former Southern Pacific branch. Shortline service started June 15, 1990.

The company is a subsidiary of Western Railroad Builders of Ogden, Utah.
Radio frequencies: 161.010 (Texas), 160.380 (New Mexico)
Location of enginehouse: Perryton, Texas, and Hurley, N. M.
Locomotives: 9

No.	Builder	Model	New	Builder No.
2072	EMD	GP7	12/53	18905 1974
2163	EMD	GP7	2/51	12205 1979
2164	EMD	GP7	12/50	13166 1979
2171	EMD	GP7	10/50	13164 1979
2182	EMD	GP7	2/51	12202 1980

No.	Builder	Model	New	Builder No.
4291	EMD	GP7	8/52	16884
4292	EMD	GP7	5/53	18238
5315	EMD	SD45	12/66	32547 1981
5316	EMD	SD45	12/66	32538 1981

ST RAIL SYSTEM

Iron Horse Park
North Billerica, MA 01862

Reporting marks: ST
Phone: 508-663-1030

ST Rail System (formerly Guilford Transportation Industries) owns and operates the Springfield Terminal, Boston & Maine, and Maine Central railroads, and the Portland Terminal Company. Operations extend from the Albany, New York, area to central Maine. Traffic includes pulp, paper products, coal, agricultural commodities, and general freight — about 163,000 cars a year.
Employees: 1,000

STATE UNIVERSITY RAILROAD CO.

Reporting marks: SUR

The State University Railroad is operated by Norfolk Southern for freight service from a Norfolk Southern connection at Glenn, North Carolina, to Carrboro (Chapel Hill), 10.2 miles. The company was chartered April 12, 1879, and the railroad opened about January 1, 1882. The Southern Railway and its successor, Norfolk Southern, have leased and operated the railroad since 1924.

STEELTON & HIGHSPIRE RAILROAD CO.

Front and Swatara Streets
Steelton, PA 17113

Reporting marks: SH
Phone: 717-986-2455

The Steelton & Highspire is a switching road with 26 miles of track between Steelton and Highspire, Pennsylvania. It connects with Conrail at Steelton. It handles about 10,000 cars annually. It started operations in 1917 and is owned by Bethlehem Steel.
Radio frequencies: 160.425, 161.190, 160.740
Locomotives: 6

No.	Builder	Model	New	Builder No.
70	EMD	SW9	4/50	11376
71	EMD	SW7	10/50	12918
72	EMD	SW9	12/52	17226
73	EMD	SW9	6/56	21831
77	EMD	SW1200	1957	23266
79	EMD	SW9	1957	22272

Freight cars: 30 gondolas

STERLING BELT LINE RAILROAD

12th and Commerce Streets
Wellsville, OH 43968

Reporting marks: SBLN
Phone: 216-532-1544
Fax: 216-532-4587

Sterling Belt Line is a switching line at Wellsville, Ohio, operating former Conrail trackage acquired in February 1984. Traffic is less than 50 cars a year. It is owned by Sterling China Co.

STEWARTSTOWN RAILROAD CO.

Pennsylvania Avenue
P. O. Box 155
Stewartstown, PA 17363

Reporting marks: STRT
Phone: 717-993-2936

The Stewartstown Railroad operates excursion service between Stewartstown and New Freedom, Pennsylvania, 7.4 miles. Rail is 70 to 115 pound.

The Stewartstown was incorporated September 22, 1884, and opened September 10, 1885. From 1923 until 1935, the company operated the New Park & Fawn Grove Railroad between Stewartstown and Fawn Grove. That line was abandoned in 1935, and regular passenger service ended by 1952.

The Stewartstown Railroad suspended service on June 22, 1972, because of hurricane damage to the connecting Penn Central line. Freight service resumed on January 14, 1985, when the company leased the former Penn Central line from New Freedom to York. That lease ended on September 30, 1992, and the company no longer has a freight connection.

Excursion trains started on July 4, 1985. The company is independent.

Location of enginehouse: Stewartstown, Pa.
Locomotives: 3

No.	Builder	Model	New	Builder No.
9	Plymouth	ML-8	5/43	4490
10	GE	44-ton	8/46	28503
11	EMD	SW8	9/57	654

Plymouth 35-tonner No. 9 used to pull freight on the Stewartstown Railroad, but the line now carries only passengers. Photo by Jim Shaw.

STOCKTON TERMINAL & EASTERN RAILROAD

1330 North Broadway Avenue
Stockton, CA 95205

Reporting marks: STE
Phone: 209-466-7001
Fax: 209-466-1862

The Stockton Terminal & Eastern operates freight service from connections with the Santa Fe, Union Pacific, Southern Pacific, Tidewater Southern, and Central California Traction Company at Stockton, California, to Linden, 13.79 miles. Rail is 60 to 90 pound. Traffic consists of more than 4,000 cars of produce and general commodities a year.

The Stockton Terminal & Eastern Railroad was incorporated October 29, 1908, to build a 27-mile line from Stockton to Jenny Lind. The road opened from Stockton to Bellota, 18.5 miles, in 1910. It was sold under foreclosure on January 18, 1919, to E. F. Davis, who operated it until December 31, 1926, when the present corporation took over. It was cut back to Linden in the 1950s.

The company has been owned by the Stockton Terminal Co. (the Beard family) since 1958.

Radio frequency: 160.455
Location of enginehouse: Stockton, Calif.
Locomotives: 5

No.	Builder	Model	New	Builder No.
505	Alco	S-1	4/42	69686
507	Alco	S-1	5/42	69691
557	Alco	S-2	12/43	71289
560	Alco	S-2	2/50	77018
564	Alco	S-4	5/51	78778

Freight cars: 270 insulated boxcars

Stockton Terminal & Eastern Alco S-4 No. 564 pulls a short train at Stockton, California. Photo by Jim Shaw.

STOURBRIDGE RAILROAD CO.

356 Priestly Avenue
Northumberland, PA 17857

Reporting marks: SBRR
Phone: 717-473-7949

The Stourbridge Railroad operates freight service from Honesdale, Pennsylvania, to a connection with Conrail at Lackawaxen, 24.6 miles. Rail is 100 to 119 pound. Traffic includes paper, lumber, utility poles, carbon black, chemicals, and petroleum wax — 1,500 cars a year. Occasional excursion trains are operated for the Wayne County Chamber of Commerce.

The line was built in part by the Jefferson Railroad, which completed its line to Honesdale July 13, 1868. That company was acquired by the Erie Railroad in 1870. When Conrail was formed, this line was purchased by the Pennsylvania Department of Transportation, which designated the Lackawaxen & Stourbridge to operate it, on June 30, 1989.

The company is controlled by Richard Robey, and is affiliated with the North Shore Railroad.
Radio frequency: 160.455
Location of enginehouse: Honesdale, Pa.
Locomotives: 2

No.	Builder	Model	New	Builder No.
54*	EMD	BL2	4/49	8165
430	EMD	SW7	5/50	11630

* 54 is owned by the Wayne County Chamber of Commerce

STRASBURG RAIL ROAD CO.

Route 796
P. O. Box 96
Strasburg, PA 17579

Reporting marks: SRC
Phone: 717-687-7522
Fax: 717-687-6194

The Strasburg Railroad operates irregular freight service and scheduled excursion trains from Strasburg, Pennsylvania, to a connection with Conrail at Leaman Place, 4.61 miles. Rail is 112 pound. Freight traffic is less than 100 cars a year and includes plastic pellets and lumber. Most of the railroad's income is derived from excursion trains.

The company is the oldest railroad company operating in the United States under its original charter. It was chartered June 9, 1832, and was run by local interests until 1957, when service ended due to severe storm damage. The railroad filed for abandonment, but it was purchased by a group of railroad buffs and restored to operation. Because freight potential was so limited, excursion trains started in 1959, and from the start passenger revenue exceeded freight income. The Strasburg is one of the most successful excursion lines in the United States. It is independent.
Radio frequency: 161.235
Location of enginehouse: Strasburg, Pa.
Locomotives: 6

No.	Builder	Model	New	Builder No.
1	Plymouth	20-ton	10/26	2452
31	BLW	0-6-0	7/08	32894
33	GE	44-ton	6/48	29964
89	CLC	2-6-0	3/10	922
90	BLW	2-10-0	6/24	57812
475	BLW	4-8-0	6/06	28343

The company also has a 1920 Mack-Brill railcar and a 1915 Sanders railcar. Other non-operational items are on display.

TACOMA EASTERN RAILWAY CO.

2501 East D Street, Room 202
P. O. Box 4
Tacoma, WA 98401

Reporting marks: TE
Phone: 206-383-2626

Tacoma Eastern provides freight service from a connection with Union Pacific at Tacoma Junction (Fife) to Morton, Washington, 66.3 miles; from Frederickson to Maytown and Chehalis, 55 miles; and from Park Junction to National, 3.5 miles. It connects with Union Pacific at Tacoma Junction and Centralia and with Burlington Northern at Centralia and Chehalis. Mainline rail runs from 85 to 132 pound.

Traffic is handled from Tacoma and Frederickson and includes aircraft parts, aggregate, and forest products. Currently two excursion railroads operate over portions of the line: the Mount Rainer Scenic Railroad (Mineral to Eatonville Junction) and the Chehalis-Centralia Railroad Association (at Chehalis).

The line was built in part by the Tacoma Eastern Railroad Co., chartered in 1899. By 1918 the company was under the control of the Chicago, Milwaukee & St. Paul. In 1980 the Milwaukee Road sold it to the Weyerhaueser Company, whose private carrier, the Chehalis Western Railroad, operated the line from 1981 to 1992.

In 1990 Weyerhaeuser donated a small portion of the property to the City of Tacoma and sold the remainder to the city for $3.1 million in 1995. Tacoma has contracted with Tacoma Eastern Railroad to operate the line. The operating company is independent.
Radio frequencies: 160.635, 160.245, 160.995
Location of enginehouse: Western Junction, Wash.
Locomotives: leased as required

TACOMA MUNICIPAL BELT LINE RAILWAY

2601 East West Road
P. O. Box 11007
Tacoma, WA 98411

Reporting marks: TMBL
Phone: 206-922-6631
Fax: 206-922-9088

The Tacoma Municipal Belt Line is a switching road at Tacoma, Washington, operating 25 miles of track. It connects with Burlington Northern and Union Pacific. Rail is 70 to 130 pound. Traffic runs 50,000 cars a year.

The railroad started as a passenger trolley line in 1889. Freight operations were added in 1918, and passenger service ended in 1948. The current operation under the Tacoma Department of Public Utilities started in 1955. The line has always been owned by the City of Tacoma.
Radio frequencies: 161.070, 161.145, 161.295
Locomotives: 6

No.	Builder	Model	New	Builder No.	Rebuilt
1201	EMD	SW9	4/52	11722	
1202	EMD	SW9	2/51	13138	
1203	EMD	SW1200	2/65	29786	
1204	EMD	SW1200	2/63	27859	
2000	EMD	GP20	9/52	17372	1969
2001	EMD	GP20	9/52	17386	1969

TENNESSEE RAILWAY CO.

Reporting marks: TENN

Tennessee Railway is operated for freight service from Oneida to Devonia, Tennessee, 44.65 miles. Branch lines total 12 miles.

The first Tennessee Railway was chartered April 19, 1904, to purchase and operate a private lumber railroad. The company was placed in receivership in 1913 and reorganized on June 29, 1918, as the Tennessee Railroad. The company was again placed in receivership on July 1, 1959. It was purchased by Southern Railway and reorganized under its present name in 1973. The line is presently operated as part of Norfolk Southern.

TENNESSEE SOUTHERN RAILROAD CO., INC.

100 Railroad Street
P. O. Box 32
Mount Pleasant, TN 38474

Reporting marks: TSRR
Phone: 615-379-5824
Fax: 615-379-5826

Tennessee Southern operates freight service from a connection with CSX at Godwin (Natco), Tennessee, to Florence, Alabama, 86 miles. A branch extends from Columbia to Pulaski, Tenn., 22.4 miles. Rail is 70 to 132 pound. Traffic includes chemicals, scrap, cement, lumber, paper products, fertilizer, and manufactured products — less than 9,000 cars a year.

The main line from Godwin to Florence was built by the Nashville & Florence Railroad, chartered in 1879. The company was acquired by the Louisville & Nashville in 1882, and merged with the Tennessee & Alabama Railroad to form the Nashville, Florence & Sheffield Railroad in 1887. By 1900 the property had been absorbed by L&N. The Pulaski branch was built by the Nashville & Decatur Railroad in the early 1860s. N&D was acquired by the L&N in the 1870s.

CSX sold and leased this line to the Tennessee Southern on February 20, 1989. The company is controlled by Shortlines, Inc. (Don Denbo, Dennis Prince, and others).

Radio frequency: 160.755
Location of enginehouse: Pulaski, Tenn.
Locomotives: 15

No.	Builder	Model	New	Builder No.
201	AT&SF	CF7	1974	
514	EMD	GP9	11/58	24956
523	EMD	GP30	6/62	27356
706	EMD	GP7	10/52	17030
1726	EMD	GP9	2/57	22771
1782	EMD	GP9	4/56	21088
2329	EMD	GP7	2/53	17766
2506	AT&SF	CF7	8/74	
2558	EMD	GP30	10/62	27429
2593	EMD	GP30	10/63	27563
5981	EMD	GP9	10/55	21029
6173	EMD	GP9	11/56	22556
6487	EMD	GP9	10/56	22231
6583	EMD	GP9	1/58	24365
9424	EMD	GP18	7/63	28287

Freight cars: 47 hopper cars

TENNKEN RAILROAD CO., INC.

1200 East Cherry Street
Dyersburg, TN 38024

Reporting marks: TKEN
Phone: 901-286-2530
Fax: 901-285-9042

Tennken operates freight service from a connection with the Illinois Central at Dyersburg, Tennessee, to Hickman, Kentucky, 52 miles. Rail is 70 to 115 pound.

Traffic includes about 3,500 cars a year of plastic resins, carbon black, grain, steel coils, and limestone.

This former Illinois Central branch line was acquired by the Hickman River City Development Corporation following its abandonment in 1983. Tennken service started on December 5, 1983.

The operating company is controlled by Henry and Bruce Hohorst and is affiliated with the West Tennessee Railroad.
Radio frequency: 160.365, 160.935
Location of enginehouse: Dyersburg, Tenn.
Locomotives: 3

No.	Builder	Model	New	Builder No.
9433	EMD	GP28	7/64	28941
9434	EMD	GP28	7/64	28942
9435	EMD	GP28	7/64	28943

Tennken 9434 switches cars of carbon black at Dyersburg, Tennessee. Photo by Edward Lewis.

TERMINAL RAILWAY, ALABAMA STATE DOCKS

251 North Water Street
P. O. Box 1588
Mobile, AL 36633

Reporting marks: TASD
Phone: 205-441-7300
Fax: 205-441-7306

Terminal Railway, Alabama State Docks, is a switching road operating 75 miles of track at the ports of Mobile and Chickasaw, Alabama. It interchanges with Burlington Northern, CSX, Illinois

Central, and Norfolk Southern. Rail is 100 pound. It handles nearly 70,000 cars a year. The line opened in 1928. It is owned by the state of Alabama.

Radio frequencies: 161.070, 161.100

Locomotives: 8

No.	Builder	Model	New	Builder No.
761	EMD	MP15DC	8/76	756150-1
771	EMD	MP15DC	10/77	776002-1
772	EMD	MP15DC	10/77	776002-2
801	EMD	MP15DC	10/80	796300-1
802	EMD	MP15DC	10/80	796300-2
803	EMD	MP15DC	10/80	806003-1
821	EMD	MP15DC	6/62	816033-1
822	EMD	MP15DC	6/62	816033-2

Freight cars: 700 boxcars

TEXAS & NEW MEXICO RAILROAD

1111 South Leech Street
Hobbs, NM 88241

Reporting marks: TNMR
Phone: 505-393-0258
Fax: 505-393-0689

The Texas & New Mexico operates freight service from a connection with Union Pacific at Monahans, Texas, to Lovington, New Mexico, 107 miles. Rail is 85 pound. Traffic includes LP gas, liquid asphalt, aggregate, cotton, and scrap metal — about 3,900 cars a year.

The line was built by the Texas-New Mexico Railway, which was incorporated on November 19, 1927, and completed to Lovington on July 20, 1930. By then it was under the control of the Texas & Pacific.

Union Pacific sold the property to the present operator, and shortline service started September 18, 1989. The company is a division of the Austin & Northwestern Railroad, which is a subsidiary of RailTex, Inc.

Radio frequency: 161.520
Location of enginehouse: Eunice, N. M.
Locomotives: 2

No.	Builder	Model	New	Builder No.	Rebuilt
202	EMD	GP9	6/55	20523	
2053	EMD	GP7	11/53	18899	1973

Freight cars: 106 gondolas

TEXAS & NORTHERN RAILWAY CO.

P. O. Box 1000
Lone Star, TX 75668-1000

Reporting marks: TN
Phone: 214-656-3761
Fax: 214-656-3295

The Texas & Northern operates freight service from a connection with Kansas City Southern at Daingerfield, Texas, to Lone Star, 7.6 miles. Rail is 119 pound. Traffic consists of steel and related commodities and totals nearly 20,000 cars a year.

The company was incorporated August 4, 1948, by Lone Star Steel Company to take over operation of its private railroad.

Radio frequency: 161.100
Location of enginehouse: Lone Star, Texas

Locomotives: 11 plus 2 slugs

No.	Builder	Model	New	Builder No.
1, 2	T&N	Slug	1950, 1951	
24	Alco	S-2	12/43	70064
53	Alco	S-1	6/53	80616
54	Alco	S-1	6/51	78809
55	Alco	S-1	5/51	78767
56	Alco	S-1	7/52	80059
992-995	AT&SF	CF7	1970-1974	
997	EMD	GP7	11/50	11051
998	EMD	MP15	12/75	756085-1
999	EMD	MP15	12/75	756085-2

Freight cars: 13 gondolas (plus 1,200 flatcars for on-line use)

TEXAS & OKLAHOMA RAILROAD CO.

1060 Wayne Avenue
Indiana, PA 15701

Reporting marks: TXOR
Phone: 412-349-3333
Fax: 412-349-6119

The Texas & Oklahoma owns a rail line from Maryneal, Texas, to a connection with Santa Fe at Sweetwater, 17 miles, and on to Chillicothe and the Oklahoma border, 189 miles. Service is currently being provided only south of Crowell, and most traffic is in the Sweetwater-Maryneal area. Rail ranges from 70 to 90 pound. Traffic is primarily cement and related commodities plus some grain and cotton — about 4,000 cars a year.

The line was built by the Kansas City, Mexico & Orient Railway and opened by 1912. The company was reorganized in 1914 and 1924. The Santa Fe purchased the KCM&O in 1928 and merged it in 1941. The Texas & Oklahoma purchased the Maryneal-Red River portion of the old KCM&O on June 1, 1991. It operated an extension of the line in Oklahoma until 1992, when that line was sold to Oklahoma Department of Transportation and operations taken over by Grainbelt. The ICC has authorized abandonment of the track from Chillicothe to the Oklahoma border.

Texas & Oklahoma Railroad is owned by Joe Kovalchick. It is operated under contract by American Railroads Corporation (Texas North Orient).

Location of enginehouse: Sweetwater, Texas
Locomotives: 4 (provided by American Railroads Corp.)

No.	Builder	Model	New	Builder No.	Rebuilt
200	EMD	GP9	4/55	20518	
203	EMD	GP9	7/56	22075	
204	EMD	GP9	7/56	22074	
9525	EMD	GP38	8/69	35169	

TEXAS CITY TERMINAL RAILWAY CO.

P. O. Box 591
Texas City, TX 77592

Reporting marks: TCT
Phone: 409-945-4461
Fax: 409-948-9160

Texas City Terminal is a terminal road with 30 miles of track at Texas City, Texas. It connects with Santa Fe, Burlington Northern, Southern Pacific, and Union Pacific. Rail is 115 pound. It

handles nearly 26,000 cars a year. The company was incorporated in January 1921 as successor to the Texas City Transportation Company (which started in 1893). It is owned jointly by Santa Fe and Union Pacific.
Radio frequencies: 160.620, 160.725

Locomotives: 3

No.	Builder	Model	New	Builder No.
35	EMD	MP15DC	11/82	827028-1
36	EMD	MP15DC	11/82	827028-2
37	EMD	MP15DC	11/82	827028-3

TEXAS, GONZALES & NORTHERN RAILWAY CO.

816 St. Peter Street
Gonzales, TX 78629

Reporting marks: TXGN
Phone: 210-672-9259
Fax: 210-672-9884

The Texas, Gonzales & Northern provides freight service from a connection with Southern Pacific Railroad at Harwood, Texas, to Gonzales, 12.2 miles. Rail ranges from 75 to 113 pound. Traffic includes cottonseed hulls, crude oil, grain, animal feed, and clay slurry — about 2,000 cars a year.

The line was built by the San Antonio & Aransas Pass Railway, which was acquired by Southern Pacific. Shortline service started on November 13, 1992. The company is a subsidiary of TNW Corporation and is affiliated with the Texas North Western Railroad.
Radio frequency: 160.455
Location of enginehouse: Gonzales, Texas
Locomotives: 1

No.	Builder	Model	New	Builder No.
92	EMD	SW1200	3/65	29794

TEXAS MEXICAN RAILWAY CO.

1200 Washington Street
P. O. Box 419
Laredo, TX 78042

Reporting marks: TM
Phone: 512-722-6411
Fax: 512-723-7406

Texas Mexican operates freight service from the international border at Laredo, Texas, to Corpus Christi and Flour Bluff, 172.9 miles. It connects with National Railways of Mexico, Southern Pacific, and Union Pacific.

Traffic includes farm products, waste, scrap, pulp, and paper products. It amounts to about 42,000 carloads a year, much of it moving between the United States and Mexico.

The line was built by the Corpus Christi, San Diego, & Rio Grande Narrow Gauge Railroad, which was chartered March 13, 1875. The present name was adopted June 25, 1881. The road was briefly under the control of National Railways of Mexico, but in 1902 NdeM's interest was transferred to a New York bank. It was sold in 1982 to Transportacion Maritima Mexicana and Mexrail, Inc. Recently 49 percent of the road's stock was acquired by Kansas City Southern.

Radio frequencies: 160.695, 161.220, 161.130
Location of enginehouse: Laredo, Texas
Locomotives: 20

No.	Builder	Model	New	Builder No.
850	EMD	GP7	6/50	10537
852	EMD	GP7	5/51	11937
853	EMD	GP9	10/58	24771
854	EMD	GP18	1/63	27856
855	EMD	GP18	1/63	27857
856	EMD	GP28	9/65	30711
857	EMD	GP38	11/66	32461
858	EMD	GP38	6/67	32673
859	EMD	GP38	8/71	37424
860	EMD	GP38	8/71	7373-1
861	EMD	GP38-2	9/74	74625-1
862	EMD	GP38-2	9/74	74625-2
863	EMD	GP38-2	6/78	77607-1
864	EMD	GP38-2	9/79	786233-1
865	EMD	GP38-2	7/80	796326-1
866	EMD	GP38-2	11/80	806017-1
867	EMD	GP38-2	5/85	847025
868	EMD	GP35	3/64	28525
869	EMD	GP60	5/90	896051-1
870	EMD	GP60	10/91	907148-1

Freight cars: 789

GP38-2 No. 867 and two sister units head up a serious road freight on the Texas Mexican Railway near Oilton, Texas. Photo by Jim Shaw.

TEXAS NORTH WESTERN RAILWAY CO.

HCR 1, Box 9
Sunray, TX 79086-9702

Reporting marks: TXNW
Phone: 806-935-7474

Texas North Western operates freight service from Etter Junction, Texas, where it connects with the Santa Fe, to Morse and Pringle, 43 miles. Rail is 80 to 110 pound. Traffic consists of about 2,000 cars a year of carbon black, oil, and grain.

This is a former Rock Island line built between 1926 and 1930. The present operator started service November 22, 1982, between Etter Junction and Liberal, Kansas, about 110 miles. By 1987, the line had been cut back to its present size.

The company is controlled by TNW Corp. of Dallas and is affiliated with the Texas, Gonzales & Northern Railway.
Radio frequency: 160.455
Location of enginehouse: Sheerin, Texas
Locomotives: 2

Texas North Western SW7s No. 89 and 88 await assignment at Sunray, Texas, in May 1994. Photo by Jim Shaw.

No.	Builder	Model	New	Builder No.
88	EMD	SW7	6/50	10437
89	EMD	SW7	10/50	9159

TEXAS NORTHEASTERN DIVISION, MID-MICHIGAN RAILROAD

425 North Walnut Street
P. O. Box 1296
Sherman, TX 75091-1296

Reporting marks: TNER
Phone: 214-893-9492
Fax: 214-868-2875

The Texas Northeastern operates freight service from Texarkana to Sherman, Texas, 155 miles, from Sherman to Denison, 10 miles, and from Bells to Trenton, 14 miles. It connects with Kansas City Southern, Southern Pacific, and Union Pacific at Texarkana, with Kiamichi Railroad at Paris, with Burlington Northern and Southern Pacific at Sherman, with Burlington Northern, Southern Pacific, and Union Pacific at Denison, and with the Dallas, Garland & Northern at Trenton. Traffic amounts to about 16,000 cars a year of grain, food products, and paper products.

The route is a former Texas & Pacific line. Shortline service started October 22, 1990. The company is owned by RailTex, Inc.
Radio frequency: 160.815
Location of enginehouse: Sherman, Texas
Locomotives: 6

No.	Builder	Model	New	Builder No.	Rebuilt
25	EMD	SW1500	10/68	34234	
2153	EMD	GP7	2/51	12210	1979
2166	EMD	GP7	10/52	17462	1979
2219	EMD	GP7	6/53	18554	1980
5060	EMD	GP38	11/67	33691	
5076	EMD	GP38	11/67	33701	

TEXAS, OKLAHOMA & EASTERN RAILROAD CO.

412 East Lockesburg Avenue
De Queen, AR 71832

Reporting marks: TOE
Phone: 501-642-1309
Fax: 501-642-1368

Radio frequencies: 160.230 (road), 160.605, 160.785, 161.445
Location of enginehouse: De Queen, Ark.
Locomotives: 10

No.	Builder	Model	New	Builder No.
D-12	EMD	GP40	3/71	36879
D-13	EMD	GP40	9/71	38243
D-14	EMD	GP40	9/71	38570
D-15	EMD	GP40-2	12/72	72654-1
D-16	EMD	GP40-2	11/73	73619-1
D-20	EMD	GP40-2	9/74	74604-1
D-22	EMD	GP35	4/65	30136
D-23	EMD	GP40	9/68	34339
D-24	EMD	GP40	8/68	34300
D-25	EMD	GP40	10/67	33505

Freight cars: 2,280

The Texas, Oklahoma & Eastern extends from a connection with the De Queen & Eastern at West Line, Arkansas, to a connection with the Kamichi Railroad at Valliant, Oklahoma, 39.82 miles. Rail is 90, 100, and 115 pound. Traffic is primarily forest products and totals more than 45,000 cars a year.

The company was incorporated October 21, 1910, and the railroad opened from Valliant to Broken Bow, 24 miles, on July 15, 1911, and from Broken Bow to West Line in 1921. Passenger service ended in 1948.

The line is operated in conjunction with the De Queen & Eastern. Both railroads are owned by Weyerhaeuser Company.

TEXAS SOUTH-EASTERN RAILROAD CO.

P. O. Box 366
Diboll, TX 75941

Reporting marks: TSE
Phone: 409-829-5613
Fax: 409-829-4814

Radio frequency: 160.920
Location of enginehouse: Diboll, Texas
Locomotives: 3

No.	Builder	Model	New	Builder No.
22	GE	70-ton	5/56	32569
301	BLW	DS-4-4-750	7/50	74813
1007	BLW	VO-1000	8/44	71934

Freight cars: 117 boxcars, 19 flatcars

The Texas South-Eastern provides switching service from Diboll, Texas, to Lufkin, 10.3 miles, and from Blix to Vair, 7.2 miles. It connects with the Southern Pacific at Diboll and Lufkin, and with the Angelina & Neches River at Lufkin. Rail is 60 to 75 pound. Traffic is lumber and forest products — 2,200 cars a year.

The company was incorporated October 9, 1900, and has been controlled by Temple-Inland, Inc., since 1992.

TEXAS TRANSPORTATION CO.

312 Pearl Parkway
P. O. Box 1661
San Antonio, TX 78296

Reporting marks: TXTC
Phone: 210-226-0231
Fax: 210-226-0304

Texas Transportation Company is an electrically operated 1.1-mile switching line at San Antonio, Texas. It connects with Southern Pacific.

Traffic consists of less than 1,000 cars of food products a year. The railroad was built in 1889 and became a common carrier in October 1932. It is owned by Pearl Brewing Company.

Locomotives: 2

No.	Builder	Model	New	Builder No.
1	BLW/Westinghouse	50-ton electric	12/17	47450
2	Texas Electric	45-ton electric	1955	

THERMAL BELT RAILWAY

2114 Williams Wood Drive
Morganton, NC 28655

Reporting marks: TBRY
Phone: 704-433-7409

Thermal Belt provides freight service from a CSX connection at Bostic, North Carolina, to Gilkey and Alexander Mills, 16 miles total. Rail is 85 pound. Traffic includes plastic, grain, and forest products — under 500 cars a year.

The road includes former Southern Railway and CSX lines. The Southern line between Alexander Mills and Gilkey was opened in 1887 by the Charleston, Cincinnati & Chicago Railroad. Southern ceased operating the line in 1989. The CSX line from Bostic to Forest City was built by the Central Carolina Railroad in 1886. Shortline service started on April 2, 1990.

The property is owned by the Rutherford Railroad Development Corporation, and the operating company is owned by Southeast Shortlines, Inc. (Don McGrady).

Radio frequency: 161.175

Locomotives: 1

No.	Builder	Model	New	Builder No.	Rebuilt
1	EMC	SW	7/38	718	1978

Thermal Belt SW1 No. 1 pulls a string of bulk lumber and grain cars past an industry at Forest City, North Carolina. Photo by Jim Shaw.

TOLEDO, PEORIA & WESTERN RAILWAY CORP.

1990 East Washington Street
East Peoria, IL 61611

Reporting marks: TPW
Phone: 309-698-2600
Fax: 309-698-2679

The Toledo, Peoria & Western operates freight service from a connection with the Santa Fe at Fort Madison, Iowa, by trackage rights on Santa Fe 15.5 miles to Lomax, Illinois, then on its own rails to Kokomo, Indiana, 318.7 miles. A 4.9-mile branch extends from Crandall to Morton, Illinois. Total mileage operated is 350. TP&W connects with Bloomer Shippers Connecting Railroad, Burlington Northern, Central Railroad of Indianapolis, Chicago & Illinois Midland, Chicago & North Western, Conrail, CSX, Illinois Central, Kankakee, Beaverville & Southern, Norfolk Southern, Peoria & Pekin Union, Soo Line (CP Rail System), Southern Pacific, and Union Pacific. Rail ranges from 100 to 136 pound. The TP&W moves over 55,000 cars of agricultural commodities, auto parts, coal, steel, chemicals, and double-stack containers annually.

The line opened in 1860; the history of the companies operating it is full of foreclosures, reorganizations, leases, and sales. In 1960 as the Toledo, Peoria & Western Railroad it came under the joint ownership of the Santa Fe and the Pennsylvania. In 1976 it extended its line from Effner, Ind., east to Logansport by acquiring the connecting ex-PRR route. In 1979 the Santa Fe acquired full ownership of the TP&W and merged it on December 31, 1983.

The current owners acquired the line from Santa Fe and reincorporated the TP&W on February 3, 1989. The company is independent (the New York, Susquehanna & Western acquired a 40 percent interest in 1995).

Radio frequencies: 161.310, 161.400
Location of enginehouse: East Peoria, Ill.
Locomotives: 21

No.	Builder	Model	New	Builder No.	Rebuilt
1500	EMD	F-7	6/52	16592	
1601	EMD	GP7	1951	14313	
1602	EMD	GP7	5/53	18244	
2002-2019	EMD	GP20			1977-1984

TOMAHAWK RAILWAY, LP.

301 South Marinette Street
P. O. Box 130
Tomahawk, WI 54487

Reporting marks: TR
Phone: 715-453-2303
Fax: 715-453-3518

Tomahawk Railway operates freight service from Tomahawk, Wisconsin, to Wisconsin Dam, 6 miles, and from Tomahawk to Bradley, 5.4 miles. It connects with Wisconsin Central at Bradley and Tomahawk. Rail is 115 pound. Traffic is paper, pulpwood, coal, and scrap paper — about 10,000 cars a year.

The Marinette, Tomahawk & Western Railway was incorporated October 4, 1894, and opened November 27, 1895. It purchased the Wisconsin & Chippewa Railway in June 1898 and was reorganized as the Marinette, Tomahawk & Western Railroad on November 16, 1912. Passenger service ended in 1918.

The present company, formed in 1992, is a partnership controlled by Rail Management, the general partner.

Radio frequencies: 160.290, 160.740
Location of enginehouse: Tomahawk, Wis.
Locomotives: 3

No.	Builder	Model	New	Builder No.
80	EMD	SW8	11/51	15516
83	EMD	SW1500	5/70	36486
87	EMD	SW1500	1968	1415-1

TONAWANDA ISLAND RAILROAD, INC.

3909 Witmer Road
Niagara Falls, NY 14305-1239

Reporting marks: TIRL
Phone: 716-282-7651

The Tonawanda Island Railroad operates a 3.5-mile switching line from North Tonawanda to Tonawanda Island, New York. It connects with Conrail and CP Rail System (Delaware & Hudson). Rail is 105 pound. Traffic is lumber and manufactured products — under 150 cars a year.

The line is former Conrail trackage acquired in 1983. Tonawanda Island Railroad began operation February 14, 1983. It was acquired by the L&H Railroad Co. (Cory Sanoin) in 1988.
Radio frequency: 27.125
Location of enginehouse: Tonawanda, N. Y.
Locomotives: 1 (plus 1 Whiting Trackmobile)

No.	Builder	Model	New	Builder No.	Rebuilt
1	70-ton	CLC	6/50	2635	

TOPPENISH, SIMCOE & WESTERN RAILROAD

10 Asoton Avenue
P. O. Box 889
Toppenish, WA 98948

Reporting marks: TSWR
Phone: 509-865-1911

The Toppenish, Simcoe & Western operates limited freight and excursion service from a connection with Washington Central at Wesley Junction (near Toppenish) to White Swan, Washington, 20.56 miles. Freight traffic amounts to less than 500 cars a year of forest products, fertilizer, and grain. The line was built about 1912 by the Toppenish, Simcoe & Western Railroad, which was absorbed by the North Yakima & Valley (part of Northern Pacific) in 1914. Burlington Northern sold the line to the Washington Central in October 1986. Washington Central discontinued service in 1993, and the Toppenish, Simcoe & Western started service July 16, 1993. The railroad is owned by the Yakima Valley Rail & Steam Museum, a nonprofit corporation.
Location of enginehouse: Toppenish, Wash.
Locomotives: 1

No.	Builder	Model	New	Builder No.
2070	Alco	MRS-1	9/53	80386

TOWANDA-MONROETON SHIPPERS LIFELINE, INC.

RD 1, Box 18
Monroeton, PA 18832

Reporting marks: TMSL
Phone: 717-265-6469

The Towanda-Monroeton Shippers Lifeline operates freight service as needed between Monroeton, Pennsylvania, and a connection with Conrail at Towanda, 6.3 miles. Rail is 90 pound. Traffic includes feed, agricultural products, and wood and is less than 500 cars a year.

The company was formed in November 1975 to help promote restoration of service on the Lehigh Valley's State Line & Sullivan branch, which had been washed out in June 1972. When no operator could be found, TMSL agreed to provide service. The ICC approved the operation February 9, 1977, and service started between South Towanda and Monroeton. In 1987 the company took over the rest of the branch, 1.6 miles, from South Towanda to Towanda.

Most of the property is owned by Pennsylvania Department of Transportation, and the operating company is owned by J. T. Zadrusky.

Location of enginehouse: Monroeton, Pa.

Locomotives: 1

No.	Builder	Model	New	Builder No.
26	EMC	SW1	2/39	909

Towanda Monroeton Shippers Lifeline SW1 No. 26 is painted in a scheme reminiscent of the old Lehigh Valley. Photo by Jim Shaw.

TRANSKENTUCKY TRANSPORTATION RAILROAD INC.

205 Winchester Street
Paris, KY 40361

Reporting marks: TTIS
Phone: 606-987-1589
Fax: 606-987-1625

Transkentucky Transportation operates freight service between CSX connections at Paris and Maysville, Kentucky, 49.6 miles. Rail is 105 to 132 pound. Traffic is overhead coal moving from eastern Kentucky coal fields on CSX to Maysville for transloading to barge at the Transcontinental Terminal facility. The road carries 35,000 cars annually.

The line was the Maysville branch of the Kentucky Central Railroad, built around 1875. It was acquired by the Louisville & Nashville in 1891. Transkentucky Transportation purchased the line from the L&N in 1979. The company is controlled by American Commercial Marine Service (CSX Transportation).

Radio frequencies: 160.665, 161.265, 161.445

Location of enginehouse: Paris, Ky.

Locomotives: 20

No.	Builder	Model	New	Builder No.
242-244	GE	U-28-B	3/66	35908-35910
246	GE	U-28-B	4/66	35912
247	GE	U-28-B	2/66	35865
251	GE	U-28-B	2/66	35859
253	GE	U-28-B	2/66	35868
254	GE	U-28-B	10/66	36078
255-257	GE	U-28-B	10/66	36101-36103
258	GE	U-28-B	12/66	36116-7
259	GE	U-28-B	12/66	36116-8
260	GE	U-28-B	12/66	36116-9
261	GE	U-28-B	8/66	36013
5758	GE	U-36-B	7/71	37804
5763	GE	U-36-B	8/71	37809
5791	GE	U-36-B	2/72	38284
5793	GE	U-36-B	2/72	38286
5797	GE	U-36-B	2/72	38290

TRINIDAD RAILWAY, INC.

16 East Granite
Butte, MT 59701

Reporting marks: TRI
Phone: 406-782-4233

On December 31, 1992, Trinidad Railway acquired Colorado & Wyoming's line from Jansen, Colorado, where it connects with the Santa Fe and Burlington Northern to New Elk Mine (Stonewall), 30 miles. Traffic is coal. Santa Fe has been given trackage rights to operate this property.

TRONA RAILWAY CO.

13068 Main Street
Trona, CA 93562

Reporting marks: TRC
Phone: 619-372-2312
Fax: 619-372-2484

The Trona Railway operates freight service from Trona, California, to a connection with the Southern Pacific at Searle, 30.55 miles. Rail is 100 to 115 pound. Traffic includes sulfuric acid, soda ash, potash, salt cake, borax, coal, minerals, and military equipment — 18,000 cars a year.

The company was incorporated March 12, 1913, and the railroad opened on September 6, 1914. Passenger service ended in 1937. North American Chemical acquired this line from Kerr-McGee Chemical Corporation in 1990.

Radio frequencies: 161.085, 161.190
Location of enginehouse: Trona, Calif.
Locomotives: 6

No.	Builder	Model	New	Builder No.
3001	EMD	SD45-2	5/74	74603-6
3002	EMD	SD45-2	5/74	74603-7
3003	EMD	SD45-2	5/74	74603-8
3004	EMD	SD45-2	5/74	74603-9
3005	EMD	SD45-2	5/74	74603-10
3006	EMD	SD45-2	8/74	74601-10

Trona turned its old Baldwins out to pasture and leased rebuilt SD45-2s like No. 3002 shown at Searle, California, in October 1993. Photo by Jim Shaw.

TULARE VALLEY RAILROAD CO.

P. O. Box 26421
Salt Lake City, UT 84126

Reporting marks: TVRR
Phone: 801-972-8330

On December 21, 1992, Tulare Valley Railroad acquired several Santa Fe branch lines totaling 140 miles in California's San Joaquin Valley:
• Ducor to Cutler (Porterville branch), 52 miles
• Corcoran to Calwa, 66 miles
• Wyeth to Orange Cove and Minkler, 9.4 miles
• Hammond to Cameo, 6 miles

The company contracted with San Joaquin Valley Railroad to operate these lines, and traffic information is shown for that railroad. Since starting service, Tulare Valley Railroad has abandoned the segments between Corcoran and Tulare, 14.7 miles, and between Visalia and Cutler, 13.3 miles. It is controlled by Morris Kulmer, Kern Schumucher, and Michael Van Wagenen.

TULSA-SAPULPA UNION RAILWAY CO.

701 East Dewey
Sapulpa, OK 74066

Reporting marks: TSU
Phone: 918 224-1515
Fax: 918-224-3049

The Tulsa-Sapulpa Union Railway operates freight service from Tulsa to Sapulpa, Oklahoma, 10 miles. It connects with Santa Fe, Sand Springs, and Union Pacific at Tulsa, and with Burlington Northern at Sapulpa. Rail ranges from 70 to 110 pound. Traffic includes sand, soda ash, lime, pulpboard, plastic resin, steel, and boilers — about 4,000 cars a year.

The Sapulpa & Interurban Railway built a line from Sapulpa to Mounds in 1908. The company went bankrupt in 1912 and merged with the Oklahoma Union Railway, which had built a line from Tulsa to Sapulpa. The Mounds-Sapulpa line was abandoned in 1928, and the company went bankrupt the following year. Passenger service was ended in 1933, and the company reorganized as the Sapulpa Union Railroad in 1934. The present name was adopted in 1943. The railroad converted from electric to diesel operation April 11, 1960. The company is independent.

Radio frequency: 161.070
Location of enginehouse: Sapulpa, Okla.
Locomotives: 4

No.	Builder	Model	New	Builder No.
101	EMD	SW1	5/40	1075
102	EMD	SW1	4/47	4730
104	EMD	SW9	2/52	15685
107	EMD	SW7	8/50	11475

TURTLE CREEK INDUSTRIAL RAILROAD, INC.

2658 Jefferson Street
P. O. Box 518
Export, PA 15632

Reporting marks: TCKR
Phone: 412-327-0280
Fax: 412-327-0113

The Turtle Creek Industrial Railroad operates freight service from a connection with Conrail at Trafford, Pennsylvania, to Export, 10.7 miles. Rail is 130 pound. Traffic includes lumber, steel products, and machinery and totals nearly 500 cars a year.

The line is former Conrail track, once the Pennsylvania Railroad's Export branch. It was built in 1890 by the Turtle Creek Valley Railroad, which was acquired by the Pennsylvania before 1900.

Turtle Creek Industrial Railroad acquired it in June 1982 following Conrail's decision to abandon it. The company is controlled by Dura-Bond Coating Co.
Radio frequencies: 463.800, 468.700
Location of enginehouse: Export, Pa.
Locomotives: 3

No.	Builder	Model	New	Builder No.
unnumbered	GE	50-ton	6/48	29871
462	EMD	SW1	8/49	7509
550	EMD	NW2	10/49	8534

TUSCOLA & SAGINAW BAY RAILWAY CO., INC.

308 West Main Street, Suite 303
P. O. Box 550
Owosso, MI 48867-0550

Reporting marks: TSBY
Phone: 517-725-6644
Fax: 517-723-8226

The Tuscola & Saginaw Bay operates 405 miles of line in Michigan:
• Ann Arbor to Thompsonville, Michigan, 222.8 miles, on the former Ann Arbor main line
• Ashley to Middleton, 12 miles, ex-Grand Trunk Western
• Owosso to St. Charles, 20 miles, ex-New York Central
• Cadillac to Petoskey, 91.2 miles, ex-Pennsylvania Railroad
• Walton Junction through Traverse City to Grawn and Williamsburg, ex-Pennsylvania to Traverse City and ex-Chesapeake & Ohio (Pere Marquette) beyond

Principal interchanges are with Ann Arbor at Ann Arbor, CSX at Annpere, Mid-Michigan at Alma, and Grand Trunk Western and Central Michigan at Durand. Traffic consists of about 10,000 cars a year of sand, grain, food products, chemicals,

EMD NW2 No. 1977 switches cars at Richville Junction on the Tuscola & Saginaw Bay in July, 1990. This line is now operated by the Huron & Eastern, and No. 177 has moved to Owosso. Photo by Jim Shaw.

petroleum products, auto parts, agricultural products, and general commodities.

The company was incorporated in 1977 and was designated by Michigan authorities to operate 44 miles of former New York Central branches near Vassar. Service started October 1, 1977. In October 1982 Michigan designated the company operator of the former Ann Arbor line from Ann Arbor to Alma, 97 miles, and in 1983 added the rest of the Ann Arbor in Michigan (Alma to Frankfort), which had been operated by Michigan Interstate, plus the north end of the Michigan Northern itself (Cadillac to Petoskey, plus branches to Traverse City and Charlevoix). In January 1991 the operation of the original cluster of lines at Vassar was turned over to the Huron & Eastern Railroad. The railroad is controlled by J. E. Shepherd and L. M. McCloud.

Radio frequencies: 160.575, 161.100
Location of enginehouses: Owosso and Cadillac, Mich.
Locomotives: 11

No.	Builder	Model	New	Builder No.
385	EMD	GP35	3/64	28991
387-394	EMD	GP35	3/64	28993-29000
1977	EMD	NW2	7/42	1695
2126	GE	25-ton	1/53	31777

Freight cars: 90 covered hoppers

TWIN CITIES & WESTERN RAILROAD CO.

2925 12th Street
East Glencoe, MN 55336

Reporting marks: TCW
Phone: 612-864-7200
Fax: 612-864-7220

Twin Cities & Western provides freight service from a connection with Burlington Northern at Appleton, Minnesota, to Hopkins, 145 miles. In addition the company operates by trackage rights over CP Rail System (Soo Line) from Hopkins to St. Paul, connecting there with Burlington Northern, Chicago & North Western, CP Rail System, Minnesota Commercial, and Wisconsin Central; and from Appleton to Milbank, South Dakota, connecting with the Sisseton Milbank Railroad. Twin Cities & Western connects with Minnesota Central at Norwood. It operates a total of 218 miles. Traffic includes grain, sugar, and other food products, coal, fertilizer, agricultural implements, and crushed rock — about 17,000 cars a year.

The Appleton-Hopkins line was part of the Milwaukee Road main line west of Minneapolis. It was built by the Hastings & Dakota Railway between 1872 and 1879. Twin Cities & Western bought the track from Soo Line on July 27, 1991. The company is controlled by Charles Clay, Douglas Head, and Kent Shoemaker, and is affiliated with the Red River Valley & Western Railroad.

Radio frequencies: 160.860, 160.875, 161.460
Location of enginehouse: Glencoe, Minn.
Locomotives: 8

No.	Builder	Model	New	Builder No.	Rebuilt
401	EMD	GP10	10/50	11046	1975
402	EMD	GP10	4/51	13336	1974
403	EMD	GP10	1/56	20784	1972
404	EMD	GP10	9/57	23208	1971
405	EMD	GP10	12/54	19769	1973
406	EMD	GP10	1/56	20782	1973
407	EMD	GP10	3/54	19239	1977
408	EMD	GP10	12/57	23817	1975

Freight cars: 242 covered hoppers

TWIN STATE RAILROAD CO. — *See Lamoille Valley Railroad*

TYBURN RAILROAD CO.

P. O. Box 7060
Penndel, PA 19047-7060

Reporting marks: TYBR
Phone: 215-757-3793
Fax: 215-757-7006

Tyburn Railroad provides switching service on a half mile of track from a connection with Conrail at Fair to Fairless (Tyburn Yard), near Morrisville, Pennsylvania. Rail is 100 pound. About 1,000 cars a year of chemicals, stone, soda ash, and salt make up the road's traffic.

The company also operates a half mile of track at Red Rose yard in Lancaster, Pa., connecting with Conrail.

Tyburn Railroad is controlled by Adelaide, Edward, and Gerard McHugh and William McNulty.

Radio frequencies: 161.385, 160.335
Locomotives: 2

No.	Builder	Model	New	Builder No.
390	GE	45-ton	2/42	15149
400	GE	44-ton	10/47	29070

TYSON RAILROAD, INC.

2210 Oaklawn Drive
Springdale, AR 72764

Reporting marks: TSNR
Phone: 501-756-4000

The Tyson Railroad acquired 1.6 miles of CSX track at Ivalee, Alabama, in 1989. The company is controlled by its principal shipper, Tyson Foods, producer and packer of chicken and poul-try products. Traffic is poultry feed totaling about 3,000 cars a year. Tyson is selling the line back to CSX.

Locomotives: 1

No.	Builder	Model	New	Builder No.
293	EMD	SW900	5/60	25895

UNION COUNTY INDUSTRIAL RAILROAD CO.

356 Priestly Avenue
Northumberland, PA 17857

Reporting marks: UCIR
Phone: 717-473-7949

Union County Industrial Railroad operates freight service from a connection with Conrail at Milton, Pennsylvania, to New Colum-bia, 3.9 miles. In addition it provides freight service over the West Shore Railroad from West Milton through Lewisburg to Mifflinburg and Winfield, 18 miles. Rail is 85 to 140 pound. Traffic includes grain, grain products, fertilizer, woodpulp, steel, food products, and scrap paper — about 1,000 cars a year. The Lewisburg &

Buffalo Creek Railroad operates excursion trains between Lewisburg and Winfield.

Union County acquired the Milton-West Milton-New Columbia line, a former Reading branch, from Conrail and began service April 4, 1995. It also took over the freight lines formerly operated by West Shore Railway Services: West Milton through Lewisburg to Winfield (ex-Reading) and Lewisburg to Mifflinburg (ex-Pennsylvania Railroad).

Conrail ended service on the Mifflinburg line in late 1981. West Shore assumed operations in December 1983 and acquired operating rights on the Winfield line on May 5, 1988. West Shore, which owns the track, is controlled by Julia Sanders. Union County Railroad is owned by Richard Robby, and is affiliated with the North Shore Railroad.

Radio frequencies: 154.600, 154.570
Location of enginehouse: Winfield, Pa.
Locomotives: 3

No.	Builder	Model	New	Builder No.
1500	EMD	SW8	2/53	16193
2233	EMD	GP30	4/63	28141
9425	EMD	SW1	11/50	11219

UNION RAILROAD CO.

135 Jamison Lane
P. O. Box 68
Monroeville, PA 15146

Reporting marks: URR
Phone: 412-829-3461
Fax: 412-829-6607

Union Railroad is a switching line operating 170.3 miles of track (27.9 route miles) in and around North Bessemer, Duquesne, and McKeesport, Pennsylvania (southeast of Pittsburgh). It connects with Bessemer & Lake Erie, Conrail, CSX, Wheeling & Lake Erie, and McKeesport Connecting. It handles about 190,000 cars a year.

The company was incorporated July 2, 1894, and began operations in 1896. It acquired the Monongahela Southern in 1937. Union Railroad was owned by U. S. Steel until 1988, when it was purchased by Transtar, Inc.

Radio frequencies: 160.260, 160.500, 160.620, 160.350
Locomotives: 42
Freight cars: 242 gondolas

MP15 No. 17 and four sister engines pull a Union Railroad coal train through Hall, Pennsylvania. Photo by Jim Shaw.

UPPER MERION & PLYMOUTH RAILROAD CO.

P. O. Box 404
Conshohocken, PA 19428

Reporting marks: UMP
Phone: 610-828-7536
Fax: 610-828-6970

The Upper Merion & Plymouth is a switching road operating 15 miles of track (5 route miles) between Conshohocken and Swedeland, Pennsylvania. It connects with Conrail at Swedeland. Rail is 100 and 115 pound. It carries about 6,800 cars a year.

The company was incorporated July 9, 1907, and was ac-quired in 1990 by Lukens Steel, which also owns the Brandywine Valley Railroad.

Radio frequency: 160.485
Locomotives: 3

No.	Builder	Model	New	Builder No.
9007	GMD	SW9	1/51	A124
9008	EMD	NW2	1/47	4588
9009	EMD	SW7	6/50	10434

Freight cars: 2,564

UTAH CENTRAL RAILWAY CO.

Union Station, Room 205
Ogden, UT 84401

Reporting marks: UCRY
Phone: 801-627-3823

Utah Central is a switching railroad with a mile of track between Ogden and Stratford, Utah. It serves the Ogden Commercial Industrial Park and nearby industries. It connects with Southern Pacific at Transfer Yard and with Union Pacific at Relico. It began common carrier service on October 17, 1995; it was previously a contract carrier.

Locomotives: 3

No.	Builder	Model	New	Builder No.
202	EMD	SW8	12/51	15738
1237	GE	44-ton	2/53	31875
1244	GE`	44-ton	2/53	31882

UTAH RAILWAY CO.

340 Hardscrabble Road
Helper, UT 84526

Reporting marks: UTAH
Phone: 801-472-3407
Fax: 801-265-3744

Utah Railway operates freight service from Hiawatha, Utah, to Utah Railway Junction, 25.3 miles, then by trackage rights on Denver & Rio Grande Western (Southern Pacific) to Provo, 72.3 miles, where it connects with Southern Pacific and Union Pacific. Some eastbound cars are also interchanged at Utah Railway Junction. Rail is 90 to 115 pound. Traffic is coal, mostly moving in 84-car unit trains, totaling nearly 50,000 cars a year.

The company was incorporated January 24, 1912, and the railroad opened in October 1914. The Denver & Rio Grande operated the line until 1917, when independent service started. The company is owned by Arava Natural Resources, Inc., a subsidiary of Mueller Industries.

Radio frequencies: 160.560, 161.145
Location of enginehouse: Martin, Utah

Locomotives: 12

No.	Builder	Model	New	Builder No.
9001	EMD	SD40	7/70	36752
9002	EMD	SD40	7/70	36754
9003	EMD	SD40	6/70	36701
9004	EMD	SD40	6/70	36755
9005	EMD	SD40	7/70	36748
9006	EMD	SD40	7/70	36749
9007	EMD	SD40	7/70	36751
9008	EMD	SD40	6/70	36704
9009	EMD	SD40	2/69	34745
9010	EMD	SD40	2/69	34759
9011	EMD	SD40	7/69	34969
9012	EMD	SD45	5/72	7391-1

Utah SD40 No. 9005 and three other SD40s pull a unit coal train through Martin, Utah, in September 1992. Photo by Jim Shaw.

VALDOSTA RAILWAY, LP.

P. O. Box 789
Lake Park, GA 31636

Reporting marks: VR
Phone: 912-559-7984
Fax: 912-559-7015

Valdosta Railway operates freight service from connections with CSX and Norfolk Southern at Valdosta, Georgia, to Clyattville, 10 miles. Rail is 115 pound. Traffic includes wood chips, forest products, paper products, and chemicals — about 8,500 cars a year.

The Valdosta Southern Railroad Co. was incorporated August 30, 1951, to purchase a branch being abandoned by the Georgia & Florida Railroad. The portion of the line from Clyattville to Madison, Florida, was abandoned March 31, 1972. The entire property was sold in 1992 to the Valdosta Railway, which is a limited partnership controlled by Rail Management, the general partner.

Radio frequency: 160.680
Location of enginehouse: Clyattville, Ga.
Locomotives: 2

No.	Builder	Model	New	Builder No.
184	EMD	GP7	8/50	9081
1284	EMD	GP10	1/55	20151

VANDALIA RAILROAD CO.

1318 South Johanson Road
Peoria, IL 61607

Reporting marks: VRRC
Phone: 309-697-1400

The Vandalia Railroad is a switching line with 2.54 miles of former Illinois Central Gulf track at Vandalia, Illinois. It connects with Conrail. Rail is 90 pound. Traffic is under 500 cars a year of plastic, animal feed, fertilizer, limestone, and steel pipe.

The ICG abandoned this line, part of Illinois Central's original main line, in 1981. The Vandalia Railroad restored service on December 21, 1983. The company was purchased by Pioneer RailCorp in October 1994.

Radio frequency: 160.545
Locomotives: 2

No.	Builder	Model	New	Builder No.
56	Alco	T-6	3/58	82860
104	EMD	SW9	3/51	9786

VENTURA COUNTY RAILWAY CO.

250 East Fifth Street
P. O. Box 432
Oxnard, CA 93032

Reporting marks: VCY
Phone: 805-486-4428
Fax: 805-483-2541

Ventura County Railway operates freight service from a connection with the Southern Pacific at Oxnard, California, to South Oxnard, Wilds, and Port Hueneme, 9 miles. Rail is 90 pound.

Traffic includes produce, imported automobiles, and general commodities — 5,000 cars a year. The company was incorporated May 11, 1911, as successor to the Bakersfield & Ventura Railroad. Passenger service ended in 1926. The company is independent.

Radio frequency: 161.355

Location of enginehouse: Oxnard, Calif.
Locomotives: 3

No.	Builder	Model	New	Builder No.	Rebuilt
9	Alco	S-6	12/55	81428	
100	EMD	GP7	6/52	16379	
unknown	EMD	SW14			1995

VERMONT RAILWAY, INC.

One Railway Lane
Burlington, VT 05401

Reporting marks: VTR
Phone: 802-658-2550
Fax: 802-658-2553

The Vermont Railway operates freight and TOFC service from Burlington, Vermont, south through Rutland to Hoosick Junction, New York, 131.6 miles. It connects with New England Central at Burlington, Green Mountain and Clarendon & Pittsford at Rutland, and ST Rail System (Boston & Maine) at Hoosick Junction. Rail is 90 to 105 pound. Service between North Bennington, Vt., and Hoosick Junction was suspended early in 1993. Traffic includes ground limestone, petroleum products, feed, salt, lumber, grain, coal, cement, and other commodities; the total is about 13,500 cars a year. An independent operator runs excursion trains out of Burlington on Vermont Railway tracks.

The line was built in two segments. The track between Rutland and Burlington was opened by the Rutland & Burlington Railroad in 1849. The Rutland-Bennington line was built by the Western Vermont Railroad, chartered in 1845 and completed in 1853. It was later reorganized as the Bennington & Rutland and was acquired by the Rutland Railroad (successor to the Rutland & Burlington) in 1900.

The Rutland ceased operating in October 1961 because of a bitter strike, and it abandoned its line. The Vermont Railway was incorporated October 25, 1963, to operate a portion of the Rutland that had been purchased by the state of Vermont. Operation began on January 6, 1964.

The rail line is owned by the state of Vermont and leased to the Vermont Railway, which is owned by the J. L. Wulfson Estate and others.

Radio frequencies: 160.290, 160.440, 160.710, 161.010
Location of enginehouses: Burlington and Rutland, Vt.
Locomotives: 4

No.	Builder	Model	New	Builder No.
201	EMD	GP38-2	12/72	72655
301	EMD	GP40	5/67	33098
501	EMD	SW1500	9/66	31990
801	EMD	GP18	4/61	26655

Freight cars: 2 boxcars, 10 covered hoppers

VIRGINIA SOUTHERN DIVISION, NORTH CAROLINA & VIRGINIA RAILROAD

Railroad Avenue
P. O. Box 12
Keysville, VA 23947

Reporting marks: VSRR
Phone: 804-736-8862
Fax: 804-736-9968

The Virginia Southern operates freight service from a connection with Norfolk Southern at O&H Junction (Oxford), North Carolina, to a second Norfolk Southern connection at Burkeville, Virginia, 78 miles. Rail is 85 to 100 pound.

Traffic includes pulpwood, wood chips, coal, and sugar — about 7,000 cars a year.

The line was built in part by the Richmond, Danville & Piedmont Railway in the 1870s. It later became part of the Richmond & Danville, then the Southern Railway.

Norfolk Southern has leased this line to the present operator under its Thoroughbred Short Line Program. Virginia Southern service started on November 28, 1988. It is a subsidiary of RailTex.

Radio frequency: 161.310
Location of enginehouse: Keysville, Va.
Locomotives: 3

No.	Builder	Model	New	Builder No.
200	EMD	GP40	8/68	34083
512	EMD	GP40	8/68	34089
618	EMD	GP9	10/56	22424

Virginia Southern handles a lot of wood chips as evidenced in this view of yellow-and-green GP9 No. 618 at Keysville, Virginia, in May 1991. Photo by Jim Shaw.

WABUSH LAKE RAILWAY and ARNAUD RAILWAY

P. O. Box 878
Sept-Îles, PQ G4R 4L4
Canada

Reporting marks:
Phone: 418-964-3008
Fax: 418-962-9876

The Wabush Lake Railway and the Arnaud Railway both connect with the Quebec North Shore & Labrador, the former at Ross Bay Junction, Newfoundland (Labrador), 224 miles north of Sept-Îles, and the latter at Arnaud Junction, Quebec, 8 miles out of

Sept-Îles. The Wabush Lake Railway runs west from Ross Bay Junction on a stretch of line operated jointly with QNS&L to Wabush Lake (near Labrador City), where it connects with Northern Land Company's line, then 1 mile farther to Wabush Mines.

The Arnaud Railway runs west from Arnaud Junction, then south to the St. Lawrence River at Pointe Noire, 21 miles.

Traffic on the two roads is primarily iron ore moving from the Wabush mine to the Arnaud Railway via the QNS&L. Neither provides common-carrier service now. The two railroads were built in 1963. They are controlled by Cliffs Mining Company (Cleveland Cliffs Inc.).

Radio frequencies: 160.860, 160.980, 160.050, 160.395
Enginehouses: Pointe Noire, Que., and Wabush Lake, Newfoundland
Locomotives: 11

No.	Builder	Model	New	Builder No.
901, 902	MLW	RS-18	1961	83279, 83280
903	MLW	RS-18	1962	83306
904-911	MLW	RS-18	1964	84822-84829

WACCAMAW COAST LINE RAILROAD CO., INC.

1551 Depot Road
P. O. Box 2202
Conway, SC 29526

Reporting marks: WCLR
Phone: 803-347-5301
Fax: 803-248-5790

The Waccamaw Coast Line operates freight service from a connection with Carolina Southern at Conway, South Carolina, to Myrtle Beach, 14.1 miles. Rail is 85 pound. Traffic includes stone, coal, wood chips, pulpwood, forest products, and brick — about 7,500 cars a year.

The line is a former Atlantic Coast Line branch acquired from CSX by Horry County and leased to the Horry County Railroad in November 5, 1984. On October 10, 1987, the county leased the railroad to the Waccamaw Coast Line.

The operating company is controlled by the Carolina Southern Railroad.
Radio frequencies: 461.450, 466.450
Location of enginehouse: Chadbourn, S. C.
Locomotives: pooled with Carolina Southern

The Waccamaw Coast Line uses a paint scheme reminiscent of the old Atlantic Coast Line, although the CF7 looks strangely out of place in Coast Line purple. Photo by Garreth M. McDonald.

WALKERSVILLE SOUTHERN RAILROAD, INC.

P. O. Box 651
Walkersville, MD 21793

Reporting marks: WS
Phone: 301-898-0899

The Walkersville Southern plans to operate from a connection with Maryland Midland at Walkersville, Maryland, to Frederick, 5 miles. At present there is minimal freight traffic on the line.

The property was acquired from the Penn Central estate by the state of Maryland in 1982 and has been out of service ever since. The operating company is independent.

Location of enginehouse: Walkersville, Md.
Locomotives: 1

No.	Builder	Model	New	Builder No.
1	Plymouth	18-ton	12/42	4615

WALKING HORSE & EASTERN RAILROAD CO., INC.

P. O. Box 1317
Shelbyville, TN 37160

Reporting marks: WHOE
Phone: 615-684-7376
Fax: 615-684-6318

The Walking Horse & Eastern operates freight service from Shelbyville, Tennessee, to a connection with CSX at Wartrace, 7.76 miles. Rail is 100 pound. Traffic includes plastic, LP gas, and metal products — under 500 cars a year.

The line was built by the Nashville & Chattanooga Railroad in 1853 and became part of the Nashville, Chattanooga & St. Louis. Seaboard System abandoned the branch on May 1, 1985, and it was acquired by the Bedford Railroad Authority, which designated the Walking Horse & Eastern to operate it. The operating company is controlled by G. R. Abernathy.

Radio frequency: 160.635
Location of enginehouse: Shelbyville, Tenn.
Locomotives: 2

No.	Builder	Model	New	Builder No.
1186	EMD	SW9	1/53	16250
1585	EMD	NW2	10/48	5839

Freight cars: 47 boxcars

Walking Horse & Eastern NW-2 No. 1585 awaits a call to duty at Wartrace, Tennessee. The road's logo is a Tennessee walking horse, painted on the cab. Photo by Jim Shaw.

WARREN & SALINE RIVER RAILROAD CO.

325 West Cedar Street
P. O. Box 390
Warren, AR 71671

Reporting marks: WSR
Phone: 501-226-6717
Fax: 501-226-5534

The Warren & Saline River operates freight service from a connection with the Union Pacific at Warren, Arkansas, to Cloquet, 8 miles. Rail is 85 to 90 pound. Traffic is outbound lumber and forest products — more than 5,000 cars a year.

The company was incorporated March 25, 1920, to take over the property of the Warren, Johnsville & Saline River Railroad (incorporated August 7, 1905), a logging road. The company purchased 2 miles of the Warren & Ouachita Valley Railroad at Warren in 1978. Operations between Cloquet and Hermitage were discontinued in 1985. Potlatch Forests, Inc. has owned the company since June 1959.

Radio frequencies: 451.625, 456.625
Location of enginehouse: Warren, Ark.
Locomotives: 2

No.	Builder	Model	New	Builder No.
538	EMD	SW1200	12/50	11668
539	EMD	SW1	7/49	7575

Warren & Saline River SW1 No. 539 switches chip hoppers at the Potlatch mill in Warren, Arkansas. This locomotive was purchased from the Warren & Ouachita Valley and was former Rock Island No. 539. Photo by James Gunning.

WARREN & TRUMBULL RAILROAD CO.

136 South Fifth Street
Coshocton, OH 43812

Reporting marks: WTRM
Phone: 614-622-8092

The Warren & Trumbull operates from a connection with CSX at Deforest Junction, Ohio, to North Warren, 5.28 miles. Rail is 131 pound. Annual traffic is more than 500 cars a year of scrap metal, and steel products.

The line was acquired from Conrail by the Mahoning Valley Economic Development Rail Corporation, which leased the property to the railroad. Shortline service started on March 15, 1994. The operating company is controlled by Summit View Corporation (Jerry Jacobson), and is affiliated with the Ohio Central Railroad System.

Location of enginehouse: Deforest Junction, Ohio
Locomotives: 1 engine

No.	Builder	Model	New	Builder No.
52	EMD	SW9	4/53	12866

WASHINGTON CENTRAL RAILROAD CO., INC.

6 East Arlington
P. O. Box 109
Yakima, WA 98907

Reporting marks: WCRC
Phone: 509-453-9166
Fax: 509-452-9346

The Washington Central operates freight service on several lines in south-central Washington
• Pasco to Cle Elum
• Yakima to Naches
• Yakima to Moxee City
• Gibbon to Zillah
• Connell to Moses Lake Airbase
• Warden to Othello
• Bassett Junction to Schrag

In 1992 the company took over several short Union Pacific lines in the Yakima valley. Total mileage operated is 302. Rail is predominantly 112 and 132 pound on the main lines. Traffic includes food, forest, and agricultural products amounting to more than 34,000 cars a year.

Washington Central connects with Burlington Northern at Pasco and Connell, with Union Pacific at Kennewick, and with Toppenish, Simcoe & Western at Toppenish.

Most of Washington Central's lines are former Northern Pacific line trackage acquired from Burlington Northern; the Warden-Othello line and part of the line to Moses Lake are ex-Milwaukee Road. Washington Central started operation October 13, 1986. The company is controlled by Nick B. Temple.

Radio frequencies: 160.770, 161.295
Location of enginehouses: Yakima, Gibbon, Warden, and Kennewick, Wash.
Locomotives: 16

No.	Builder	Model	New	Builder No.
100	EMD	F7A	6/52	16595
101	EMD	F7B	2/53	17914
102	EMD	F7A	6/52	16596
201	EMD	SW1200	1966	31230
202	EMD	SW1200	1965	29801
203	EMD	SW1200	1966	31222
211	EMD	SW1200	1965	29784
212	EMD	SW1200	1965	29788
301	EMD	GP9	1957	22737
302	EMD	GP9	1957	22719
401	AT&SF	CF7	1973	
402	AT&SF	CF7	1971	
2087	EMD	GP38	12/67	33718
2184	EMD	GP38	5/70	36477
4491	EMD	GP7	8/52	16896
4492	EMD	GP7	6/52	16846

Freight cars: 1399 boxcars, flatcars, gondolas, and covered hoppers

Washington Central GP9 No. 301 pulls a short train of empty woodchip and lumber cars near Thrall. Photo by Albert Farrow.

WASHINGTON COUNTY RAILROAD CORP.

P. O. Box 1267
Trenton FL 32693

Reporting marks: WACR
Phone: 904-463-1103
Fax: 904-463-1104

Washington County Railroad operates freight service from a connection with the New England Central at Montpelier Junction, Vermont, through Montpelier to Barre, Websterville, and Graniteville, 14 miles. Rail is 80 to 90 pound. Traffic includes transit cars, lumber, granite, and other commodities — under 500 cars a year.

Rail service in the area started in November 1873 when the Wells River Railroad opened its line. The company was reorganized in 1877 as the Montpelier & Wells River Railroad, and merged into the Barre & Chelsea (which traces its origins to the Barre Railroad formed in 1888) in January 1945. The Barre & Chelsea abandoned its line in 1957, and its lines in and around Montpelier were purchased by the newly organized Montpelier & Barre Railroad. The Montpelier & Barre received permission to abandon in 1980, and the state of Vermont purchased its tracks. The Washington County Railroad was formed in 1980 to operated that line. It is a subsidiary of CSF Acquisitions Company (Clyde Forbes).

Radio frequency: 161.190 (not in use)
Location of enginehouse: Montpelier, Vt.
Locomotives: 2

No.	Builder	Model	New	Builder No.
25	Alco	S-1	8/44	71662
29	Alco	S-1	5/49	76737

WATERLOO RAILWAY CO.

Reporting marks: WLO

The company owns a line from a connection with the Illinois Central at Water Valley Junction, Mississippi, to a connection with the Mississippi & Skuna Valley Railroad at Bruce Junction, 11 miles. The line is operated by Illinois Central. Traffic is overhead business moving between the IC and the M&SV.

The Waterloo Railway was organized in 1955 by Illinois Central and the Rock Island to purchase the property of the Waterloo, Cedar Falls & Northern Railway, an interurban connecting Cedar Rapids, Waterloo, and Waverly, Iowa. IC purchased Rock Island's half interest in 1968 and merged the operations with its own Iowa Division in 1970. By 1980 nearly all the WCF&N line had been abandoned and the Waterloo Railroad had dwindled to switching operations at Cedar Rapids and Waterloo.

The Waterloo Railway is a 1985 reorganization of the Waterloo Railroad Co. It appears to be an example of reuse of a corporate structure for convenience.

Freight cars: 1,258 boxcars, 150 covered hoppers

WCTU RAILWAY CO.

7551-A Crater Lake Highway
White City, OR 97503

Reporting marks: WCTR
Phone: 503-826-2631
Fax: 503-826-4420

WCTU Railway operates a 13-mile switching line at White City, just north of Medford, Oregon. It connects with the Central Oregon & Pacific and handles about 4,000 cars a year. Rail is 85 pound. The White City Terminal & Utility Co. started operations in November 1954. The present name was adopted soon after Union Tank Car Co. acquired control in 1974.

Radio frequencies: 160.680, 160.800
Locomotives: 2

No.	Builder	Model	New	Builder No.
5117	GE	70-ton	9/51	31162
5119	GE	70-ton	5/55	32284

Freight cars: 3,033

WELLSBORO & CORNING RAILROAD CO., INC.

356 Priestley Avenue
Northumberland, PA 17857

Reporting marks: WCOR
Phone: 717-473-7949

The Wellsboro & Corning operates freight service from connections with Conrail and CP Rail System (Delaware & Hudson) at Gang Mills, near Corning, New York, to Wellsboro Junction and Wellsboro, Pennsylvania, 35 miles. Rail is 80 to 127 pound. Traffic is 700 cars a year and includes sand, soda ash, chemicals, grain, food products, sugar, lumber, and light bulbs. The Tioga Central Railroad operates excursion trains over this line.

The north end of the line, from Corning to Lawrenceville, was built in 1841 by the Tioga Coal, Iron Mining & Manufacturing Company. That company was reorganized as the Corning & Blossburg Railroad in 1851, and as the Blossburg & Corning Railroad in 1854. The south end of the line, from Lawrenceville to Wellsboro, was built by the Wellsboro & Lawrenceville Railroad, which opened its line in 1871. The two roads merged in 1873 to form the Corning, Cowanesque & Antrim Railroad, which was leased to the Fall Brook Railroad in 1892. Fall Brook was leased to New York Central in 1899.

Wellsboro & Corning 800 awaits switching chores at Wellsboro, Pennsylvania. Photo by Jim Shaw.

The line was included in the Conrail core system but lost importance over the years. When Conrail abandoned the south end of its route through the "Grand Canyon of Pennsylvania," this former main line became a low-density branch. Conrail sold the line on December 30, 1992, to Growth Resources of Wellsboro (GROW), which designated the Wellsboro & Corning to operate the line. The company is controlled by Richard Roby.

Radio frequency: 160.455
Location of enginehouse: Wellsboro, Pa.
Locomotives: 1 engine

No.	Builder	Model	New	Builder No.
800	EMD	SW8M	9/51	14056

WEST MICHIGAN RAILROAD CO.

1318 South Johanson Road
Peoria, IL 61607

Reporting marks: WJ
Phone: 309-697-1400

The West Michigan Railroad provides freight service from a connection with CSX at Hartford, Michigan, to Paw Paw, 14.6 miles. The load limit is 220,000 pounds. Traffic is food and agricultural products, and the company expects to move about 500 cars a year.

The line was built by the 3-foot gauge Toledo & South Haven Railroad, opened on October 1, 1877. In 1894 the company was reorganized as the South Haven & Eastern, and in April 1903 it came under control of the Pere Marquette. From 1911 to 1914 the line was leased to Michigan United Railways, an interurban company.

The Kalamazoo, Lake Shore & Chicago purchased the line from CSX in 1986 and started operations on August 5, 1987. After March 1993 it operated under Chapter 11 bankruptcy protection. It suspended operations May 26, 1995, because of lack of funds. On June 24, 1995, the ICC authorized the West Jersey Railroad to operate the line as a Directed Rail Carrier. West Jersey began service in August 1995, changed its name to West Michigan Railroad, and purchased the line on October 10, 1995. It is a subsidiary of Pioneer RailCorp.

Radio frequencies: 160.815, 160.215
Location of enginehouse: Paw Paw, Mich.
Locomotives: 2

No.	Builder	Model	New	Builder No.
7803	Alco	RS-3	8/52	80161
7804	Alco	RS-3	8/52	80184

WEST TENNESSEE RAILROAD CORP.

One Depot Street
Trenton, TN 38382

Reporting marks: WTNN
Phone: 901-855-1131
Fax: 901-855-4622

The West Tennessee Railroad operates freight service from a Norfolk Southern connection at Lawrence, Tennessee, to Kenton, 43 miles. It connects with CSX at Humbolt. Rail is 90 to 115 pound.

Traffic includes grain, scrap, steel billets, coil steel, and frozen chickens — 6,500 cars a year.

The line was part of the main line of the Mobile & Ohio Railroad between Mobile, Alabama, and Columbus, Kentucky, built as early as 1861. In 1940 it became part of the Gulf, Mobile & Ohio, and in 1972 part of Illinois Central Gulf.

Gibson County Railroad Authority acquired the line in August

1984 following its abandonment. Shortline service started on October 5, 1984.

The operating company, controlled by H. G. Hohorst and Bruce Hohorst, is affiliated with the Tennken Railroad.
Radio frequencies: 160.245, 161.070, 161.475
Location of enginehouse: Trenton, Tenn.
Locomotives: 5

No.	Builder	Model	New	Builder No.
1850	Alco	RS-11	4/56	81943
1851	Alco	RS-11	4/56	81944
1852	Alco	RS-11	4/56	81945
1853	Alco	RS-11	4/56	81946
2054	Alco	RSD-12	4/56	81947

WEST TEXAS & LUBBOCK RAILROAD CO., INC.

211 South Sixth Street
Brownfield, TX 79316

Reporting marks: WTLR
Phone: 806-637-6954
Fax: 806-637-8074

The West Texas & Lubbock operates freight service from a connection with the Santa Fe at Lubbock, Texas, to Seagraves, 65 miles. A branch line runs from Doud to Whiteface and Coble, 39.8 miles — a total of 111 miles are operated. Rail is 90 pound. Traffic includes salt cake, chemicals, fertilizer, grain, cotton, and LP gas — about 4,500 cars a year.

The line was built by the South Plains & Santa Fe and opened into Seagraves on July 1, 1918. The branch to Whiteface opened on December 1, 1925. The company was leased by the Panhandle & Santa Fe in January 1931. Santa Fe turned over the line to the Seagraves, Whiteface & Lubbock Railroad on April 2, 1990. The West Texas & Lubbock, a subsidiary of RailAmerica, acquired it on November 1, 1995.
Radio frequency: 160.785
Location of enginehouse: Brownfield, Texas
Locomotives: 5

No.	Builder	Model	New	Builder No.
105	EMD	GP7	1/51	12064
113	EMD	GP7	11/51	14991
118	EMD	GP7	12/52	17086
4538	EMD	GP9	3/57	23542
4543	EMD	GP9	3/57	23544

Freight cars: 33 boxcars

WESTERN KENTUCKY RAILWAY, LLC

P. O. Box 66
Sturgis, KY 42459

Reporting marks: WKRL
Phone: 502-664-9938
Fax: 502-664-9941

The Western Kentucky Railway owns a line running from a CSX connection at Princeton, Kentucky, to Waverly, 69 miles, plus a branch line from Blackford to Providence, 9.5 miles, and several short mine branches near Providence. A total of 92 miles are owned. Rail is 112 to 132 pound. Traffic is primarily coal — 20,000 cars a year. The line is currently embargoed from Blackford to Waverly.

The line was built in large part by the Ohio Valley Railway and acquired by Illinois Central. In March 1982 the Tradewater Railway Company, a subsidiary of Costain Coal, Inc., bought the property from Illinois Central. On January 1, 1995, the coal company sold the Tradewater Railway to Rail Management & Consulting Corporation, which organized the current operator to run the line.

Radio frequency: 160.635
Location of enginehouse: Pyro Mine, Ky.
Locomotives: 8

No.	Builder	Model	New	Builder No.	Rebuilt
1338	EMD	GP18	1/60	25455	
1342	EMD	GP18	1/60	25459	
1347	EMD	GP18	10/61	26936	
3419	EMD	GP9	5/54	19480	
4544	EMD	GP7	1957	23556	
4547	EMD	GP7	1957	23566	
4548	EMD	GP7	2/59	25054	
4549	EMD	GP7	2/59	25058	

Freight cars: 232 hopper cars (additional reporting mark TWRY)

WESTERN PLANT SERVICES, INC.

P. O. Box 2494
Richmond, CA 94801

Reporting marks: WPS
Phone: 510-235-7713

The company provides local switching service on 15 miles of track at Richmond, California. It connects with Southern Pacific and Santa Fe.
Locomotives: 2

WESTERN RAIL ROAD CO.

2682 Wald Road
P. O. Box 311475
New Braunfels, TX 78131-1475

Reporting marks: WRRC
Phone: 210-625-8084
Fax: 210-625-5834

The company operates a 1.9-mile railroad from a connection with the Union Pacific at Dittlinger, Texas, to Stonetown. Rail is 136 pound. Traffic is crushed rock, and other aggregates, and cement and totals about 27,000 cars a year.

The company was incorporated March 22, 1974, as the PB Railroad, Inc. The ICC authorized construction of the line on May 9, 1975, and work started in September. The present name was adopted in November 1975. Sunbelt Management of Houston controls the railroad.

Radio frequency: 160.335
Location of enginehouse: Dittlinger, Texas
Locomotives: 3

No.	Builder	Model	New	Builder No.
534	EMD	SW1	7/49	7479
1007	EMD	SW1	11/39	978
9617	EMD	SW9	5/57	23363

Freight cars: 408 hopper cars, 55 gondolas

WHEELING & LAKE ERIE RAILWAY

100 East First Street
P. O. Box 96
Brewster, OH 44613

Reporting marks: WE
Phone: 216-767-3401

The Wheeling & Lake Erie has acquired and is leasing former Norfolk & Western lines from Connellsville, Pennsylvania, to Cleveland, Ohio, 342 miles, and to Carey and Bellevue, Ohio. There are a number of branch lines, and the company has trackage rights over CSX from Connellsville to Hagerstown, Maryland, 180 miles. It operates a total of 878 miles. It connects with Conrail, CSX, Norfolk Southern, and seven short lines. Traffic is primarily coal, steel, and chemicals — 87,000 cars a year.

The routes purchased include the former Wheeling & Lake Erie Railway, which was leased by the Nickel Plate in 1949, and the former Akron, Canton & Youngstown, which was purchased by the Norfolk & Western in 1964 (at the same time it merged the Nickel Plate). The current Wheeling & Lake Erie leases the Pittsburgh & West Virginia Railway, which N&W leased in 1964.

The current W&LE began operations May 12, 1990. It is owned by Wheeling Acquisition Corporation (principals are Chris Rooney, James Hanscom, and William Fergeson).
Radio frequencies: 161.025, 161.250, 160.440, 160.665, 161.565
Locomotives: 47
Freight cars: 1,275
Principal Shop: Brewster, Ohio

WHITE PASS & YUKON CORPORATION, LTD.

General Office: P. O. Box 4070
Whitehorse, YT Y1A 3T1, Canada
Passenger Office: P. O. Box 435
Skagway, AK 99840

Reporting marks: WPY
Phone: 403-668-7621
Phone: 907-983-2217

The White Pass & Yukon Corporation controls a 3-foot gauge line extending from Skagway, Alaska, to Carcross, Yukon Territory, 67.5 miles. Rail is 90 pound. It currently carries no freight but operates excursion between Skagway and Bennett, British Columbia, 40.6 miles. In 1994 it carried 140,000 passengers.

The line was built by three companies during the Klondike Gold Rush of the 1890s. The Pacific & Arctic Railway & Navigation Co. built the Alaska portion of the line. The British Columbia-Yukon Railway and the British Yukon Railway built lines in British Columbia and the Yukon Territory respectively. Construction started at Skagway on May 27, 1898. Rails reached White Pass on February 20, 1899, and Whitehorse on July 29, 1900.

The three companies were controlled by the White Pass & Yukon Railway, which was registered under the English Companies Act in 1898. That company was liquidated in 1951, and its assets were acquired by the White Pass & Yukon Corporation.

Freight and passenger service ended when the railroad closed in 1982. In 1988 the company reopened for seasonal passenger excursion service. The company is independent.

Radio frequencies: 160.305 (train), 160.425 (yard)
Enginehouse: Skagway, Alaska
Locomotives: 16

No.	Builder	Model	New	Builder No.
73	Baldwin	2-8-2	1947	73352
90	GE	84-ton, 800 hp	1954	32060
91	GE	84-ton, 800 hp	1954	32061
92	GE	84-ton, 800 hp	1956	32709
93	GE	84-ton, 800 hp	1956	327010
94	GE	84-ton, 800 hp	1956	32711
95	GE	86-ton, 900 hp	1963	34592
96	GE	86-ton, 900 hp	1963	34593
97	GE	86-ton, 900 hp	1963	34594
98	GE	86-ton, 900 hp	1966	35790
99	GE	86-ton, 900 hp	1966	35791
100	GE	86-ton, 900 hp	1966	35792
108	MLW	DL535E, 1200 hp	1971	M6054-01
109	MLW	DL535E, 1200 hp	1971	M6054-02
110	MLW	DL535E, 1200 hp	1971	M6054-03
114	MLW	DL535E, 1200 hp	1982	M6123-04

WICHITA, TILLMAN & JACKSON RAILWAY CO., INC.

4420 West Vickery Boulevard
Suite 110
Fort Worth, TX 76107

Reporting marks: WTJR
Phone: 817-737-7288
Fax: 817-732-2610

The Wichita, Tillman & Jackson operates freight service from a connection with Burlington Northern (and Union Pacific by trackage rights over Burlington Northern) at Wichita Falls, Texas, to connections with BN and Farmrail at Altus, Oklahoma, 77.6 miles. It connects with Grainbelt at Frederick, Okla. Rail is 60, 90, and 110 pound. A separate line runs from a connection with Union Pacific at Waurika, Okla., to Walters, 24 miles. Rail on that line is predominantly 85 pound.

Traffic is primarily grain, plus fertilizer, gypsum board, sand, soda ash, and chemicals used in glass manufacture. Annual traffic runs about 8,200 cars.

The Wichita Falls-Altus line is a former Missouri-Kansas-Texas branch built by the Wichita Falls & Northwestern Railway between 1906 and 1909. WF&NW came under control of MKT by 1912. The state of Oklahoma owns the track between Altus and the state line.

The Waurika-Walters line is a former Rock Island branch built around 1900 and purchased by the state when the RI was abandoned. It was leased for a period to the Oklahoma-Kansas-Texas, a subsidiary of the MKT.

The Wichita, Tillman & Jackson began operation on January 14, 1991. It is a subsidiary of Rio Grande Pacific Corporation.

Radio frequencies: 160.275, 161.265
Location of enginehouse: Wichita Falls, Texas
Locomotives: 6

No.	Builder	Model	New	Builder No.
4364	EMD	GP7	11/50	11991
4367	EMD	GP7	6/50	9914
4370	EMD	GP7	11/51	14250
4443	EMD	GP7	10/51	13323
4451	EMD	GP7	11/51	14243
4454	EMD	GP7	6/50	10190

WILLAMETTE & PACIFIC RAILROAD, INC.

110 West Tenth Avenue
Albany, OR 97321

Reporting marks: WPRR
Phone: 503-924-6565
Fax: 503-924-6580

The Willamette & Pacific operates freight service from a connection with Southern Pacific at Albany, Oregon, to Toledo, 75 miles; from Dawson through Alpine Junction to Newberg, 84.9 miles; and on short branches to Dallas and Willamina. Willamette & Pacific leases a total of 183.8 miles and has an additional 41.2 miles of trackage rights from Albany to Eugene, where most interchange takes place. Rail ranges from 75 to 136 pound. Traffic is primarily forest products, paper products, scrap, and steel — 35,000 cars a year.

The Albany-Toledo line was built by the Willamette Valley & Coast Railroad, which was chartered in 1879. The company was reorganized successively as the Oregon Pacific, the Oregon, Corvalis & Eastern, and the Corvalis & Eastern. In 1915 Southern Pacific acquired control.

The line south from Newberg south was built between 1880 and 1890 by Southern Pacific as its West Side Division. It was electrified from 1917 to 1929.

Willamette & Pacific operates these lines under a long-term lease from Southern Pacific effective February 22, 1993. It is a subsidiary of Genesee & Wyoming Industries, Inc.

Radio frequency: 160.770
Location of enginehouse: Albany, Ore.
Locomotives: 22

No.	Builder	Model	New	Builder No.	Rebuilt
1501	EMD	SD7	11/52	17145	
1551	EMD	SW1500	12/69	35293	
1801	EMD	GP9	4/59	25130	1977
1803	EMD	GP9	1/57	22920	
1852	EMD	SD9	5/55	20216	
2301-2317	EMD	GP39-2	10/74	74602-1–74602-17	

Freight cars: 99 gondolas

WILLAMETTE VALLEY RAILWAY CO.

635 North Walnut Street
Independence, OR 97351

Reporting marks: WVR
Phone: 503-838-4184
Fax: 503-838-5740

The Willamette Valley Railway operates freight service from a connection with Southern Pacific at Woodburn, Oregon, to Stayton, 29.7 miles. A second line runs from Mill City to Albany, 48 miles total. About 3,300 cars a year of lumber, plywood, and other commodities make up the road's traffic.

The Stayton line was built by the Oregonian Railroad, which was absorbed by Southern Pacific in 1890. The Mill City line was built in part by the Oregon & California and Oregon Pacific railroads. The lines were leased from Southern Pacific and shortline service starting February 22, 1993. The Willamette Valley Railway is independent.

Radio frequencies: 160.530, 160.560, 161.070
Location of enginehouse: Albany and Woodburn, Ore.
Locomotives: 3

No.	Builder	Model	New	Builder No.	Rebuilt
3859	EMD	GP9	2/59	25152	1978
4364	EMD	SD9	2/55	19940	1973
4433	EMD	SD9	4/55	20204	1977

WILLAMINA & GRAND RONDE RAILWAY CO.

635 North Walnut Street
Independence, OR 97351

Reporting marks: WGR
Phone: 503-838-4184

The Willamina & Grand Ronde operates a switching line at Willamina, Oregon, and owns 0.6 mile of track at Independence.

The track at Willamina was built in 1922 by the Willamina & Grand Ronde Railway (Spaulding-Miami Lumber Co.), and operated by that company until 1955, when the Longview, Portland & Northern Railroad acquired it. The LP&N operated the line as its Grand Ronde Division until March 1980, when it was sold to the Willamina & Grand Ronde Railroad — which was merged into the Willamette Valley Railroad on March 10, 1986, and sold again on March 1, 1988. Part of the Willamina & Grande Ronde was a line to Fort Hill, which was sold in 1995 to the Hampton Railway. The track at Independence is a remnant of the Valley & Siletz Railroad, which was built about 1918.

The Willamina & Grand Ronde is affiliated with Willamette Valley Railway.

Radio frequencies: 160.530, 160.560, 161.070
Location of enginehouse: Willamina, Ore.
Locomotives: 1

No.	Builder	Model	New	Builder No.
2890	EMD	GP9	9/59	25646

Freight cars: 277 covered hoppers, 10 gondolas, 115 flatcars

WILMINGTON & WESTERN RAILWAY CORP.

P. O. Box 5575
Wilmington, DE 19808

Reporting marks: WWRC
Phone: 302-998-7178

The Wilmington & Western operates freight service from a connection with CSX at Landenberg Junction, Delaware, to Hockessin, 10.2 miles. Rail is 90 pound. Traffic includes bricks and lumber — 100 cars a year. Excursion service is operated over the line by the Wilmington & Western Railroad.

The line was built by the Wilmington & Western Railroad in 1872. The company was absorbed by Baltimore & Ohio in 1883. Passenger service ended in 1929.

After B&O abandoned the line in 1982, the Octoraro Railway provided freight service on the line until May 1984, when the Wilmington & Western started service. The company is independent.

Radio frequency: 160.755
Location of enginehouse: Marshallton, Del.
Locomotives: 2

No.	Builder	Model	New	Builder No.
114	EMD	SW1	2/40	1021
8408	EMD	SW1	8/40	1106

WILMINGTON TERMINAL RAILROAD, LP.

1717 Woodbine Street
Wilmington, NC 28401

Reporting marks: WTRY
Phone: 910-343-0461
Fax: 910-251-8159

Wilmington Terminal provides switching service on 7 miles of track leased from the North Carolina Ports Railway Commission at Wilmington, North Carolina. It connects with CSX and handles about 5,000 cars of steel, chemicals, and paper products a year.

The company started operation on October 1, 1986. It is a partnership controlled by Rail Management, the general partner.
Radio frequency: 160.320
Locomotives: 3

No.	Builder	Model	New	Builder No.
1203	EMD	SW1200	2/66	31231
1204	EMD	SW1200	3/66	31117
1205	EMD	SW1200	3/66	31240

WINAMAC SOUTHERN RAILWAY CO.

500 North Buckeye Street
P. O. Box 554
Kokomo, IN 46901

Reporting marks: WSRY
Phone: 317-459-3196

Winamac Southern Railway provides freight service from Kokomo, Indiana, to Bringhurst, 47.5 miles. It also operates 2.4 miles of belt trackage around Kokomo and a branch from Van to Winamac, 25.7 miles. Traffic is primarily agricultural and runs about 2,400 cars a year.

The company is controlled by Daniel R. Frick, owner of JK Line, and the railroad is operated in conjunction with the Central Railroad of Indianapolis, which provides locomotives.

WINCHESTER & WESTERN RAILROAD CO. (VIRGINIA DIVISION)

126 East Piccadilly Street
P. O. Box 264
Winchester, VA 22601

Reporting marks: WW
Phone: 703-662-2600
Fax: 703-667-3692

Winchester & Western's Virginia Division operates freight service from Gore, Virginia, 18 miles to a junction with CSX, then 2 more miles by trackage rights on CSX to downtown Winchester. Rail is 90 to 132 pound.

The company also operates a line from Winchester to Conrail and Norfolk Southern connections at Hagerstown, Maryland (39 miles, including 6 miles of trackage rights on Conrail from Williamsport to Hagerstown). There is an additional CSX interchange at Martinsburg, West Virginia. Rail is 100 to 130 pound.

Traffic is outbound sand, limestone, aluminum, scrap, and brick, and inbound paper, plastic, lumber, wallboard steel, and minerals. The total is about 10,000 cars a year.

The first operating company serving the area was the original Winchester & Western Railroad, which was chartered in 1916 and opened the following year. The company failed and was sold January 26, 1926, to two companies that consolidated their holdings through merger on August 1, 1929, as the Winchester & Wardensville Railroad. In August 1934 the ICC approved abandonment of the outer end of the line — from Rock Enon, Va., to Wardensville, W. Va. — and passenger service was discontinued at the same time.

A new Winchester & Western Railroad (the present company) was incorporated February 17, 1940, and on March 1, 1941, it took over operation of the Winchester & Wardensville Railroad. In 1944 the line was further cut back to Gore. On December 8, 1986, the Winchester & Western took over a former Pennsylvania Railroad line from Winchester to Williamsport, Md. The north end of that line was opened by the Martinsburg & Potomac Railroad in

1873. The line was completed south to Winchester by 1889, by which time the property was under the control of the Cumberland Valley Railroad, part of the Pennsylvania system.

The Winchester & Western is owned by Unimin Corporation.

Radio frequency: 160.920

Location of enginehouse: Gore, Va.

Locomotives: 9

No.	Builder	Model	New	Builder No.
351	Alco	RS-11	11/57	82628
403	EMD	GP9	5/54	19464
445	EMD	GP9	1/55	20133
498	EMD	GP9	11/55	21924
605	Alco	RS-11	9/56	81939
709	EMD	GP9	11/56	21895
863	Alco	RS-11	2/59	83027
2910	Alco	RS-11	4/59	83407
3611	Alco	RS-11	12/56	82028

Freight cars: 322 covered hoppers, 22 boxcars

WINCHESTER & WESTERN RAILROAD CO. (NEW JERSEY DIVISION)

Burlington Road
P. O. Box 1024
Bridgeton, NJ 08302

Reporting marks: WW
Phone: 609-451-6400
Fax: 609-451-7016

Winchester & Western's New Jersey Division operates freight service from a connection with Conrail at Millville, New Jersey, to Dorchester, 13 miles, from Vineland to Mauricetown, 27 miles, and from Bridgeton Junction to Seabrook, 3.3 miles. The railroad has trackage rights over Conrail between Vineland and Millville. Rail is 90 to 130 pound.

Traffic is predominantly silica sand and aggregates plus food products, corn syrup, grain, and other commodities, and totals about 10,000 cars a year.

The Dorchester line is former Pennsylvania-Reading Seashore Lines trackage; the Mauricetown line was part of the Central Railroad of New Jersey. Both lines were included in and operated by Conrail until they were sold to the Winchester & Western on October 1, 1986. On January 15, 1987 the company took over the line of the Jersey Southern Railway between Bridgeton Junction and Seabrook.

The Winchester & Western is owned by Unimin Corporation.

Radio frequencies: 161.310, 161.070 (on Conrail only)

Location of enginehouse: Bridgeton Junction, N. J.

Locomotives: 6

No.	Builder	Model	New	Builder No.
459	EMD	GP9	7/55	20464
4575	EMD	GP9	7/55	20480
517	EMD	GP9	3/58	24508
520	EMD	GP9	3/58	24511
732	EMD	GP9	11/55	20912
811	EMD	GP9	1959	25089

WINDSOR & HANTSPORT RAILWAY CO., LTD

12 Station St.
Hantsport, NS B0P 1PO
Canada

Reporting marks: WHRC
Phone: 902-684-3415
Fax: 902-684-3415

The Windsor & Hantsport operates from a connection with Canadian National at Windsor Junction, Nova Scotia, to Kentville, 52.9 miles. Rail is 90 pound. About 23,000 cars a year of gypsum rock, grain, vegetable oil, lumber, and other commodities make up the road's traffic.

The line is part of the Dominion Atlantic Railway, which was incorporated July 22, 1895, as a consolidation of several railroad companies and was leased by Canadian Pacific in 1912.

In 1994 CP sold the line to the Windsor & Hantsport, which began service August 29, 1994. The company is a subsidiary of Iron Road Railways, Inc.

Radio frequencies: 160.755, 160.815, 161.355
Enginehouse: Windsor, N. S.
Locomotives: 8

No.	Builder	Model	New	Builder No.
8026	MLW	RS-32	8/59	82579
8027	MLW	RS-32	8/59	82580
8036	MLW	RS-32	8/59	82589
8037	MLW	RS-32	8/59	82590
8038	MLW	RS-32	8/59	82591
8041	MLW	RS-32	7/60	83303
8042	MLW	RS-32	7/60	83284
8046	MLW	RS-32	7/60	83288

Freight cars: 76 gondolas

WINSTON-SALEM SOUTHBOUND RAILWAY CO.

206 North Spruce Street
P. O. Box 20204
Winston-Salem, NC 27120-0204

Reporting marks: WSS
Phone: 910-723-3671
Fax: 910-723-8373

The Southbound operates freight service from Winston-Salem to Wadesboro, North Carolina, 90 miles. It connects with Norfolk Southern, High Point, Thomasville & Denton, and CSX. Rail is 100 to 132 pound. Traffic includes grain, aggregate, beer, forest products, paper products, coal, and coke — 21,000 cars a year. The company was incorporated January 31, 1905, and the first train operated from Winston-Salem to Wadesboro on November 24, 1910. The company stock is owned equally by CSX and Norfolk Southern. The railroad is operated independently with equipment furnished by the owners.

Radio frequencies: 160.590, 161.250

WIREGRASS CENTRAL RAILROAD CO., INC.

812 North Main Street
Enterprise, AL 36330

Reporting marks: WGCR
Phone: 334-347-6070
Fax: 334-393-6149

Wiregrass Central Railroad operates from a connection with CSX at Waterford, Alabama, to Clintonville, 23.2 miles. Rail is 85 pound. Traffic includes grain and oil mill products.

The line, which was part of the Atlantic Coast Line system, was built between 1905 and 1915. Wiregrass Central purchased it from CSX and began service on December 11, 1987. The company is controlled by Pete Claussen (Gulf & Ohio Railways).
Radio frequencies: 160.500, 161.190
Location of enginehouse: Enterprise, Ala.
Locomotives: 7

Two GP9s pull the daily freight into Enterprise, Alabama, on the Wiregrass Central. Photo by Jim Shaw.

No.	Builder	Model	New	Builder No.	Rebuilt
1026	EMD	GP7	10/50	12001	
1051	EMD	NW2	7/47	14760	
2876	EMD	GP9	4/59	25133	
3832	EMD	GP9	3/59	25118	
3872	EMD	GP9	2/59	25016	
6226	EMD	GP9	7/57	23383	
8056	EMD	GP10	12/54	19898	1970

WISCONSIN & CALUMET RAILROAD CO., INC.

5300 North 33rd Street
P. O. Box 9229
Milwaukee, WI 53209-9229

Reporting marks: WICT
Phone: 414-438-8820
Fax: 414-438-8826

The Wisconsin & Calumet operates freight service on several lines totaling 318 miles in southeast Wisconsin and nearby Illinois:
• from connections with Chicago & North Western and Soo Line (CP Rail System) at Janesville, Wisconsin, west to Monroe, 38.8 miles
• from a connection with the Chicago Central & Pacific near Freeport, Illinois, north through Monroe to connections with C&NW and Soo Line at Madison, 60.9 miles
• from Madison southeast to Janesville, then northeast to Waukesha, where it interchanges with Wisconsin & Southern and Wisconsin Central
• trackage rights on Metra from Fox Lake, Ill., to the Belt Railway of Chicago's Clearing Yard in Chicago

Traffic includes sand, coal, grain, salt, food products, and general commodities amounting to 7,000 cars a year.

The company started operation on January 31, 1985, over

ex-Milwaukee Road and ex-Illinois Central trackage previously operated by the Chicago, Madison & Northern and the Central Wisconsin Railroad. From 1986 to 1990 it operated a former Milwaukee Road line from Madison west to Prairie du Chien.

The property is owned by the state of Wisconsin and the Wisconsin River Transit Commission. The operating company has been controlled by William Gardner since August 1993. The railroad is operated as part of the Wisconsin & Southern Railroad, which provides locomotives.

Radio frequencies: 160.575, 161.145
Location of enginehouse: Janesville, Wis.

WISCONSIN & SOUTHERN RAILROAD SYSTEM

5300 North 33rd Street
P. O. Box 9229
Milwaukee, WI 59209-9229

Reporting marks: WSOR
Phone: 414-438-8820
Fax: 414-438-8826

The Wisconsin & Southern operates freight, TOFC, and COFC service from a connection with CP Rail System (Soo Line) at North Milwaukee, Wisconsin, to Oshkosh, 94 miles. Branch lines run from Granville to Menomonee Falls (4 miles), Iron Ridge to Mayville (7.5 miles), Horicon to Cambria (26.1 miles), and Brandon to Markesan (11.6 miles). Additional connections are made with the Chicago & North Western at Granville, with Fox River Valley at Germantown, Wisconsin Central at Slinger and Rugby Junction, and with Wisconsin & Calumet at Waukesha (by trackage rights on Wisconsin Central). Rail is 90 pound or heavier. Traffic includes food products, grain, fertilizer, machinery, limestone, lumber, steel, plastic, sand, salt, pulpboard, paper, and chemicals and amounts to 15,000 cars a year.

Wisconsin & Southern's lines are former Milwaukee Road branches acquired by the Wisconsin Department of Transportation and managed by the East Wisconsin Counties Railroad Consortium. The company, which also operates the affiliated Wisconsin & Calumet Railroad, started service on July 1, 1980. It was acquired by William Gardner (Northern Rail Car Corporation) in August 1988.

Employees: 110

Radio frequencies: 160.575, 161.145
Location of enginehouse: Horicon, Wis.
Locomotives: 20

No.	Builder	Model	New	Builder No.	Rebuilt
10A	EMD	E9A	9/55	20494	
10C	EMD	E9A	4/56	21605	
801	EMD	E8A	7/50	11482	
1009	EMD	NW2	9/48	6581	
1200	EMD	SW1200	11/54	20076	
1201	EMD	SW1200	11/54	20049	
2001	EMD	GP7	9/52	16990	1980
2002	EMD	GP7	10/52	17460	1981
3501	EMD	GP35	5/64	29558	
4490	EMD	GP9	4/59	25220	
4491	EMD	GP9	11/60	26348	
4492	EMD	GP9	3/59	25213	
4493	EMD	GP9	3/59	25110	
4494	EMD	GP9	7/59	25321	
6547	EMD	GP35	2/64	28489	
6579	EMD	GP35	5/64	29553	
6585	EMD	GP35	5/64	29559	
6604	EMD	GP35	1/65	29709	
6620	EMD	GP35	3/65	29725	
6661	EMD	GP35	8/65	30173	

Freight cars: 688

WISCONSIN CENTRAL LTD.

General Office: One O'Hare Center
P. O. Box 5062
Rosemont, IL 60017
Operating Office: P. O. Box 96
1625 Depot Street
Stevens Point, WI 54481

Reporting marks: WC
Phone: 708-318-4600
Fax: 708-318-4578
Phone: 715-345-2499
Fax: 715-345-2482

Wisconsin Central operates 2,050 miles of track in Wisconsin, upper Michigan, eastern Minnesota, northern Illinois, and Ontario.

Traffic is paper, paper products, forest products, and aggregate amounting to about 240,000 cars a year.

Wisconsin Central purchased most of its lines from the Soo Line Railroad in October 1987 at a price of $122 million plus $9 million for various equipment. Financing was arranged by Irving Trust Co. Service started October 11, 1987.

Soo Line had previously spun off the routes as a subsidiary, the Lake States Transportation Company, and they were operated separately for a short time before the Wisconsin Central purchase. They are in large part the lines of the Wisconsin Central Railroad that was leased by the Soo Line in 1909 and merged in 1961.

Wisconsin Central acquired the Green Bay & Western, and Fox River Valley & Western railroads in 1994 and operates them as the Fox Valley & Western. In 1995, Wisconsin Central acquired the Algoma Central Railway, which it operates separately.

Wisconsin Central has also extended itself outside North America. In 1993 purchased a 27 percent interest in New Zealand Railways, took over its operation, and renamed it Tranz Rail. In December 1995 it began acquisition of Great Britain's Rail Express Systems Limited, which operates mail trains and special and excursion trains throughout Britain.

Radio frequencies: 160.785, 161.295, 160.260, 160.335
Enginehouse: Stevens Point, Wis.
Locomotives: 114
Freight cars: 10,462
Principal Shop: Fond du Lac, Wis.

WYE TRANSPORTATION CORP.

1920 Leonard Avenue
P. O. Box 369004
Columbus, OH 43236

Reporting marks: WYEC
Phone: 614-253-8511

The Wye Transportation Corporation is a switching line at East Columbus, Ohio. It operates former Conrail trackage and connects with Conrail. Service started April 5, 1984. The company is independent.

WYOMING COLORADO RAILROAD CO., INC.

452 Snowy Range Road
Laramie, WY 82070

Reporting marks: WYCO
Phone: 307-721-2907

Wyoming Colorado operates three separate lines. One extends from a connection with Union Pacific at Laramie, Wyoming, to Hebron, Colorado, 108 miles. Rail is 112 to 115 pound. Seasonal excursion trains are also operated on this line. The second line extends from a Union Pacific connection at Wolcott Junction to Saratoga, Wyoming, 24.3 miles. Rail is 131 to 133 pound. The third line, the Oregon Eastern Division, runs from a Union Pacific connection at Ontario, Oregon, to Celatom, 21 miles. Traffic on all three divisions consists primarily of forest products — 1,000 cars a year.

The Hebron line was built by the Laramie, Hahn's Peak & Pacific between 1904 and 1914. In 1914 the company was reorganized as the Colorado, Wyoming & Eastern Railway, and 10 years later it became the Laramie, North Park & Western. Union Pacific leased the railroad in 1936 and merged it in 1951.

The Saratoga line was built and operated by the Saratoga & Encampment Railroad between 1908 and 1928. Union Pacific leased it from November 1921 to October 1926. The company was reorganized as the Saratoga & Encampment Valley in May 1928 and remained under Union Pacific control until August 1951 when it was merged into Union Pacific.

Wyoming Colorado bought the two lines from Union Pacific in November 1987 and began service on December 19, 1987. It bought UP's Ontario-Burns line on November 6, 1989, and abandoned the 120 miles from Celatom to Burns in June 1992. The company is a subsidiary of Western Railroad Builders, Inc.

Radio frequency: 160.380
Location of enginehouse: Laramie and Wolcott Junction, Wyo.; Ontario, Ore.
Locomotives: 7

No.	Builder	Model	New	Builder No.
1365	EMD	GP9	7/59	25325
1510	EMD	F7A	1952	
1511	EMD	F7B	1952	
1512	EMD	F7A	1952	19065
1607	EMD	GP7	1/52	15634
1608	EMD	GP7	1/52	15635
6083	EMD	SD9	3/53	17124

Except for switching a warehouse in Laramie, the Wyoming Colorado makes its living operating a seasonal excursion train between Laramie and Fox Park. FP7As No. 1510 and 1512 head a southbound excursion near Centennial, Wyoming. Photo by Jack Armstrong.

YADKIN VALLEY RAILROAD CO.

P. O. Box 1218
Rural Hall, NC 27045

Reporting marks: YVRR
Phone: 910-969-6055
Fax: 910-969-9168

Yadkin Valley provides freight service from a connection with Norfolk Southern at Rural Hall, North Carolina, to North Wilkesboro, and from Mount Airy through Rural Hall to Brook Cove, a total of 101.7 miles. Rail is 85 to 100 pound. Traffic, about 11,000 cars a year, is primarily feed ingredients, coal, lumber, and building materials.

The North Wilkesboro line was completed by the North Western North Carolina Railroad (Richmond & Danville Railroad) on August 30, 1890. The Mount Airy line was completed by the Cape Fear & Yadkin Valley Railroad in June 1888. The company was absorbed by Southern in 1899.

Yadkin Valley is affiliated with Gulf & Ohio Railways (Pete Clausen), and is operating the lines under NS's Thoroughbred Short Line Program. It started operations on December 11, 1989.

Radio frequency: 160.980
Location of enginehouse: Rural Hall, N. C.
Locomotives: 10

No.	Builder	Model	New	Builder No.	Rebuilt
201	EMD	GP7	11/52	17048	
202	EMD	GP7	10/52	17039	
203	EMD	GP7	4/53	18051	
204	EMD	GP9	3/57	22930	
205	EMD	GP9	3/55	20344	
206	EMD	GP9	2/57	22781	
673	EMD	GP9	2/59	24825	
696	EMD	GP9	4/59	24848	
8092	EMD	GP10	4/53	17722	1975
8220	EMD	GP10	9/56	22545	1973

It takes six Geeps including a leased NS unit to pull the daily freight on the Yadkin Valley Railroad shown near Tobaccoville, North Carolina, in November 1992. Photo by Jim Shaw.

YOLO SHORTLINE RAILROAD CO.

1965 East Main Street
Woodland, CA 95776

Reporting marks: YSLR
Phone: 916-666-9646
Fax: 916-666-2919

The Yolo Shortline provides freight service from a connection with the Union Pacific at West Sacramento, California, to Clarksburg, 11 miles, and to Woodland, 17 miles. Rail is 60, 70, 85, 112, and 119 pound. Traffic includes coke, alcohol, sugar, tomato products, flour, and grain — under 2,000 cars a year. Seasonal excursion trains are operated between Woodland and West Scramento.

The Clarksburg line is made up of part of the former Sacramento Northern Railway Sacramento-Oakland main line (opened in 1913 by the Oakland, Antioch & Eastern), part of SN's Holland branch, opened in 1929, and a short spur of that line to a sugar beet plant at Clarksburg. The Woodland branch is a former Sacramento Northern branch built in 1911. Yolo Shortline bought the Clarksburg line from Union Pacific on February 4, 1991, and the Woodland line was acquired September 27, 1992. The company is controlled by Roger Stabler and Dave Magaw.
Radio frequency: 160.260
Location of enginehouse: Woodland, Calif.
Locomotives: 6

No.	Builder	Model	New	Builder No.
50	GE	50-ton	6/53	31801
101	Alco	S-1	5/42	69692
131	EMD	GP9U	1/57	24075
132	EMD	GP9U	4/54	19441
133	EMD	GP9U	5/56	21420
1233	BLW	0-6-0	7/18	49160

YORKRAIL, INC.

96 South George Street, Suite 400
York, PA 17401

Reporting marks: YKR
Phone: 717-771-1700
Fax: 717-854-6275

Yorkrail operates from connections with the Maryland & Pennsylvania and Conrail at York to a connection with CSX at Porters, Pennsylvania, 16 miles. Traffic consists of 7,000 cars a year of grain, paper, chemicals, and general freight.

The line is a former Western Maryland branch built in 1892 and 1893 by the Baltimore & Harrisburg Railway Eastern Extension. CSX sold it to Yorkrail on February 17, 1989. Yorkrail is a subsidiary of Emons Transportation Group, Inc.
Radio frequencies: 160.500 (road), 161.370 (switching)
Location of enginehouse: West York, Pa.
Locomotives: 4

No.	Builder	Model	New	Builder No.
1750	EMD	GP7	6/57	23018
1752	EMD	GP7	6/57	23011
1754	EMD	GP7	10/56	22234
1756	EMD	GP7	10/56	22230

Freight cars: 74 boxcars, 13 gondolas, 6 covered hoppers

YOUNGSTOWN & AUSTINTOWN RAILROAD CO.

136 South Fifth Street
Coshocton, OH 43812

Reporting marks: YARR
Phone: 614-622-8092

The Youngstown & Austintown operates 3.54 miles of former Erie track at Austintown, Ohio. It connects with Conrail and CSX. Rail is 90 to 140 pound. Traffic includes food products, lumber, fabricated steel, steel coils, and sand — over 500 cars a year.

The property was acquired from Conrail by the Economic Development Rail Corporation on January 29, 1985. It is now owned by the Mahoning Valley Economic Development Council. The operating company is part of the Ohio Central Railroad System (J. J. Jacobson).

Radio frequency: 160.845
Locomotives: 3

No.	Builder	Model	New	Builder No.
14	Alco	S-4	6/41	69487
19	Alco	S-4	1/52	79525
71	EMD	GP7	4/53	17982

YREKA WESTERN RAILROAD CO.

300 East Miner Street
P. O. Box 660
Yreka, CA 96097

Reporting marks: YW
Phone: 916-842-4146
Fax: 916-842-4148

Yreka Western operates freight service from Yreka, California, to a connection with the Central Oregon & Pacific at Montague, 8.86 miles. Rail is 75 pound. Traffic includes wood chips, forest products, and propane, under 500 cars a year. "Blue Goose" excursion service started in June 1986.

The Yreka Railroad was incorporated May 28, 1888, and opened January 9, 1889. The Yreka Western Railroad was incorporated August 24, 1933, to acquire the property of the Yreka Railroad — operations started on April 18, 1935. The company is owned by Kyle Railways, Inc.

Radio frequency: 161.070
Location of enginehouse: Yreka, Calif.
Locomotives: 4

No.	Builder	Model	New	Builder No.
18	BLW	2-8-2	9/14	41709
19	BLW	2-8-2	3/15	42000
20	EMD	SW8	3/53	17335
21	EMD	SW8	3/53	17337

Yreka Southern hauls freight and passengers through a scenic area of northern California. SW8 No. 21 is pulling a longer-than-average freight out of Yreka, California. Photo by Jim Shaw.

OWNERSHIP AND CONTROL

This list of shortline holding companies and group operators does not include companies affiliated with Class 1 railroads or non-operating or leased subsidiaries.

Aberdeen & Rockfish Railroad Company
P. O. Box 917, Aberdeen, NC 28315
Phone: 910-944-2341
    Dunn-Erwin Railway Division
    Pee Dee River Railway Division

Abernathy, Richard G.
P. O. Box 1317, Shelbyville, TN 37160
Phone: 615-684-7376
    Sequatchie Valley Railroad
    Southern Alabama Railroad
    Walking Horse & Eastern Railroad

Alcoa (Aluminum Company of America)
425 Sixth Avenue, Pitttsburgh, PA 15219
Phone: 412-553-4172
    Bauxite & Northern Railway
    Massena Terminal Railroad
    Point Comfort & Northern Railway
    Rockdale, Sandow & Southern Railroad

American Railroads Corporation
207 South Cook Street
Barrington, IL 60010
Phone: 708-382-0500
    Gulf, Colorado & San Saba Railway
    Texas & Oklahoma Railroad

Arkansas Shortline Railroads, Inc.
P. O. Box 150, Dardanelle, AR 72834
Phone: 501-968-6455
    Caddo, Antoine & Little
      Missouri Railroad
    Dardanelle & Russellville Railroad
    Ouachita Railroad

Bethlehem Steel Corporation
1170 Eighth Avenue, Bethlehem, PA 18018
Phone: 215-694-5972
    Conemaugh & Black Lick Railroad
    Patapsco & Black River Railroad
    Philadelphia, Bethlehem &
      New England Railroad
    South Buffalo Railway
    Steelton & Highspire Railroad

CAGY Industries, Inc.
P. O. Box 6000, Columbus, MS 39703
Phone: 601-328-6331
    Columbus & Greenville Railway
    Chattooga & Chickamauga Railway
    Redmont Railway

Central Properties, Inc.
P. O. Box 505, Kokomo, IN 46901
Phone: 317-868-8107
    Central Railroad Co. of Indiana
    Central Railroad Co. of Indianapolis
    Winamac Southern Railway

Champion International Corporation
1 Landmark Square, Stamford, CT 06921
Phone: 203-357-8500
    Angelina & Neches River Railroad
    Moscow, Camden &
      San Augustine Railroad

Claussen, Pete (Gulf & Ohio Railways)
401 Henely Street, Suite 5
Knoxville, TN 37902
Phone: 615-525-9400
    Atlantic & Gulf Railroad

    Georgia & Florida Railroad
    H&S Railroad
    Mississippi Delta Railroad
    Nash County Railway
    Wiregrass Central Railroad
    Yadkin Valley Railroad

Corman, R. J.
P. O. Box 788, Nicholasville, KY 40356
Phone: 606-885-9457
    R. J. Corman Railroad Corp.
    R. J. Corman Railroad Co. —
      Memphis Div.
    R. J. Corman Railroad Co. —
      Cleveland Div.
    R. J. Corman Railroad Co. —
      Western Ohio Line

Cornell, Sloan
P. O. Box 4745, Gettysburg, PA 17325
Phone: 717-334-2411
    Gettysburg Railroad
    Knox & Kane Railroad

CSF Acquisitions Co. (Clyde Forbes)
P. O. Box 1267, Trenton, FL 32693
Phone: 904-463-1103
    Florida West Coast Railroad
    Lamoille Valley Railroad
    New Hampshire & Vermont Railroad
    Twin State Railroad
    Washington County Railroad

Dingman, Robert O.
50 Commercial Street, Gowanda, NY 14070
Phone: 716-532-5242
    New York & Lake Erie Railroad
    Oil Creek & Titusville Lines

St. Lawrence & Raquette River
Railroad
**Durden, K. E./Rail Switching Service/
Rail Management & Consulting Corp./
Green Bay Packaging**
P. O. Box 28300, Panama City, FL 32411
Phone: 904-230-8331
    A&G Railroad
    Atlantic & Western Railway, LP
    The Bay Line Railroad
    Copper Basin Railway
    East Tennessee Railway
    Galveston Railway
    Georgia Central Railway
    KWT Railway
    Little Rock & Western Railway
    Tomahawk Railway
    Valdosta Railway
    Western Kentucky Railway
    Wilmington Terminal Railroad
**Emergent Group
(formerly National Railway Utilization)**
P. O. Box 17526, Greenville, SC 29606
Phone: 803-235-8056
    Peninsula Terminal Company
    Pickens Railroad
Emons Transportation Group, Inc.
96 S. George Street, Suite 520
York, PA 17401
Phone: 717-771-1700
    Maryland & Pennsylvania Railroad
    St. Lawrence & Atlantic Railroad
    YorkRail
Farmrail System (George Betke)
P. O. Box 17501, Clinton, OK 73601
Phone: 405-323-1234
    Farmrail Corp.

Finger Lakes Railway — jointly with
Genesee & Wyoming
Grainbelt Corp.
Fay, Gordon, and George Bartholomew
4110 Centerpointe Drive, Suite 207
Fort Myers, FL 33916
Phone: 813-275-6060
    Bay Colony Railroad
    Seminole Gulf Railway
Frick, Daniel R.
P. O. Box 68, Monterey, IN 46960
Phone: 219-542-2031
    JK Lines
    Winamac Southern Railway —
      operated by Central Properties
Genesee & Wyoming Industries, Inc.
71 Lewis Street, Greenwich, CT 06830
Phone: 203-629-3722
    Allegheny & Eastern Railroad
    Bradford Industrial Rail
    Buffalo & Pittsburgh Railroad
    Dansville & Mount Morris Railroad
    Finger Lakes Railway — jointly with
      Farmrail
    Genesee & Wyoming Railroad
    GWI Switching Services
    Louisiana & Delta Railroad
    Portland & Western Railroad
    Rochester & Southern Railroad
    Willamette & Pacific Railroad
Genesee Valley Transportation Co.
8364 Lewiston Road
Batavia, NY 14020-1245
Phone: 716-343-5398
    Delaware Lackawanna Railroad
    Depew, Lancaster & Western Railroad
    Genesee & Mohawk Valley Railroad

Lowville & Beaver River Railroad
Mohawk, Adirondack &
    Northern Railroad
Georgia Pacific Corporation
P. O. Box 757, Crossett, AR 71635
Phone: 501-567-8562
    Amador Central Railroad
    Arkansas, Louisiana &
      Mississippi Railroad
    Ashley, Drew & Northern Railway
    Blue Rapids Railway
    Chattahoochee Industrial Railroad
    Fordyce & Princeton Railroad
    Gloster Southern Railroad
    Old Augusta Railroad
Gulf & Ohio Railways — *see Claussen, Pete*
Hohorst, Henry
113 East River Road, Rumson, NJ 07760
Phone: 908-842-0912
    Tennken Railroad
    West Tennessee Railroad
Indiana & Ohio Rail Corporation
8901 Blue Ash Road, Cincinnati, OH 45242
Phone: 513-891-9191
    Cincinnati Terminal Railway
    Indiana & Ohio Railroad
    Indiana & Ohio Railway
    Indiana & Ohio Central
International Paper Co.
6400 Poplar, Memphis, TN 38197
Phone: 901-763-6226
    Longview, Portland & Northern Railway
    Mississippi Export Railroad
**Ironhorse Resources, Inc.
(Gregory B. Cundiff)**
P. O. Box 99, O'Fallon, IL 62269
Phone: 618-632-4400

BSDA Railroad
Railroad Switching Service of Missouri
Rio Valley Switching Co.
Southern Switching Co.

Iron Road Railways (Robert T. Schmidt)
1828 L Street, N.W., Suite 402
Washington, DC 20036
Phone: 202-296-0535
    Bangor & Aroostook Railroad
    Canadian American Railroad
    Iowa Northern Railway
    Windsor & Hantsport Railway

James River Corporation
P. O. Box 2218, Richmond, VA 23217
Phone: 804-782-8325
    Berlin Mills Railway
    Meridian & Bigbee Railroad

Kyle Railways
8687 Via de Ventura, Scottsdale, AZ 85258
Phone: 602-443-3939
    Arizona Eastern Railway
    California Western Railroad
      (Mendocino Coast Railway)
    Eastern Alabama Railway
    Kyle Railroad
    Port Railroads
    San Joaquin Valley Railroad
    San Pedro & Southwestern Railroad
    Tulare Valley Railroad — operator
    Yreka Western Railroad

Laurinburg & Southern Railroad Co.
P. O. Box 1929, Laurinburg, NC 28353
Phone: 910-276-0786
    Red Springs & Northern Railroad

LTV Steel/Jones & Laughlin Steel
4166 Second Avenue, Pittsburgh, PA 15219
Phone: 412-227-4903

Mahoning Valley Railway
Monongahela Connecting Railroad
Aliquippa & Southern Railroad
Chicago Short Line Railway
Cuyahoga Valley Railway
Midland Terminal Co
River Terminal Railway

Lukens Industries
50 South First Avenue, Coatesville, PA 19320
Phone: 215-383-3202
    Brandywine Valley Railroad
    Upper Merion & Plymouth Railroad

Magma Copper Co.
7400 North Oracle Road, Suite 200
Tucson, AZ 85704
    Magma Arizona Railroad
    San Manuel Arizona Railroad

May, Steven
475 Slocum Road, Exeter, PA 18643
Phone: 717-693-7565
    Luzerne & Susquehanna Railway
    Owego & Harford Railway

Ohio Railroad System (J. J. Jacobson) —
Summit View Corporation
136 S. Fifth Street, Coshocton, OH 43812
Phone: 614-622-8092
    Columbus & Ohio River Railroad
    Ohio & Pennsylvania Railroad
    Ohio Central Railroad
    Ohio Southern Railroad
    Warren & Trumbull Railroad
    Youngstown & Austintown Railroad

OmniTRAX, Inc. — Patrick Broe
252 Clayton Street, Suite 400
Denver, CO 80206
Phone: 303-393-0033
    Central Kansas Railway

Chicago Rail Link
Chicago, West Pullman &
    Southern Railroad
Council Bluffs Railway
Georgia Woodlands Railroad
Great Western Railway of Colorado
Great Western Railway of Oregon
Kansas Southwestern
Manufacturers' Junction Railway
Newburg & South Shore Railroad
Northern Ohio & Western Railway

Parkinson, David L.
1470 Railroad Avenue
Saint Helena, CA 94574
Phone: 707-963-8831
    Arizona & California Railroad
    California Northern Railroad

Pinsly Railroad Company
53 Southampton Road
Westfield, MA 01085
Phone: 413-568-6426
    Arkansas Midland Railroad
    Florida Central Railroad
    Florida Midland Railroad
    Florida Northern Railroad
    Greenville & Northern Railroad
    Pioneer Valley Railroad

Pioneer RailCorporation
1318 South Johanson Road, Peoria, IL 61607
Phone: 309-697-1400
    Alabama Railroad
    Alabama & Florida Railroad
    Decatur Junction Railroad
    Fort Smith Railroad
    Minnesota Central Railroad
    Mississippi Central Railroad
    Vandalia Railroad

Potlatch Corporation
P. O. Box 3591, San Francisco, CA 94111
Phone: 415-981-5980
    Duluth & Northeastern Railroad
    Prescott & Northwestern Railroad
    St. Maries River Railroad
    Warren & Saline River Railroad
RailAmerica, Inc.
1800 Diagonal Road, Suite 600
Alexandria, VA 22314
Phone: 703-683-7600
    Delaware Valley Railway
    Huron & Eastern Railway
    Saginaw Valley Railway
    South Central Tennessee Railroad
RailLink, Inc.
1 Park West Circle, Suite 201
Midlothian, VA 23113
Phone: 804-379-4664
    Carolina Coastal Railway
    Commonwealth Railway
RailTex, Inc.
4040 Broadway, Suite 200
San Antonio, TX 78209
Phone: 210-841-7600
    Austin Railroad d/b/a
        Austin & Northwestern Railroad
    Blue Rapids Railway — operated by
        Northeast Kansas & Missouri
    Cape Breton & Central Nova
        Scotia Railway
    Central Oregon & Pacific Railroad
    Chesapeake & Albemarle Railroad
    Dallas, Garland & Northern Railroad
    Goderich-Exeter Railway
    Grand Rapids & Eastern Railroad
    Indiana Southern Railroad

    Michigan Shore Railroad
    Mid-Michigan Railroad
    Northeast Kansas & Missouri Railway
    Texas Northeastern Railroad
    Missouri & Northern Arkansas Railroad
    New England Central Railroad
    New Orleans Lower Coast Railroad
    North Carolina & Virginia Railroad
    Virginia Southern Railroad Division
    Salt Lake City Southern Railroad
    San Diego & Imperial Valley Railroad
    South Carolina Central Railroad
    Carolina Piedmont Division
    Georgia & Alabama Division
    Georgia Great Southern Division
    Georgia Southwestern Division
    Texas & New Mexico Railroad
Rail-West, Inc.
P. O. Box 917, McMinnville, OR 97128
Phone: 503-434-9400
    Willamette Valley Railway
    Willamina & Grande Ronde Railway
**Reading & Northern System
(Andrew Muller, Jr.)**
P. O. Box 218, Port Clinton, PA 19549
Phone: 610-562-2100
    Blue Mountain & Reading Railroad
    East Mahanoy & Hazleton Railroad
    Reading, Blue Mountain &
        Northern Railroad
Rio Grande Pacific Corporation
4420 West Vickery Boulevard, Suite 110
Fort Worth, TX 76107
Phone: 817-737-7288
    Idaho Northern & Pacific Railroad
    Nebraska Central Railroad
    Wichita, Tillman & Jackson Railway

Robey, Richard
356 Priestley Avenue
Northumberland, PA 17857
Phone: 717-473-7949
    Nittany & Bald Eagle Railroad
    North Shore Railroad
    Shamokin Valley Railroad
    Stourbridge Railroad
    Union County Industrial Railroad
    Wellsboro & Corning Railroad
    West Shore Railroad
**South Carolina Public Railways
Commission**
P. O. Box 279, Charleston, SC 29402
Phone: 803-727-2067
    East Cooper & Berkeley Railroad
    Port Royal Railroad
    Port Terminal Railroad of South
        Carolina
    Port Utilities Commission of
        South Carolina
Stone Container Corporation
150 North Michigan Avenue
Chicago, IL 60601
Phone: 312-346-6600
    Apache Railway
Tarantula Corporation
6300 Ridglea Place, Suite 1200
Fort Worth, TX 76116
Phone: 817-763-8297
    Fort Worth & Dallas Railroad
    Fort Worth & Dallas Belt Railroad
    Fort Worth & Western Railroad
Temple Inland Corporation
    Sabine River & Northern Railroad
    Texas South-Eastern Railroad

TNW Corporation
HCR 1, Box 9, Sunray, TX 79086
Phone: 806-935-7474
    Texas, Gonzales & Northern Railroad
    Texas North Western Railway
Transtar, Inc.
(Blackstone Limited Partners)
P. O. Box 68, Monroeville, PA 15146
Phone: 412-829-3463
    Bessemer & Lake Erie Railroad
    Birmingham Southern Railroad
    Duluth, Missabe & Iron Range
      Railway
    Elgin, Joliet & Eastern Railroad
    Lake Terminal Railroad
    McKeesport Connecting Railroad
    Union Railroad

Walker, Arthur T, Estate Corporation
    Mountain Laurel Railroad
    Pittsburg & Shawmut Railroad
    Red Bank Railroad
Webb, C. R.
Coffeyville, KS 67337
Phone: 316-251-3600
    Blue Mountain Railroad
    Eastern Idaho Railroad
    Osage Railroad
    Palouse River Railroad
    South Kansas & Oklahoma Railroad
    Southeast Kansas Railroad
Western Railroad Builders, Inc.
P. O. Box 1855, Ogden, UT 84402
Phone: 801-393-4525
    Arizona Central Railroad

    Southwestern Railroad
    Wyoming Colorado Railroad
Weyerhaeuser Co.
33663 32nd Drive South
Federal Way, WA 98003
Phone: 206-924-5272
    Columbia & Cowlitz Railway
    Curtis, Milburn & Eastern Railroad
    DeQueen & Eastern Railroad
    Golden Triangle Railroad
    Mississippi & Skuna Valley Railroad
    Texas, Oklahoma & Eastern Railroad
Wulfson family
1 Railway Lane, Burlington, VT 05401
Phone: 802-658-2550
    Clarendon & Pittsford Railroad
    Vermont Railway

NON-OPERATING RAILROADS

The railroad companies listed below share one characteristic: They no longer operate rail service but they still have a corporate existence. Some are in various stages of abandonment; others are just in suspension or are abandoned except for the formalities.

BUFFALO CREEK RAILROAD CO.

Reporting Marks: BC
Buffalo Creek Railroad acquired the property of the Buffalo Creek & Gauley Railroad from Dundon, to Widen, West Virginia, 18.6 miles, in November 1991. The company is controlled by William T. Bright and is affiliated with the Elk River Railroad. Neither Buffalo Creek nor Elk River is currently in service.

CENTRAL NEW YORK RAILROAD CORP.

1 Railroad Avenue   **Reporting Marks:** CNYK
Cooperstown, NY 13326   **Phone:** 315-732-1774
The Central New York, which is owned by the Delaware Otsego Corporation, owns a line extending from a connection with New York, Susquehanna & Western (Northern Division) at Richfield Junction, New York, to Richfield Springs, 21.7 miles — a former Lackawanna branch. Operations were suspended in early 1988. On August 21, 1995, the ICC approved abandonment.

ELK RIVER RAILROAD INC.

300 Greenbrier Road
P. O. Box 460
Summersville, WV 26651

Reporting Marks: ELKR
Phone: 304-872-3000
Fax: 304-872-3033

Elk River Railroad owns a line extending from a CSX connection at Burnsville Junction, near Gilmer, West Virginia, to Hartland, 61 miles. It also connects with the Buffalo Creek Railroad at Dundon. Rail is 85 to 132 pound. There is potential coal traffic if mining operations are developed. The road is not currently in service.

The line was built by the Charleston, Glendennin & Sutton, chartered in 1893. It became part of the Coal & Coke Railway in 1903, and that became part of Baltimore & Ohio by 1918. CSX, successor to Chessie System and B&O, suspended service on this line in 1988 and sold the property to the current operator in August 1989. The company is owned by William T. Bright.

Location of enginehouse: Gassaway, W. Va.

Locomotives: 1

No.	Builder	Model	New	Builder No.	Rebuilt
1	ICG	GP10	12/57	23837	1974

KCT RAILWAY CORP.

P. O. Box 26421
Salt Lake City, UT 84126

Reporting Marks: KCTV
Phone: 801-972-8330

KCT Railway was formed in May 1990 to acquire several Santa Fe branch lines totaling about 148 miles. It does not currently operate any of its track and most sections have been formally abandoned. The company is affiliated with A&K Railroad Materials Co.

LEELANAU TRANSIT CO.

P. O. Box 631
Sutton's Bay, MI 49682

Reporting Marks: LTCR

Leelanau Transit owns a "landlocked" rail line from Rennies, Michigan, just north of Traverse City, to Sutton Bay, 31 miles. The line has not provided freight service since 1973, and its connection with the Chesapeake & Ohio was removed in 1982. The line was built by the Traverse City, Leelanau & Manistique Railway about 1903. It was leased to and operated for many years by the Manistee & Northeastern Railway, then C&O. Excursion trains were started in 1991 by the Leelanau Scenic Railroad, a separate company. The company is independent.

Locomotives: 2 (owned by Leelanau Scenic Railroad)

No.	Builder	Model	New	Builder No.
5258	EMD	SW9	11/51	15517
5298	EMD	NW2	5/48	5556

LOUISVILLE & WADLEY RAILWAY CO.

P. O. Box 71
Louisville, GA 30434

Reporting Marks: LW
Phone: 912-252-5980

Louisville & Wadley owns a line from a connection with Norfolk Southern at Wadley, Georgia, to Gibson Junction, 2 miles. Rail is 56 to 80 pound. Rail service is suspended.

The company was incorporated September 18, 1961, to purchase the property of the Louisville & Wadley Railroad, which had been incorporated on August 24, 1872. The rail line opened in October 1879, and passenger service lasted until 1953.

Service to Louisville was discontinued in 1971 due to bridge failure, but substitute service is available. The railroad is owned by B. D. Gibson.

Freight cars: 46 plain and insulated boxcars

LUDINGTON & NORTHERN RAILWAY

2840 Bay Road
Saginaw, MI 48603

Reporting Marks: LUN
Phone: 602-385-3456

The Ludington & Northern owns a rail line from a connection with the CSX at Ludington, Michigan, to North Epworth, 2.79 miles. Rail is 90 pound. Service has been suspended for several years.

The company was incorporated July 18, 1901, and constructed a line from Ludington to Epworth, 4.5 miles. Operations were discontinued for a period in the mid-1930s. The company is independent.

THE OLYMPIC RAILROAD CO.

6429 129th Ave., S.E.   **Reporting Marks:** OLYR
Bellevue, WA 98006   **Phone:** 206-644-2534

The Olympic Railroad owns terminal trackage at Port Townsend, Washington, and connects by barge with Burlington Northern and Union Pacific at Seattle. The railroad is not currently in operation.

The line was built by The Port Townsend Southern Railroad. It was sold to the Milwaukee in May 1975. After Milwaukee Road discontinued its western operations, Seattle & North Coast operated it until it went bankrupt and closed in June 1984. The current operator took over on June 5, 1988.

Locomotives: 1

No.	Builder	Model	New	Builder No.
52	EMD	SW1	3/40	1045

Freight cars: 145 boxcars

SOUTHERN SAN LUIS VALLEY RAILROAD

2255 Lava Lane   **Reporting Marks:** SSLV
Alamosa, CO 81101   **Phone:** 719-589-4925
   Fax: 719-589-5559

The Southern San Luis Valley Railroad owns a mile of track between Blanca and McClintock, Colorado. It connects with the Denver & Rio Grande Western at Blanca. Rail is 65 pound. Service is suspended. The San Luis Valley Southern Railway was incorporated July 3, 1909, and opened a line from Blanca to the Colorado-New Mexico border on September 1, 1910. The company was reorganized as the San Luis Valley Southern Railway in 1948, and the present name was adopted December 11, 1953. The railroad is controlled by Colorado Aggregates Co.

Location of enginehouse: Blanca, Colo.

Locomotives: 2

No.	Builder	Model	New	Builder No.
1	Plymouth	ML-8	5/41	4161
D500	SLVS	20-ton	11/55	

TUCSON, CORNELIA & GILA BEND RAILROAD CO.

2600 North Central Avenue   **Reporting Marks:** TCG
Phoenix, AZ 85004-3014   **Phone:** 602-234-8100

The Tucson, Cornelia & Gila Bend owns a rail line from a connection with the Southern Pacific at Gila Bend, Arizona, to Ajo, 43.3 miles. Rail is 70 pound.

The railroad was incorporated May 10, 1915, and opened for traffic on February 20, 1916. Passengers were carried into the mid 1980s. Service was suspended on April 12, 1985, when copper mining was curtailed in the Ajo area. Phelps Dodge Corporation owns the company.

Location of enginehouse: Ajo, Ariz.

Locomotives: 2

No.	Builder	Model	New	Builder No.
52	EMD	NW2	6/47	4845
53	EMD	SW7	1/51	13981

WINIFREDE RAILROAD CO.

P. O. Box 70   **Reporting Marks:** WNFR
Winifrede, WV 25214   **Phone:** 304-949-1837

The Winifrede Railroad owns a line from West Carbon (Winifrede), West Virginia, to a connection with CSX at Winifrede Junction, 6.75 miles. Rail is 85 and 100 pound. Service was suspended in 1989.

The company was incorporated November 15, 1881, and the railroad opened for business the following year. It is controlled by Carbon Industries.

Radio frequency: 160.830

Location of enginehouse: West Carbon, W. Va.

Freight cars: 200 covered hoppers

SHORT LINES NO LONGER IN EXISTENCE

The short line industry is undergoing constant change. Some short lines have grown enough to make themselves attractive buyout candidates for their connecting trunk lines, while others dependent on a single source of revenue and traffic have seen that source vanish and found themselves facing hard times and abandonment. Still others have been sold to and reorganized by new owners. This section covers U. S. railroads that have disappeared since 1985. Railroads controlled or owned by a Class 1 carrier for a number of years are shown with the owning road's initials following their name.

Abbeville Grimes Railway: Abbeville to Grimes, Alabama, 26.7 miles. Assets sold to A&G Railroad on January 1, 1994.

Aberdeen & Briar Patch Railway: Aberdeen to Star, North Carolina, 34.46 miles. Sold to Aberdeen, Carolina & Western June 1987.

Ahnapee & Western Railway: Casco Junction to Algoma, Wisconsin, 14 miles. Service ended about 1987 due to a failed bridge. As of October 25, 1990, no longer a common carrier.

Akron & Barberton Belt Railroad: East Akron to Barberton and Rittman, Ohio, 19.44 miles. Assets sold to the Akron Barberton Cluster Railway on July 21, 1994.

Alabama Industrial Railroad: Huntsville to Norton, Alabama, 13.2 miles. A former Louisville & Nashville branch line operated from June 1984 to February 18, 1985, when the owner, Huntsville & Madison County Railroad Authority, took over operation.

Alabama Southern Railroad: York to Lilita, Alabama, 10.3 miles. Acquired the Sumpter & Choctaw Railroad from the Southern Railway early in 1985 and filed for abandonment April 29, 1985, without operating.

Allegheny Railroad: Erie to Emporium, Pennsylvania, 149.2 miles. Property acquired by Allegheny & Eastern November 25, 1992.

Andalusia & Conecuh Railroad: Andalusia to Gantt, Alabama, 8.7 miles. Started operations in June 1983 and abandoned its line on October 17, 1987. A 2-mile piece at Andalusia is operated by the Alabama & Florida Railway.

Alabama & Florida Railroad: Reorganized as Alabama & Florida Railway November 23, 1992.

Anthracite Railway: The Perkiomen branch was turned over to the Blue Mountain & Reading Railroad in mid-1988, and the Kutztown and Boyertown branches followed on July 1, 1989.

Arcata & Mad River Railroad: Korblex to Korbel, California, 7.7 miles. Discontinued service in 1983 following suspension of service on the Northwestern Pacific. Abandoned on May 24, 1985. Service resumed in 1994 by the North Coast Railroad.

Arkansas & Louisiana Missouri Railway: Monroe, Louisiana, to Crossett, Arkansas, 54.4 miles. Property acquired by Arkansas, Louisiana & Mississippi Railroad on September 27, 1991.

Arkansas Western Railway (KCS): Heavener, Oklahoma, to Waldron, Arkansas, 31.8 miles. Merged into Kansas City Southern on July 1, 1992.

Atlanta & St. Andrews Bay Railway: Panama City, Florida, to Dothan, Alabama, 81 miles. Assets sold to The Bay Line on January 1, 1994.

Baltimore & Annapolis Railroad: Baltimore (Clifford) to Glen Burnie, Maryland, 6 miles. Property acquired by Maryland Mass Transit Administration in October 1991. Freight service is operated by Canton Railroad.

Bath & Hammondsport Railroad: Hammondsport to Bath and Wayland, New York, 21.2 miles. Assets sold to Steuben County Industrial Development Agency in February 1993, then leased to Champagne Railroad for continued operation.

Belton Railroad: Belton to Smith, Texas, 6.2 miles. Assets sold to Georgetown Railroad on June 3, 1991.

Borinstein Railroad: Switching line at Indianapolis, Indiana. Out of business about 1994.

Brillion & Forest Junction Railroad: Forest Junction to Brillion, Wisconsin, 6.7 miles. Former Chicago & North Western branch line operated from June 1978 until abandonment on April 4, 1985, because of loss of lease.

Buffalo Creek & Gauley Railroad: Dundon to Widen, West Virginia, 18.6 miles. Sold to Buffalo Creek Railroad November 1991.

Buffalo Ridge Railroad: Sioux Falls, South Dakota to Agate (Worthington), Minnesota, 62 miles. Service ended June 1992. The property is owned by local I.D.A. and is now operated by the Nobles Rock Railroad.

Butte, Anaconda & Pacific Railway: Butte to Brown, Montana, 31.9 miles. Abandoned spring 1985. The property was acquired by the state of Montana and is operated by the Rarus Railway.

C&J Railroad: Hopkinsville to Gracy, Kentucky, 33.5 miles. The company filed for bankruptcy in March 1987 and made its last run on November 12, 1987.

Cadillac & Lake City Railroad: Limon to Cimarron Hills, Colorado (near Colorado Springs), 68.7 miles. Operated until December 1989, when the company declared bankruptcy.

Cadiz Railroad: Cadiz to Gracey and Princeton, Kentucky, 28.9 miles. Abandonment approved November 23, 1988.

Cambria & Indiana Railroad: Clover to Revloc, Pennsylvania, 27.9 miles. Coal lines closed and the last revenue run was made on July 15, 1994. Abandoned November 11, 1994.

Camino, Placerville & Lake Tahoe Railroad: Placerville (Smith Flat) to Camino, California, 8.05 miles. Last run June 17, 1986. The company has abandoned operations.

Carolina & Northwestern Railroad: Hickory to Lenoir, North Carolina, 22.3 miles. Property sold to a local authority and leased to Caldwell County Railroad on September 26, 1994.

Cedar Valley Railroad: Albert Lea, Minnesota, to Mona Junction (Waterloo), Iowa, 94.3 miles. Assets sold to Cedar River Railroad December 31, 1991.

Central Louisiana & Gulf Railroad: Hodge to Alexandria, Louisiana, 71 miles. The company started operations in April 1981 over a former Rock Island branch line and was absorbed by MidLouisiana Rail Corporation in July 1987.

Central Wisconsin Railroad: Madison to Freeport, Wisconsin, 60.4 miles, and Waukesha to Mineral Point, 128.2 miles. Operations over these former Milwaukee Road lines ceased January 3, 1985, because of insurance problems.

Chaparral Railroad: Paris to Farmersville, Texas, 60.1 miles. Abandoned in 1995.

Charles City Rail Lines: Switching line at Charles City, Iowa. Ceased operations February 24, 1994, due to lack of funds.

Chattahoochee Valley Railway: West Point, Georgia, to McGinty, Alabama, 9.45 miles. Operations abandoned early in 1992.

Chelatchie Prairie Railroad: Rye Junction to Chelatchie Prairie, Washington, 29.5 miles. Former Longview, Portland & Northern line, acquired July 22, 1981. Abandonment was authorized on August 29, 1985, and part of the line is now operated by Lewis & Clark Railway.

Chicago, Missouri & Western Railway: Declared bankruptcy April 1, 1988. Chicago-St. Louis line sold to SPCSL Corp. (SP) in November 1989; Kansas City line sold to Gateway Western Railroad January 8, 1990.

Chillicothe-Brunswick Rail Maintenance Authority: Chillicothe to Brunswick, Missouri, 37 miles. Property leased to Wabash & Grand River Railway on April 1, 1990.

Chillicothe Southern Railroad: Chillicothe to Brunswick, Missouri, 39 miles. Removed on July 24, 1987, by owner, Green Hills Rural Development Authority, which continues to operate the line as Chillicothe-Brunswick Rail Maintenance Authority.

Cimarron River Valley Railway: Camp to Cushing, Oklahoma, 25.5 miles. Discontinued operations in April 1989 and received abandonment authority July 22, 1989.

Cliffside Railroad: Cliffside to Ellenboro, North Carolina, 8.1 miles. Service ended in 1987 and the line was formally abandoned in January 1992.

Colleton County Railroad: H&B Junction to Walterboro, South Carolina, plus a short branch, 28 miles. Organized to take over a Seaboard System branch line effective November 1, 1986. On January 20, 1988, it was merged into Hampton & Branchville.

Colorado & Eastern Railroad: Operated several track segments in Colorado, Iowa, and Missouri. Reorganized in February 1987 as Great Northern Transportation Co. and each line segment given its own name.

Columbia & Silver Creek Railroad:
• Columbia to Silver Creek, Mississippi, 28.7 miles. Operation taken over by Gloster Southern on November 1, 1988.
• Taylorsville to Saso, Mississippi, 10 miles. Abandoned about 1992.

Connecticut Rail Systems (P&W): Merged into Providence & Worcester September 1, 1993.

Cooperstown & Charlotte Valley Railway: Cooperstown to Cooperstown Junction, New York, 16.4 miles. Discontinued common carrier service April 25, 1989, after several years of minimal activity. Abandonment approved in July 1995.

Corinth & Counce Railroad: Corinth, Mississippi, to Counce, Tennessee, 16.5 miles. Assets sold to Tennrail December 31, 1991.

Council Bluffs & Ottuma Railway: Switching operation at Council Bluffs, Iowa. Assets sold to Council Bluffs Railroad in May 1991.

Crosbyton Railroad: Lubbock to Crosbyton, Texas, 36.14 miles. Started operations in January 1990 and was abandoned before the year was out. Traffic was minimal.

Crystal City Railroad: Gardendale to Carrizo Springs, Texas, 55 miles. Last train operated February 13, 1995. Abandonment approved by the ICC June 1995.

Curtis, Milburn & Eastern Railroad: CM&E Junction to Curtis, Washington. Abandoned in February 1993.

Davenport, Rock Island & North Western Railway: Switching and terminal company at Davenport, Iowa, and Rock Island, Illinois. Ended service June 29, 1995; operations taken over by its owners, Burlington Northern and CP Rail (Soo Line).

Denver Terminal Railroad: Switching line at Denver, Colorado. Operated from October 1993 to September 1994. Operated briefly as Platte Valley Railway, then assets sold to Denver Rock Island Railroad.

Denver Terminal Railway: Switching line at Denver, Colorado. Property sold to Denver Railway in July 1989.

Des Moines Union Railway: Switching line at Des Moines, Iowa. Company merged into Norfolk & Western Railway March 2, 1989.

Detroit & Mackinac Railway: Bay City to Cheyboygan, Michigan, plus branch lines, 348 miles. Most of the line was sold to Lake States Railway February 17, 1992, and the rest was abandoned.

Duval Transportation of the Carolinas, Inc.: Mullins to Whiteville, North Carolina, and Conway, South Carolina, 76 miles. Name changed to Mid-Atlantic Railroad on November 5, 1987, following a change of management.

Elkhorn & Walworth Railroad: Janesville to Elkhorn and Walworth, Wisconsin, 37.6 miles. Operations discontinued January 3, 1985, because of insurance problems.

Eureka Southern Railroad: Willits to Korblex, California, 156 miles. Assets purchased by North Coast Rail Authority on April 1, 1992, and leased to North Coast Railroad for continued service.

Fairmont & Western Railroad: Elrod to Fairmont, North Carolina, 12.78 miles. Line closed in 1988; track removed July 1989.

Falls Creek Railroad: Falls Creek to Minns Summit, Pennsylvania, 4.5 miles. Operations ended in March 1988 following the bankruptcy of its owner, Benjamin Coal Co.

Ferdinand Railroad: Ferdinand to Huntingburg, Indiana, 6.48 miles. Company assets sold to Ferdinand & Huntingburg Railroad on November 10, 1987.

Ferdinand & Huntingburg Railroad: Ferdinand to Huntingburg, Indiana, 6.5 miles. Last run March 3, 1991; road abandoned.

Fonda, Johnstown & Gloversville Railroad: Fonda to Broadalbin, New York, 19.7 miles. Operations discontinued in March 1984; abandoned July 4, 1988; track removed in 1990.

Fore River Railway: Quincy Point to East Braintree, Massachusetts, 2.14 miles. Owner leased property to Quincy Bay Terminal February 1, 1992.

Fort Smith & Van Buren Railroad (KCS): Coal Creek to McCurtain, Oklahoma, 18 miles. Merged into Kansas City Southern on July 1, 1992.

Fox River Valley Railroad: Green Bay to Milwaukee, Wisconsin, plus branch lines, 214 miles. Merged into Fox Valley & Western Ltd. on August 28, 1993.

Frankfort & Cincinnati Railroad: Frankfort to Stagg and Elsinor, Kentucky, 6.64 miles. Abandonment authorized effective November 11, 1985.

Franklin County Railroad: Franklinton to Louisburg, North Carolina, 10 miles. Short line service over a former Seaboard System branch started on November 4, 1985. Abandonment approved during 1987 and service discontinued on February 10, 1988.

Fulton County Railroad: Rochester to Monterey, Indiana, over former Erie Lackawanna main line. Operated from April 1981 to 1985 using Tippecanoe Railroad engine.

Galveston, Houston & Henderson Railroad: Absorbed by the Missouri Pacific (UP) on December 2, 1989.

Galveston Wharves: Switching line at Galveston, Texas. Sold to Galveston Railway in November 1987.

Garden City Northern Railroad: Garden City to Shallowater, Kansas, 30.6 miles. Merged into Garden City Western Railway September 1, 1991.

Georgia Eastern Railroad: Barnett to Washington, Georgia, 17 miles. Property sold to Georgia Woodlands Railroad in June 1988.

Georgia Great Southern Division: Dawson to Albany, Georgia, 22 miles. In 1994, the company abandoned track from Albany to Sasser and suspended operations on the rest.

Georgia Northern Railroad (Southern Railway): Merged into Norfolk Southern February 5, 1994.

Golden Cat Railroad: Delta to Newman Spur, Missouri, 10.8 miles. Line operated by Jackson & Southern Railroad. Ended service April 30, 1993, when shipper-owner closed plant. Abandoned in November 1993.

Graham County Railroad: Robbinsville to Topton, North Carolina, 12 miles. The line was abandoned November 1, 1970, but freight service resumed January 8, 1974. In 1975 a flood forced suspension of service again. Service was restored in May 1982 and operated until January 9, 1984, when it was again discontinued. Formal abandonment came in February 1987.

Graysonia, Nashville & Ashdown Railroad: Nashville to Ashdown, Arkansas, 31.55 miles. Merged into Kansas City Southern July 2, 1993.

Great Southwest Railroad (MP): Switching line at Grand Prairie, Texas. Merged into the Missouri Pacific on Nov. 24, 1986.

Green Bay & Western Railroad: Kewaunee, Wisconsin, to Winona, Minnesota, 254 miles. Merged into Fox Valley & Western Ltd. on August 28, 1993.

Hartford & Slocomb Railroad: Dothan to Hartford, Alabama, 22 miles. Abandoned from Hartford to Taylor and the balance sold to H&S Railroad July 1, 1992.

Helena Southwestern Railroad: West Helena to Helena, Arkansas, 4 miles. Rail assets sold to P. E. Barnes & Sons, Ltd., for continued operation as a private carrier in April 1987.

Hillsboro & North Eastern Railway: Hillsboro to Union Center, Wisconsin, 6.5 miles. Embargoed in April 1985 and abandonment approved in February 1987.

Hillsdale County Railway: Coldwater, Michigan, to Montpelier, Ohio, and branches, 95 miles total. Assets sold to Indiana Northeastern December 22, 1992.

Holton Interurban Railway (SP): El Centro to Holtville, California, 10.49 miles. Absorbed by Southern Pacific December 1985.

Horry County Railway: Conway to Myrtle Beach, South Carolina, 14.1 miles. Removed by property owner (Horry County) and operations transferred to Waccamaw Coast Line Railroad in November 1987.

Indiana & Ohio Eastern Railroad: Vauces to Fire Brick and Red Diamond, Ohio, 77.2 miles. Sold to Great Miami & Scioto Railway January 1, 1994.

Indiana Eastern Railroad & Transportation Co. (Hoosier Connection): Emporia to Carthage, Indiana, 21.55 miles. Service ended December 31, 1984, and property taken over by Indiana Midland Railway effective January 8, 1985.

Indiana Midland Railway: Emporia to Carthage, Indiana, 21.55 miles. Operation taken over by Carthage, Knightstown & Shirley Railroad in April 1987.

Interstate Railroad (Southern Railway): Wentz to Miller Yard, Virginia, 90 miles. Absorbed by Norfolk Southern in 1992.

Iowa Railroad: Bureau, Illinois, to Council Bluffs, Iowa, 379 miles plus several branch lines (the former Rock Island main line). Operated from October 19, 1981, through November 2, 1984, when the line was taken over by the Iowa Interstate Railroad. Iowa Railroad continued to operate a switching operation at Council Bluffs, Iowa, until all assets were auctioned off in 1987.

Iowa Southern Railroad: Council Bluffs to Blanchard, Iowa, 61.5 miles. Line cut back to Council Bluffs August 22, 1988, and remaining property sold to Council Bluffs & Ottuma Railroad in August 1990.

Iowa Terminal Railroad: Waller to Charles City and Marble Rock, Iowa, 15.7 miles. and Mason City to Clear Lake, 10.4 miles. The Charles City line was sold to Trains Unlimited and leased to the Cedar Valley Railroad in September 1986, and the Mason City line was sold to Iowa Traction Railroad in April 1987.

Iron Cliffs Railway: Switching line between West Ishpeming and Pluto, Michigan, 3.2 miles. Started service in 1991 and died a short time later.

J&J Railroad: Hardin to Murray, Kentucky, 8.34 miles. Sold to Hardin Southern Railroad on October 1, 1993.

Jackson & Southern Railroad: Delta to Jackson, Missouri, 18 miles (plus Golden Cat Railroad). Railroad closed down April 30, 1992.

Jersey Southern Railway: Bridgton Junction to Seabrook, New Jersey, 3.3 miles. Operations transferred to Winchester & Western effective February 1, 1987.

Johnsonburg, Kane, Warren & Irvine Railroad: Irvine to Warren, Pennsylvania, 55 miles. Started July 15, 1982, over state-owned trackage (some ex-Conrail) and sold to Allegheny Railroad September 1, 1985.

Kansas City Public Service Freight Operation: Switching line at Kansas City, Missouri. Inoperative since the mid-1970s; abandoned in 1981. The company then relocated on 7.4 miles of line at Dodson, Missouri. It abandoned all operations effective July 1, 1989.

Kansas City Terminal Railway: Operation taken over by Gateway Western on April 2, 1994.

Kewash Railroad: Washington to Keota, Iowa, 14.8 miles. Abandoned in December 1988 following several years of inactivity.

Kelly's Creek & Northwestern Railroad: Cedar Grove to Lewis, West Virginia, 7.9 miles. Operations ended February 1993. Line abandoned in January 1995.

Klamath Northern Railway: Gilchrist to Gilchrist Junction, Oregon, 10.6 miles. Service ended September 10, 1991. No longer a common carrier.

Lackawanna Railway: Scranton to Mount Pocono, Pennsylvania, 33 miles. Lease ended August 27, 1993. Now operated by Delaware Lackawanna Railroad.

Lackawanna Valley Railroad: Scranton to Carbondale, Pennsylvania, 22,3 miles. Lease ended August 27, 1993. Now operated by Delaware Lackawanna Railroad.

Lackawaxen & Stourbridge Railroad: Lackawaxen to Honesdale, Pennsylvania, 24.6 miles. Lease terminated on June 30, 1989, and operation transferred to Stourbridge Railroad.

Lake Erie, Franklin & Clarion Railroad: Clarion to Summerville, Pennsylvania, 15 miles. Permission to abandon received and operations suspended September 16, 1992.

Lake Superior Terminal & Transfer Co. (BN, C&NW, and Soo Line): Switching line at Superior, Wisconsin. Operations taken over by Burlington Northern on January 1, 1987. Company dissolved September 23, 1987.

Lakeside Transportation: Moberly to Excello, Missouri, 15.3 miles. Started December 1993 and ended September 1994.

Laona & Northern Railway: Laona to Laona Junction, Wisconsin, 7.42 miles. Abandonment authorized November 14, 1983. A portion of the line at Laona was operated by the Nicolet Badger Northern Railroad.

Lenawee County Railroad: Adrian to Riga, Michigan, 18 miles. Traffic embargoed effective September 30, 1990; line abandoned.

Live Oak, Perry & South Georgia Railway (Southern Railway): Foley through Perry, Florida, to Adel, Georgia, 81 miles. Merged into Norfolk Southern February 5, 1994.

Louisiana Midland Railway: Switching line at Packton and Ferriday, Louisiana. Property sold at sheriff's sale July 1, 1986.

Mahanoy & Hazleton Railway (the first company of that name — another company with a similar name is now operating): York

Junction to Delano, Pennsylvania, 11 miles. In May 1987 Panther Valley took over operation of this line.

Marinette, Tomahawk & Western Railroad: Tomahawk to Wisconsin Dam, Wisconsin, 11.4 miles total. Assets sold to Tomahawk Railway in December 1991.

Marion County Railway: Mullins to Marion, North Carolina, 6.3 miles. Acquired from the Seaboard System in July 1984 and operated until March 1985. The line has not been abandoned but most of the rail has been removed.

Marquette & Huron Mountain Railroad: Marquette to Buckroe, Michigan, 10.43 miles. Line sold at auction on January 14, 1985, following the death of its owner.

McCloud River Railroad: Mount Shasta to Burney, California, 96 miles. Assets sold to McCloud Railway July 1, 1992.

McCormick, Ashland City & Nashville Railroad: Nashville to Chapmansboro, Tennessee, 19 miles. Owner, Cheatham County Rail Authority, turned over lease to Central of Tennessee Railway & Navigation Co. in 1992.

Mercersburg Railway: Marion to Mercersburg, Pennsylvania, 13.5 miles (ex-Conrail). Operations ran from November 1, 1978, to October 1, 1980, when the line was turned back to Conrail. The line was abandoned by 1981.

Michigan Interstate Railroad: Reorganized as Ann Arbor Railroad effective October 7, 1988.

Michigan Northern Railway: Petoskey to Mackinaw City, Michigan, 33 miles. Last run January 11, 1986, and is now inactive.

Mid-Atlantic Railroad: Mullins to Chadbourn, South Carolina, 76 miles. Assets sold to Carolina Southern Railroad February 7, 1995.

MidLouisiana Railroad: Gibsland to Winnfield, Louisiana, 64.3 miles. Merged into Kansas City Southern January 1, 1994.

MidSouth Rail: Shreveport, Louisiana, to Meridian, Mississippi, plus branches, 399 miles. Merged into Kansas City Southern January 1, 1994.

Mineral Wells & Eastern Railway: Weatherford to Mineral Wells, Texas, 22 miles. Operations abandoned in fall 1992.

Minneapolis, Northfield & Southern Railroad: Minneapolis to Northfield, Minnesota, 45 miles plus branches. Acquired by Soo Line in January 1982 and merged October 1, 1985.

Minnesota Transfer Railway: Switching line at Minneapolis and St. Paul, Minnesota. Property sold to Minnesota Commercial Railway in January 1987.

Mississippian Railway: Amory to Fulton, Mississippi, 24 miles. The property was sold to Itawamba County Development Authority October 1986. It is now operated by Mississippian Railway Cooperative.

Montour Railroad: Montour Junction to Gilmore, Pennsylvania, 23 miles. Operations were suspended during 1983 and abandonment approved May 22, 1986.

Monongahela Railway: Brownsville, Pennsylvania, to Rivesville, West Virginia, 162 miles. Operations taken over by Conrail on May 1, 1993.

Moxahala Valley Railway: New Lexington to Glass Rock, Ohio, 31.7 miles. Operations transferred by state of Ohio to Ohio Southern in September 1986.

Muncie & Western Railroad: Switching line at Muncie, Indiana. Service ended and abandonment application filed March 1995.

Natchez Trace Railroad: Grand Junction, Tennessee, to Oxford, Mississippi, 56.5 miles. Assets sold to Pioneer Railcorp and name changed to Mississippi Central in March 1993.

Nevada Northern Railroad: Cobre to McGill, Nevada, 150.5 miles. Service ended about 1983 when copper mines closed. The railroad was bought by Los Angeles Department of Water & Power. It was leased to Northern Nevada Railroad, which resumed service in January 1995.

Nicolet Badger Northern Railroad: Wabeno to Tipler, Wisconsin, 37.8 miles. Ceased operations in February 1995.

North Carolina Ports Commission: Wilmington operation leased to Wilmington Terminal Co. and Morehead City operation leased to Carolina Rail Service on October 1, 1986.

North Central Oklahoma Railroad: Chickasha to Mountain View and Richards Spur, Oklahoma, 76 miles (ex-Rock Island). Operated from January 1982 to October 1982, when a portion of its property was acquired by the Oklahoma-Kansas-Texas. Limited operations to Mountain View continued until April 15, 1985. AT&L Railroad took over part of the line in June 1985.

North Central Oklahoma & Midlands Railway: Blackwell to Tonkawa, Oklahoma, 8.2 miles. Formed about 1988 but never operated.

North Louisiana & Gulf Railroad: Hodge to Gibsland, Louisiana, 40 miles. Sold to MidLouisiana Rail Corporation in July 1987.

North Stratford Railroad: North Stratford, New Hampshire, to Beecher Falls, Vermont, 23 miles. Last revenue trip April 8, 1989. Operations abandoned. Partial service restored by New Hampshire Central Railroad in 1993.

Northern Missouri Railroad: Burlington Junction to Lock Springs, Missouri, 93 miles. Began operation February 13, 1984; discontinued operations in June 1986.

Northwestern Pacific Railroad (SP): Schellville to Eureka, California, 328 miles. Lines north of Willits sold to Eureka Southern November 1, 1984. Company merged into Southern Pacific October 1, 1992. Lines south of Willits are now operated by California Northern.

Octoraro Railway: Wilmington, Delaware, to Modena and Nottingham, Pennsylvania, 56 miles. Lease canceled by Pennsylvania Department of Transportation on July 1, 1994. Now operated by Delaware Valley Railroad.

Oklahoma Central Railroad: Switching line at El Reno, Oklahoma. Service ended in 1988 and line abandoned.

Oregon & Northwestern Railroad: Hines to Seneca, Oregon, 50.2 miles. Service ended in March 1984 due to flood damage to connecting UP line. Several miles of switching track at Burns sold to Wyoming Colorado Railroad. No longer a common carrier as of April 25, 1990.

Oregon, California & Eastern Railway: Klamath Falls to Bly, Oregon, 65.4 miles. Service ended in April 1990 and railroad abandoned.

Oregon, Pacific & Eastern Railway: Cottage Grove to Culp Creek, Oregon, 16.6 miles. Abandoned in October 1994.

Ottumwa Connecting Railroad: Switching line at Ottumwa, Iowa. Began operations in August 1984 over a former N&W line

and was given abandonment authority effective August 15, 1985. Property acquired by Ottumwa Terminal Railroad.

Ottumwa Terminal Railroad: Property sold to Council Bluffs & Ottumwa Railroad in August 1989.

Panther Valley Railroad: Lease terminated by Carbon County Railroad Commission and property leased to C&S Railroad on March 10, 1990.

Petaluma and Santa Rosa Railroad (SP): Santa Rosa to Sebastopol and Petaluma, California, 16.9 miles. Abandoned by owner and operator Northwestern Pacific (SP) in 1985.

Pigeon River Railroad: South Milford to Ashley Heights, Ohio, 9.3 miles. Line taken over by Indiana Northeastern Railroad December 22, 1992.

Pioneer & Fayette Railroad: Switching line at Franklin Junction, Ohio. Service ended about 1991 and assets sold by 1994.

Pittsburgh & Lake Erie Railroad: Connellsville, Pennsylvania, to Youngstown, Ohio, 181 miles including several branch lines. Assets sold to Three Rivers Railway (CSX) September 13, 1992.

Pittsburgh & Ohio Valley Railway: Switching line at Neville Island, Pennsylvania. Line sold to CSX in December 1993.

PL&W Railroad: Youngstown, Ohio, to Darlington, Pennsylvania, 38.5 miles. Taken over by Ohio & Pennsylvania Railroad June 14, 1995.

Pocono Northeast Railway: Switching line in Scranton and Wilkes-Barre area of Pennsylvania, 93 miles. Ceased operations on September 17, 1993. Service taken over by Delaware-Lackawanna, then Luzerne & Susquehanna Railroad following purchase by local agency.

Port Huron & Detroit Railroad: Port Huron to Marine City, Michigan, 19.1 miles. Acquired by Chessie System on December 13, 1984, and merged into CSX five years later.

Port of Tacoma: Switching line at Tacoma, Washington. Operation merged with Tacoma Municipal Belt Line in September 1984.

Portland Traction Co.: Switching line at Portland, Oregon. Reported to have made its last run on November 1, 1990, and property abandoned.

Prairie Trunk Railway: Springfield to Shawneetown, Illinois, 74 miles (ex-Baltimore & Ohio). Operations suspended in June 1984 and abandoned effective July 3, 1985.

Rahway Valley Railroad: Cranford to Springfield, New Jersey, 5 miles. Last run April 21, 1992; line abandoned.

Rocky Mountain Railcar & Railroad: Switching railroad in and around Rocky Mountain Arsenal northeast of Denver. Assets sold at public auction on August 15, 1995.

Sacramento Northern Railway (WP, UP): Sacramento to Chico, California, 91.8 miles, and Concord to Pittsburg, California, 13.3 miles, plus branches. Merged into Union Pacific January 1, 1988.

Saltville Railroad: Glade Springs to Saltville, Virginia, 4 miles. Railroad closed January 25, 1991.

San Francisco Belt Railroad: Switching line along San Francisco waterfront. Closed spring 1993 due to lack of traffic.

Shore Fast Line, Inc.: Winslow Junction to Atlantic City, New Jersey, 30.7 miles and branches. Assets sold to Southern Railroad of New Jersey on December 9, 1991.

Sisseton Southern Railroad: Sisseton to Milbank, North Dakota, 38 miles. Operating lease terminated June 30, 1989, and operations taken over by Sisseton-Milbank Railroad.

South Central Florida Railroad: Sebring to Lake Harbor, Florida, 82.2 miles. Assets sold to South Central Florida Express on September 17, 1994.

SouthRail: Regional railroad operating 686 miles of former Illinois Central trackage in Mississippi, Alabama, and Tennessee. Merged into Kansas City Southern on January 1, 1994.

Spencerville & Elgin Railroad: Ohio City to Lima, Ohio, 30 miles. Assets leased to Indiana Hi-Rail in March 1991. Service ended on October 28, 1993.

St. Lawrence Railroad: Lease terminated by Ogdensburg Bridge & Port Authority effective April 1, 1990, and operation turned over to St. Lawrence & Raquette River Railroad.

Staten Island Railway: Cranford Junction, New Jersey, to St. George, New York, 12.2 miles. Last run April 21, 1992; railroad abandoned.

Strouds Creek & Muddlety Railroad (CSX): Allingdale to Ravens, West Virginia, 21.3 miles. Merged into CSX in 1992.

Sugar Loaf & Hazleton Railroad: Harleigh Junction to Gowen Colliery, Pennsylvania, 3.8 miles. Operations ceased in 1989.

Sunset Railway: Bakersfield to Taft, California, 48 miles. Assets sold in part to Tulare Valley on December 21, 1992; balance of line to Taft abandoned.

Sumter & Choctaw Railway: Lilita to Bellamy, Alabama, 3.55 miles. Operations discontinued early in 1983 and abandonment authority granted in August 1986.

T&P Railway: Topeka to Parnell, Kansas, 41 miles. Line purchased from the Santa Fe in 1991 and abandoned in May 1993.

Tennessee, Alabama & Georgia Railway (Southern Railway): Chattanooga, Tennessee, to Flintstone, Georgia; Ewing to Gadsden, Alabama, 30 miles. Merged into Norfolk Southern in 1991.

TennRail: Corinth, Mississippi, to Counce, Tennessee, 16.5 miles. Merged into Kansas City Southern on January 1, 1994.

Terre Haute, Brazil & Eastern Railroad: Terre Haute to Limedale, Indiana, 30 miles. Company closed following bankruptcy. Last run February 26, 1993.

Texas Central Railroad: Gorman to Dublin, Texas, 24.1 miles. Operations taken over by CenTex Rail Link August 15, 1994.

Texas-New Mexico Railway (MP): Monahans, Texas, to Lovington, New Mexico, 107.57 miles. Absorbed by owner, Missouri Pacific, in 1977.

Three Rivers Railway (CSX): Former P&LE trackage taken over for operation by CSX on September 17, 1993.

Tidewater Southern Railway (WP, UP): Stockton to Turlock, California, 47.9 miles. Merged into Union Pacific January 1, 1988.

Tioga Central Railroad: Owego to Harford, New York, 26 miles. Owner, Tioga County Industrial Development Agency, leased the line to Owego & Harford Railway on May 1, 1992.

Tradewater Railway: Princeton to Blackford and Waverly, 69 miles. The assets were sold to Western Kentucky Railway on January 1, 1995.

Union Railroad of Oregon: Union Junction to Union, Oregon, 2.9 miles. The sole industry served by the railroad closed, and the railroad received ICC approval to abandon on August 31, 1995.

Unity Railways: Unity Junction to Renton, Pennsylvania, 3.9

miles. Ceased common-carrier service in July 1990. Formal abandonment took place in August 1994.

Valley & Siletz Railroad: Switching line at Independence, Oregon, that had operated 40.6 miles to Valsetz until the early 1980s. Abandonment authorized April 28, 1985. Property sold to the Willamette Valley Railroad in January 1985.

Visalia Electric Railroad (SP): Exeter to Elderwood, California, 21.3 miles. Merged into SP on October 1, 1992; later abandoned.

Wabash & Erie Railroad and Wabash & Ohio River Railroad: Took over Indiana Hi-Rail on June 26, 1994, but the transaction was rejected by the ICC, which ordered Indiana Hi-Rail to resume operations.

Wabash & Grand River Railway: Kelly to Chillicothe, Missouri, 37 miles. Lease terminated December 1, 1993, following severe flood damage to line. Service resumed under operation of the owner, Green Hills Rural Development Authority.

Ware Shoals Railroad: Shoals Junction to Ware Shoals, South Carolina, 5.17 miles. Service discontinued July 25, 1985.

Warren & Ouachita Valley Railway: Warren to Banks, Arkansas, 16 miles. Abandoned following the abandonment of its owner, the Rock Island, in April 1980. A portion of the line at Warren was acquired and is operated by the Warren & Saline River Railroad.

Warrenton Railroad: Warren Plains to Warrenton, North Carolina, 3 miles. Operations suspended August 31, 1985, following closing of Seaboard System connection. The rails were still in place in 1992 and the line has not been formally abandoned.

Weatherford, Mineral Wells & Northwestern Railway (T&P, MP): Weatherford to Mineral Wells, Texas, 21.9 miles. Absorbed by Missouri Pacific (UP) January 1, 1988. Property sold to the city of Mineral Wells in fall 1989.

West Jersey Short Line: Swedesboro to Salem and Port Salem, New Jersey, 18 miles. Lease transferred to Pioneer Railroad, West Jersey Division, on September 30, 1988. Line renamed West Jersey Railroad in September 1990.

West Jersey Railroad: Swedesboro to Salem and Port Salem, New Jersey, 18 miles. Started service in September 1988. Lease transferred to Southern Railroad of New Jersey on May 1, 1995.

West Shore Railroad: Operated by the Union County Industrial Railroad.

West Virginia Northern Railroad: Tunnelton to Kingwood, West Virginia, 10.4 miles. Operations suspended March 17, 1991, and abandonment was approved in May 1993. The road is now being operated for passenger excursions.

White Pass & Yukon: Skagway to White Pass, Alaska, and Whitehorse, Yukon Territory, 110.7 miles. Operations suspended in late 1983, and a permanent closing announced in September 1985. Reopened for tourist operation in 1990.

Willamette Valley Railroad: Switching line at Independence, Oregon. Abandonment approved in December 1993.

Willamina & Grande Ronde Railroad: Willamina to Fort Hill, Oregon. Merged into Willamette Valley Railroad March 10, 1986.

Wisconsin & Michigan Railway: Mellen to Bessemer, Michigan, 33 miles. Service started in 1992 and ended February 12, 1995.

Wisconsin Western Railroad: Madison to Pairie du Chien, Wisconsin, plus branch line, 115 miles (ex-Milwaukee Road). Operation started in July 1982 and continued until January 3, 1985, when it was discontinued because of insurance problems.

Wolfeboro Railroad: Wolfeboro to Sanbornville, New Hampshire, 12 miles. Abandonment approved April 6, 1986.

Wyandotte Southern Railroad: Switching line with 3.9 miles of track at Wyandotte, Michigan. Abandoned in June 1986. The last run was June 25, 1986.

Yakima Valley Transportation Co.: Switching line operating in and around Yakima, Washington. Applied to abandon April 26, 1984, and discontinued operations November 11, 1985. The city of Yakima continues to operate trolley excursions over a portion of this company's line.

Yancey Railroad: Kona Junction to Burnsville and Bowditch, North Carolina, 12.6 miles. Operations suspended late in 1982 and assets auctioned in May 1985. Most equipment was removed by summer 1984. Rails were still in place in 1993.

Youngstown & Southern Railroad: Youngstown, Ohio, to Darlington, Pennsylvania, 35.5 miles. Assets sold to PL&W Railroad on May 1, 1993.

INDEX OF RAILROADS BY STATE

Batten Kill, 38
Bradford Industrial Rail, 48
Buffalo & Pittsburgh, 52
Buffalo Southern, 53
Champagne, 73
Clarendon & Pittsford, 84
Danbury Terminal, 98
Dansville & Mount Morris, 98
Depew, Lancaster & Western, 103
Finger Lakes, 120
Genesee & Wyoming, 128
Livonia, Avon & Lakeville, 179
Lowville & Beaver River, 184
Massena Terminal, 191
Middletown & New Jersey, 197
Mohawk, Adirondack & Northern, 205
New England Central, 215
New York & Lake Erie, 221
New York Cross Harbor, 222
New York, Susquehanna & Western, 222
Ontario Central, 237
Ontario Midland, 238
Owego & Harford, 241
Rochester & Southern, 268
St. Lawrence & Raquette River, 271
Somerset, 286
South Brooklyn, 287
South Buffalo, 287
ST Rail System, 296
Tonawanda Island, 311
Wellsboro & Corning, Vermont Railway, 322

NORTH CAROLINA

Aberdeen & Rockfish, 13
Aberdeen, Carolina & Western, 14
Alexander, 18
Atlantic & Western, 35
Beaufort & Morehead, 42
Caldwell County, 55
Cape Fear, 61
Carolina Coastal, 62
Carolina Rail Services, 63
Carolina Southern, 64
Chesapeake & Albemarle, 77
Clinton Terminal, 85
Dunn-Erwin, 107
Great Smoky Mountains, 141
High Point, Thomasville & Denton, 149
Laurinburg & Southern, 176
Nash County, 212
North Carolina & Virginia, 227
Red Springs & Northern, 263
State University, 296
Thermal Belt, 309
Virginia Southern, 323
Wilmington Terminal, 336
Winston-Salem Southbound, 339
Yadkin Valley, 344

NORTH DAKOTA

Dakota, Missouri Valley & Western, 95
Red River Valley & Western, 262

OHIO

Akron Barberton Cluster, 16
Ann Arbor, 24
Ashland, 32
Ashtabula Carson Jefferson, 33
Bessemer & Lake Erie, 44
Blue Rock Transportation, 48
Camp Chase Industrial, 57
Central Railroad of Indiana, 71
Cincinnati Terminal, 83

Columbus & Ohio River, 89
Cuyahoga Valley, 93
Great Miami & Scioto, 140
Indiana & Ohio, 156
Indiana & Ohio Central, 157
Indiana Hi-Rail, 157
Indiana Northeastern, 159
Lake Terminal, 173
Mahoning Valley, 186
Newburgh & South Shore, 223
Nimishillen & Tuscarawas, 224
Northern Ohio & Western, 231
Ohi-Rail, 233
Ohio & Pennsylvania, 233
Ohio Central, 234
Ohio Southern, 235
Pigeon River, 247
River Terminal, 265
R. J. Corman (Cleveland), 266
R. J. Corman (Western Ohio), 266
Sterling Belt Line, 297
Warren & Trumbull, 326
Wheeling & Lake Erie, 333
Wye Transportation, 342
Youngstown & Austintown, 346

OKLAHOMA

AT&L, 34
Farmrail, 119
Grainbelt, 138
Hollis & Eastern, 150
Kiamichi, 167
Northwestern Oklahoma, 231
Osage, 239
Sand Springs, 277
South Kansas & Oklahoma, 289
Southeast Kansas, 291
Southwestern, 295
Texas Oklahoma & Eastern, 308

Tulsa-Sapulpa Union, 314
Wichita, Tillman & Jackson, 334

OREGON

Blue Mountain, 47
Central Oregon & Pacific, 70
City of Prineville, 83
East Portland Traction, 111
Great Western, 143
Hampton, 147
Idaho Northern & Pacific, 154
Longview, Portland & Northern, 180
Molalla Western, 206
Mount Hood, 209
Peninsula Terminal, 246
Portland & Western, 252
Port of Tillamook Bay, 253
WCTU, 329
Willamette & Pacific, 335
Willamette Valley, 335
Willamina & Grand Ronde, 336
Wyoming Colorado (Oregon Eastern), 343

PENNSYLVANIA

Aliquippa & Southern, 20
Allegheny & Eastern, 21
Allegheny Valley, 21
Bessemer & Lake Erie, 44
Bradford Industrial Rail, 48
Brandywine Valley, 49
Bristol Industrial Terminal, 50
Buffalo & Pittsburgh, 52
C&S, 73
Chestnut Ridge, 78
Conemaugh & Black Lick, 90
Delaware-Lackawanna, 100
Delaware Valley, 101